Salesforce in Action

A guide to administrator essentials and advanced
Salesforce features across sales, service, and marketing cloud

Andy White

bpb

www.bpbonline.com

First Edition 2026

Copyright © BPB Publications, India

ISBN: 978-93-65892-222

LIMITS OF LIABILITY AND DISCLAIMER OF WARRANTY

To View Complete
BPB Publications Catalogue
Scan the QR Code:

www.bpbonline.com

Dedicated to

To my wonderful wife, without whose help I could have finished this book in half the time, and to my gorgeous children, Ava, Erin, and Daniel. Without whose feigned interest, I would never have finished it and Jesus Christ

About the Author

Andy White has 15 years of professional experience in information technology, which covers Salesforce and other technologies. His knowledge and experience in Salesforce have been condensed into this book. Throughout his career, he has developed a strong reputation for expertise, problem-solving, and a practical approach to complex challenges.

However, he is not your typical techie. Outside of his professional work, Andy places great importance on family life and values. He is also a qualified chef and an accomplished amateur painter, having done several solo exhibitions around London. One of his recent works was commissioned for a woman's birthday, which shows that she is unable to visit her favorite woodlands due to a recent severe disability. This reflects his belief that creativity and personal connections are as valuable as professional achievement.

About the Reviewers

❖ **Stanley Sequeira** is a 25x certified Salesforce Application and System Architect with 19 years of experience in architecting and delivering innovative solutions across diverse industries. With a proven track record in leading technical teams and managing complex projects, Stanley excels in designing and implementing Salesforce solutions that enhance business processes and customer experiences. His expertise spans integrations, Enterprise Territory Management, Public Sector Solutions, and clinical trial management. Stanley's proficiency in Salesforce Sales, Service, Experience, and Data Clouds, coupled with his hands-on experience in data migrations, reporting, and mobile solutions, underscores his ability to drive impactful results. Certified in multiple Salesforce disciplines, he brings a wealth of knowledge and a strategic mindset to every project, ensuring successful outcomes and client satisfaction.

❖ **Chamil Madusanka** holds the distinction of being the very first Sri Lankan Salesforce MVP, a title he has proudly held since 2019. A certified Salesforce professional, Chamil embarked on his Salesforce journey in 2011. In 2012, he took the pioneering step of founding the Sri Lankan Salesforce Ohana, a community-driven initiative. He leads the Colombo Developer community group under the Sri Lankan Salesforce Ohana. Chamil's vision is to elevate Salesforce competency within Sri Lanka, fostering a nurturing environment for Salesforce professionals and students to flourish within the Salesforce ecosystem.

Currently, Chamil holds the roles of head of Salesforce practice and Salesforce Architect at iTelasoft (Pvt) Ltd. His professional trajectory includes notable tenures at Dazeworks Technologies (Pvt) Ltd, Rizing (formerly known as Attune Lanka (Pvt) Ltd), and Sabre Technologies (Pvt) Ltd (where he started Salesforce Journey). He served as a visiting lecturer at the University of Moratuwa, Sri Lanka, offering his expertise in subjects such as innovation management and multidisciplinary design.

Chamil's remarkable contributions extend beyond his roles, as evidenced by his authorship of three impactful works. His invaluable expertise has been instrumental as a technical reviewer for four distinct books focusing on Salesforce technologies. These publications stand as a testament to his commitment to knowledge sharing and his dedication to enhancing the Salesforce landscape.

Educationally, Chamil secured a BSc in computer science from the **University of Colombo School of Computing** (**UCSC**), Sri Lanka, and an MBA in management of technology from the University of Moratuwa, Sri Lanka. His academic journey kindled his fascination with cloud computing, semantic web technologies, ontology-based systems, innovation management, knowledge management, innovation performance, and market orientation geographically, hailing from the ancient city of Polonnaruwa in Sri Lanka, Chamil currently resides in Colombo, within the western province of the country. Beyond his tech pursuits, he finds solace in consuming technology literature and playing and watching cricket.

Acknowledgement

There are a few people I would like to thank for their support whilst writing this book. I would like to thank Robin Barwell for allowing me to include the diagram on the CPQ configuration. I have used this in various CPQ projects, and it has saved me hundreds of hours as well as several successful projects.

I would also like to thank the team at BPB Publications for being supportive in correcting my English and giving guidance.

Preface

This book is basically everything you need to know about Salesforce. It never ceases to amaze me how badly Salesforce can be configured. This book is not only how but also why Salesforce should be setup. The basic rule is to keep it simple, use configuration and not code. This book emphasizes the very basic skills you will need to know as a Salesforce Administrator, but puts it into the larger view of the various Salesforce products.

Chapter 1: Introduction to Salesforce- This is about getting a free Salesforce environment to play around with, getting familiar with logging into Salesforce, and the basic navigation around the user interface. In particular, it will show you how to configure Salesforce from a basic layout.

Chapter 2: Basic Admin Essentials- This chapter covers the typical tasks faced by a Salesforce Administrator on a daily basis. It includes checking the user's role and profile, as well as being able to login as them. It includes a high-level view of the Salesforce environment and how to diagnose common issues.

Chapter 3: Customizing User Interface- This chapter is about making users want to use Salesforce. It includes how to create a user interface with all the relevant information needed by the user. It also includes ways to monitor users, but in a friendly way to ensure they are using Salesforce to its full potential.

Chapter 4: Creating Object with Custom Fields and Relationships- This chapter is the basics of modifying Salesforce. It shows how Salesforce can easily be configured to meet various business requirements. It also goes into depth on various aspects that an administrator should be aware of, such as sharing and visibility to information, as well as basic checks that should be in place before making updates to a live environment.

Chapter 5: Adding Users and Assigning Correct Access Levels- Security is essential for any business. It can make headline news when the wrong information gets out. This chapter is about securing your Salesforce environment so people only get to see what they need to see.

Chapter 6: Automating Salesforce with Flows– This chapter introduces Salesforce Flows, which will give you a basic understanding of how automation will allow users freedom to do what they need to do, whilst Salesforce can take care of the background routine work.

Chapter 7: Salesforce Security Model– This chapter builds on the previous one, but since so many problems arise with setting up the correct security in Salesforce, it is essential that administrators have a good understanding of the Salesforce security model. This chapter shows how to configure an entire Salesforce org, but demonstrates how to test it.

Chapter 8: Reports, Dashboards, and Basic Tableau– This chapter is about how to show the data to various users, from when they login to presentations to senior management.

Chapter 9: Various Salesforce Tools– It can be very time-consuming to do various tasks in Salesforce. Fortunately, there are many tools available to save you time and hassle. This chapter goes through the most useful tools you can use to ensure that you are using Salesforce to its best capabilities.

Chapter 10: Various Salesforce Features– This chapter gives an overview of numerous Salesforce features that are not immediately obvious. For example, you can use Salesforce to run a call center or manage an online commercial website. If you do not know that these features are there, then you are missing out. Salesforce can meet a wide variety of business needs. The aim is to have a true 3600 customer view, and the more you can do in Salesforce, the better.

Chapter 11: Basics of Apex and Lightning Web Components– This chapter gives an overview of customizing Salesforce using code. Although configuration is the best way of achieving most functionality, it is useful to be able to code Salesforce for specific requirements. In addition, being able to integrate Salesforce with other external systems is also necessary. This chapter gives an overview of the key skills and areas you will need to know.

Chapter 12: Einstein AI– This chapter shows how to use AI with Salesforce. In particular, it focuses on Agentforce, which is Salesforce's native AI capability. This is an area Salesforce will expand upon over the next few years, but this chapter will give a basic introduction, including the ability to assist Sales and Service users.

Chapter 13: Preparing for Salesforce Certifications– It is important to be certified with Salesforce. This chapter gives hints and tips on how to become certified with Salesforce and provides a general plan for your career growth.

Chapter 14: Broader Salesforce Ecosystem– It is easy to think of Salesforce as a stand-alone solution, but there are many Salesforce products. This chapter gives an overview of the various other products that you should be aware of. It also gives a quick introduction to how to use and configure these products.

Chapter 15: Further Readings– This chapter gives an overview based on experience. It has not always been easy working as an IT consultant, and some lessons learned have been painful. This chapter is to give you some basic insight into ways to convince senior management, as well as to avoid being marched into **human resource (HR)**.

Code Bundle and Coloured Images

Please follow the link to download the
Code Bundle and the *Coloured Images* of the book:

https://rebrand.ly/9de0d2

The code bundle for the book is also hosted on GitHub at
https://github.com/bpbpublications/Salesforce-in-Action.
In case there's an update to the code, it will be updated on the existing GitHub repository.

We have code bundles from our rich catalogue of books and videos available at
https://github.com/bpbpublications. Check them out!

Errata

We take immense pride in our work at BPB Publications and follow best practices to ensure the accuracy of our content to provide with an indulging reading experience to our subscribers. Our readers are our mirrors, and we use their inputs to reflect and improve upon human errors, if any, that may have occurred during the publishing processes involved. To let us maintain the quality and help us reach out to any readers who might be having difficulties due to any unforeseen errors, please write to us at: errata@bpbonline.com

Your support, suggestions and feedbacks are highly appreciated by the BPB Publications' Family.

Piracy

If you come across any illegal copies of our works in any form on the internet, we would be grateful if you would provide us with the location address or website name. Please contact us at business@bpbonline.com with a link to the material.

If you are interested in becoming an author

If there is a topic that you have expertise in, and you are interested in either writing or contributing to a book, please visit www.bpbonline.com. We have worked with thousands of developers and tech professionals, just like you, to help them share their insights with the global tech community. You can make a general application, apply for a specific hot topic that we are recruiting an author for, or submit your own idea.

Reviews

Please leave a review. Once you have read and used this book, why not leave a review on the site that you purchased it from? Potential readers can then see and use your unbiased opinion to make purchase decisions. We at BPB can understand what you think about our products, and our authors can see your feedback on their book. Thank you!

For more information about BPB, please visit www.bpbonline.com.

Join our Discord space

Join our Discord workspace for latest updates, offers, tech happenings around the world, new releases, and sessions with the authors:

https://discord.bpbonline.com

Table of Contents

CHAPTER 1
Introduction to Salesforce

Introduction

This book is aimed at people who want to learn Salesforce. It is based on practical examples and many hands-on examples. All you will need is a laptop and a good internet connection.

The target audience for this book can be divided into two categories: user of Salesforce who needs Salesforce for their job, and system administrators who need to know the best way to meet the requirements of the business and the users.

However, Salesforce is best navigated by knowing what can be done and what should not be done. There are many ways to get things wrong, and there is always the best way to get something right. It will save you time and embarrassment if you get Salesforce right the first time. If you want to make a career in Salesforce or simply want to get hands-on experience, then this book is for you. Salesforce can be configured for small companies and global companies. Both seek the same thing: a simple, reliable way to make people's jobs easy and enjoyable. This book aims to show you how this is done.

This chapter gives an overview of what Salesforce is, how to get access to your own Salesforce environment, and a start on the recommended training material.

It also covers basic navigation around the Salesforce user interface, an introduction to configuring it, key concepts, and the core understanding of how it works. This chapter will set the foundations for the subsequent chapters in this book and also give some basic tips for understanding how to read this book with step-by-step examples.

Structure

In this chapter, we will cover the following topics:

- Introducing Salesforce
- Getting free Salesforce environment
- Navigating user interface
- Setting up your Salesforce environment
- Basic concepts in Salesforce

Objectives

By the end of this chapter, you will have learned how to register with your own Salesforce instance, how to navigate your way around, and how to start the configuration of Salesforce. You will also be able to understand how Salesforce works from both a user's view and how Salesforce could be configured to meet different requirements. You will also learn how to setup your own user profile, and it will end with a short quiz.

Introducing Salesforce

Let us look at what the term Salesforce denotes. For starters, the term is used to refer to a couple of things:

- A company
- A website
- A technology

Salesforce was started in 1999 by *Marc Benioff*, who had the vision for a completely cloud-based, configurable **customer relationship management** (**CRM**) system. Salesforce pioneered the way for configuration-based development, i.e., the mouse-driven clicks, not code approach to delivering business solutions.

Salesforce ecosystem

It has evolved over the years from a glorified address book to an online environment where you can configure pretty much anything.

Salesforce is a cloud-based system that gives ready-made solutions to a wide range of business applications. The basic Sales and Service Cloud is the core product that can then be configured to meet a specific business need. It is important to note that Salesforce works best when the out-of-the-box configuration is used and not customized using code. The Salesforce ecosystem consists of various objects that form the basis of the sales process used by most businesses, and then the service process used to maintain the customer relationship.

If you want a CRM system, then it is pretty much good to go; however, if you want to build mobile apps, a call center, an online shop, or multiple websites, then it is all there. Salesforce is also very scalable, going from a small number of users to tens of thousands.

This book aims to balance beginner-level content with advanced insights. The aim is to give you hands-on exercises but also to point you in the direction you may wish to take. To cover everything in Salesforce would be impossible and would quickly go out of date. As such, it is better to get you started and give you the confidence and structure to allow yourself to take you further. As much as possible, the key topics are discussed, which will allow you to research and learn them as you wish. This chapter is about starting with Salesforce, finding your way around, and getting help if needed. Many of the subjects in this chapter require more detail, but this will be covered later, or a suitable reference or resource will be provided.

However, like anything, it takes time to get there. The more time you spend practicing configuring Salesforce, the better you will be. It is recommended that you dedicate three to five hours a day to familiarizing yourself with the basics of Salesforce within a month. Obviously, it can take years to become an expert in certain areas, but this book will cover most of them sufficiently to get you started.

Undoubtedly, some of the chapters are very useful, such as *Chapter 6, Automating Salesforce with Flows,* or *Chapter 12, Einstein AI,* but you can only understand them once you have learned the basics.

Benefits of using Salesforce

Salesforce removes a lot of the complexity that other CRM applications required in the past. It was the first cloud-based CRM, meaning that businesses did not need to host their own servers. Salesforce was also the first cloud-based platform that provided easy configuration of its CRM solution, which allowed it to be configured to meet a vast range of business needs. Over the past two decades, Salesforce has continually led innovation in many areas such as **artificial intelligence (AI)**, internal collaboration, application integration, and more. Salesforce has demonstrated itself to be a leader in cloud-based technologies, including the first server-side language called **Apex**.

Salesforce pricing model

Users of Salesforce are charged per user per month. The monthly subscription is based on many factors, such as what edition of Salesforce you are using and the number of users, as well as other factors, such as feature licenses, paid third-party applications, and bundling with other Salesforce products. For relevant prices, search on *Google* for Salesforce pricing plans.

Getting free Salesforce environment

There are two key areas to get you started with Salesforce:

- A free Salesforce Developer Edition account
- Trailhead

Now, let us look at how we can get a free Salesforce Developer account.

Get a free Salesforce environment; just Google free Salesforce Developer Edition, which will give you everything you need to get started. Follow these steps:

1. The link is **https://developer.salesforce.com/signup**. Enter the details requested.

2. You will need to enter your email address and other details.

3. However, the username needs to be in the format of an email address, but it can be anything like `learningsalesforce@anything.com`.

4. Do not enter your actual email address, as you are likely to have many Salesforce orgs (i.e., Salesforce environments) assigned for you to work on over time, and you cannot reuse the username.

5. Complete the form, and you will be sent an email with the details you need to access your new free Salesforce account.

6. Keep the details in this email in a safe place, as you may need to refer to them.

Getting free Salesforce training

Trailhead is a free training environment. Salesforce is keen to make sure people know and understand their various products. Just Google Salesforce Trailhead for 1000's of online courses and examples. The link is **https://trailhead.salesforce.com/**, and it helps if you login using your Salesforce Developer account created previously above. Search the various courses and get points and badges. Examples are shown in the following figure:

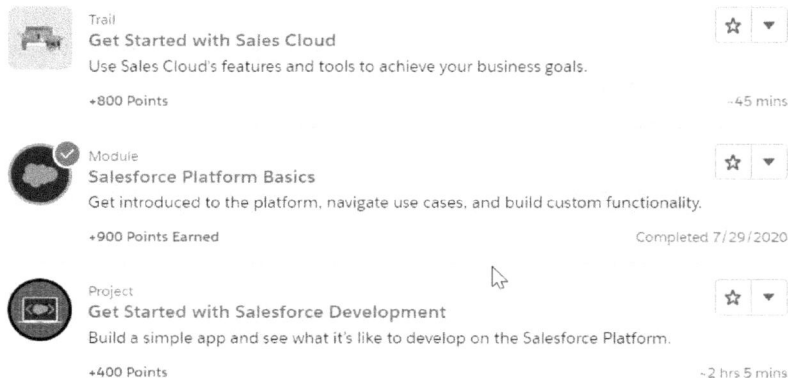

Trail
Get Started with Sales Cloud
Use Sales Cloud's features and tools to achieve your business goals.
+800 Points ~45 mins

Module
Salesforce Platform Basics
Get introduced to the platform, navigate use cases, and build custom functionality.
+900 Points Earned Completed 7/29/2020

Project
Get Started with Salesforce Development
Build a simple app and see what it's like to develop on the Salesforce Platform.
+400 Points ~2 hrs 5 mins

***Figure 1.1**: Example of Trailhead training challenges*

To login to a Salesforce Trailhead, it is generally more reliable not to use the login button at the top of the screen, but to use the login at the bottom of the screen on an actual trail, as shown in the following figure:

Figure 1.2: Linking your Salesforce environment to Trailhead

There are other resources, such as *Salesforce Ben* and many great tutorials (*YouTube ApexHours*), but with a free Salesforce environment and 1000 tutorials on Trailhead, you will soon get the confidence and experience to get started with Salesforce as a career.

You may be thinking this book is simply going through online resources, but it is quite the opposite. This book is primarily experience-based, so it includes many areas that are not so obvious or have various pitfalls. Online resources are simply described so you can do them yourself.

Salesforce AppExchange

There is also the AppExchange (**https://appexchange.salesforce.com/**), which is similar to the *Google Play Store* or the *Apple App Store*. This has thousands of apps you can add to Salesforce, often for free. This allows you to add specific functionality that Salesforce may not offer out-of-the-box.

Navigating user interface

This subject is covered in more detail in *Chapter 3, Customizing User Interface*, but a basic overview is given here. In summary, the user interface is highly configurable on a user level basis. This is to say, the screen can be made to suit each user-based on their setup.

To get started, login to your new free edition of Salesforce created previously in the section *Getting free Salesforce training*, and then you will see a screen similar to *Figure 1.3*. With a new Salesforce org (i.e., an instance of Salesforce), various prompts will help you get started. It is advised that you make the most of these whilst they are available and go slowly through them, as they point out the key features of Salesforce for first time users.

Salesforce users can be divided into two categories:

- People using Salesforce to do their job.
- Administrators are those people responsible for building out Salesforce for the users.

This book is aimed at administrators or people starting out in various areas of Salesforce, but it is helpful to be able to see both sides. When a user first logs into Salesforce, they will see a screen similar to the one in the following figure:

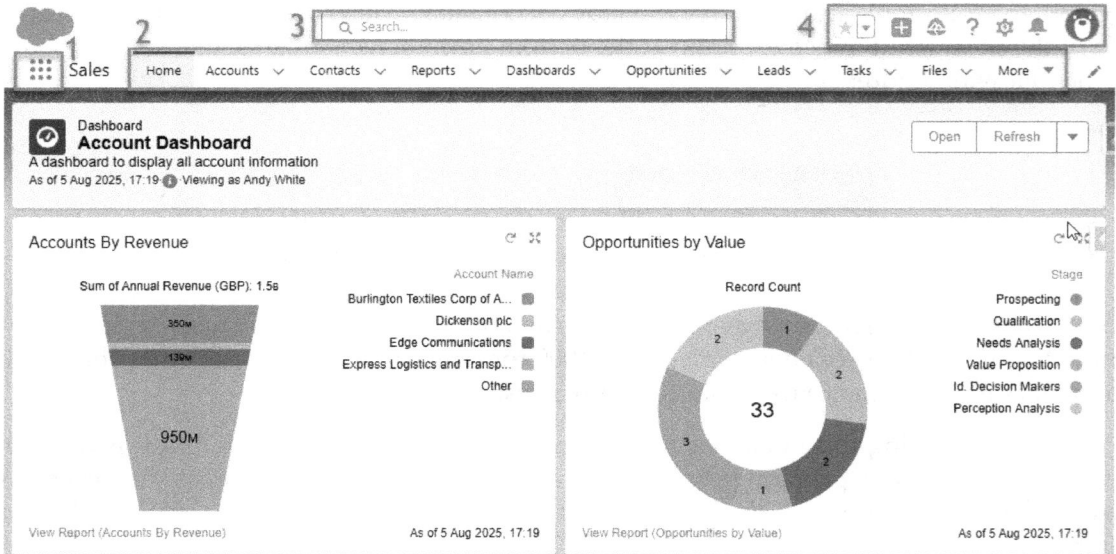

Figure 1.3: *Salesforce home screen layout*

In the illustration above, the following are numbered. Please select from each of the above as outlined in the following instructions:

1. The **App Launcher**; choose one of the different apps available: **Service, Sales**, or whichever looks interesting (refer to *Figure 1.4*).

2. Click the **View All** link on the **App Launcher** to see a list of all the apps available, as shown in the following figure:

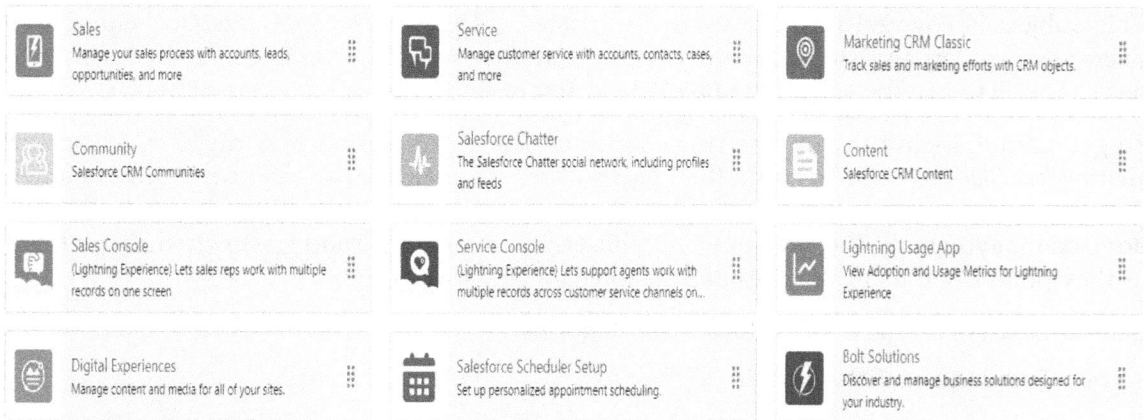

Figure 1.4: *The App Launcher*

3. Across the top are tabs, which will change depending on the app you have selected.

Note: **Various tabs can exist in many other apps, so you will see the Accounts and Contacts tabs appearing in both the Sales and the Service apps, whilst the Sales app will also have the Opportunities tab, and the Service app will have the Cases tab. These are covered in more detail in the section titled 'Salesforce objects' later in this chapter.**

4. The Global Search Box is useful in finding records inside Salesforce. For example, if we type in **Tim Barr**, then Salesforce will show any records with *Tim Barr*; in this case, it is a contact in Salesforce.

5. The global search should not be confused with the search in the setup discussed in the following. Global search is for searching the data in Salesforce, whilst the setup search is for finding configuration settings used throughout this book.

6. There are various icons in the top right-hand corner. Hover your mouse over various icons to get a description. In particular, notice the gear or cog icon, which is for the configuration settings in Salesforce.

7. Select this, then press **Setup** to open a screen that gives you access to all your options. This will be the bulk of what has been covered in this guide. When this book says press **Setup**, it means press this gear icon and select **Setup**. The other icons are:

   a. The star is to bookmark a particular page so you can find it easily.

   b. The + symbol is for global actions to quickly and easily do something in Salesforce without having to navigate to a specific page.

   c. The big question mark **?** is also there to provide you with help. The help is specific to the page, so if you get stuck on a particular part of Salesforce, then the Help button is there for you.

   d. The bell icon is for notifications. Messages you need to check.

   e. The profile icon (which can be an image of you) is your details kept in Salesforce.

Starting with the configuration setup

If you press the gear icon in the area highlighted by the number *4* in *Figure 1.3* above, you will see the **Setup** page, as shown in the following figure:

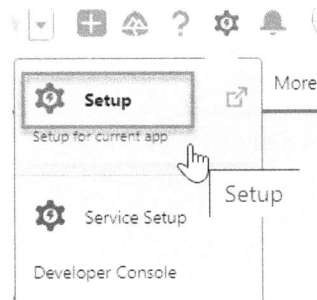

Figure 1.5: *Select Setup to change the configuration of Salesforce*

Note: The other menu options available may change depending on what screen you are currently on in Salesforce, but you will always see Setup.

After you press **Setup**, you enter the configuration screen of Salesforce. This shows you what you have most recently worked on and, most importantly, the **Setup** menu, as shown in the following figure:

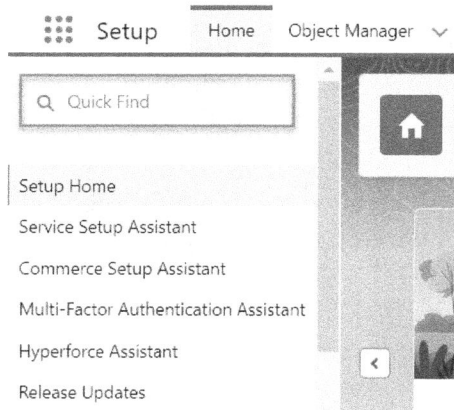

Figure 1.6: Setup configuration menu

The menu on the left is for accessing all the configuration settings in Salesforce. Since there are a lot of options, if you know what you are looking for, then the quickest way is to use **Quick Find**, which is highlighted above in the figure. For example:

1. Type **Integration** to see all the various integration settings available.

2. Also, type in **Users** or **Lead** to see the relevant options. Type in **Company information**, which will give you details on your Salesforce instance and all the features that are available to you.

Note: You have just used the two search features in Salesforce. The global search is for finding data or records in Salesforce, whilst the setup search is for finding features that can be configured.

Setting up your Salesforce environment

The following sections are to give you a high-level overview of Salesforce, the different applications, and a basic understanding of configuration. There will be more details in the following chapters.

Overview of Salesforce applications

Salesforce has many different products covered in *Chapter 14, Broader Salesforce Ecosystem*, but the two main ones are Sales Cloud and Service Cloud:

- Sales Cloud helps you get new customers, orders, build campaigns, and manage new opportunities.
- Service Cloud helps keep customers by engaging with them on questions or problems they may have, and helps maintain the customer relationship.

The two products work together and are built on the Salesforce Lightning Platform, which is the underlying technology. They are not separate, though. They are both included in your Salesforce Developer Edition and use the same objects (similar to tables). The two most important objects are:

- **Accounts**: These are typically businesses.
- **Contacts**: These are the people who often (but not always) belong to an account.

Arguably, other objects (such as users, profiles, opportunities, cases, and more) are equally important as Salesforce needs them to work, but accounts and contacts are at the center of much of the functionality, and a lot of Salesforce functionality relies on them.

Basic Salesforce terminology

Learning Salesforce is relatively straightforward, but there will be some specific terms and concepts that should be explained to help new users understand Salesforce, the language used in this book, and online resources.

To make this guide easier to understand, some key terms and concepts are listed here in alphabetical order, but not necessarily in order of importance. Let us look at them:

- **Apex**: This is the development language used for writing custom code in Salesforce, typically triggers and classes. Some basics are covered in *Chapter 11, Basics of Apex and Lightning Web Components*.
- **API**: **Application program interface** (**API**), refers to how one system can send or receive data (securely) between separated online (cloud) systems. Some basics are covered in *Chapter 11, Basics of Apex and Lightning Web Components*.
- **Certifications**: There are many certifications you can get as your career develops with Salesforce. The choice is up to you, but the basic Salesforce Administrator certification is a good place to start. Certifications require maintenance exams to ensure you are still up to date with the latest Salesforce release.
- **CRM**: It is the core functionality of Salesforce when used for Sales and Service. It allows users to view data they have for customers and to see the related information, such as sales opportunities or cases to resolve.
- **Einstein**: Salesforce AI is built into the platform. It is useful for enriching data, assisting users in predicting possible sales to customers, generating email responses, assisting in data enrichment, or even helping write code and flows. This is the largest area of growth within Salesforce currently and is changing continuously.

- **Field-level security (FSL)**: It covers who can see what for fields on an object. This is covered in *Chapter 7, Salesforce Security Model*.

- **Hyperforce**: Salesforce originally hosted its own **platform as a service** (**PaaS**), meaning the infrastructure was taken care of by Salesforce behind the scenes. Although this was a proven success, they were not the only company to do this, and data residency (i.e., the country in which the data actually sits) was an issue. **Amazon Web Services** (**AWS**) had many more locations and a scalable and flexible architecture that could handle the volumes of data and the security required. As a result, Salesforce has moved a lot of the back-end data and some functionality onto the AWS infrastructure. This transition is known as **Hyperforce**.

- **Logging in**: You can login to Salesforce via **https://login.salesforce.com/**. This will also work with your Developer Edition Salesforce org. There are also custom domains (known as **MyDomain**, such as `mydomain.salesforce.com`, which are customizable when setting them up). For a sandbox (i.e., a test environment), `test.salesforce.com` is often used. These are discussed later in this book.

- **Lightning Web Components (LWC)**: These are used to build custom functionality that combines basic web skills (such as HTML, CSS, JavaScript, etc.) with Apex. Some basics are covered in this guide. It allows you to build very bespoke features into Salesforce. This is generally considered a replacement for Visualforce pages, the traditional form of developing Salesforce, but it does not work well on mobile devices.

- **Managed package**: It is the package that is an installed application from a third-party (typically via the AppExchange). These are often locked, so you cannot configure them other than what the third-party vendor allows. They also come with their namespace, which is shown in the URL (see namespace definition in the following).

- **Native (or non-native)**: Although Salesforce is a stand-alone environment, it is possible to build (or install) features that run outside of Salesforce. Native means it is inside Salesforce (and built on the Lightning Platform), whilst non-native means it is built outside of Salesforce but is integrated into Salesforce.

- **Objects**: They are the basic building blocks of Salesforce. They are primarily tables where you keep data with additional functionality depending on the object. They can be standard (i.e., already in your Salesforce org) or custom (i.e., you have made them), and related to each other to allow users to navigate related information easily. The most common objects are:

  o   Accounts

  o   Contacts

  o   Leads

  o   Opportunities

  o   Cases and users

There are also some other objects that are less common, such as external objects and custom metadata types, which you would not need to use in this book, but should be aware of their existence.

*   **Org**: It is also called an **instance**. This is short for organization and refers to your own Salesforce stand-alone environment. There are different types of org; the live one is often called **production**, and copies can be made of it into a sandbox. There are also others, such as scratch org, which are similar to a sandbox but expire after a short period of time (typically 7 to 30 days). Scratch orgs are generally used by developers.

*   **Org Wide Defaults (OWD)**: These are the access rights provided to each object in Salesforce. They are either Private (so only the record owner can see them) or Public/ Read Write, meaning everyone can see them. The settings are stored in **Setup | Security | Sharing Settings**. The security model is discussed in *Chapter 7, Salesforce Security Model*.

*   **Releases**: Salesforce has three updates every year. This is to make sure that Salesforce is secure and new features are available. These are winter, spring, and summer. You get release notes beforehand to inform you of Salesforce's new features. If you have a Salesforce certification, you are required to keep it up to date by taking a short exam after the release.

*   **SaaS**: This means that all the functionality is in the cloud and not running locally on your laptop or device. Related acronyms are PaaS and **infrastructure as code (IaaS)**, which refer to PaaS or IaaS. Salesforce is **software as a service (SaaS)**.

*   **Salesforce editions**: Although the Developer Edition of Salesforce is free, it is limited. You can only have two users, limited data, and many features are missing (for example, creating a sandbox). It is worth noting that Salesforce comes at different licensing costs depending on the edition you have paid for. These range from Starter Edition (up to 10 users and limited functionality) to Enterprise and Unlimited Edition. Salesforce will combine license costs for a company to ensure it remains competitive with other alternatives. To compare them, Google compares Sales Cloud editions.

*   **Sandbox**: Salesforce does not recommend (or prohibits in many cases) doing configuration or development work in the live (also known as **production**) environment. Instead, it allows you to copy the live environment into a sandbox, i.e., a safe place to do your work and test it before going into the live (production) environment. However, your Developer Edition of Salesforce would not come with sandbox environments. To login to a sandbox, use **https://test.salesforce.com/**

*   **Setup**: This is the key to accessing Salesforce configuration. If you are a system administrator (which you are), then you will see a small cog icon at the top right-hand side of your screen. This book will often say setup, which means press this cog icon.

- **Salesforce Object Query Language (SOQL)**: It is a concise code used to get data from a Salesforce object. It typically uses **SELECT** (something, **FROM** object, **WHERE** condition). This is covered in *Chapter 11, Basics of Apex and Lightning Web Components*. There is also **Salesforce Object Search Language** (**SOSL**), which is used for searching text across multiple objects.

Basic concepts in Salesforce

In this section, we will look at basic concepts that will be used throughout this book. This will cover the basics of user access, Salesforce objects, and different ways the data can be viewed in Salesforce.

Roles and profiles

Every user in Salesforce needs access, which is controlled by roles and profiles. Since users will have different jobs, Salesforce needs to be configured for them. This is controlled by a combination of:

- **Roles**: What the user can see.
- **Profiles**: What the user can do. Profiles are meant to be kept as simple as possible, with tweaks to them done using **Permission Sets** (and **Permission Set Groups**).

To access them, follow these instructions:

1. Click the gear icon to enter **Setup**.

2. Use the **Quick Find** feature and enter **Users** as shown in *Figure 1.6*. To have a look at the different users available.

3. If you select a user, you will also see what role and profile they have been assigned.

   If you select your own record, you will see that your profile is a system administrator, which means you can configure all aspects of Salesforce. Refer to the following figure to see the users with basic information. Press the **Edit** link to see more details about the user:

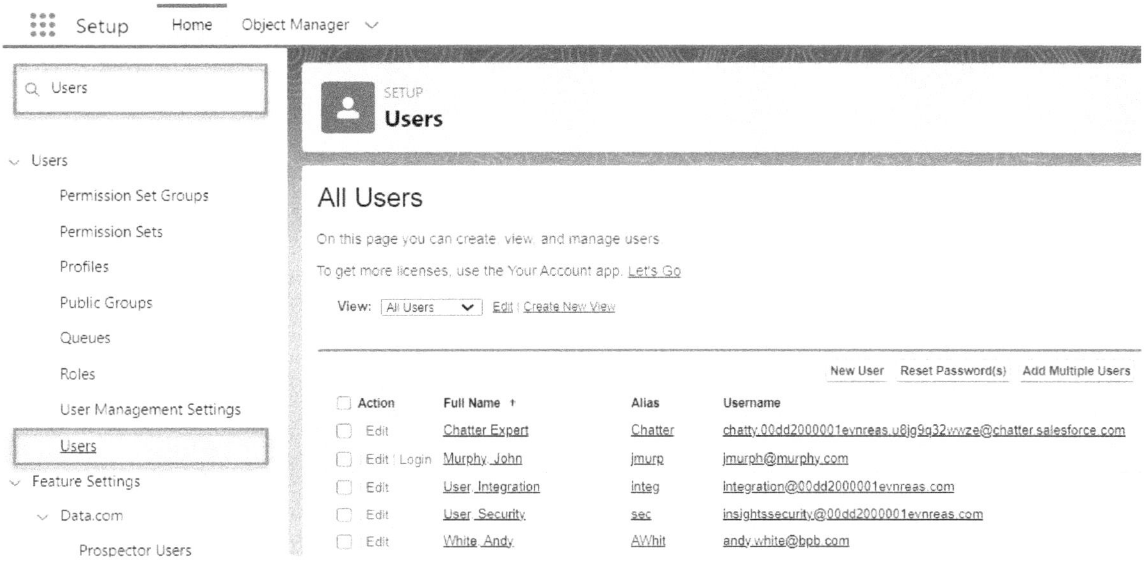

Figure 1.7: Finding users in configuration setup

Note: **When creating a new profile, the best practice is to copy a standard profile and give it a specific name; however, create as few profiles as possible. Use Permission Sets (and Permission Set Groups) to tweak a profile. This will be covered later; for now, you do not need to understand them in detail, but this is the very basics of providing user access to Salesforce.**

Every user must have a profile, but not necessarily a role. The combination of roles and profiles determines what every user can see and do in Salesforce. In particular, what is shown on the screen via page layouts (discussed later).

Salesforce Classic vs. Salesforce Lightning

When Salesforce first came out, it was built in a way that made sense then. However, with the rise of mobile phones and other devices, Salesforce needed a more responsive experience to ensure users had the flexibility to use Salesforce how they liked.

Salesforce has rebuilt the entire look and feel of the Lightning Platform (previously called **Force.com**). The underlying structure remains the same, but it is far more adaptive to various uses.

Users still have the option to return to the original Classic interface, but the default view is now Lightning Experience. It is worth being aware of the two ways to view Salesforce, as configuration is easier in the Classic version, and some parts of Lightning still use the classic interface. The user interface is chosen per user, which means the user can decide which version to use.

To change to Classic, follow these steps:

1. Go to the view profile icon in the top right-hand corner.

2. Select **Switch to Salesforce Classic**, as shown in the following figure:

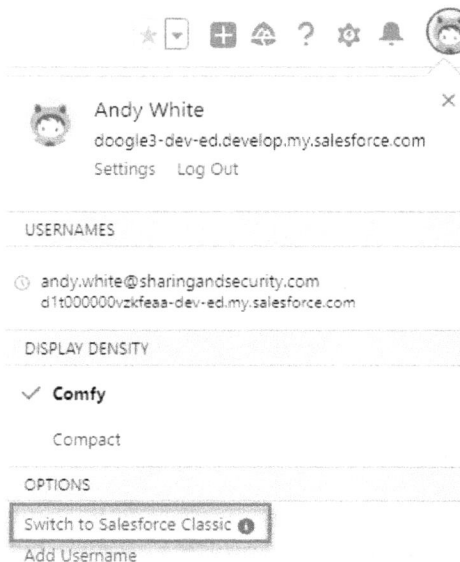

Figure 1.8: Switching from Salesforce Lightning to Salesforce Classic

3. You can easily move between the two versions by pressing the **Switch to Lightning Experience** link at the top of the page. This will return you to Salesforce Lightning, which is used for the majority of this book. Refer to the following figure:

Figure 1.9: Switching from Salesforce Classic to Lightning

As a system administrator, it is well worth being aware of the two different ways Salesforce can be seen. It can help greatly with resolving user issues. For example, a user may not be able to see something and come to you for help. If you switch to Salesforce Classic, then it will be visible and work fine. In this case, check the configuration for the Lightning page, or if it is also a problem in Classic, start by checking the page layout assignment and security settings covered in *Chapter 5, Adding Users and Assigning Correct Access Levels,* and *Chapter 7, Salesforce Security Model.*

Salesforce objects

This requires some understanding of the relationships between objects in Salesforce. An object is a table of data, similar to a spreadsheet; only the columns are fields, and the rows are the data.

There are many standard objects in Salesforce, and you can create your own, which are called **custom objects**. The most fundamental standard objects are:

- **Accounts**: These are basically businesses or organizations.

- **Contacts**: These are typically people who are employees of an account, but they do not have to be.

- **Cases**: These are for storing records of contacts who have problems or issues.

- **Opportunities**: These are for potential future sales for the account.

Other important objects depend on your use of Salesforce. For example, the campaign object is for marketing purposes, whilst the asset object is useful for goods (or services) sold but no longer belongs to an account.

Hence, if you have a contact in Salesforce (i.e., a person), then this is stored on the contact object. However, an account (i.e., a company) will have many contacts working for it. This is a one-to-many relationship, i.e., one **Accounts** will have many **Contacts**. Likewise, an account may have many opportunities. This creates a related list in Salesforce, which is shown on the **Related** tab, as shown in the following figure:

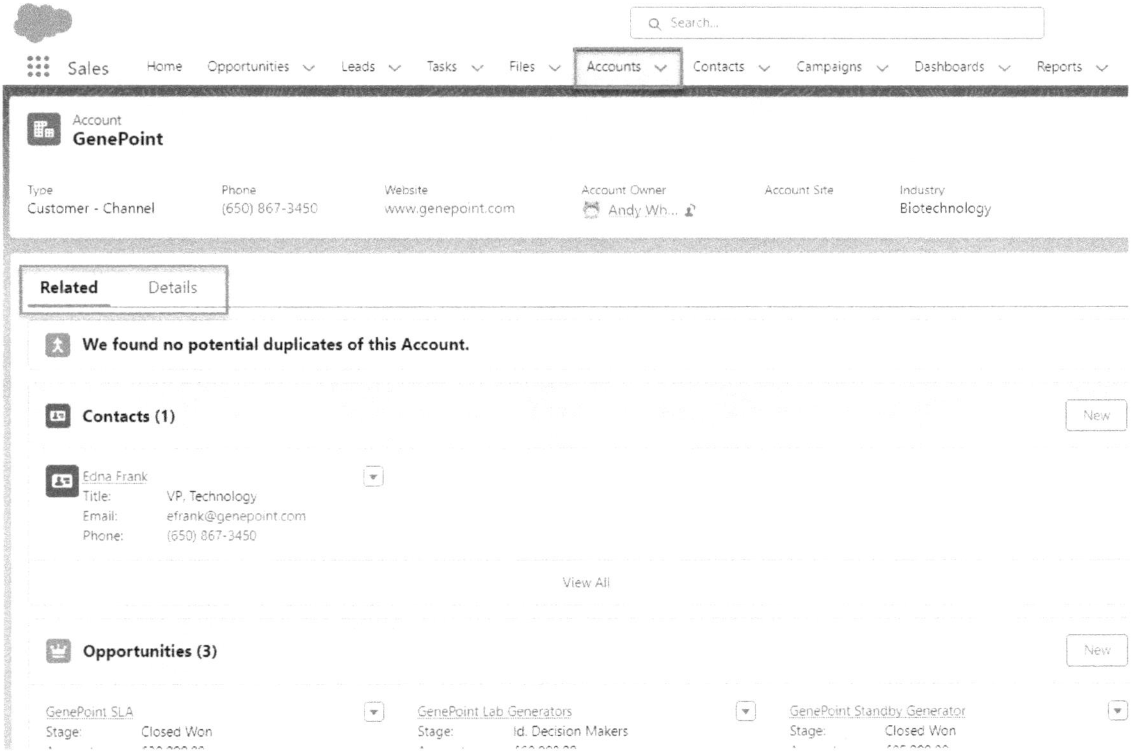

Figure 1.10: *Showing related and detailed information*

In the above illustration, the accounts object is selected in the tab; then, a specific account is chosen (in this case, **GenePoint**). The two tabs highlighted are:

- **Related**: The various **Contacts** and **Opportunities** on this account. Since an account will likely have many contacts, this makes a list, as does the opportunity.

- **Details**: The specific fields are on the account, such as name, address, phone, etc.

The layout of the page can be configured in many different ways:

1. The quickest way to change the layout is by pressing **Setup | Edit Page**, as shown in *Figure 1.11*:

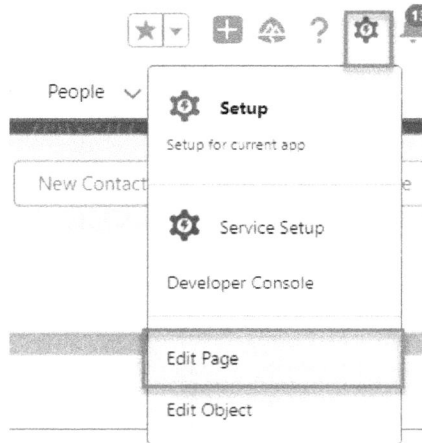

Figure 1.11: Edit Page layout directly from Setup

2. This then displays the page layout for the **Page** you were on, as shown in *Figure 1.12*. Drag the layout about, but do not press **Save** just yet.

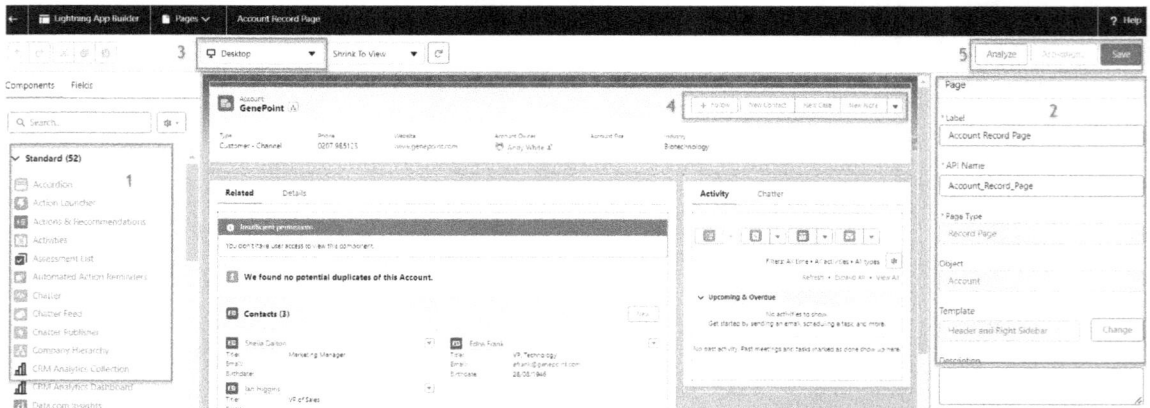

Figure 1.12: Page layout in configuration mode

In *Figure 1.12,* the following areas have been numbered:

1. **Component pane**: Various components can be added to the page. These can be standard Salesforce components or custom components (called LWX).

2. **Component properties**: By pressing a component, the properties (i.e., what configuration options are available) give a list of options available to change different settings on the component.

3. **Preview**: View the page for a laptop, tablet, or mobile device. This allows you to see how Salesforce would appear on different devices and for other users.

4. **Add button**: such as macros or quick actions, to easily automate users' tasks.

5. **Activate**: If you save the page, you need to make it active before users can see it.

Objects and relationships

As mentioned, Salesforce builds relationships between the various objects. This helps users to have all the related information readily available. There are two beneficial relationships that are used throughout basic administration tasks:

- **Master-detail**: This is a firmly bound relationship where the detail (child) record is bound to the master (parent) record. As such, if you delete the parent record, then the child records are also deleted. Master-detail also has specific properties, such as inheriting the sharing model from the parent and being able to do roll-up summary fields. These are discussed later.

- **Lookup relationship**: Although similar to master-detail, this simply looks up a record on the master. If the master is deleted, then the child remains. Also, the child object does not inherit the sharing model from the parent.

In most cases, a lookup relationship is sufficient. Details of the above are covered in *Chapter 4, Creating Object with Custom Fields and Relationships*.

Schema Builder

This section is optional but useful throughout the book. If you want to see the relationships between the objects in Salesforce, Schema Builder is a very useful tool for showing all the objects, fields, and relationships between them:

1. Go to Setup and type **Schema Builder** into the search setup.

2. Select the **Objects** you wish to view on the left-hand side, as shown in *Figure 1.13*.

3. This shows the objects and their relationship to each other, as shown in the following figure:

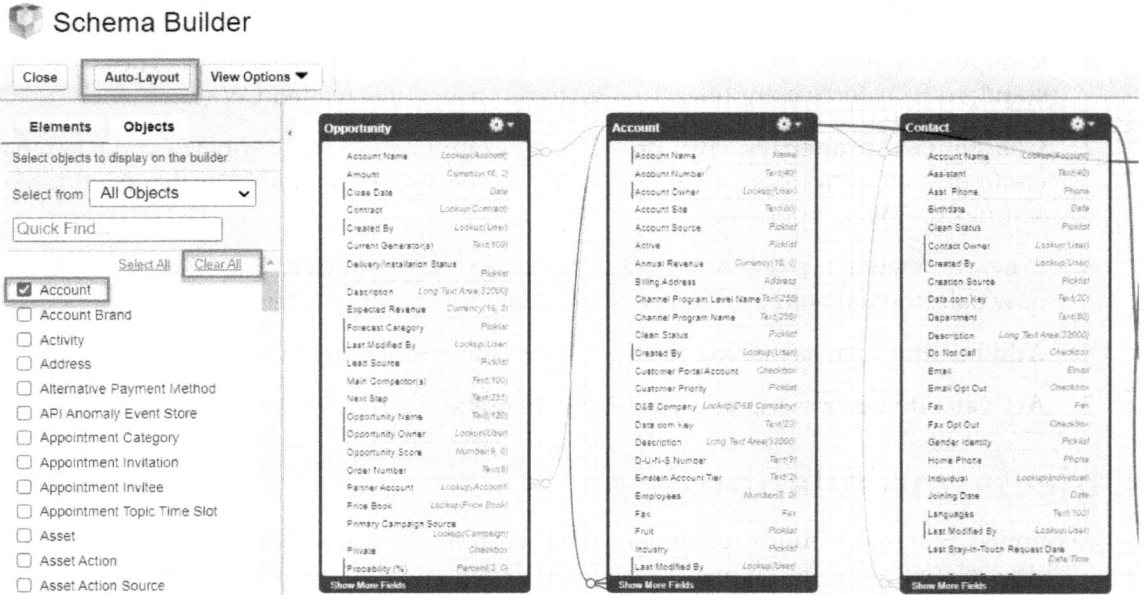

Figure 1.13: Schema Builder

Let us understand *Figure 1.13* in detail:

1. Start by pressing the **Clear All** link to create a blank display (i.e., no objects are shown).

2. Then, from the list on the left, select **Account, Contact, Opportunity**, and **Case**.

3. Finally, press the **Auto-Layout** option to help arrange them on the screen.

4. If you hover your mouse over the lines connecting the objects, you can see information about how they are related.

Objects and their relationships are being emphasized because this directly relates to the user interface. If an object is related to another one, it can appear on the same screen as the parent object (i.e., the one it is related to).

Salesforce list views

Salesforce gives users the choice to see what records they want to see when they first go to a tab in Salesforce. The following figure is for **Opportunities**. The options for what you want to see are listed in the menu:

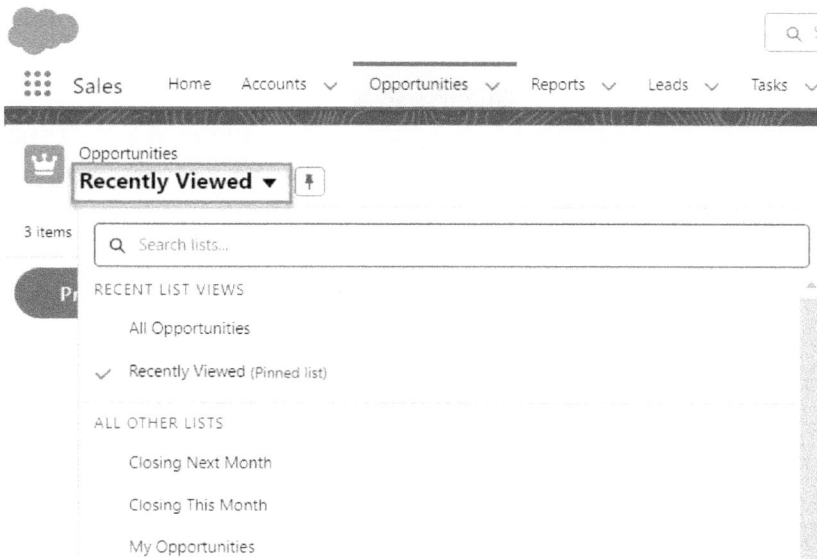

Figure 1.14: List views

To change the criteria for the filters (i.e., what you want to include or exclude), use the small cog icon as shown in the following figure:

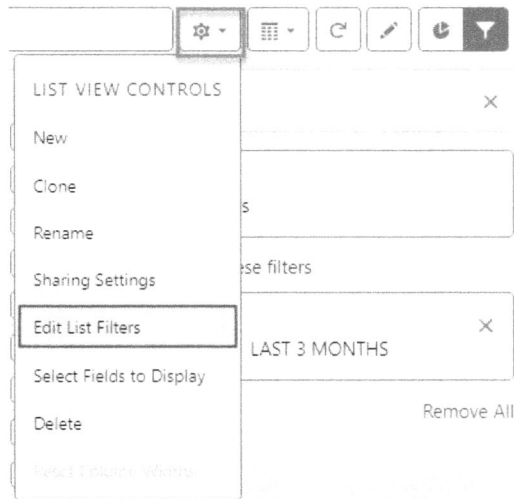

Figure 1.15: Editing list views

The figure above has **Edit List Filters** and **Select Fields to Display**. This allows you to filter only the fields you wish to display and choose which fields appear when you select the list view. For example, a list view can show only records owned by you, a date range, or any field on the object. Views can be shared, too, as shown in *Figure 1.15*.

The following figure shows **Sharing Settings**, which allow you to select from the following options:

Sharing Settings

Who sees this list view?

○ Only I can see this list view

◉ All users can see this list view ❶

○ Share list view with groups of users ❶

| Cancel | Save |

Figure 1.16: Choosing who should see the list view

Changing your profile settings

Follow these steps to change your profile settings:

1. When you first login to Salesforce, you only have the basic information setup for gaining access.

2. You may wish to add more information or check the settings. This is done by clicking the view profile icon in the top-right of the screen, as shown in the following figure:

Andy White ✕

doogle3-dev-ed.develop.my.salesforce.com

Settings Log Out

Figure 1.17: View your own profile

3. If you press the blue character (called **Astro Nomical**) icon, you can update your image and enter basic information.

4. Alternatively, press the **Settings** link shown in *Figure 1.17*, which appears, and a menu of various settings which are outlined as follows:

    a. There are quite a few settings here, but two useful ones are pressing the **Settings** link and selecting **Grant Account Login Access**. This allows other users to grant the Salesforce system administrator access to their account. This is useful for resolving users' issues. It also allows Salesforce support access to your instance if you need it.

b. Other users should follow these steps to grant access to you as an administrator or to give Salesforce access.

c. Grant admin access and select the time period you wish to grant access to your administrator or Salesforce, and press Save.

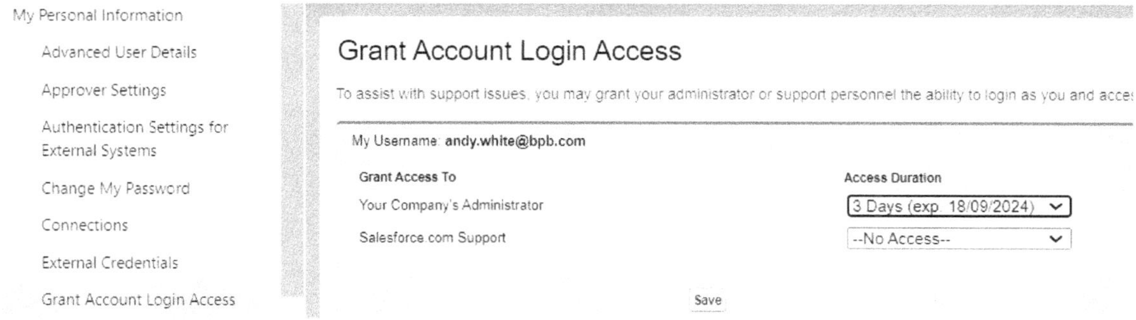

Figure 1.18: Giving access to your Salesforce account

d. **Language and time zone** allow you to switch Salesforce to your preferred language and ensure the time zone is correct for you.

Tasks, events, and Chatter

Salesforce comes with various features to allow users to collaborate with other users and to do their job easily. Salesforce Activities are an additional feature that can be shown on the page layout to allow collaboration on an **Activity**. If you go to the Sales Cloud and choose an **Opportunity** record, you will see the following activities, as shown in the following figure:

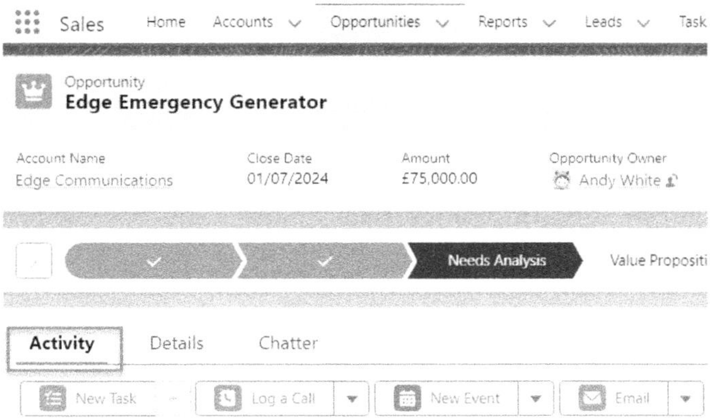

Figure 1.19: Activity-related list

Activities can be performed on any object and allow users to keep a record of what actions have been done by the user related to the record. An **Activity** is typically either a task or an event. Let us look at this in detail:

- **New Task**: Similar to an activity, but there is no date associated with the record. It is simply a list of something that needs to be done and assigned to someone.

- **Events**: These are like tasks, but come with a time and date associated with them. These can be seen on the Calendar included with Salesforce.

- **Log a Call**: Allows users to enter details of a call (or details of other communications) and puts a timeline to show when and what was done.

- **Email**: This requires some configuration first, typically setting up decent email templates and ensuring the Exchange Server (or similar) is configured with Salesforce. However, the email sent enters the same timeline as other activities, allowing you to keep a record of how users engage with customers.

In addition to the activities above, there are other features in Salesforce for keeping track of the progress of users doing their work:

- **Chatter**: Salesforce has an internal instant messaging system called **Chatter**. It has various features, such as a conversation feed and the ability to send and add files. Chatter can be on a particular record or in a group, making collaboration easy. Other options are **Poll** or **Question**, which are similar to the functionality found in *WhatsApp*.

  Note: **Chatter can also be used for collaboration with non-Salesforce users or even external customers. They can be added to Chatter groups.**

- **Notes & Attachments**: All objects support **Notes & Attachments**. For example, if you go to an account record and select the **Related** tab, you will see the following:

Figure 1.20: *Notes & Attachments*

Although **Notes & Attachments** are out-of-the-box functionality, if you are creating a new custom object, then you need to enable them when creating the object (and not afterwards).

- **Files**: Salesforce recommends using the Files feature instead of **Notes & Attachments** since these have better sharing capabilities across the Salesforce org and also have useful features such as preview mode without having to download the file.

You can use both **Notes & Attachments** and files, but it is possible to migrate from one to the other or use a combination of both. This will depend on the company you work for, the age of their Salesforce, and other requirements. There are apps on the AppExchange (such as Magic Mover) that can assist with this. It is possible to use both **Files** and **Notes & Attachments** by enabling the file **General Settings**, as shown in *Figure 1.21*:

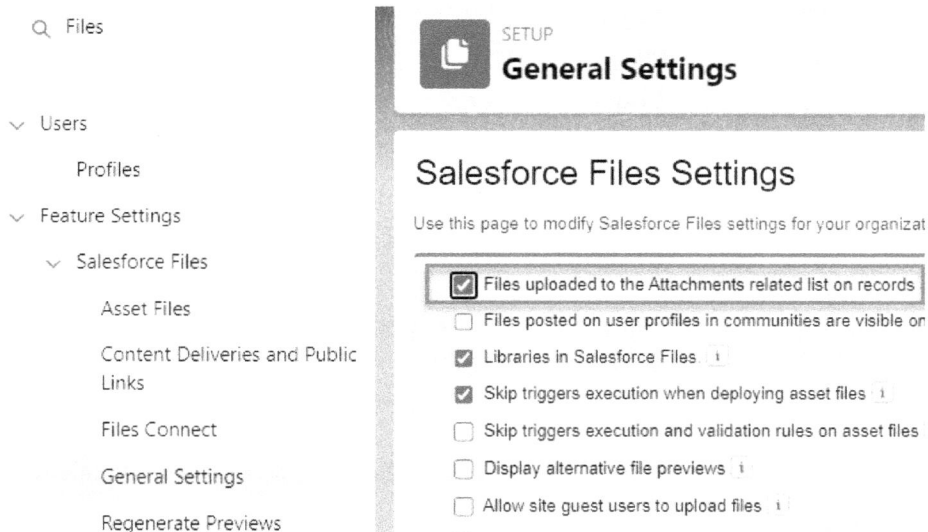

Figure 1.21: *Allowing Notes & Attachments with files*

Conclusion

You have managed to complete the chapter and should have a basic understanding of Salesforce. This chapter would have shown you how to get access to Salesforce and an introduction to Trailhead's training material.

You would have also learned how to navigate the basic Salesforce interface, including access to different apps as well as the tabs. Each tab would have the details section as well as the related lists. You would have also seen that the related lists are, in fact, other Salesforce objects that have a relation with the tab you are on. These relationships (either master-detail or lookup) have been explained.

This should give you the confidence to go into Setup and learn how to find various configuration settings. You will use this throughout this book, as we will discuss it in more detail in the upcoming chapter.

Multiple choice questions

1. **Salesforce uses objects, which can be standard or custom objects. Which objects are standard in Salesforce?**

    a. Accounts, Contacts, Projects

    b. Users, Accounts, Cases

    c. Contacts, Sales, Service

    d. Accounts, Profiles, Tabs

2. **Salesforce uses roles and profiles to:**

    a. Give users access to specific areas of Salesforce

    b. Control which fields are displayed on the page

    c. Allow users different levels of access to data

    d. Give users access to their records

    e. All of the above

3. **Are Files preferable to Notes & Attachments? Is it true or false?**

    a. True

    b. False

4. **All users must have a role to gain access to Salesforce. Is it true or false?**

    a. True

    b. False

5. **Schema Builder is used for:**

    a. Viewing who has access to which objects in Salesforce

    b. Looking at individual objects and which role or profile has access to them

    c. Viewing objects in Salesforce, the fields and relationships between them

    d. Creating apps and tabs that can be used

6. **Trailhead is just one of many resources available for learning Salesforce. Is it true or false?**

    a. True

    b. False

7. **The language used by Salesforce for doing custom development is called:**

    a. React

    b. Apex

    c. Flex

    d. ActionScript

8. **How many times is Salesforce updated each year?**

    a. Two times

    b. Three times

    c. Four times

    d. Six times

9. **Salesforce has various products, but the two main ones are:**

    a. Sales and Marketing Cloud

    b. Salesforce and Admin Cloud

    c. Sales and Service Cloud

    d. Service and Developer Cloud

10. **LWC uses traditional web skills such as HTML, CSS, and JavaScript as well as APEX. Is it true or false?**

    a. True

    b. False

11. **What is the name of a development environment in Salesforce?**

    a. Scratch box

    b. Developer environment

    c. Configuration workbench

    d. Sandbox

Answers

1   **b**

2   **e**

3   **a**

4   **b**

5   **c**

6   **a**

7   **b**

8   **b**

9   **c**

10   **a**

11   **d**

Join our Discord space

Join our Discord workspace for latest updates, offers, tech happenings around the world, new releases, and sessions with the authors:

https://discord.bpbonline.com

Chapter 2
Basic Admin Essentials

Introduction

Having got a basic understanding of Salesforce in the previous chapter, this chapter is about starting to configure Salesforce and some of the basic settings. By the end of this chapter, you will have a good foundation for understanding how Salesforce is configured for basic tasks.

This chapter also goes through the process that is typical for many companies using Salesforce. The process of getting new potential sales on the lead object and then progressing through an opportunity. With some configuration, you can then create a quote around the opportunity. If the sale is successful, then this allows users to create and order, which then allows users to take care of their customers using Service Cloud.

Although this is a very high-level overview, it helps administrators understand why they are often asked to do configurations by understanding the end-to-end process of creating sales in the Sales Cloud and looking after customers in the Service Cloud.

Structure

In this chapter, we will discuss the following topics:

- Understanding what is in your Salesforce org
- Main Salesforce object model

- Relationship between Sales and Service Cloud
- Basic Salesforce customization
- Administration essentials
- Data management

Objectives

The main objective of this chapter is to allow you to gain familiarity with Salesforce and how to navigate to certain areas, such as Salesforce Setup and Object Manager. The aim is to build a foundation for the rest of this book. Many of the sections in this chapter will assume knowledge from throughout this book, so it is important that you are familiar with the basic concepts, which are explained in this chapter.

The aim is to allow you to understand the basic principles required for a Salesforce Administrator and give you confidence to go through some of the more in-depth chapters that follow.

Understanding what is in your Salesforce org

If you are using the Developer Edition Salesforce org, then it will be straight out-of-the-box. However, you may also find yourself working on Salesforce orgs that have been used for several years or configured for a specific purpose.

To get an overview of what features are in your Salesforce org, go to **Setup | Company Information** as shown in the following figure:

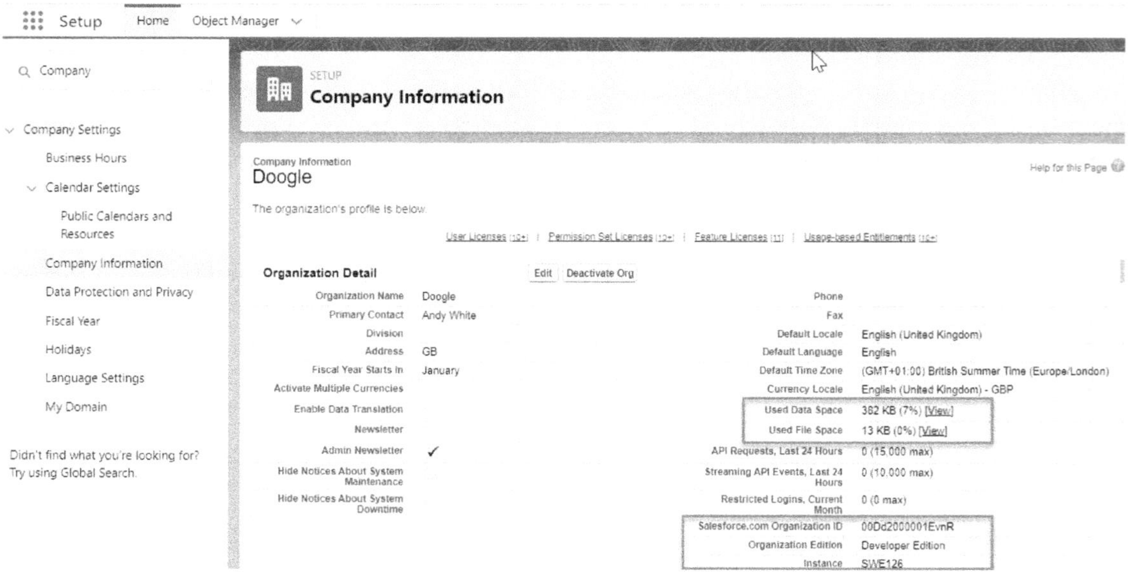

Figure 2.1: Company Information and org properties

The above basic information is shown:

- **Used Data Space**: The amount of data stored in records, i.e., the actual fields in Salesforce. Click the **View** link to see the storage usage.

- **Used File Space**: Anything attached to an object in Salesforce, such as a document, image, etc. Click the **View** link to see the storage usage.

- **Salesforce.com Organization ID**: This is useful when raising a case with Salesforce to identify the org you might be having an issue with. It is also useful in other areas.

- **Organization Edition**: This is often useful for ensuring the edition can support features you wish to add or use.

- **Instance**: The name of the server hosting your Salesforce instance. This is useful for **https://trust.salesforce.com/**, discussed in *Chapter 9, Various Salesforce Tools*.

  Further down the page, you will see:

  o **User licenses**:

    - Permission set licenses

    - Managed packages

    - Feature licenses

The first two are often used when adding additional functionality from Salesforce or a third-party vendor. Feature licenses show you how much of your Salesforce resources are being used, and are helpful to see if you are reaching some of Salesforce's limits.

Doing health check on your Salesforce org

If starting at a new company with an old Salesforce org, the AppExchange has Salesforce Org Check, which can be run in either a full-copy sandbox or in production. There are more sophisticated tools (such as CodeScan or SonarQube), but Salesforce Org Check will indicate the level of technical debt (i.e., bad configuration) in the org.

The image for Org Check on the AppExchange is shown in the following figure:

Figure 2.2: Org Check on the Salesforce AppExchange

Main Salesforce object model

Although it is a relatively simple process to create custom objects in Salesforce, it is important to understand the Salesforce standard objects first. Since there are many of them, it is better to use the available objects before creating custom objects. Objects can always be renamed (go to **Setup | Rename Tabs and Labels**), but be aware that there may be built-in functionality on the object that might not be wanted, or could even be a bonus.

The following figure is a high-level illustration of the core objects in Salesforce. It is simplified for illustrative purposes:

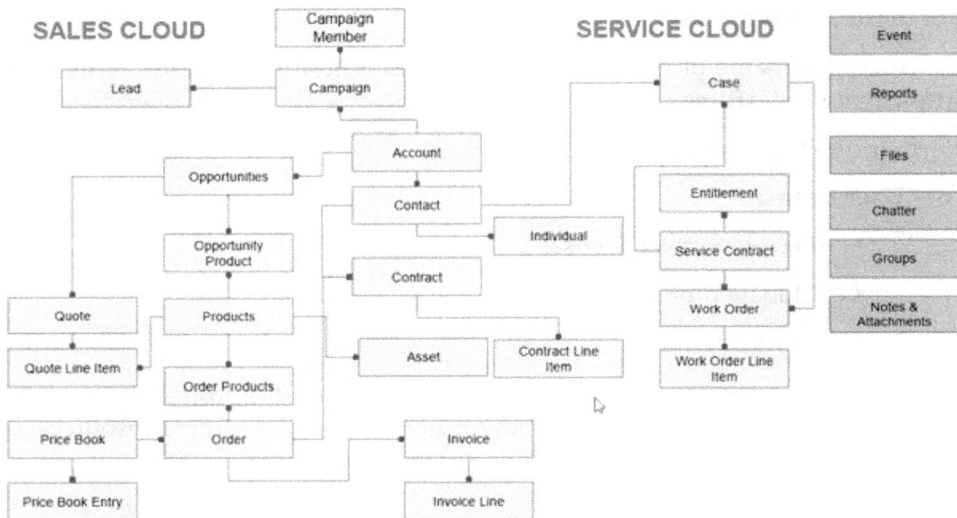

Figure 2.3: *Salesforce object model, showing the main objects and their relationships*

The above figure shows objects generally used for the Sales Cloud on the left-hand side and those for the Service Cloud on the right-hand side. Those in the middle are used for both. The objects that stand-alone on the right-hand side are used in many places, so the connections are not illustrated to keep the figure simple, likewise with accounts and contacts, since most records in Salesforce will have some relationship with accounts or contacts.

Although *Figure 2.3*, often called an **entity relationship diagram** (**ERD**) or **object model diagram** (**OMD**), may look uninviting to someone new to IT or Salesforce, it is possibly the most useful diagram to be familiar with, as it shows you how objects in Salesforce relate to each other. It is useful for building reports, designing flows, knowing which related lists can be added to the user interface, and also for coding. In fact, a good working knowledge of the objects and how they relate is useful for almost all configurations in Salesforce.

The relationship between master-detail (or parent-child, or one-to-many as it is often called) is shown in the following figure, meaning that the parent object (on the left) has many records from the child object (on the right), for example, an Account can have many Contact:

Figure 2.4: Master-detail relationship

There are many other objects that are not shown. To easily view them and the relationship between objects, go to the Schema Builder outlined in *Chapter 1, Introduction to Salesforce.*

Note: Some objects are a combination of two connected objects. These are known as junction objects in Salesforce since they allow a many-to-many relationship between objects. For example, in Figure 2.3, the Opportunity Product object allows a Products to be used many times for many Opportunities.

Refer to the following figure:

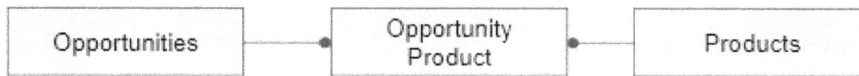

Figure 2.5: Many-to-many relationship known as a junction object

It is also possible to have a relationship known as **looking up** (called a **lookup relationship**) to the same object. For example, an account has a lookup relationship to itself, meaning an account can have a parent account, which allows you to build out a headquarters account with many subsidiary (or smaller) depots or subsidiary branch accounts. You can see this on an account record with the tiny icon, which shows the account hierarchy based on this functionality.

Relationship between Sales and Service Cloud

The following sections show a scenario to illustrate the typical lifecycle of a company that sells its goods and services using Salesforce to manage the end-to-end process. In other words, this is where the journey begins for a possible lead, which is converted into an opportunity, which can be turned into an order.

Should the customer have any further questions or issues, a case can be raised in Service Cloud to keep the customer happy.

Note: This section is to give you more of an understanding than a hands-on exercise. Feel free to follow along in your own Salesforce org, but the steps to allow you to convert opportunities to quotes and orders require additional configuration, which is typically met by sophisticated configuration or adding configure, price, quote (CPQ) or Revenue Lifecycle Management (RLM) functionality. Once you have completed this book, you will look at the steps described in the following section and find them in a logical progression.

Lead object

The lead object is where the sales journey starts. It is simply an object to store information about a potential new sale. This could come from a campaign, a website, a phone call, social media, a trade show, or anything else. Since it is likely to contain a lot of unnecessary information, it is a stand-alone object until it is qualified and progresses to an opportunity. Note that there is no relationship between lead and opportunity, but if the lead is sufficiently likely, then it is converted to an opportunity.

Figure 2.3 does not show the relationship between lead and opportunities since the conversion is done automatically by Salesforce.

To do this, go to leads in your Salesforce org and press the **Convert** button (sometimes hidden on the list on the top right-hand side). This creates an opportunity with the essential information copied across from the lead to the opportunity record. You can control which fields are mapped from lead to opportunity in **Setup | Object Manager | Leads | Fields and Relationship**, and select the **Map Lead Fields** button. This offers mapping to accounts, contacts, and opportunity fields.

Lead also comes with special features, such as Web-to-Lead, discussed in *Chapter 10, Various Salesforce Features*.

Opportunity object

The opportunity object is really where the lead is official. You can add a new opportunity without creating a lead first, but the opportunity object stores the information about the possible future sale. It could be something the company sells, a service, or a combination. It will have the various financial fields, and two required fields:

- **Stage**: From initially being entered into Salesforce to being Closed Won or Closed Lost, indicating whether the opportunity was successful or not.

- **Close date**: This is needed to provide forecasting, i.e., to show how an opportunity is progressing over time.

These are needed to build out the sales pipeline. A sales pipeline allows the company to see its anticipated revenue in the future.

The stage is particularly important as it is displayed by a series of chevrons at the top of the page called the **opportunity path**. This is configured in **Setup | Path Settings**.

There are different ways to view the sales pipeline, but the simplest way is to go to the **Opportunity** tab, select **All Opportunities** from the list view, and press the **Kanban** view as shown in the following figure:

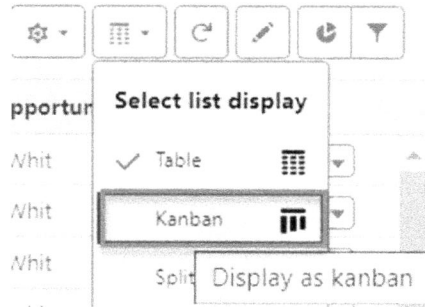

Figure 2.6: *Changing the view from table to Kanban*

Opportunity comes with special features such as opportunity teams or big deal alerts discussed in *Chapter 10, Various Salesforce Features*.

Note: **Many objects use a path to show progress at various stages. Salesforce has a fun feature called a confetti shower, which can be launched when a path reaches a milestone, such as an opportunity being won. This is covered in Chapter 10, Various Salesforce Features.**

Product object

Products are either physical things sold by the company, or they can also refer to services offered by the company. The collection of products is often referred to as the **product catalogue**.

Before you can add products to an opportunity or order, you first need to create the products in Salesforce. Your Developer Edition org will come with various products already installed. To see the **Products**, go to **App Launcher** and select the **Products** object.

To create a product, you simply need to press the **New** button and optionally include a photo of it using the URL from the image stored in the file object. If you are working for a company, there may well be many products already available, but you may need to ensure it is kept up to date.

Opportunity product object

These are the products or services needed to fulfil the opportunity. The products are either products or services that the company wishes to sell. These can be added to the opportunity on the **Products** related list as shown in the following figure:

Related

Figure 2.7: Adding products to the opportunity

When adding products, you are also asked to add the quantity and other information if you want.

As mentioned above, an opportunity product is a junction object, which means it acts as a many-to-many object, storing products for an opportunity, effectively the products or services the customer has requested, with the prices shown.

Price book object

The price book object can also be found via the app menu and comes with a standard price book. It stores information about the price of the products.

You can create multiple price books to reflect discounts for certain customers, regional differences, or even different currencies using the Salesforce multi-currency feature, as described briefly below. Once you have a price book open, you add products by using the price book entry related list.

Two features which are useful when configuring price books are:

- **Multi-currency**: Having currencies such as *US Dollars, Euros*, or the *Japanese Yen* can co-exist in the same Salesforce org. To do this, start with **Setup | Manage Currencies**.

- **Advanced currency management**: A step further by giving exchange rates for various time ranges. This allows financial figures to be calculated on exchange rates between fixed dates.

Note: **Price books can be active or inactive, and if using multi-currency, they require the currency of the price book to be the same as the contract being used on the opportunity or the order.**

This is covered in more detail in *Chapter 10, Various Salesforce Features*.

Further considerations

If you are following along with the configuration, so far, everything should work out-of-the-box. However, for the next steps, some configuration is required. This is optional, but converting opportunities into quotes and orders is additional Salesforce functionality available in CPQ, which is not available in a Salesforce Developer org. You can either register for a free Salesforce CPQ training environment or add this manually as described in the following. The steps in the following are not providing true CPQ functionality; in fact, far from it, since CPQ is quite complex. However, it is making orders and quotes available on the opportunity object, but also manages the transfer of records between them.

Note: **At the time of writing, CPQ is being superseded by Salesforce RLM. CPQ is not going to go away, but Salesforce is a continually evolving platform with new features built as the platform progresses.**

The following are the steps to add quotes and orders to the opportunity:

1. **Adding quote functionality**: Go to **Setup** | **Quote Settings**, then tick **Enable Quotes**. For the next step, assign it to all the page layouts and press **Save**.

2. **Adding order functionality**: Go to **Setup** | **Object Manager** | select the order object | select **Fields & Relationships**, then find the **Opportunity** field (it will be a field of type: `Lookup Relationship`). Press the **Opportunity** field to edit it and press the **Set Field-Level Security** button at the top of the page. Check the visible box for everything and press **Save**.

Optional: The configuration described below is covered in more detail in *Chapter 3, Customizing User Interface*. The two steps above would have done the necessary configuration, but both the order and quote-related lists will be right at the bottom of the opportunity page layout and hard to see.

To improve the page layout, go to **Setup** | **Object Manager** | select **Opportunity**. On the left-hand menu, choose **Page Layout** and choose the **Opportunity Layout**. Add the order-related list to the page layout (refer to *Chapter 3, Customizing User Interface* if needed) and move the order and quote-related list to the top of the page, just below the product-related list, and press **Save**. You should see **Orders** and **Quotes** on the opportunity objects as shown in the following figure:

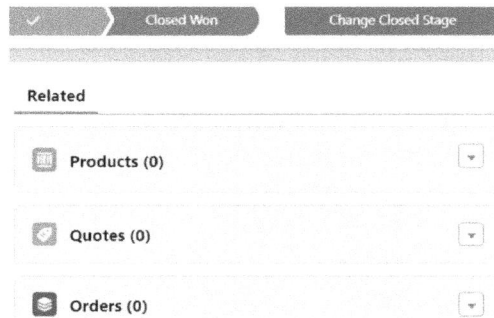

Figure 2.8: Showing Products, Quotes, and Orders on an opportunity

Quote object

If you cannot see the quote on the opportunity page, simply go to **Quotes** in the **App Launcher**. Quotes are similar to orders in many ways, but provide the ability to send customers a quote before they place an order.

The only required field is **Quote Name**. Save the quote and go to the actual quote. If you successfully completed the setup of quotes and orders, you would see that the quote is already populated with a link to the opportunity.

On the related list, you will also see **Quote Line Items** where you can **Add Products** to the quote, as shown in the following figure:

Figure 2.9: Quote Line Items

Order object

Orders are the basis of sales. These can be linked to quotes or invoices, but can be processed without either. With orders enabled on the opportunity, the new order can be created with the products and prices setup previously.

Similar to adding a quote, with the **Orders** related list on the opportunity, press the **New** button. Once, follow the order creation wizard, as shown in the following figure:

Figure 2.10: Adding an order to an opportunity

If you cannot save an order as it requires a **Contract Number**, go to the order page layout and press the wrench icon to prevent it from being required, as shown in the following:

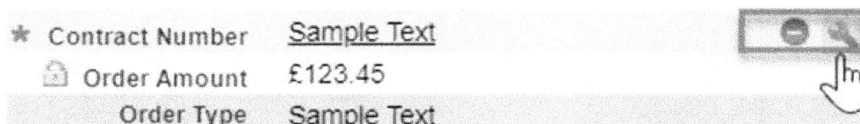

Figure 2.11: Adding an order without adding a Contract Number

Asset object

Assets are the products previously ordered but now belong to the account. Once the order has been fulfilled (and paid), then the assets need to be created. Assets are useful to provide **service level agreements** (**SLAs**) so that assets can have service warranties or the customer can contact support for issues with a product they have previously bought.

To view assets, go to the **App Launcher** and enter **Assets**. If you are in a Developer Edition org, you will not find any assets since they need to be created as part of completing an order. However, you can create one by selecting an existing product and assigning it to an account.

Case object

The case object is central to how Salesforce manages customer support and services. It is used to record information to support customers should there be a fault with a product they have purchased, or simply need some information. In *Figure 2.3*, we have moved over from the Sales Cloud to the Service Cloud, which allows cases to be created. Cases come with various features, such as a status to update users of Salesforce, and can be logged manually by a user or automatically, such as Web-to-Case or Email-to-Case. Cases can also be assigned to queues, which allow them to be dealt with in an organized manner, or escalation rules to ensure they are dealt with to meet SLAs. All of this is configurable, but a typical case record is shown in the illustration in the following figure:

Cases (3)

00001000		▼	00001017	
Contact Na...	Rose Gonzalez		Contact Na...	Sean Forbes
Subject:	Starting generator after electrical fa...		Subject:	Shutting down of generator
Priority:	High		Priority:	Medium

Figure 2.12: Adding a case, an account, or a contact record

Summary of Salesforce objects

Not described here in detail are objects that are not part of the direct sales to service lifecycle. For example, the campaign object is useful for managing and tracking marketing efforts. The service contract and entitlements object offer SLAs to customers, as well as objects with line items in their names. These objects give the individual rows of products associated with the quote or order.

The above walkthrough gives an idea of the lifecycle between Sales and Service Cloud. There are many more features, but this would be typical of a company selling products to customers and maintaining the customer relationship by having the information about the account, contact, and their previous order history. This then could be used in a call center when Salesforce has Service Cloud Voice enabled, see *Chapter 14, Broader Salesforce Ecosystem*.

Basic Salesforce customization

Having gained an understanding of the main objects in Salesforce, the next step in learning is how to customize the objects by adding fields and being able to control the layout. These two skills alone will give you great control over how Salesforce is configured for users.

Adding fields to an object

This guide is for people wanting to customize Salesforce. It is hard to know where to start, but let us assume you want to add additional fields to the standard objects and to display them in a particular way.

To add a field, you will need to know what object you want to add it to. So, navigate to **Object Manager** and select **Account** as shown in the following figure:

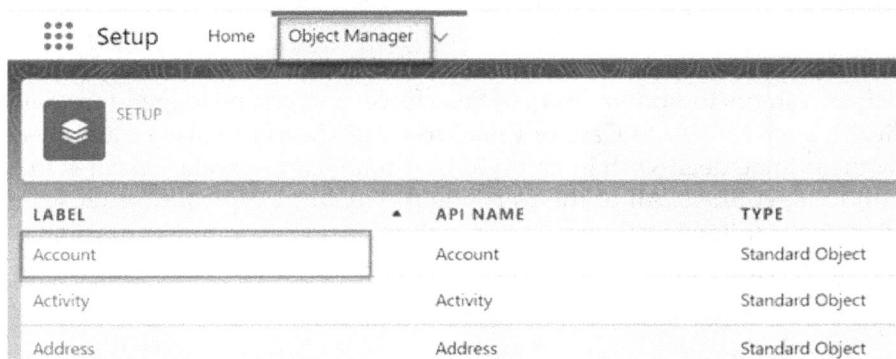

Figure 2.13: Selecting the Account object from Object Manager

Look at the options on the left-hand side, but choose **Fields & Relationships** as shown in the following figure, and press the **New** button:

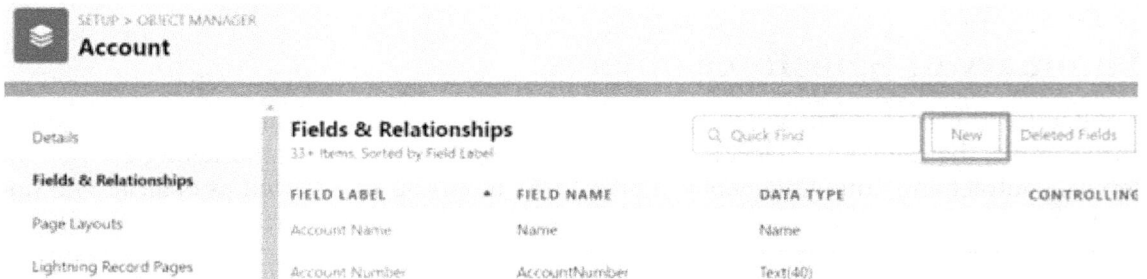

Figure 2.14: Creating a new field on the Account object

There are many different types of fields you can choose from, each with a description. It is important to familiarize yourself with each type. Although you will probably find you use some more than others, it is worth knowing what is available.

For now, choose the **Picklist** option as shown in the following figure, then **Next**:

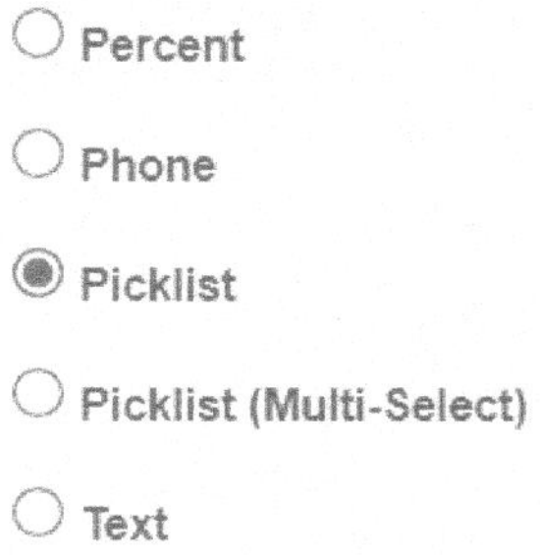

○ Percent

○ Phone

◉ Picklist

○ Picklist (Multi-Select)

○ Text

Figure 2.15: Selecting field type

Give the **Field Name**, such as `Fruit`, and list various fruits. Also, if you give a helpful **Description**, then the field gives alt text help when it is displayed on the screen, as shown in the following figure:

Field Label | Fruit | i

Values   ○ Use global picklist value set

○ Enter values, with each value separated by a new line

Mango
Grapes
Apples
Apricots
Oranges
Banana
Avocados

☑ Display values alphabetically, not in the order entered

☐ Use first value as default value i

☑ Restrict picklist to the values defined in the value set i

Field Name | Fruit | i

Description | My list of favourite fruits

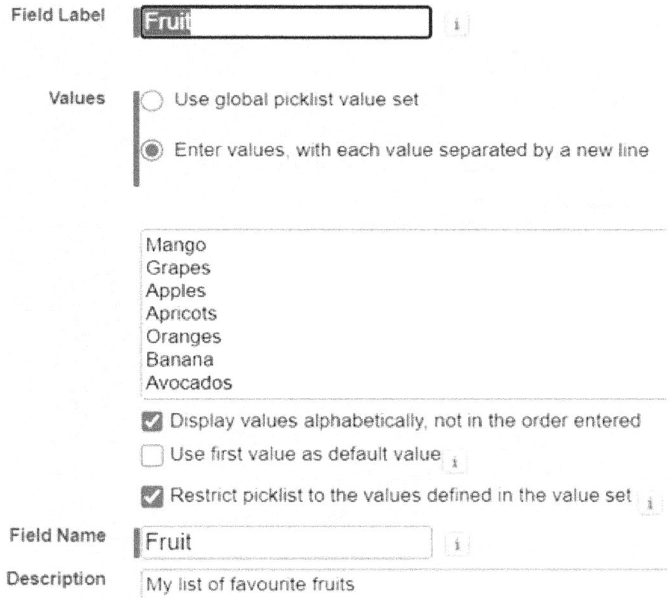

Figure 2.16: Adding picklist values to the picklist

Note the following two tips:

- Only tick the required option if you need this field completed before the record is saved. This can be set at the field-level (here) or on the page layout. If required on the field-level, then Salesforce will not save the record until a value is entered.

- If you select **Use global picklist value set**, then the picklist can be used elsewhere in Salesforce, not just on the Account object. For example, you may have a list of countries or states that are used in various features throughout Salesforce. This needs to be created beforehand from **Setup** | (search for) `Global Value Sets`. Enter the values here and then return to creating a new field and select it from the global picklist value set.

Press **Next** and **Next** and **Save**, although it takes time to understand the options.

To see the field, navigate to the **Sales** app as shown in the following figure:

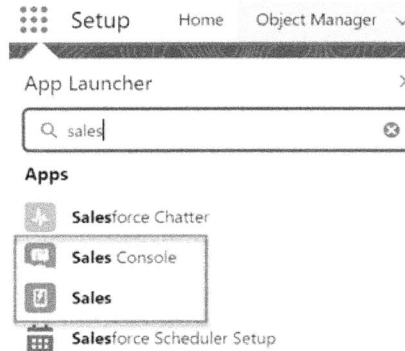

Figure 2.17: Selecting the Sales app from the App Launcher

Then, from the **Accounts** tab, select an account to see the new field on the page layout, as shown in the following figure:

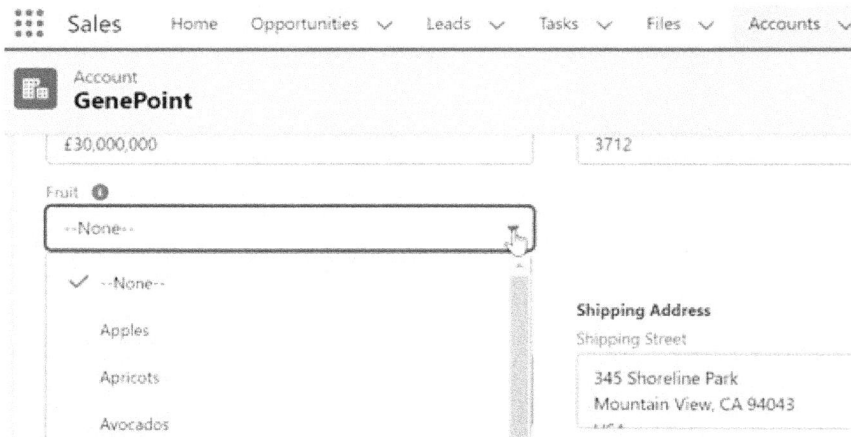

Figure 2.18: Using the newly created picklist field

Customizing the page layout

However, you may find the field is not where you would like it to be on the screen. Salesforce can take you directly into configuration for the screen by selecting the **Edit Page** option from the **Setup** cog, as shown in the following figure:

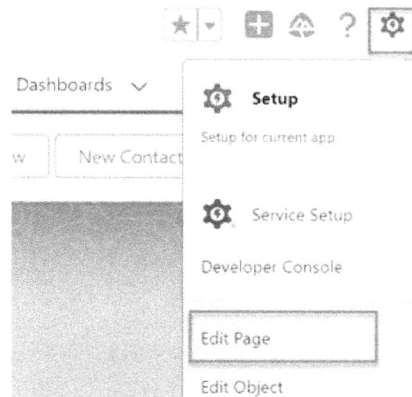

Figure 2.19: *Editing the page layout directly from the screen you are on*

This will show the page layout editor, as shown in the following figure:

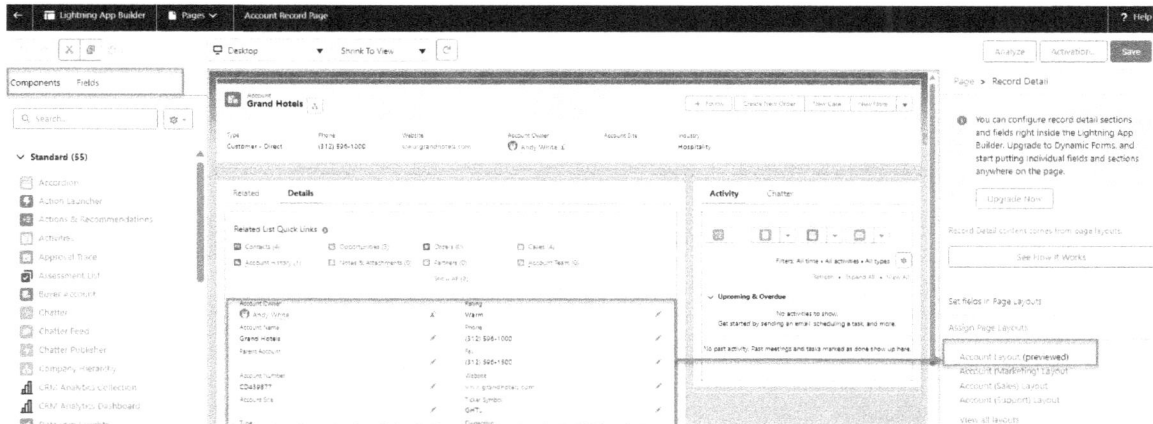

Figure 2.20: *Selecting the correct page layout for adjusting field positions and related lists*

Note: The options for adding various components, selecting fields to add (or remove), as well as the link for the layout, are highlighted in the figure. This is covered in more detail in Chapter 3, Customizing User Interface.

Selecting the **Account Layout** (highlighted on the right) brings you to the page layout configuration.

Note: You can also get to this by simply going to Setup | Object Manager, selecting the object, and choosing Page Layouts from the menu on the left-hand side.

There are options here for what you would like to do, but to re-arrange the layout, select the field you would like and simply drag it to the new location on the page, and press **Save**. Revisit the record you were looking at previously to check that you have changed the layout.

Refer to the following figure:

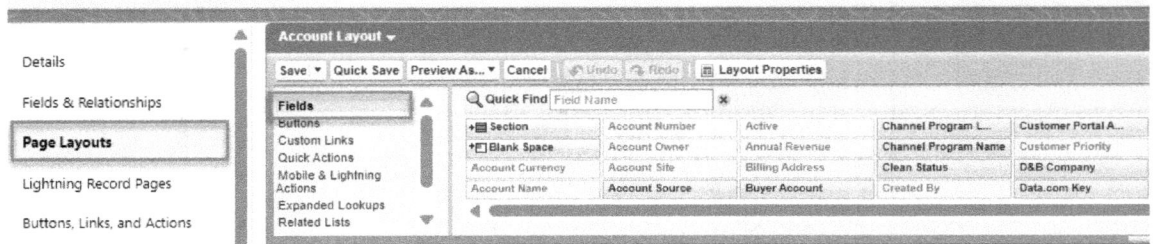

Figure 2.21: *Selecting which fields to add or remove from the page layout*

It is worth noting that adding or removing fields from a page does not necessarily prevent users from accessing the record. It could be available in reports, dashboards, or elsewhere. The Salesforce security model is discussed later, but if a user must not see fields (for example, sensitive information), then it is important to do this via **Sharing Settings** in the **Setup** menu. This will automatically prevent the user from seeing the field in the page layout and elsewhere in Salesforce.

Renaming objects

We have just learned how to modify or create objects, but the name given to a standard object might not be the name your company is familiar with. For example, the **Accounts** object might be better named **Businesses**.

To rename an object (or fields), type **Rename** into the setup search field as shown in the following figure:

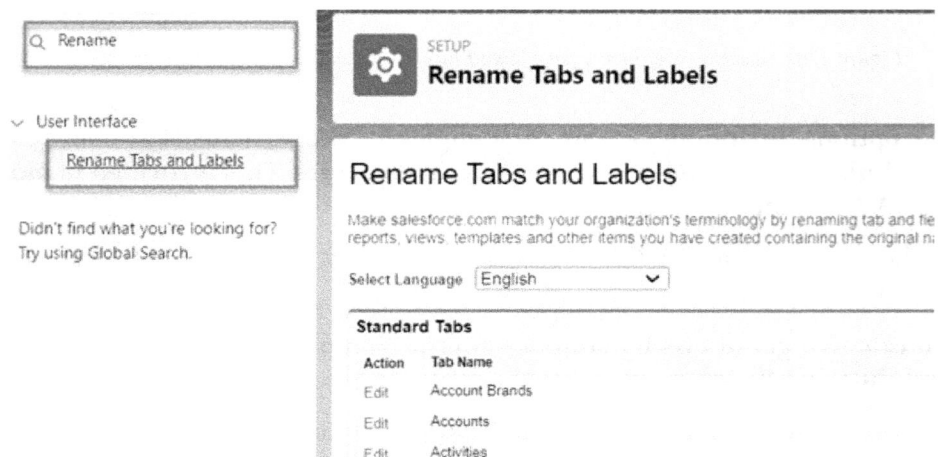

Figure 2.22: *Renaming objects tabs and labels*

Select **Edit** next to the object you wish to rename; in this case, select **Accounts**, and enter the name you would like to use, as shown in the following figure:

Figure 2.23: Renaming object names

Press **Next**, rename any fields on the object you want to change, and press **Save**.

Creating custom views

Tabs are basically a visual representation of an object. There may be fields on the object that are more important. These can be selected by creating a custom view, which can also be filtered to only show the required information. On each tab, there are views, which show the list of fields to display and a filter to select which records to show. For example, going to the **Accounts** tab, you will see **Recently Viewed**, which shows accounts you have recently looked at, as shown in the following figure:

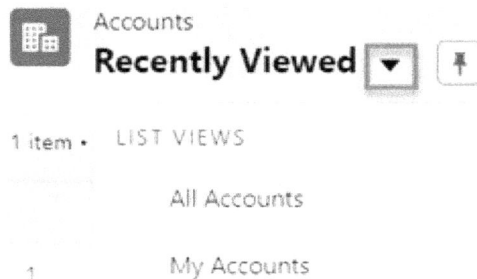

Figure 2.24: Selecting a list view

Note: **You can rearrange the order of the tabs simply by dragging them left or right to create the order you would like to see.**

Pressing the gear icon allows a **New** view to be created, as shown in the following figure:

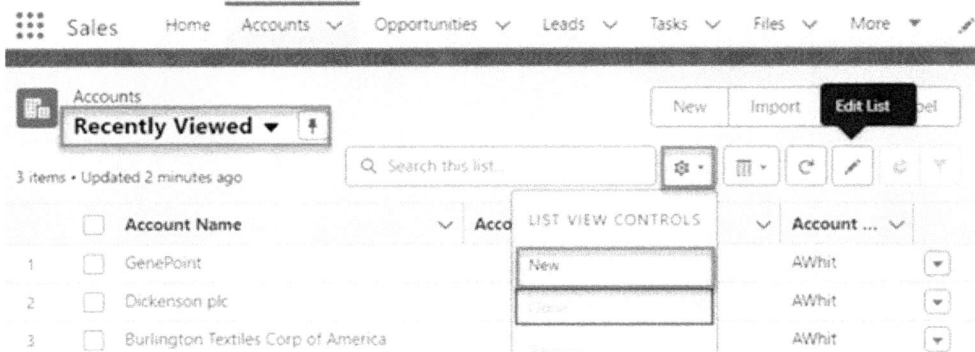

Figure 2.25: Creating a new view

For example, to create a view of **Accounts** that are high priority, create a view called `High Priority Accounts`. As an administrator, you can choose who gets to see this view with the options shown in the following figure:

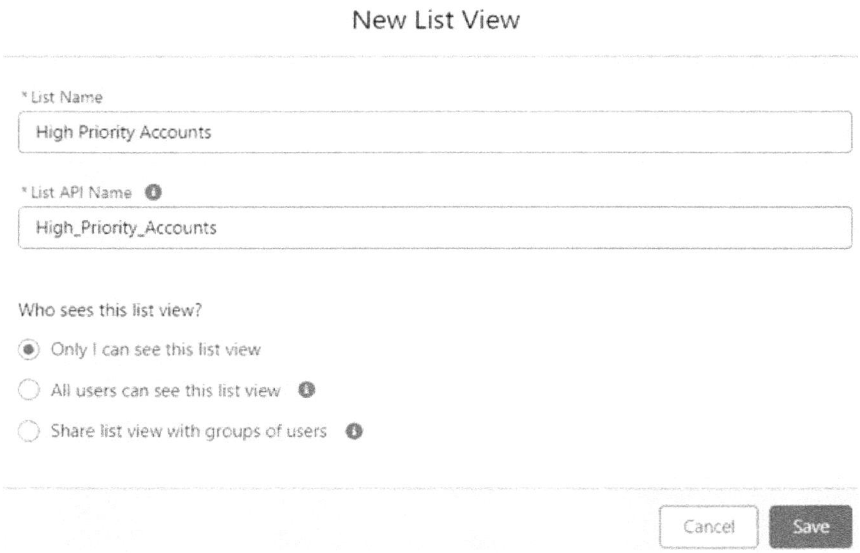

Figure 2.26: Assigning list views to different users or groups

This creates a custom view which can now be filtered for **Custom Priority** to **High**, as shown in the following figure:

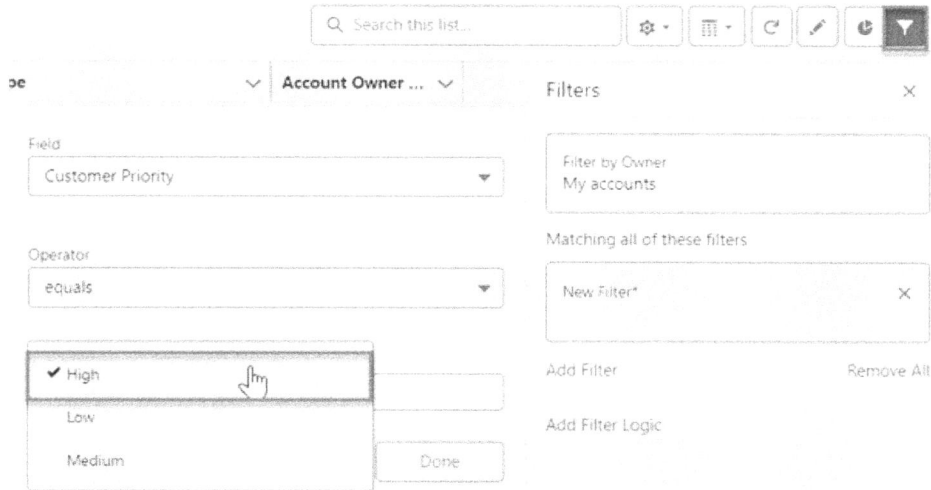

Figure 2.27: *Adding a filter to a list view*

Press the **Done** button and **Save**.

Finally, select which fields to display by choosing **Select Fields to Display,** as shown in the following figure:

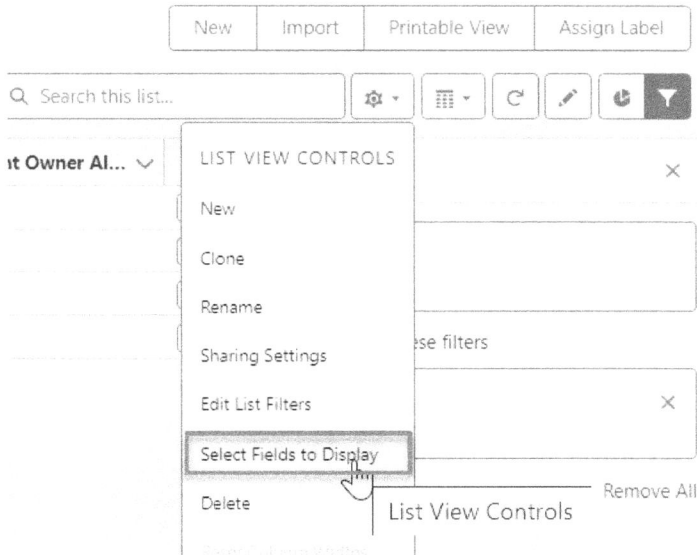

Figure 2.28: *Select the fields to display on the list view*

This shows all the fields that are available on the object. Use the left-right arrows (**1**) in the following figure to select which fields to add or remove from the new view. Order them using the up-down arrows (**2**) to get the display correctly ordered:

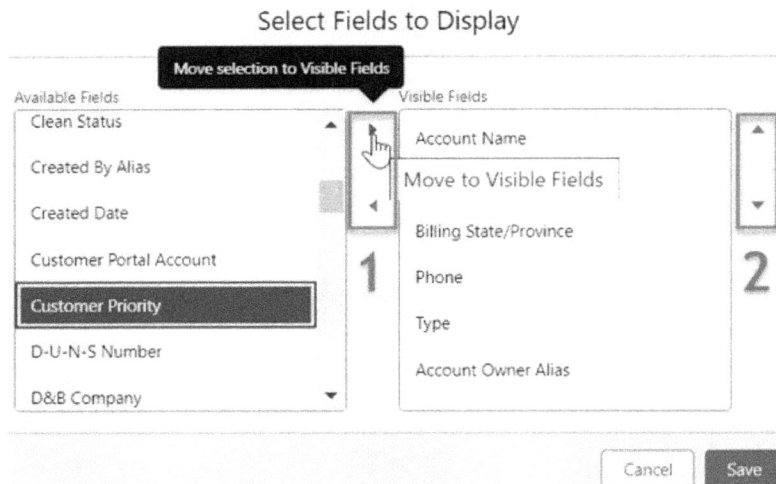

Figure 2.29: Adding fields to the list view

Press **Save**, and you will see the new view showing the fields and records that match the view filter and order as shown in the following figure:

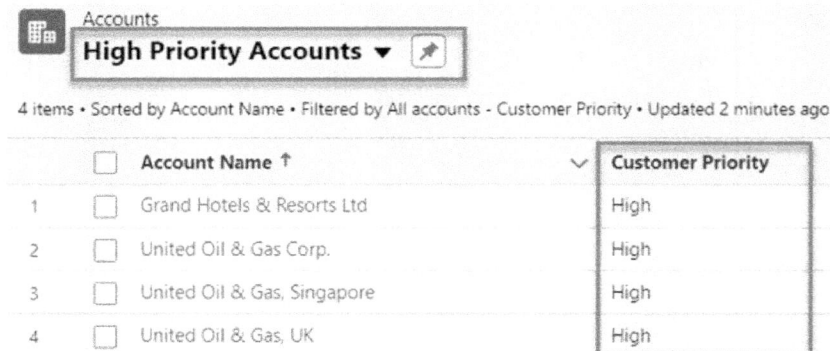

Figure 2.30: Results of a correctly configured list view

Search layouts and related lists

Related lists are the various areas on an object that show related information to the object associated with the tab. The fields displayed on a related list are controlled by the search layout. The difference is as follows:

- **Related list**: These appear on a record detail page, showing records related via a relationship lookup or master-detail relationship.
- **Search layout**: These appear in search results, lookup dialogs, recent items, and list views.

For example, on the **Accounts** tab, there are related lists for **Contacts** and **Opportunities**. However, these may not show the fields most relevant for users, which can be controlled by search layouts.

For example, selecting the related list for **Contacts** from an account shows the following figure:

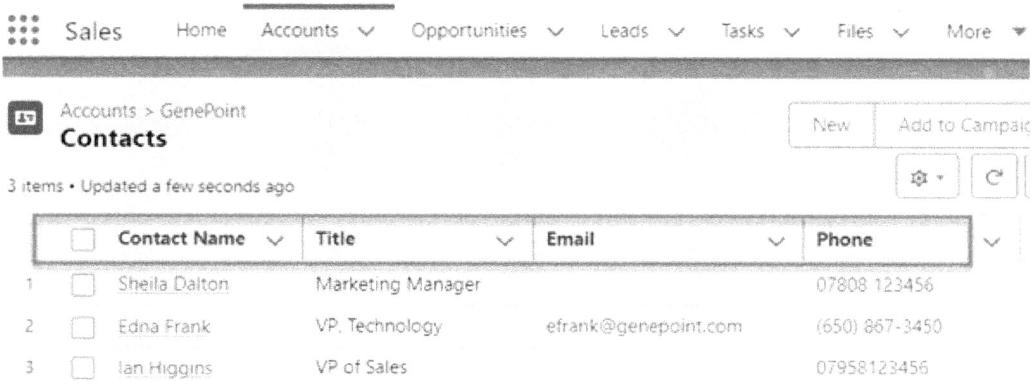

Figure 2.31: Fields displayed on a related list

For example, users would like to see the contact's birthday on the list. To do this, go to **Setup** and use quick find for **Search Layouts**. Select the object you wish to update, such as **Contact**, as shown in the following figure:

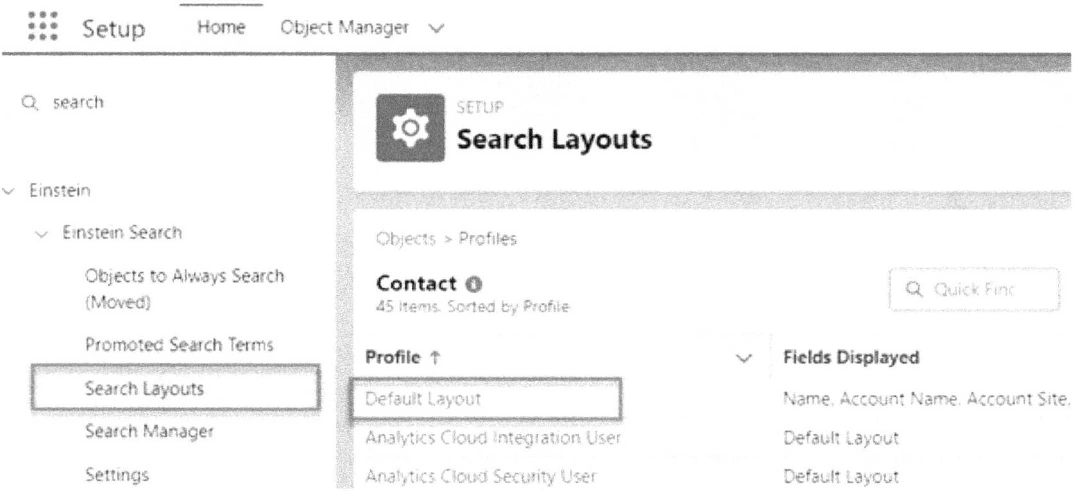

Figure 2.32: Selecting the Default Layout to modify a search layout

Select the **Default Layout** and add **Birthdate** to the list, move it up using the arrows, and press **Save**, as shown in the following figure:

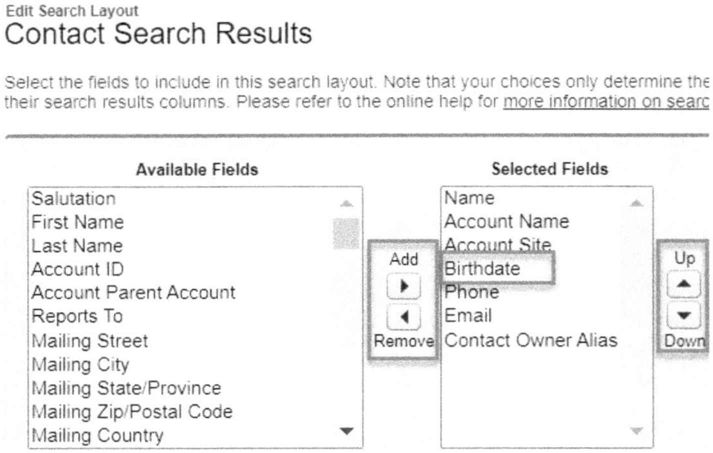

Edit Search Layout
Contact Search Results

Select the fields to include in this search layout. Note that your choices only determine the
their search results columns. Please refer to the online help for more information on searc

Available Fields		Selected Fields
Salutation		Name
First Name		Account Name
Last Name		Account Site
Account ID	**Add** ▶	Birthdate
Account Parent Account	◀	Phone
Reports To	**Remove**	Email
Mailing Street		Contact Owner Alias
Mailing City		
Mailing State/Province		
Mailing Zip/Postal Code		
Mailing Country		

(Up / Down controls to the right of Selected Fields)

Figure 2.33: Adding a new field to the search layout

Return to either the **Account** with the related list for **Contacts**, or press the **View All** link to see the changes, as shown in the following figure:

Account
Grand Hotels & Resorts Ltd

Type	Phone	Website	Account Owner	Account Site
Customer - Direct	(312) 596-1000	www.grandhotels.com	Andy White	

Related   Details

We found no potential duplicates of this Account.

Contacts (2)

Tim Barr		John Bond	
Title:	SVP, Administration and Finance	Title:	VP, Facilities
Email:	barr_tim@grandhotels.com	Email:	bond_john@grandhotels.com
Birthdate:	11/02/1958	Birthdate:	24/04/1960

View All

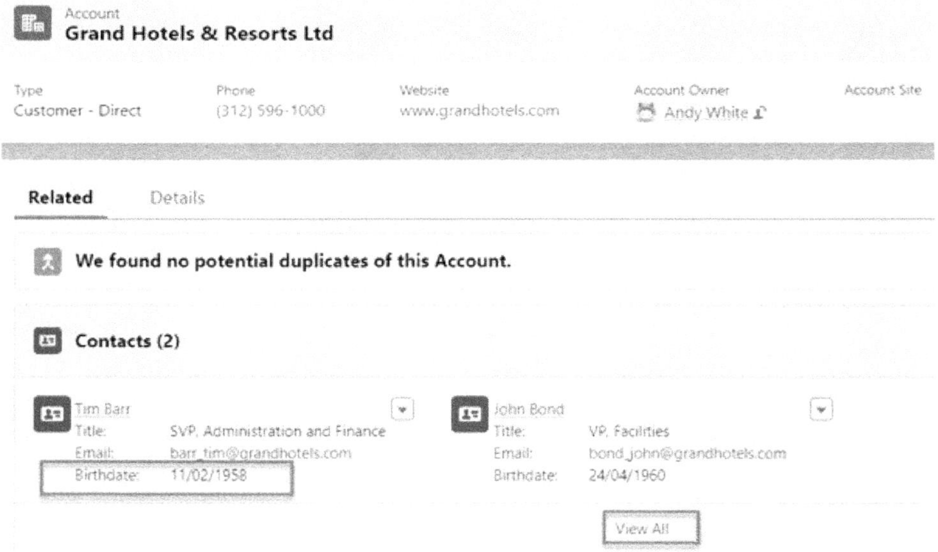

Figure 2.34: Birthdate field added to the related list on the Accounts object

Adding related lists to an object

In a similar way, the fields shown on a related list on a page layout can be added, removed, or reordered. To do this, go to **Object Manager**, select the object (accounts are used in the following figure), and go to the page layouts section as shown in the figure.

Press the small spanner icon as shown in the following figure, which shows the fields that are displayed:

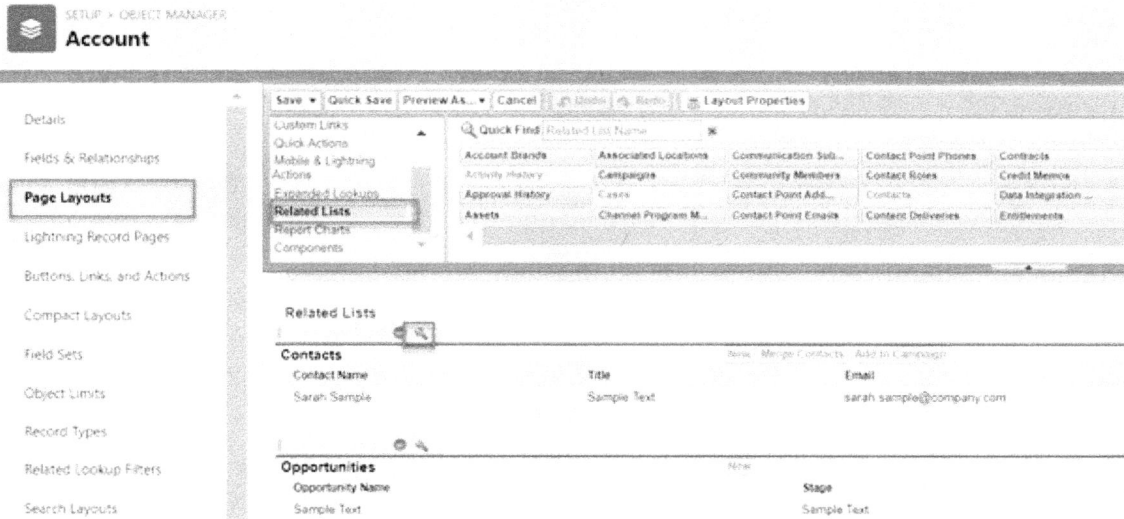

Figure 2.35: Selecting Related Lists on the Page Layouts

Add, remove, or reorder the fields, as shown in the following figure. Press **Save** on the page layout to see the results:

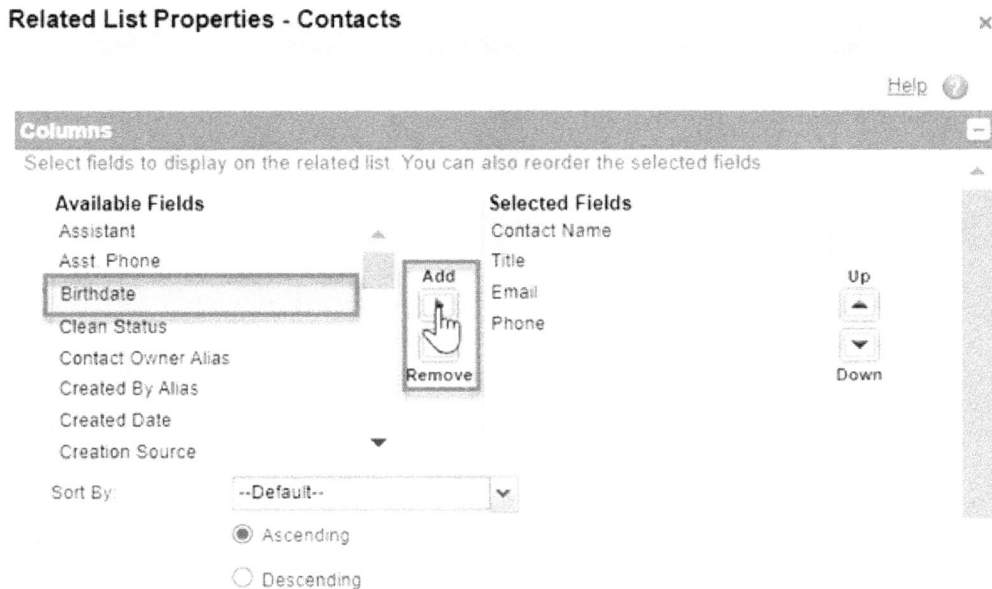

Figure 2.36: Adding a new field to a related list

Kanban view

Although lists are a great way to display a lot of data, Salesforce also offers a Kanban view. Kanban is a way of organizing records in a grid that flows from left to right, depending on a particular field value. For example, the opportunity object has a field called **stage**. When displayed in Kanban, the different stages of opportunities go from left to right to show which opportunities are at each stage.

To do this, go to the opportunity object, select **All Opportunities**, press the small icon at the top right-hand side of the screen, and select **Kanban**. Refer to the following figure:

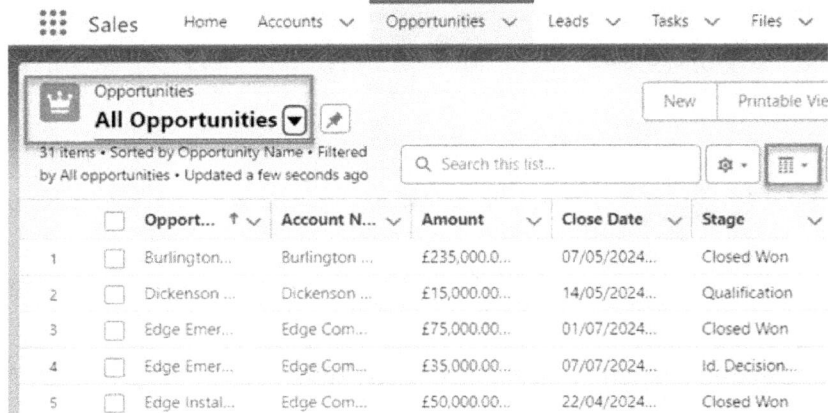

Figure 2.37: Changing to Kanban view

The display now shows all the opportunities by the stage they are at, from prospecting (on the left) to Closed Won (on the far right-hand side). The Kanban board also allows users to drag-and-drop the tiles onto different columns, effectively updating the record at the same time. The following figure shows moving an opportunity record from one stage to another:

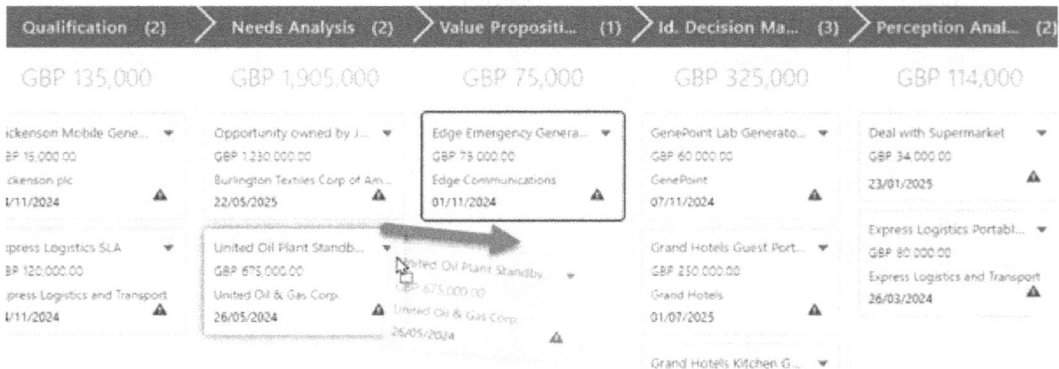

Figure 2.38: Updating an opportunity stage on a Kanban view

Modifying your personal Salesforce settings

Salesforce has its own preferences saved against your user record. To check or modify them, press the user icon, which is typically a blue head icon. Refer to the following figure:

Figure 2.39: *Changing your own profile settings*

There are quite a few settings here, but the ones most useful are:

- Pressing the blue head icon in *Figure 2.39* to update your image and enter basic information.

- Pressing the **Settings** link and selecting **Grant Account Login Access**. This allows other users to grant the Salesforce system administrator access to their account. This is useful for resolving issues that users have. It also allows Salesforce support access to your instance if you need it. Select the time you wish to grant access to your administrator or Salesforce and press **Save**.

- Pressing the first blue icon (with a Salesforce character known as **Astro Nomical**) at the top and then under **Options** select **Switch to Salesforce Classic**. This allows users to toggle between the current **Lightning Experience** user interface and the old Classic style, which was how Salesforce appeared before 2015. The Salesforce Classic user interface is shown in the following figure:

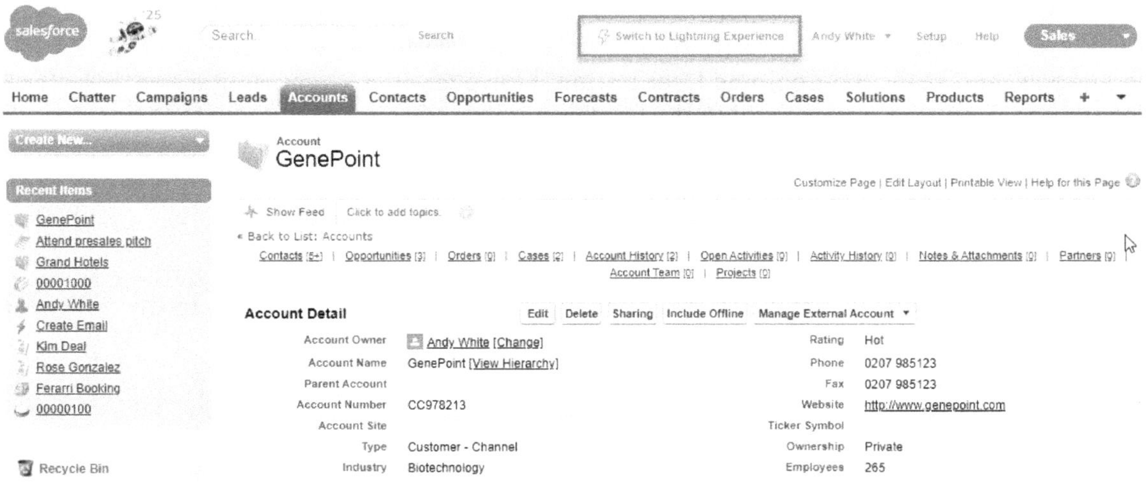

Figure 2.40: *Salesforce Classic view*

Salesforce Classic is the exact same data, objects, and security model as Salesforce Lightning, but it just has the old look of Salesforce. It is worth navigating your way around a bit to gain some familiarity.

To switch back to Salesforce Lightning Experience, press the **Switch to Lightning Experience** as highlighted in the above figure.

Administrator essentials

The range of tasks performed by a Salesforce Administrator is wide and varied. As such, they do not all fit neatly into one specific set of skills, as some tasks may impact many areas of Salesforce. In the following section, there are a few examples of things a Salesforce Administrator should know. They are included simply to help you not get caught out if you are ever asked to do something fairly basic.

This chapter should also be used in conjunction with *Chapter 9, Various Salesforce Tools,* and *Chapter 10, Various Salesforce Features,* which both include areas that Salesforce Administrators should be aware of.

Adding users to Salesforce

The security model is covered in more detail in *Chapter 7, Salesforce Security Model.* Adding users gives them access to Salesforce based on various settings. If you do not get it right, things can go wrong. Even with a thorough understanding of the security model, testing is important and should always be built into a test environment to let the users or management sign it off themselves.

Having said that, Salesforce does allow an easy way to check what a user can see or do by allowing you to login as that user.

To do this, go to the user record from **Setup | Users | Users**, find the user you would like to login as, and press the **Login as User** button. However, if you are using a new Salesforce Developer instance, then you will find a limited number of alternative users to login as.

Let us create a new user; from here, we can test the security model.

Creating a new user in Salesforce

Go to **Setup | Users | Users** (or type **Users** into the setup search). Refer to the following figure:

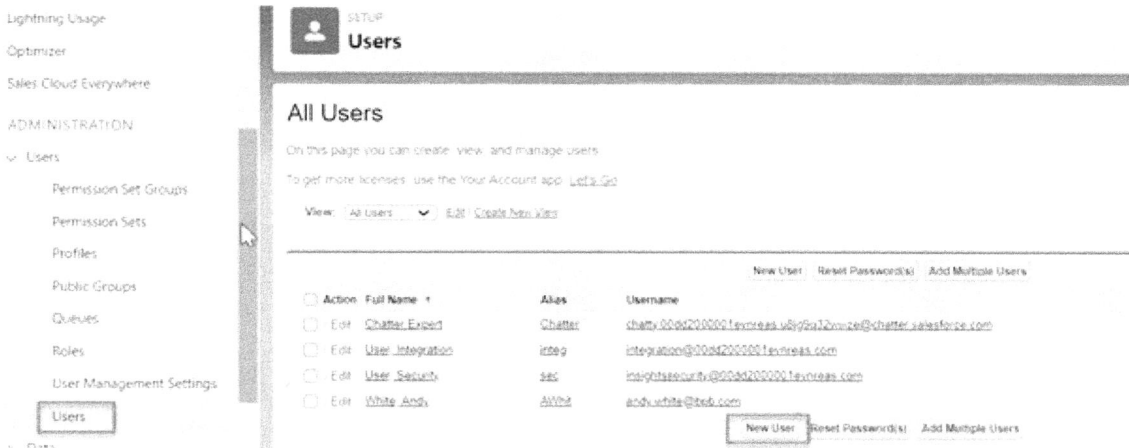

Figure 2.41: Adding a new user

Note: **If you also open up your own user record, then it is easier to copy the fields across and check that the settings are the same. The only difference is that we are going to use the profile of a standard user (instead of your profile as a system administrator).**

When adding a new user to Salesforce, you are given various options, such as their personal details and what access levels and license type are assigned to them, as illustrated in the following figure:

Figure 2.42: Selecting the license and profile of a user

Other important considerations about the above figure are:

- Use your own email address to receive access to Salesforce.

- The username needs to be in the form of an email address. It is best not to use your actual email address as Salesforce does not allow the same username to be used twice, even in another Salesforce org. Instead, be creative and think of a suitable username.

- There are various user licenses available. However, Salesforce Developer Edition only allows two Salesforce licenses.

- Finally, if you scroll to the bottom of the screen, you will also see a checkbox for **Generate new password and notify user immediately**. Ensure this is ticked.

Press **Save** and check your email inbox for confirmation of the new user account. Keep details of the username and set the password when you press the **Verify this Account** button in the email.

Now that you are logged in as the new user, go to the user settings as shown in the following figure:

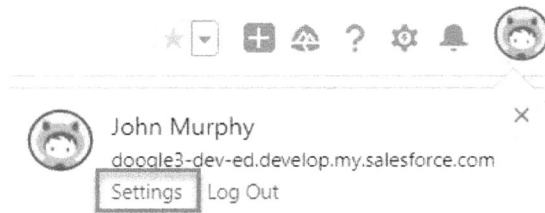

Figure 2.43: Checking user settings

Under **Grant Account Login Access**, set the support for **Your Company's Administrator** to **1 Year** as shown in *Figure 2.44* and press **Save**.

Note: **There is also the option to grant Salesforce.com Support login access if you need support from Salesforce with a case.**

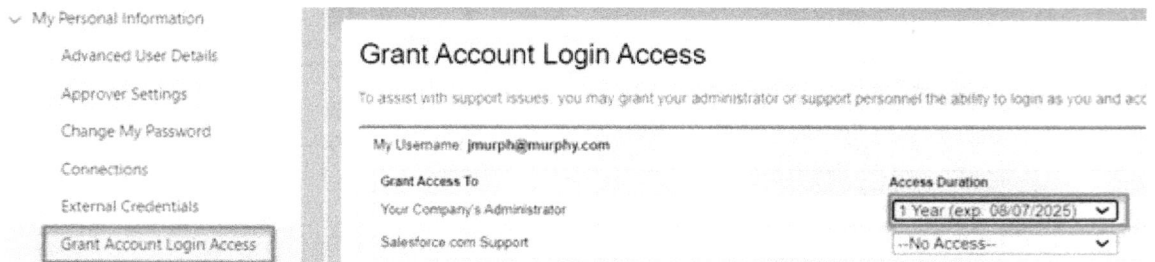

Figure 2.44: Granting user account login access

For the next step to work, you may have to log out of Salesforce and log back in again. Return to the **Users** page, and you will now see the new user with the **Login** option next to their record. Click the **Login** link as shown in the following figure:

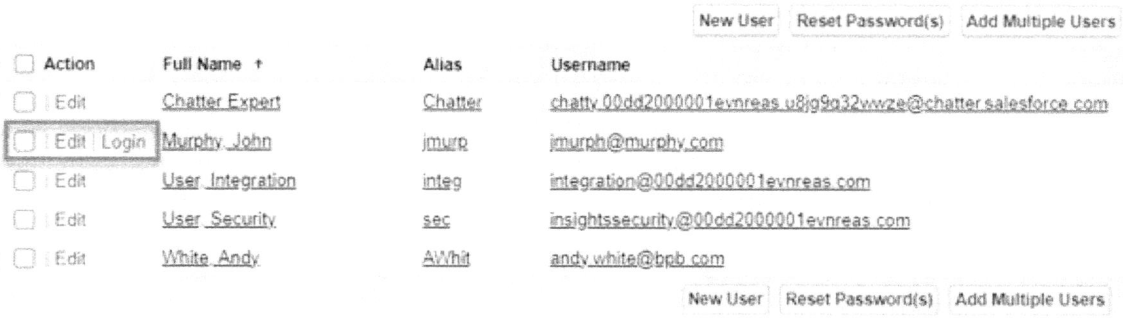

Figure 2.45: *A user account with login access provided*

You will now see that at the top of the screen, it says **Logged in as** (name) with the option to **Log out as**. You can now browse Salesforce as another user. This is useful throughout this chapter to check if the security is set correctly and working. Refer to the following figure:

Figure 2.46: *View of Salesforce user interface whilst logged in as a different user*

Setting password rules

Salesforce can allow users access based on your company's own security policies. These are found by going to **SETUP | Password Policies** as shown in the following figure:

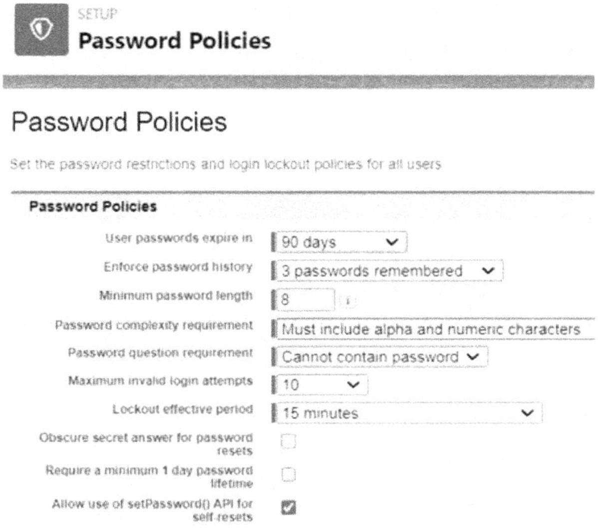

Figure 2.47: *Options available for company password policies*

For your Salesforce Developer Edition, you may wish to relax these so that the **User password expires in** and enter **Never expires**. There are also settings for setting up authentication via mobile phones or email using **Setup | Multi-Factor Authentication Assistant**.

Salesforce also supports **single sign-on** (**SSO**) and authentication using other methods such as Okta. For these settings, enter **Setup | Multi-Factor Authentication Assistant** or an Okta account and follow their documentation.

Data management

Keeping data clean in Salesforce is essential. It allows accurate reporting, a lack of miscommunication, and also helps in various Salesforce tasks, from logic and flows, Einstein 1, and more.

Some of this is down to training users to use the global search feature to check if an account or contact, or any record, already exists in Salesforce. Sometimes the data is already in Salesforce, and automation (such as converting a lead to an opportunity) means that words can be misspelled or have common acronyms instead of the whole word. If you are finding a lot of duplicates in Salesforce, then it is worth checking whether the user can see the record. If it is hidden from them (for example, the object is private), then it would be worth evaluating whether the sharing model is too restrictive. This is covered in *Chapter 7, Salesforce Security Model*.

Salesforce comes with tools to help keep the data clean. In duplicate rules, these can either:

- Block a user from saving a record.
- Advise on the duplicate and merge the details.
- Keep a report for all records, which may be duplicates.
- They are a combination of both duplicate rules and matching rules.
- To find them, go to **Setup | Duplicate Management**.
- Matching rules determine how Salesforce identifies duplicate records. They use field values and compare them for similarity. When a record is created or updated, the matching rule compares it with existing records on the same object or related object. For example, a matching rule can compare the first name, last name, and email so any similar or matching records are identified as a potential duplicate. Matching rules can be exact match or fuzzy match, meaning a company could have the name *Limited* or *Ltd* in its title.
- Duplicate rules define what happens when a matching rule is met. This could be preventing the record from being saved and putting a suitable message on the screen in front of the user. Alternatively, the user can update the record or use the existing one before saving. The least intrusive way is to allow Salesforce to complete a list of potential duplicates in the form of a report for administrators to see periodically.

The following figure shows the **Duplicate Rules** that are included with Salesforce:

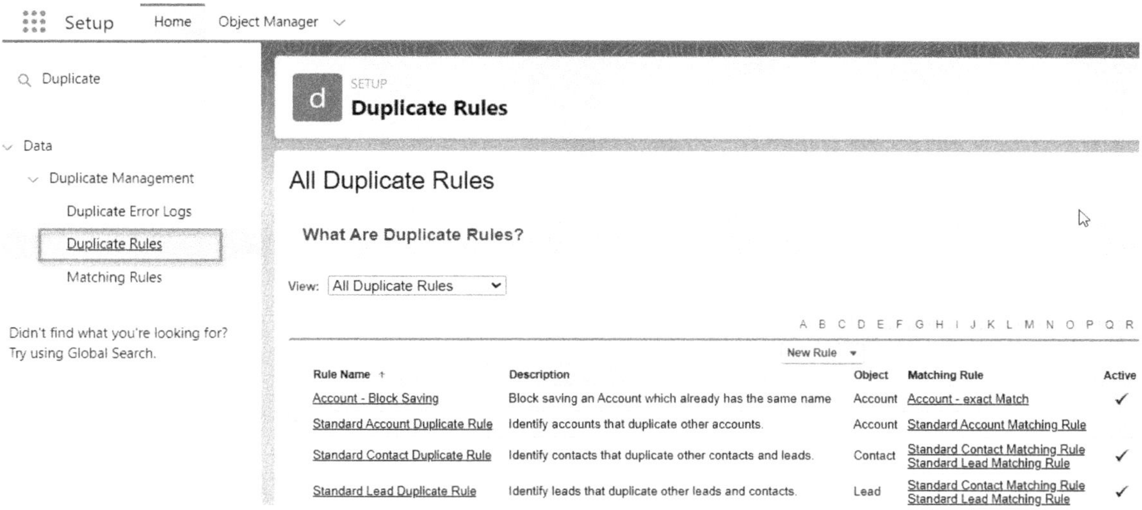

Figure 2.48: Salesforce duplicate rule

Duplicate Rules in the Developer Edition of Salesforce are not configured to do anything. They are simply placeholders. If you wanted to prevent users from entering duplicate account records, then the matching rule on the Account object would look something like the illustration in the following figure:

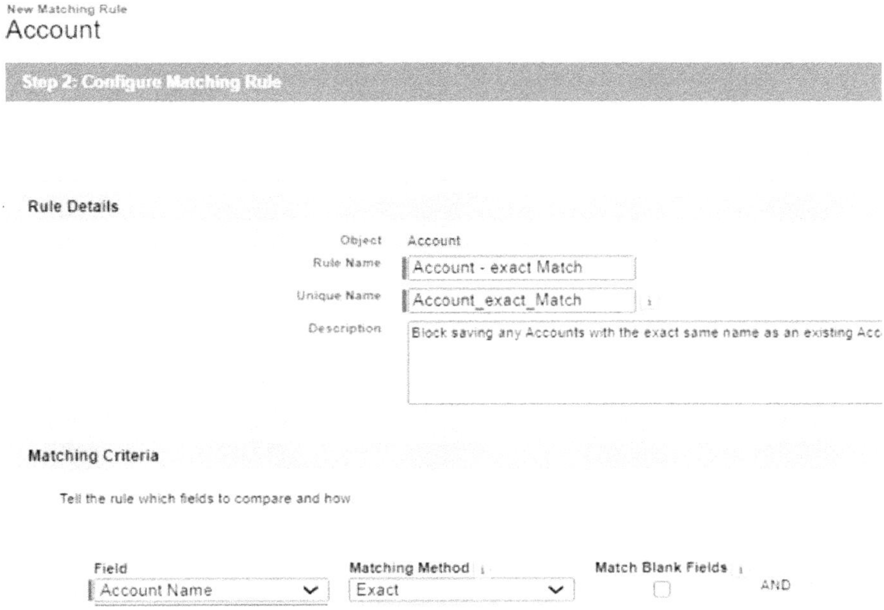

Figure 2.49: Configuring a matching rule

Press **Save** and then add a **New Duplicate Rule** on the **Account** object by going to **Setup** | **Duplicate Management** | **Duplicate Rules,** as shown in the following figure:

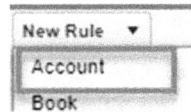

Figure 2.50: Selecting the object for the duplicate rule assignment

Enter the information as shown in the following figure, setting the action as **Block** for both creating and editing the **Account**:

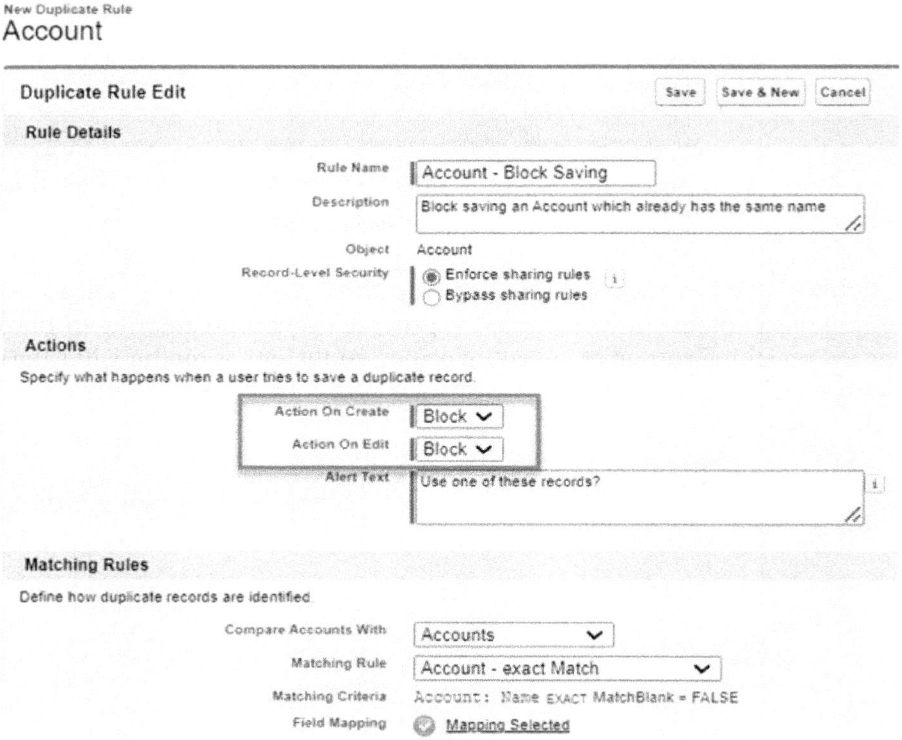

Figure 2.51: Adding duplicate rules

Finally, activate both the matching rule and the duplicate rule. Refer to the following figure:

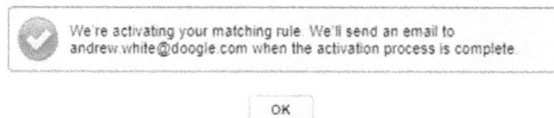

Figure 2.52: Activating duplicate rules

If you then create a new account with the name of an existing one, you will see the following message, as shown in the following figure:

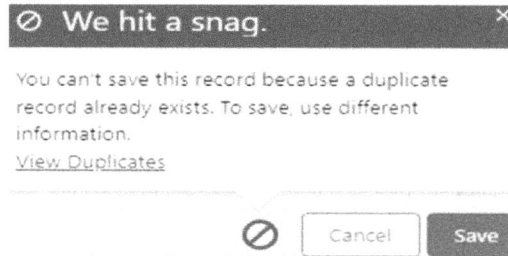

Figure 2.53: Record blocked due to duplicate rules

Duplicate management across the entire Salesforce org

Although duplicate rules are fine for simple scenarios, there may be requirements that require more complicated scenarios, which require more sophisticated logic to determine a duplicate. For example, this could be the logic that needs to be on one object to block the duplicate on a different object. There are dedicated duplicate management tools on the AppExchange, such as Cloudingo, DataGroomr, or Plauti Deduplicate, which can do sophisticated, cross-object deduplication and data cleaning. In Performance and Unlimited Editions, there are also out-of-the-box duplicate jobs, which allow you to run reports to view the results before running duplicate record sets to merge the duplicates.

Record types and page layout assignments

As mentioned, page layouts are assigned by a combination of profile and record type. Record types also allow you to apply different processes to different users and set different picklist values, depending on the record type.

If you are starting with a new Salesforce Developer Edition account, then you will not have any record types, so the page layout is assigned solely to the user's profile. These can be seen by going to **Setup** | **Object Manager** | (select the object) | **Page Layout** and pressing the **Page Layout Assignment** button on the top right-hand side of the screen. Refer to the following figure:

Figure 2.54: Page layout assignments for record types

Adding a new **Record Type**. From **Setup** | (select the object) | **Record Type** and press the **New** button.

If the requirement was only to show summary information for executives, then enter the following, as shown in *Figure 2.55*:

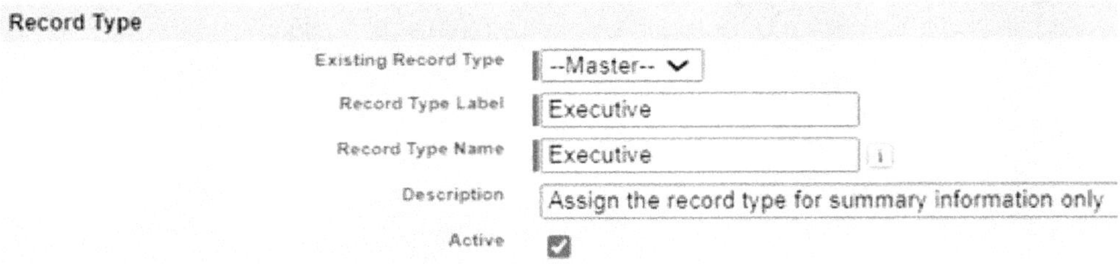

Record Type

Existing Record Type	--Master-- ⌄
Record Type Label	Executive
Record Type Name	Executive
Description	Assign the record type for summary information only
Active	☑

Figure 2.55: Setting up a new record type

Select the default values for the next two steps of the wizard. Optional to press the **Save** and **New** button to create more page layouts. For the example in the following figure three more have been created. Return to the **Page Layout Assignment** button (refer to *Figure 2.55*) to see them:

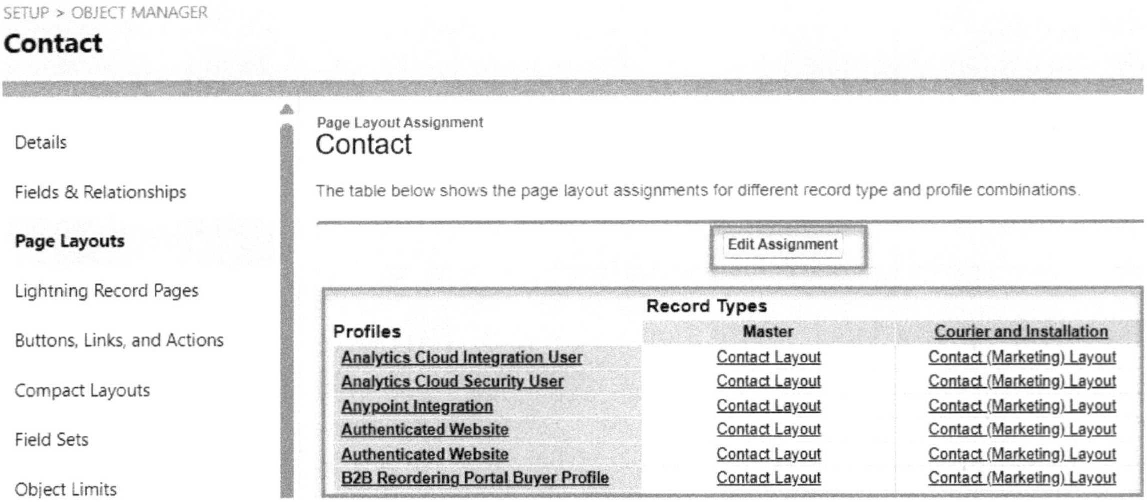

SETUP > OBJECT MANAGER
Contact

Details

Fields & Relationships

Page Layouts

Lightning Record Pages

Buttons, Links, and Actions

Compact Layouts

Field Sets

Object Limits

Page Layout Assignment
Contact

The table below shows the page layout assignments for different record type and profile combinations.

Edit Assignment

	Record Types	
Profiles	**Master**	**Courier and Installation**
Analytics Cloud Integration User	Contact Layout	Contact (Marketing) Layout
Analytics Cloud Security User	Contact Layout	Contact (Marketing) Layout
Anypoint Integration	Contact Layout	Contact (Marketing) Layout
Authenticated Website	Contact Layout	Contact (Marketing) Layout
Authenticated Website	Contact Layout	Contact (Marketing) Layout
B2B Reordering Portal Buyer Profile	Contact Layout	Contact (Marketing) Layout

Figure 2.56: Record type assignment

Press the **Edit Assignment** button in the center of the screen. The grid is now editable. Press a cell to turn it purple, and then select from the pick list saying **Page Layout To Use**. This then highlights them. Press the *Ctrl* button to make multiple selections. Once you are happy with the assignment, press **Save**. Refer to the following figure:

Page Layout To Use: [Contact (Sales) Layout ▾] 4 Selected *7 Changed*

Profiles	Record Types				(1-4 of 4)
	Master	Courier and Installation	Executive	Manufacturing	
Analytics Cloud Integration User	Contact Layout	Contact (Marketing) Layout	Contact (Sales) Layout	Contact (Support) Layout	
Analytics Cloud Security User	Contact Layout	Contact (Marketing) Layout	Contact (Sales) Layout	Contact (Support) Layout	
Anypoint Integration	Contact Layout	Contact (Marketing) Layout	Contact (Sales) Layout	Contact (Support) Layout	
Authenticated Website	Contact Layout	Contact (Marketing) Layout	Contact (Sales) Layout	Contact (Support) Layout	
Authenticated Website	Contact Layout	Contact (Marketing) Layout	Contact (Sales) Layout	Contact (Support) Layout	
B2B Reordering Portal Buyer Profile	Contact Layout	*Contact (Support) Layout*	Contact (Sales) Layout	Contact (Support) Layout	
Chatter External User	Contact Layout	Contact (Marketing) Layout	Contact (Sales) Layout	*Contact (Sales) Layout*	
Chatter Free User	Contact Layout	Contact (Marketing) Layout	*Contact (Sales) Layout*	Contact (Support) Layout	
Chatter Moderator User	Contact Layout	*Contact (Support) Layout*	Contact (Sales) Layout	Contact (Support) Layout	
Contract Manager	Contact Layout	Contact (Marketing) Layout	Contact (Sales) Layout	Contact (Support) Layout	
Cross Org Data Proxy User	Contact Layout	Contact (Marketing) Layout	Contact (Sales) Layout	Contact (Support) Layout	
Custom: Marketing Profile	Contact (Marketing) Layout	*Contact (Sales) Layout*	Contact (Sales) Layout	Contact (Support) Layout	
Custom: Sales Profile	*Contact (Sales) Layout*	Contact (Marketing) Layout	Contact (Sales) Layout	Contact (Support) Layout	
Custom: Support Profile	*Contact (Support) Layout*	Contact (Marketing) Layout	Contact (Sales) Layout	Contact (Support) Layout	

Figure 2.57: Editing record type assignment

Note: **For large orgs, the page layout column headers may go onto multiple screens. Record type is a field stored on the object. As such, Salesforce looks at this value before rendering the screen. You can add the record type field to the page layout and then change the value, which will in turn change the page layout. This can be useful for debugging UI issues when the screen does not show the user what they are expecting.**

Conclusion

This chapter has focused on various fundamental administrative tasks within Salesforce. It provided an overview of how Salesforce configuration works, offering insight into key objects and how they relate to one another. You should now have an understanding of basic configuration tasks, such as adding fields to an object, customizing views, creating users, and logging in as those users. Additionally, the chapter introduced you to basic data administration, including how to view and manage data usage within Salesforce. Lastly, you would have explored basic access configuration, learning how roles and profiles work together with record types to ensure users see the correct page layouts.

In the next chapter, you will learn how to modify the user interface to make sure Salesforce is configured in a way that users will love, as well as ensure they have the information they need, whilst ensuring they do not get access to information that they should not have.

Multiple choice questions

1. **Salesforce fields have a display name and what other name?**
    a. External reference
    b. API name

    c. Object reference

    d. Apex name

2. **A junction object is used for what purpose?**

    a. Making data available to other objects

    b. Referencing the parent object

    c. Referencing the child object

    d. Providing a many-to-many relationship between two objects

3. **List views can be shown to users based on what criteria:**

    a. Individual users, teams or the person who created the view

    b. Groups, individual users or teams

    c. Fields available on the object

    d. Filter values used to display the view

4. **If you are going into an old Salesforce environment, what is the best way to gauge the technical debt? (choose the best answer)**

    a. Look at each object and see which one is the most used.

    b. Run an app such as Org Check and get a list of bad configurations.

    c. View which objects have the most redundant fields.

    d. View login history to see which users have not used Salesforce.

5. **Salesforce connects objects so you can see related information. These are master-detail and lookup relationship. Which statement below is correct?**

    a. Master-detail copies the child record onto the parent record

    b. Lookup relationship allows users to see related information on the child object if they share the same security model

    c. Only two master-detail relationships are allowed on an object

    d. Junction objects allow one master-detail relationship but can allow several custom fields

6. **Salesforce allows you to login as other users. To do this you get the following:**

    a. The same user rights as the user

    b. Their username and password

    c. Access to connected applications, such as email

    d. A warning that you do not have access to their recently added information

7. **Data quality is important for any organization. Duplicate rules help reduce the number of records. Duplicate rules allow three levels of restriction which are:**

    a. Block saving the record, allow saving with a message, report on the duplicate

    b. Save duplicates to the duplicate object, allow for reporting

    c. Save duplicates but send a warning via email to the administrator

    d. Save all records but allow the duplicates report to show objects with duplicate data

8. **A lead can be converted into which objects?**

    a. Opportunities, campaigns and assets

    b. Accounts, contacts and activities

    c. Accounts, contacts and opportunities

    d. Opportunities and assets

9. **True or false: Assets are products which have been sold to a company and are now owned by the company?**

    a. True

    b. False

10. **Opportunities require the amount and close date. This is to provide what feature in Salesforce?**

    a. Kanban view

    b. Opportunity pipeline

    c. Big deal alerts

    d. Customizable forecasting

Answers

1	**b**
2	**d**
3	**b**
4	**c**
5	**c**
6	**a**
7	**a**
8	**c**
9	**a**
10	**b**

Join our Discord space

Join our Discord workspace for latest updates, offers, tech happenings around the world, new releases, and sessions with the authors:

https://discord.bpbonline.com

Chapter 3
Customizing User Interface

Introduction

This chapter provides an in-depth look at how the **user interface** (**UI**) can be customized to improve user presentation and interaction. To recap from *Chapters 1, Introduction to Salesforce,* and *Chapter 2, Basic Admin Essentials,* the fields, as shown on the screen, combine the user's role and profile. This allows the appropriate page layout to be shown based on record type. Fields, components, or other features can be dragged to the required position on the page. However, it is possible to do far more than provide a static layout for the user, and the features listed in the upcoming sections will significantly help with the UI and the **user experience** (**UX**).

This chapter also shows how an improved dynamic page layout can be created using Lightning record pages. This is the recommended approach to configuring Salesforce Page Layouts as Salesforce adds new features. An example is Dynamic Forms, which show or hide fields based on the user or entered data.

This chapter includes configuring various Salesforce features, such as making a custom app, configuring the home page, and other features.

Structure

This chapter covers the following topics:

- Getting started with customizing the UI

- Customizing UI on Salesforce Lightning pages

- Building an app from scratch

- Lightning record pages

Objectives

By the end of this chapter, readers will be able to customize the UI for various Salesforce users. This will include moving features to different areas on the screen, including adding, removing, and reordering the fields displayed. It will include arranging the various features and sections on the display to give a better UX.

The aim of this chapter is to allow you to confidently navigate the configurations available to customize the UI, including using Salesforce Lightning record pages to leverage the latest Salesforce features.

Getting started with customizing the UI

To understand how the UI works in Salesforce, you need to understand that much of it is still built in the Classic page layout editor (i.e., the version that came before Lightning). The reason for this is relatively simple: the two systems need to be compatible; whilst Lightning is more sophisticated with more options, if you build something in Classic, it will work in Lightning, but not always the other way around.

As a result, a lot of the core functionality is still in the Salesforce Classic page layout editor, so a good understanding of the Classic page layout editor is required to understand how to build Lightning pages and Lightning record pages. However, what you do in the Classic page layout editor will show in the Lightning UI, so your efforts are not wasted.

Overview of Salesforce Classic page layout editor

There are a few ways to get to the Classic page layout editor. Let us look at them in detail:

1. **Setup** | **Object Manager** | (select the object) | **Page Layouts**

2. **Setup** | **Edit Page** | (select the actually related list area on the canvas, on the right-hand side, under **Assign Page Layout**). Click the layout name next to the preview.

Set Related Lists in Page Layouts

Assign Page Layouts

Account Layout (previewed)
Account (Marketing) Layout
Account (Sales) Layout
Account (Support) Layout

View all layouts

Figure 3.1: Selecting the correct page layout from the editor

3. The first method is possibly simpler, but you must know precisely which page layout you are configuring. The second method is less obvious but takes you to the page layout you wish to modify.

4. The Classic page layout editor will show the page and has the following panel at the top:

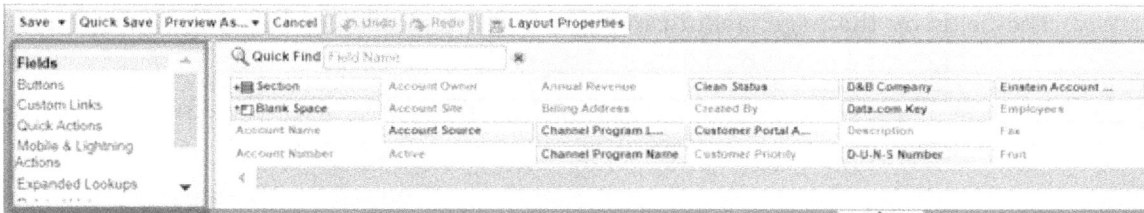

Save ▼	Quick Save	Preview As... ▼	Cancel	⤺ Undo	⤻ Redo	🖳 Layout Properties			
Fields		🔍 Quick Find	Field Name	✖					
Buttons		+🔲 Section	Account Owner	Annual Revenue	Clean Status	D&B Company	Einstein Account ...
Custom Links		+🔲 Blank Space	Account Site	Billing Address	Created By	Data.com Key	Employees
Quick Actions		Account Name	Account Source	Channel Program L...	Customer Portal A...	Description	Fax
Mobile & Lightning Actions		Account Number	Active	Channel Program Name	Customer Priority	D-U-N-S Number	Fruit
Expanded Lookups	▼	‹					

Figure 3.2: Options for adding to the page layout

5. The menu area on the left allows you to select what is shown on the right pane. Drag the component (**Fields**, **Buttons**, etc.) from the list onto the page layout.

6. When you drag onto a compatible area of the page, the section will turn to a light green color, meaning it is suitable.

7. You can drop the piece and move other parts around, too, as shown in the following figure:

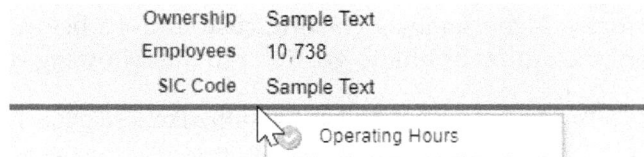

Ownership	Sample Text
Employees	10,738
SIC Code	Sample Text
	Operating Hours

Figure 3.3: Green area where new features can be added

8. Press the **Save** or **Quick Save** button once the layout is suitable.

9. The **Quick Save** button keeps you in the page layout editor, while the **Save** button returns you to the list of page layouts.

10. Then, refresh the page as seen by the user to see the updated changes.

Overview of options in page layout editor

The editor panel at the top of the page layout editor has the following categories for what can be selected. The two most commonly used ones are fields and related lists, but they are all listed here:

- **Fields**: These are the available fields on the object. If they are greyed out, they are already on the page layout. If you click them, you will be shown where they are. Fields not greyed out are available to add to the page layout. The first two blocks are for section and blank space. You can add these where you like to improve the page's look.

- **Section**: A section allows you to break the page up, give it a descriptive name, and choose from one or two columns. You can also add blank space, which allows you to enter empty screen space if you want.

  The fields on the page layout can be arranged logically by dragging and dropping them or grouped under a section, as described above.

- **Buttons**: These can be added to the page layout to perform simple actions. There are three types:

  o **Detail Page Button**: Which appears at the very top right-hand side of your screen.

  o **Detail Page Link**: This appears in the **Detail** section of the page, but appears as a Link.

  o **List Button**: This can be found in the sections of the related lists.

To create a custom button, follow these steps:

1. Go to **Setup** | (select an object) | **Buttons, Links, and Actions**. You will see a few existing examples there.

2. However, press the **New** button or the **Link** button.

3. The general process is the same as creating custom links below, with the options of where you want the button or link to go. Refer to the following figure:

Display Type   ⦿ Detail Page Link <u>View example</u>

◯ Detail Page Button <u>View example</u>

◯ List Button <u>View example</u>

Figure 3.4: *Adding a new Detail Page Link*

- **Custom links**: These allow you to put hyperlinks on your page to pull up relevant records from external sources, such *as Google Search, Google Maps, LinkedIn*, etc., by substituting URL parameters (i.e., variables in the URL). For example, if you wanted to get the Google Search results for a company name, you would put the link on the account page and would enter:

```
https://www.google.com/search?q={!Account.Name}
```

Or for Google Maps, you may wish to parse the **Account.Name** and the geolocation values (if they are stored on the **Account** record) or simply the billing address as shown in the following link:

```
http://maps.google.com/maps?q={!Account_BillingStreet}%20{!Account_
BillingCity}%20{!Account_BillingState}%20{!Account_BillingPostalCode}
```

If you wanted to get a LinkedIn search result based on someone's name, then use the following:

```
https://www.linkedin.com/search/results/all/?keywords={!Contact.Name}
```

In both cases, the exclamation mark **!** means get the results from the current page you are on in Salesforce. If you are not sure whether to use a button or a link, a link can fit neatly on the page detail and use less screen space, but a button is more visible, so it may be preferable.

Quick actions

There are two types of action:

- **Global actions**: Create global actions that are available from the Salesforce header, such as creating records or logging calls. These are found in **Setup | Global Actions**.

- **Quick actions**: These are specific to an object but add quick actions to page layouts to streamline everyday tasks, like creating records or updating existing ones, using flows or **Lightning Web Components** (**LWC**), which is discussed in *Chapter 11, Basics of Apex and Lightning Web Components*.

To find them, follow these steps:

1. Go to **Setup | (select an object) | New Action**.

2. The main reason actions are included in this book is that an existing org may have many of these. They are categorized for various scenarios, such as record creation, logging calls, and sending emails, and they still appear in the Lightning UI.

3. There are many use cases for them, and various online tutorials are available. For example, you may wish to create an order record on an account, as this would save users' time.

4. To create an order on the accounts object, go to **Setup | Object Manager | (select Account) | Buttons, Links, and Actions** and press the **New Action** button.

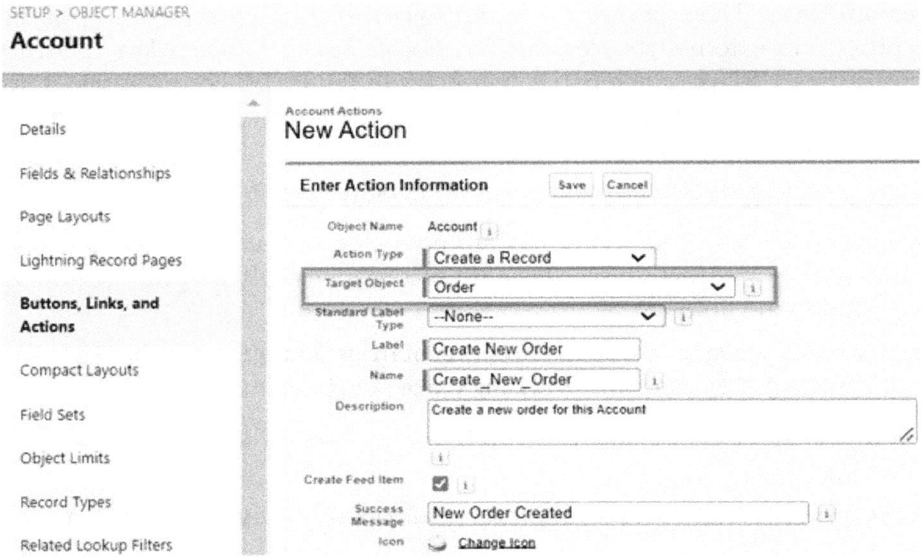

SETUP > OBJECT MANAGER
Account

Details	**Account Actions**
Fields & Relationships	## New Action
Page Layouts	**Enter Action Information** [Save] [Cancel]
Lightning Record Pages	Object Name Account ⓘ
Buttons, Links, and Actions	Action Type [Create a Record ▾]
	Target Object [Order ▾] ⓘ
Compact Layouts	Standard Label Type [--None-- ▾] ⓘ
Field Sets	Label [Create New Order]
Object Limits	Name [Create_New_Order] ⓘ
	Description [Create a new order for this Account]
Record Types	Create Feed Item ☑ ⓘ
Related Lookup Filters	Success Message [New Order Created] ⓘ
	Icon ⌣ Change Icon

Figure 3.5: Creating a custom quick action

Note: **The Target Object section below lists all the child objects of the Account object. Select Order as shown. Also, Action Type is a very powerful option, as you can select Flows and LWCs.**

5.   This then gives you the screen layout that the user will see. All required fields are included, but you can drag additional fields onto the page layout, as shown in the following figure:

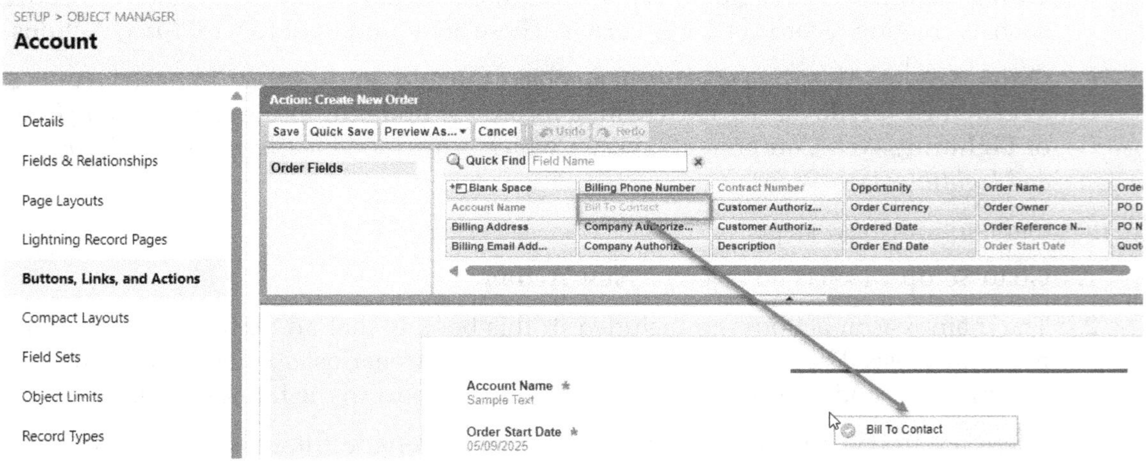

Figure 3.6: The page layout for adding a new action

6.   Press **Save**. The screen above is only the layout for the quick action. You then also need to add it to the page layout to see it working.

7. To do this, follow the same steps above, but go to **Page Layouts** (in the above diagram on the left-hand side menu) and visit an account to see the newly created quick action as shown in the following figure:

Figure 3.7: The new quick action added to the user's screen

Other notes on quick actions

Quick actions can be made compelling by combining them with other Salesforce features. In particular, quick actions can be included in the following Salesforce features:

- Salesforce Flows to allow sophisticated automation, which is covered in *Chapter 6, Automating Salesforce with Flows.*

- Adding LWC, which is covered in *Chapter 11, Basics of Apex and Lightning Web Components.*

Related lists

Related lists for sections on the page layout to show records related to the detail record. For example, an account record will have many contacts, cases, and opportunities. These are displayed on the **Related** tab and can also be ordered or filtered as required.

To modify a related list, go into the page layout and select the **Related Lists** menu item as shown below. Drag a related list to the desired location on the page layout.

Similarly, the existing related lists can be rearranged by dragging them (or removing them) as needed. In the illustration below, the related list is dragged and dropped onto the page layout. It can be placed anywhere, which is highlighted in green, as shown in the following figure:

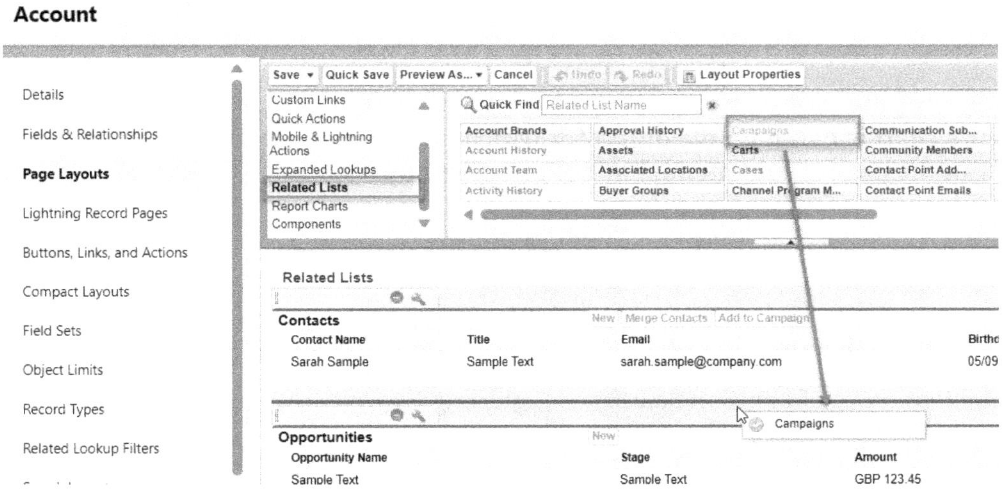

Figure 3.8: Adding a related list to the page layout

Report charts

Chapter 8, Reports, Dashboards and Basic Tableau, covers more depth in creating reports and dashboards. If you are using the Developer Edition, many of the charts can be used without further modification, although the data behind them might be lacking.

The following example shows two charts of **Accounts By Revenue** and **Opportunities By Value displayed** on an **Opportunity** record. The charts can be further configured on the page layout by pressing the **Properties** link, which gives options to **Filter by** (you would nearly always want to filter by the ID of the page you are on, for example, opportunity ID) or hide the chart with errors if it would not display.

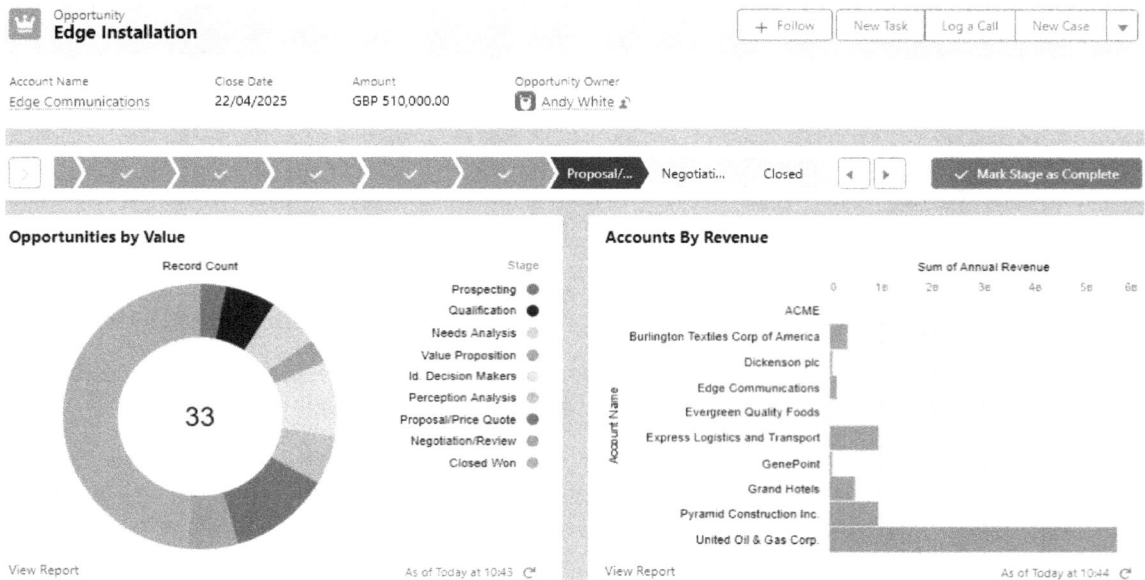

Figure 3.9: Adding a report chart to the page layout

Note: **If a chart is based on the object for which you are building the page layout, it will appear in the page layout menu, but not for other objects.**

Customizing UI on Salesforce Lightning pages

Lightning pages are the default pages when navigating Salesforce. They are the out-of-the-box visualization of what used to be Salesforce Classic, see *Chapter 2, Basic Admin Essentials*.

There are two types of pages in Salesforce Lightning Experience:

* **Lightning pages**: Rely on the same page layout as Classic but represented in Salesforce Lightning.

- **Lightning record pages**: Built to leverage the Lightning Platform, you can easily migrate from the default Lightning pages to Lightning record pages, which will be covered in later sections. Lightning record pages give you many more options and flexibility than Lightning pages. For example, Dynamic Forms must be done on Lighting record pages.

If you are working in a mature Salesforce org, you can see all the Lightning record pages by going to **Setup** | (search for) `Lightning App Builder`. You will see how many Lightning record pages exist in your org.

Customizing Salesforce Lightning pages

These are the standard Lightning pages (see above). They are the default ones when you initially have access to Salesforce.

This is best done by simply going to the page you want to customize and looking for the **Edit Page** option under the **Setup** cog. Refer to the following figure:

Figure 3.10: Editing a page directly from the record

However, this option is only available on pages that are the records of an object. It does not exist in pages in **Setup**, the main pages, the home page, and various other places, such as Calendar or Chatter. These can still be customized, but they are done via **Setup**.

It should be done in the context of the users who want the page customized and the other page layouts in the Salesforce org. For example, users from the company's sales department may have different requirements from users in the service department.

Navigate to the **Contact** tab in Salesforce and select a contact record. Select **Setup** | **Edit Page** (as shown above), and you will see a screen similar to the one shown in the following figure:

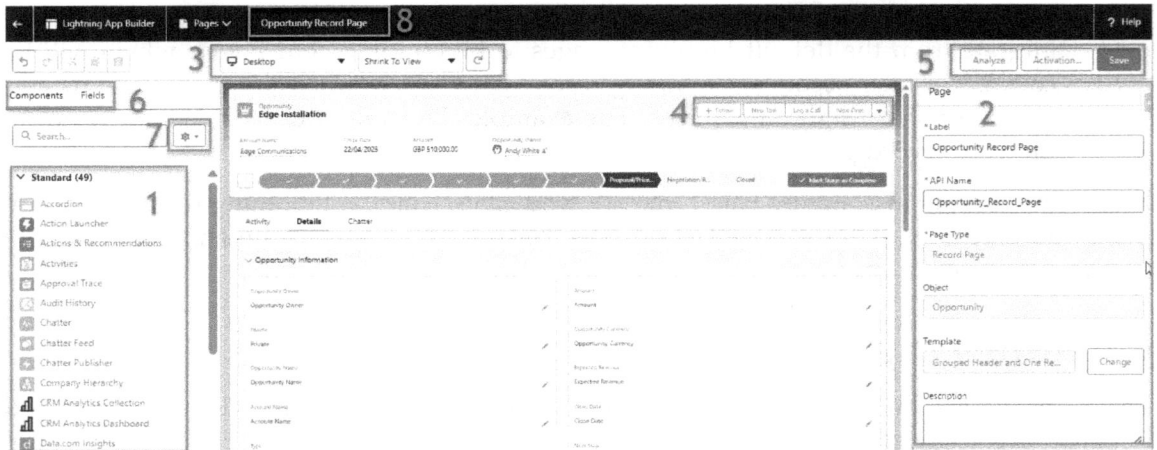

Figure 3.11: Lightning page layout editor

The illustration is a repeat of *Chapter 1, Introduction to Salesforce*, but with more detail. The areas that have been numbered are listed here in detail:

1. **Component pane**: Various components can be added to the page. These can be standard Salesforce or custom components, such as LWCs, Einstein components, those available on the AppExchange, etc. You drag-and-drop the element onto the canvas (the central area of the screen). If the area is suitable, it should be bordered in green. The list of components is extensive and can be found by doing an internet search for Standard Lightning page components, or found at: **https://help.salesforce.com/s/articleView?id=platform.lightning_page_components.htm&type=5**, but they are also described later in *Chapter 11, Basics of Apex and Lightning Web Components*.

2. **Component properties**: By pressing a component on the page canvas (the main area), the properties show what configuration options are available, which allows you to change different settings on the component. For example, you can change the highlights panel (the top section) to have a different number of buttons visible, whether it collapses by default, or other features. One of the most valuable features is to change the entire page layout at once based on the template used.

   If you click the **Page** link near the top right-hand side of the screen and then select **Template** from the properties, as listed in the following figure, you will have a wide range of different templates to choose from to change the page layout:

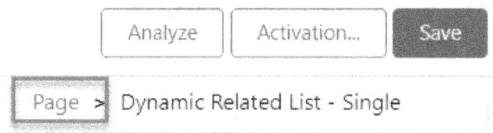

Figure 3.12: Selecting page layout component properties

3. **Preview**: View the page for a desktop, tablet, or mobile device. This allows you to see how Salesforce would appear on different devices and for other users.

4. **Add buttons**: Such as macros or quick actions, to easily automate users' tasks.

5. **Activate**: After you save the page, you must make it active before users can see it.

Lightning record pages

These are the second type of Salesforce page layout. Although similar to Lightning pages, Lightning record pages allow greater control and flexibility over the page and have more advanced features.

There are two ways to build a Lightning record page:

- Convert the original Lightning page.

- Or **Start from Scratch**. It is usually easiest and best to convert the original page to a Lightning record page.

A Lightning record page can also be created in two ways:

- On an object-level, i.e., go to **Setup | Object Manager |** (select the object) **| Lightning Record Pages** and press **New** as shown in the following figure:

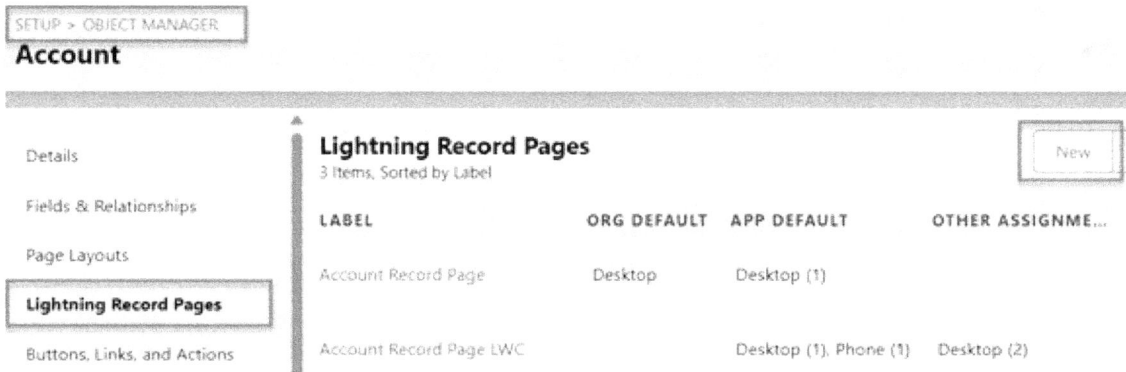

Figure 3.13: Creating Lightning record pages

- Navigate to **Setup | Lightning App Builder** and select **New** to create a new page.

Both methods will bring you to the new Lightning page screen with the options listed in the following figure:

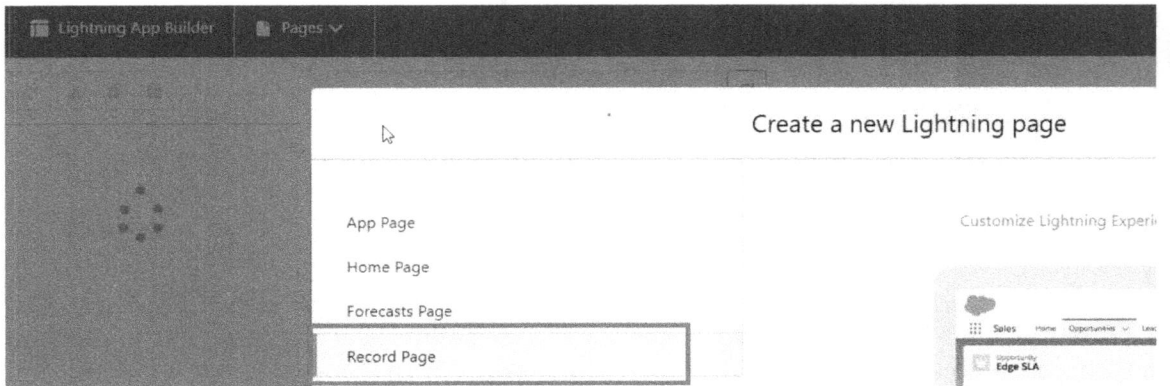

Figure 3.14: Creating a new Lightning page

The first screen gives the following options:

- **App Page**: This creates a single page that can be used in a variety of places.

- **Home Page**: This is for the Home Page, which appears as a tab and contains summary information.

- **Record Page**: This is the page on which you can see individual records.

- **Embedded Service Page**: A versatile pop-up that is embedded into various Salesforce features, such as screen pops, chats, or flows.

- **Voice Extension**: This is useful for Service Cloud Voice.

To create a new Lightning record page, complete the following steps:

1. Choose **Record Page** from the screen shown in *Figure 3.14* and press **Next**.

2. Choose a **Label** (such as `Case Lightning Record Page - Default`) and select an **Object** (such as **Case**). A Lightning record page is always associated with an object and is not a generic layout that can be applied to various objects.

3. Next, either choose the page **Template** or **Clone Salesforce Default**. Both options are suitable, so choose the layout you like; Salesforce will base the new Lightning record page on the existing Lightning page you have selected. For this example, the Salesforce default page was used with the case grouped view default for the layout.

4. Press **Done**.

   You will end up with something like the illustration shown in the following figure:

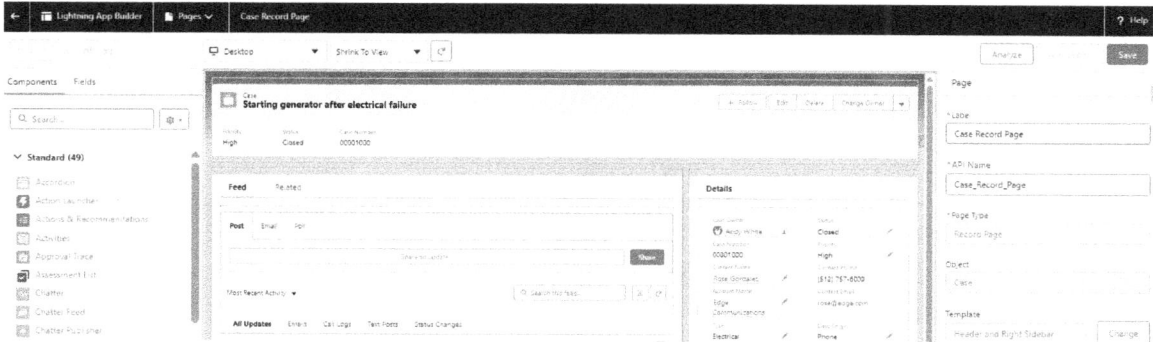

Figure 3.15: *Newly created Lightning record page*

Once done, you may wonder what the point of Lightning record pages is, as they have the same appearance as standard Lightning pages. Lightning record pages will undoubtedly become the layout of choice in the future and currently allow a more dynamic interface with greater control over the UI, with additional options on how the Lightning record page responds, which is covered in the next section.

Dynamic Forms

Dynamic Forms provide a flexible layout by displaying fields and sections more intuitively based on the users' input or selected criteria. They work on standard and custom objects, but only on Lightning record pages. They have two scenarios:

- Show or hide various fields based on the selection of a controlling field (works in real-time, so when you change a field, the dependent fields are shown).

- Show or hide sections of a page layout based on selecting a controlling field (works only upon saving the record, not changing a field value).

A Dynamic Form can only be created on a Lightning record page. Having completed the steps in the previous section, the Lightning record page can be converted to a Dynamic Form by going to the detail section in the page layout.

You will see an option at the top right-hand side saying **Upgrade Now**, as shown in the following figure:

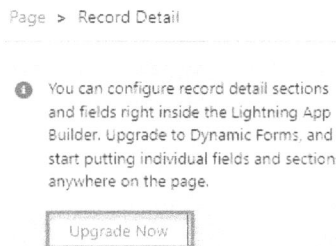

Figure 3.16: *Upgrading to allow Dynamic Forms*

Press the button and follow the three-step wizard, choosing the default page layout. In the following figure, it is the **Opportunity** page layout:

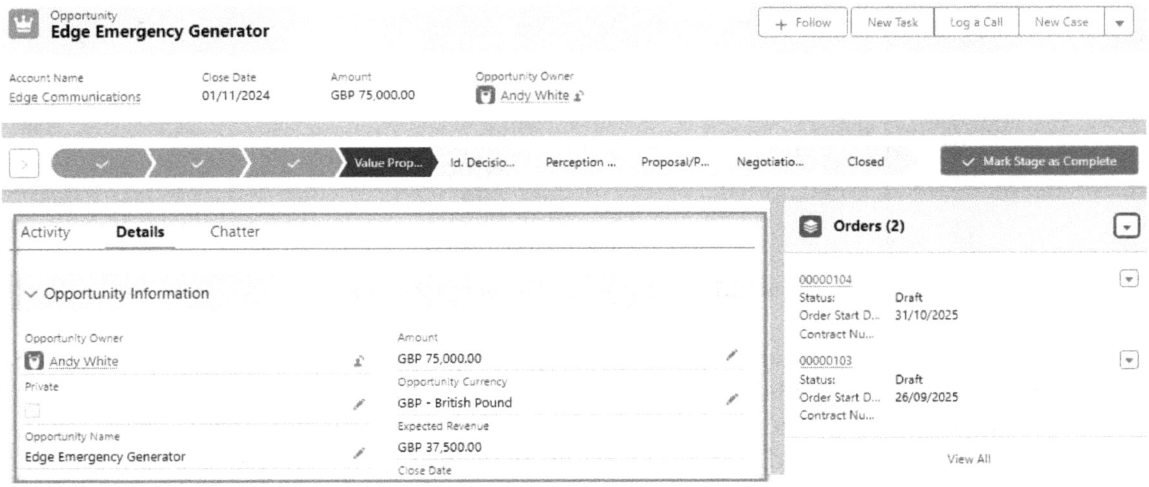

Figure 3.17: New page layout with Lightning record pages

The advantage of Lightning record pages over standard Lightning pages is that they offer more control and flexibility. Lightning record pages include conditional visibility of components and the ability to filter information within components. Standard Lightning pages focus on the overall structure and design of a page. Recent Salesforce releases often include new functionality built on Lightning record pages, so the reader should be aware of the difference.

Dynamic Form and setting field visibility

This is a fictitious example, but it could be that private opportunities are dealt with outside the pre-sales department. There is a requirement that if an **Opportunity** is **Private**, then the fields **Primary Campaign Source** and **Lead Source** are invisible. The **Private** field is a tick box on the **Opportunity** record.

Follow these steps:

1. Select the **Primary Campaign Source** field on the page layout.

2. Select the **Add Filter** button on the far right-hand side and enter the values as shown in the following figure:

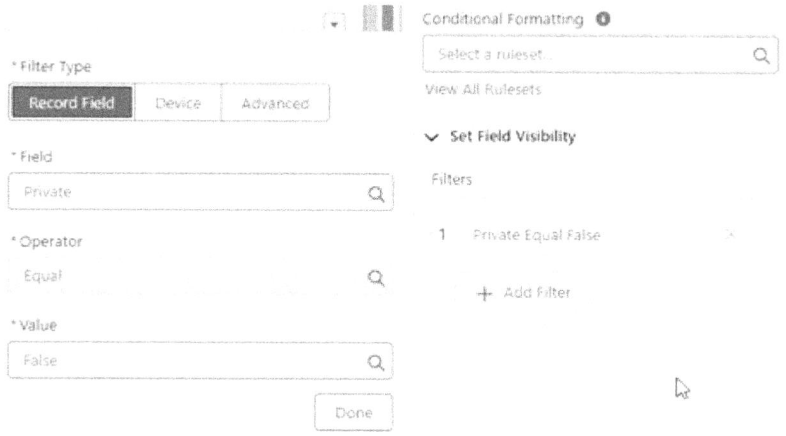

Figure 3.18: Setting field visibility for Dynamic Forms

3. Do the same for the **Lead Source** field.

4. The above makes both fields invisible if the **Opportunity** is set to **Private**. Press **Save** and **Activation** the new Dynamic Form in the Lightning record page.

5. Go to an **Opportunity** record and toggle the **Private** field on and off. The two fields go visible and then invisible to the user, as shown in the following figure:

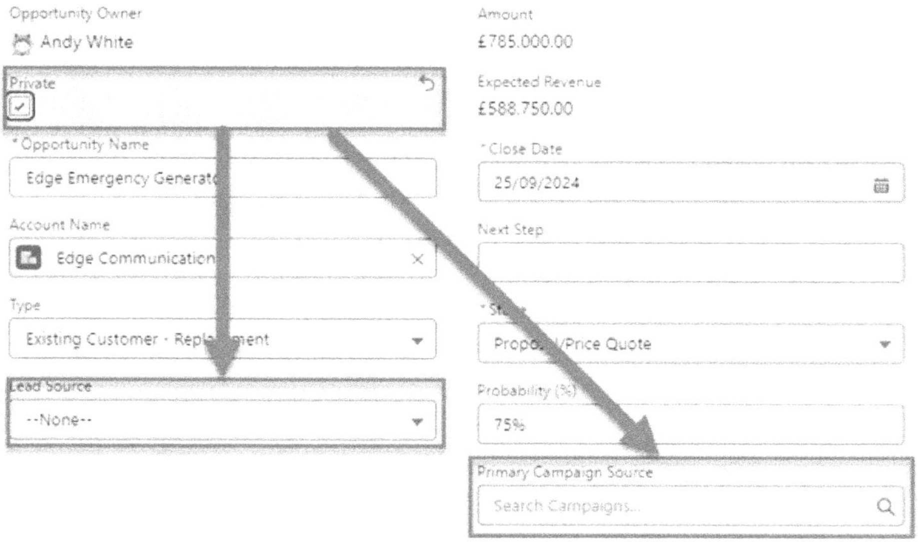

Figure 3.19: Setting field visibility for Dynamic Forms

When the **Opportunity** is set to **Private**, then the **Lead Source** and **Primary Campaign Source** fields are hidden, as shown below. Further functionality can be added using permission sets and page layout assignment, so the Sales Team do not have access to the **Private** checkbox.

Opportunity
Edge Emergency Generator

∨ Opportunity Information

Opportunity Owner		Amount	
Andy White	👤	GBP 785,000.00	
Private		Expected Revenue	
✓	🖉	GBP 588,750.00	
Opportunity Name		Close Date	
Edge Emergency Generator	🖉	25/09/2024	🖉
Account Name		Next Step	
Edge Communications	🖉		🖉
Type		Stage	
Existing Customer - Replacement	🖉	Proposal/Price Quote	🖉
		Probability (%)	
		75%	🖉

Figure 3.20: Fields hidden using Dynamic Forms

Dynamic Forms

Let us follow these steps as part of another example:

1. You can hide entire sections on the page layout in a very similar way. The main difference is that page sections are controlled when you press the **Save** button. The logic would be the same if a requirement were to hide a private information section. To do this, follow these steps:

    a. Go to the left-hand side of the page layout editor, select the **Fields** tab, and drag a **Field Section** onto the page layout as shown, and optionally give the section a **Custom Label** such as **Customer Upgrade Information**:

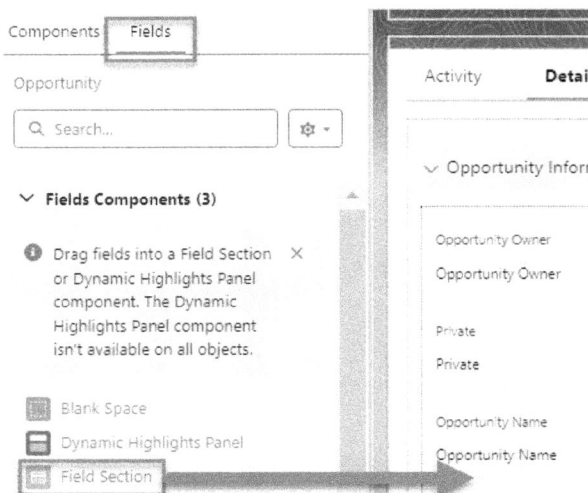

Figure 3.21: Section visibility for Dynamic Forms

    b.   Place various fields into the section. For demonstration purposes, it does not matter which ones; however, you may wish to use fields from the field list on the left-hand side.

2. Select the newly added section and choose the **Add Filter** button as in the previous example.

    Note: **You can toggle the logic using true or false values in the filter.**

3. For the example illustrated in the following figure, the section is hidden when an opportunity **Type** field is set to **Existing Customer–Upgrade**.

4. Press **Save** and **Activation** and test the opportunity record. This time, you must save the record before the section appears.

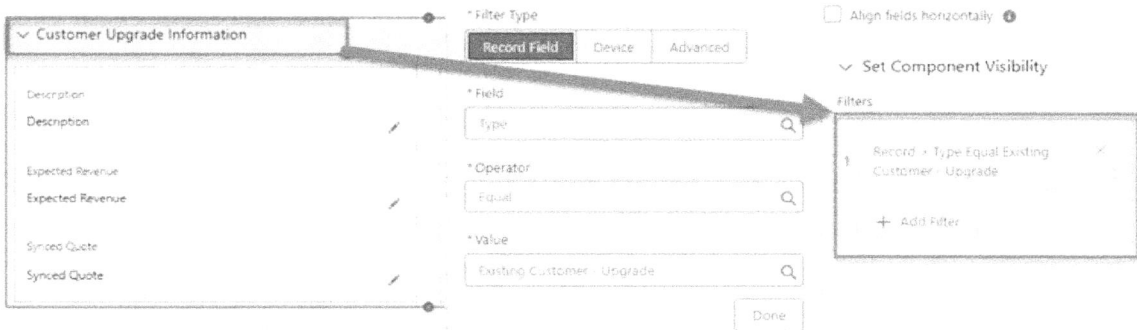

Figure 3.22: *Adding a dynamic section*

To test this functionality, go to an opportunity record and change the opportunity **Type** between **Existing Customer–Upgrade** and another value and press **Save**. The section will disappear or appear based on the opportunity **Type**, as shown in the following figure:

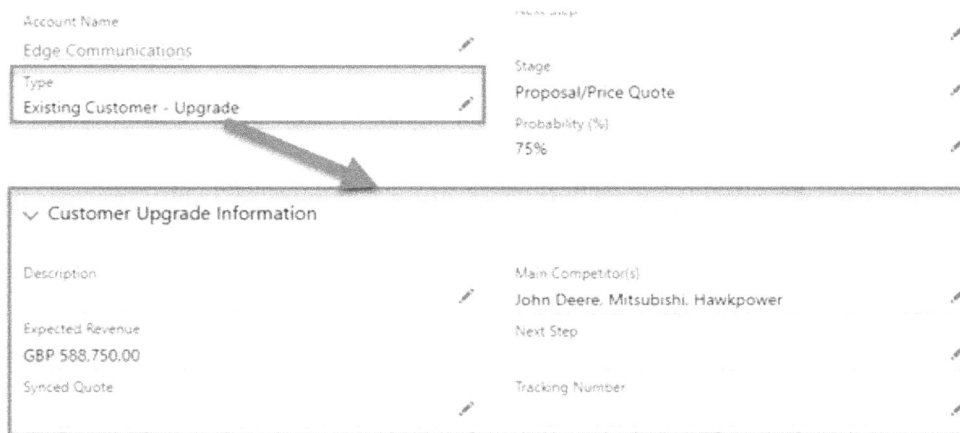

Figure 3.23: *Testing a dynamic section*

In-app guidance

Another helpful feature is in-app guidance. In-app guidance gives users directions on what steps are needed to complete a task. It can help users learn how to use new features, adopt processes, or discover products and services. To do this, follow these steps:

1. Go to **Setup | In-App Guidance** and press the blue **Add** button at the top or bottom of the screen.

   Note: **Salesforce provides a helpful video and a settings option that you may wish to view when you first setup in-app guidance.**

2. You should see another **Add** button near the top right-hand side of the screen, as shown in the following figure:

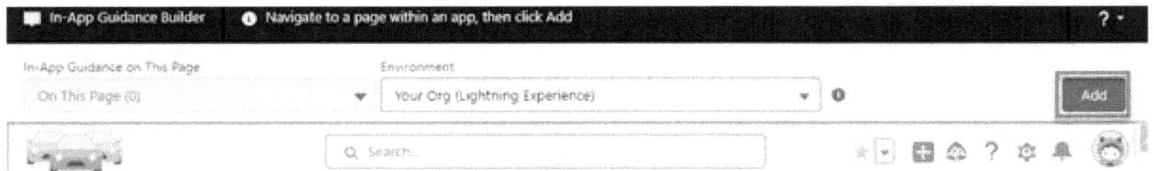

Figure 3.24: Adding in-app guidance for an app

   Note: **If you do not see the Add button, then check that the page has sufficient content to warrant in-app guidance. In which case, you will simply need to add more fields or related lists to the app.**

3. Press **Add**, and you will have the options of **Single Prompt** or **Walkthrough**.

4. From here, there are various routes depending on what you want, but for a simple **Single prompt**, press **Next** and complete the details on the right-hand side of the screen. This will populate the prompt as you go.

5. After pressing **Save**, you have the in-app guidance settings, which give options such as the date range, frequency, and number of times to show, etc.

6. Select the user profiles to which you want to apply it.

7. Once done, users will have additional helpful information when they start using new Salesforce features. Refer to the following figure:

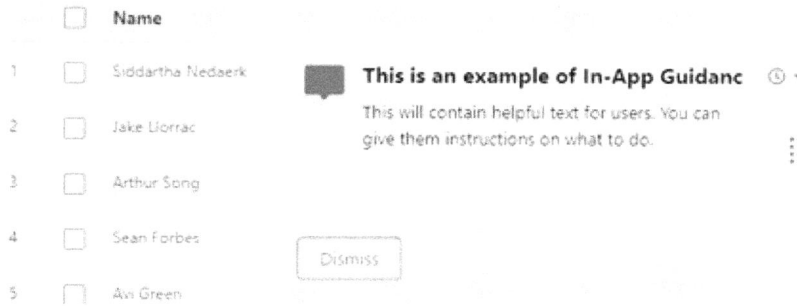

Figure 3.25: Selecting users or groups for in-app guidance

Building an app from scratch

The apps that come with the App Launcher are not limited to the ones that come with your Developer Edition org. You may want to build one from scratch. As you remember from *Chapter 1, Introduction to Salesforce*, an app is simply a collection of tabs.

However, creating a custom app may be suitable if you want to name it after the company or a particular piece of functionality, such as **Vehicle Fleet**, since you can add tabs specific to all users and grant them access to the app.

Fortunately, this is a relatively simple process. Follow these steps:

1. Go to **Setup | App Manager** to get a list of available apps.

2. On the top right-hand side of the screen, press **New Lightning App** and follow the three-stage wizard.

3. Give the app a name and description and, ideally, enter an icon or image.

4. Select the default values, but be aware that console navigation significantly impacts the UI. This is because console apps allow users to open multiple records at once, while standard apps only allow one record at a time. This is covered more in *Console apps and the utility bar* section in the chapter.

5. Utility items (optional). The utility bar is a small space, typically at the bottom left of the screen, which can add various Salesforce features, such as online status for call center agents, messages, and more. This works best with **computer telephony integration (CTI)** such as Service Cloud Voice, but add the Chatter feed to see if it works.

6. Select the tabs you want to enter for the app. This will depend on what you want to do with the app. For example, suppose the app was **Vehicle Fleet** (mentioned above). In that case, you may wish to have **Contacts**, **Vehicles** (renamed from the products object), a custom object for **Vehicle Bookings** (a junction object between **Contacts** and **Vehicles**), and a **Booking Calendar**.

7. Select the profiles that should have access to the new app. You must include yourself (your likely profile is system administrator).

8. If you ever need to adjust the settings in an app, simply go to **Setup | App Manager** and select the **Edit** option at the far-right side of the screen next to the app.

9. When you are done, you can see the new app in the **App Launcher**, which has the configuration done in the wizard in the following figure:

Figure 3.26: Building a custom app

Tip: **The app can be pushed to the top of the App Launcher list as shown in the following figure, and could be set to the default app for the users required. This is done under Setup | Users | Profiles, press Edit, and under the section Custom App Setting, select the default option against the name of the app.**

The following figure shows the making the custom app available:

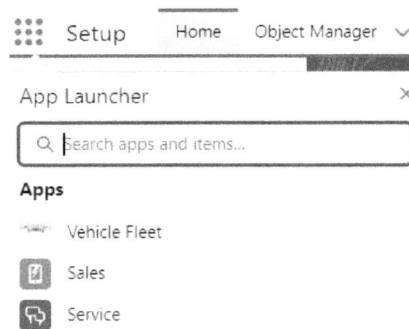

Figure 3.27: Making the custom app available

Themes and Branding

You can change Salesforce's theme by going to **Setup | Themes and Branding**. However, Salesforce comes with several included styles (try activating them on the right-hand side of the screen). The default theme is Lightning Blue if you need to return to it.

Editing highlights panel with compact layout

Salesforce allows you to keep the screen as uncluttered as possible. As a result, summary information can be displayed in the highlights panel, which is typically at the top of the screen.

This information is also useful when using Salesforce mobile (discussed further in *Chapter 10, Various Salesforce Features*. The illustration in the following shows the highlights panel for the **Contact** object:

Figure 3.28: Compact layout and highlights panel

1. This is controlled by going to **Setup** | **Object Manager** | (select the object) | **Compact Layout**.

2. Hence, for the **Contact** shown above, the **Compact Layout** is:

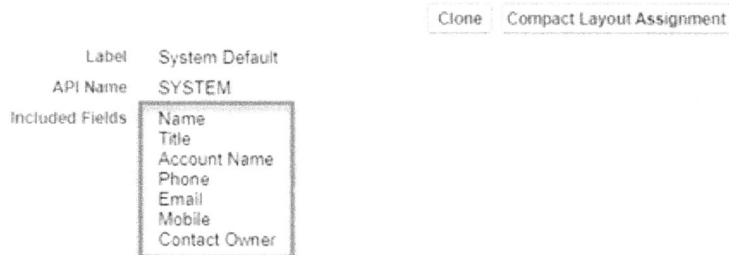

Figure 3.29: Adding fields to the compact layout

3. Since the above is the **System Default**, you need to press the **Clone** button to create a custom compact layout.

4. Then, press the **Compact Layout Assignment** button to reassign the fields shown in the highlights panel.

Console apps and utility bar

The utility bar is a thin area at the bottom of the screen that is not shown by default unless it is already configured. It is typically used in console apps, which is the option in the second step in setting up a new app, as shown in the following figure:

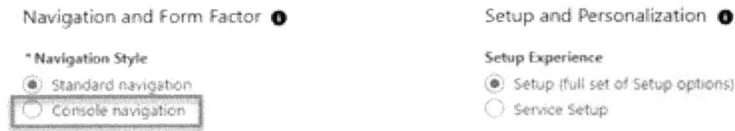

Figure 3.30: The option of creating a console app when creating a new Salesforce app

Console apps allow users to manage multiple records on a single screen, minimizing clicks and scrolling to quickly access related records. Console apps are typically used by sales or service agents to enable them to efficiently handle a large volume of data and interactions on a single screen. To view a console app, simply go to the **App Launcher** and select an app with console in the name.

For example, if you go to the **Service Console** (**App Launcher | Service Console**), you will see a small **History** icon as shown in the following figure:

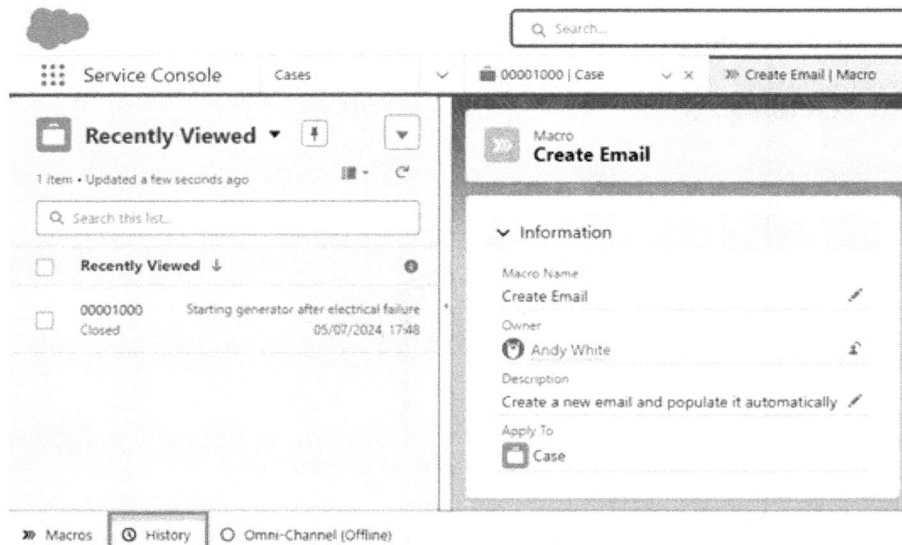

Figure 3.31: History being shown on the utility bar

However, the utility bar is handy and can be configured for a variety of functions. Typically, it will be used in a call center to add a softphone (which requires CTI functionality such as Service Cloud Voice or Genesys), but can also be used with some standard features such as Chatter. This is covered in the section *Building an app from scratch*.

To add features to the utility bar, follow these steps:

1. Go to **Setup | App Manager** and then go to the chosen app.

2. Press **Edit** on the far right-hand side, which will give the following screen, as shown in the following figure:

Figure 3.32: Adding items to the utility bar

Enhanced related lists

We covered in *Chapter 2, Basic Admin Essentials*, how to create and customize related lists. Salesforce also allows enhanced related lists that offer additional configurations, such as:

- Additional field display customization

- Filter criteria on the related list

- The ability to compact the related list

To add an enhanced related list, go to **Setup | Edit Page** as shown in the following figure:

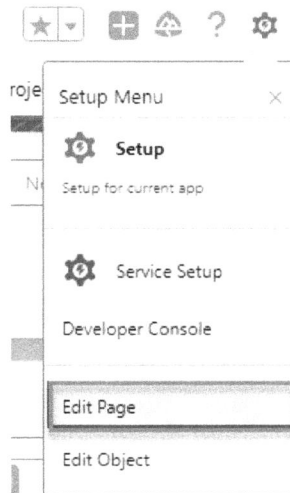

Figure 3.33: Edit Page for adding enhanced related lists

Drag the **Related List-Single** component onto the page layout and the **Related List Quick Links**, as shown in the following figure:

Figure 3.34: Adding components to the page layout

If you select the newly added components, the properties section on the right-hand side of the screen gives the following options:

- **Related List-Single**; select the object to base the related list on, select the **Number of Records to Display**, or **Upgrade to Dynamic Related Lists** to get further options.

    Refer to the following figure:

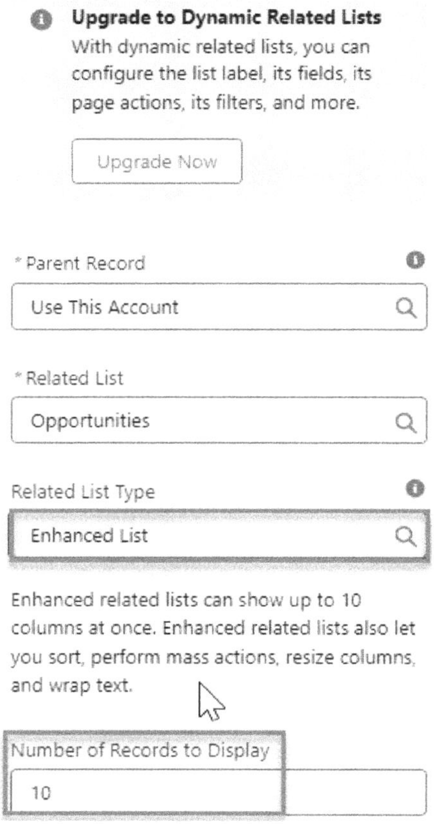

Figure 3.35: Options for enhanced related lists

- The other component added was **Related List Quick Links**. This gives you a display area at the top of the page, as shown in the following figure:

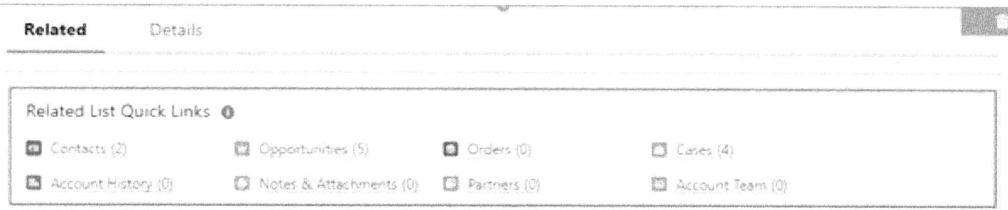

Figure 3.36: *Showing related lists on the details page*

Use the properties on the right-hand side to hide the header or set component visibility as outlined in the *Dynamic Forms* section.

Default tab in the page layout editor

Although this is simple, it is surprising how often it is ignored. If a user opens a record in Salesforce, they can see the **Details** or **Related** lists tab.

To select the **Default Tab**, go to the page layout editor, select the **Tabs** section, and use the properties to set the default:

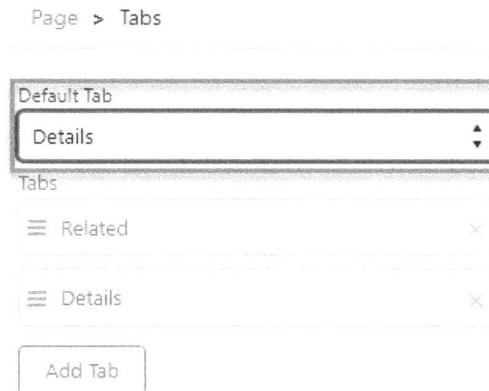

Figure 3.37: *Setting the default view for users*

Suppose you have added the **Related List Quick Links** in the previous section. In that case, you will be able to see the details and the quick links to related lists, effectively giving you all the information in one place, as shown in the following figure:

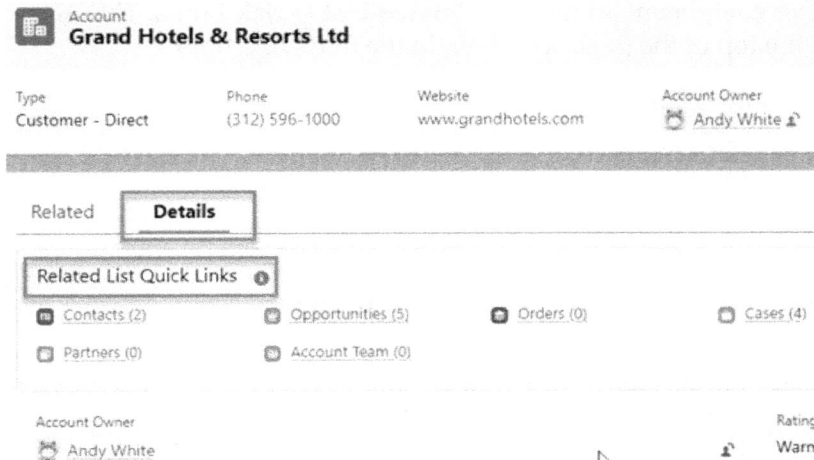

Figure 3.38: Combined view of details and related lists

Home page customization

Users typically see summary information on the home page, including dashboards, a summary of their activities, and plans for the days ahead.

It can also include recent Chatter posts, LWCs, and other features.

To customize the home page, follow these steps:

1. Go to **Setup | Lightning App Builder**, press **New**, select **Home Page**, as shown in the following figure:

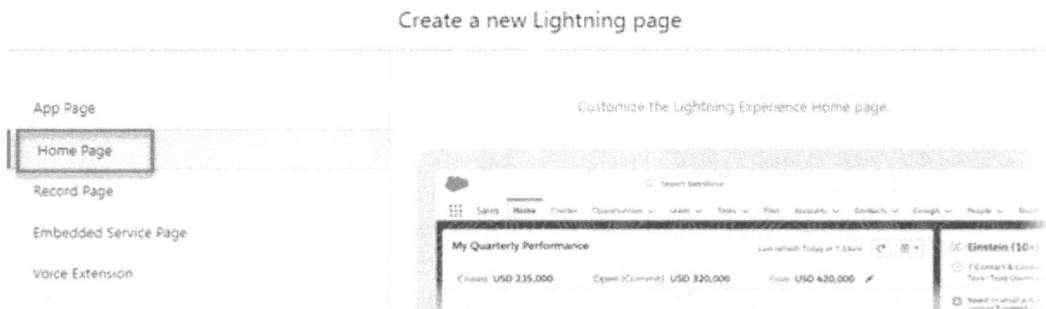

Figure 3.39: Customizing the Home Page

2. Label it, such as **Sales**, **Users**, **Home**, and then choose a template or clone the Salesforce default home page.

3. One is chosen from a template, a header, and three regions. Components for recent activities, Chatter feed, and a high-level overview of various accounts were added.

4. Once you are happy with the home page, it can be assigned as the **Org Default**, but in this case, we are only assigning it to people using the Sales app, as shown in the following figure:

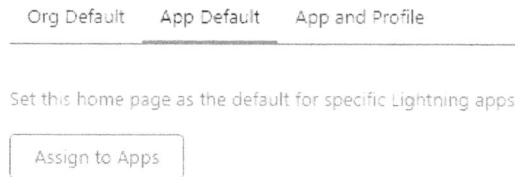

Org Default   App Default   App and Profile

Set this home page as the default for specific Lightning apps.

Assign to Apps

Figure 3.40: *Assignment of home page to various users*

5. To assign the home page to other apps, include them in the list and ensure the home page is included in the app using **App Manager**.

Search layouts

Search layouts appear in numerous places, but use the user's profile to determine what is returned when a user searches for a record.

The profile defines the fields displayed when users search for a record in the global search or look up a record in a related list.

To modify search layouts, follow these steps:

1. Go to **Setup** | **Object Manager** (select the object) | **Search Layout**.

2. Salesforce has a default layout, which is then used by the profiles in the list.

3. To create a custom search layout, press the **New** button and assign it to the profiles.

Refer to the following figure:

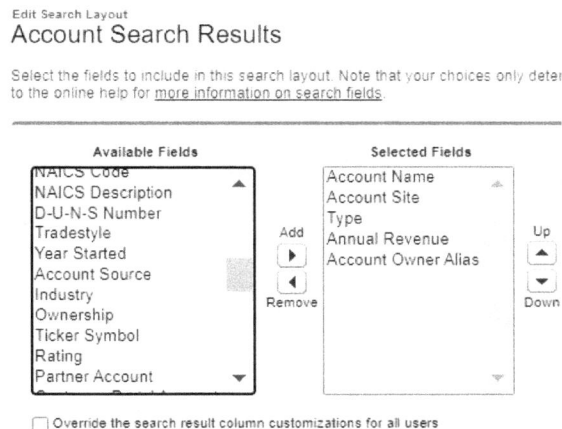

Edit Search Layout
Account Search Results

Select the fields to include in this search layout. Note that your choices only deter
to the online help for more information on search fields.

Available Fields		Selected Fields
NAICS Code		Account Name
NAICS Description		Account Site
D-U-N-S Number		Type
Tradestyle	Add	Annual Revenue
Year Started	▶	Account Owner Alias
Account Source	◀	
Industry	Remove	
Ownership		
Ticker Symbol		
Rating		
Partner Account		

Up ▲   Down ▼

☐ Override the search result column customizations for all users

Figure 3.41: *Selecting fields to add to the search layout*

Conclusion

This chapter has shown how Salesforce's UI can be customized to meet different business requirements. This has primarily been achieved by using the Salesforce Classic page layout editor, but this well-established editor is limited in its capabilities. As a result, a more advanced configuration was done using Lightning record pages. This allowed for Dynamic Forms and more granular control of the page layout.

It is recommended that Lightning record pages be used as the default way of adjusting page layout, as Salesforce will build further functionality into them while leaving the Classic page layout editor as a legacy way. However, administrators should be aware of both options.

We also built an app from scratch and set it up to have the required tabs and other features, such as the utility bar and enhanced related lists. In summary, the UI can be configured in many ways, and an administrator needs to be aware of the various options available.

In the next chapter, we will be learning how to create new objects in Salesforce, add relationships between the new objects and existing objects, and customize them by adding fields and other functionality.

Multiple choice questions

1. **The quickest way to access the page layout for a record in Salesforce is to go:**
   a. Setup | Object Manager | (select the object) | Page Layouts | (select the layout)
   b. Setup | Page Layout Editor | (select the object) | Page Layout
   c. Setup | Edit Page
   d. App Launcher | Lightning Page Layout Editor

2. **With Dynamic Forms, how do dynamic sections differ from dynamic fields?**
   a. Dynamic sections will only appear once the record has been saved
   b. Dynamic sections only show dynamic fields
   c. Dynamic sections work after the record is saved, and dynamic fields work when the user changes a field
   d. Dynamic fields criteria need to be based on a numeric, currency, or date value; dynamic sections work with all field types

3. **Lightning record pages can be which type of layout?**
   a. App page
   b. Home page
   c. Record page

   d. Embedded service page

   e. All of the above

4. **What is the difference between quick actions and global actions?**

   a. Global actions work at any location around the world; quick actions depend on the region you are in

   b. Global actions perform a wide range of functions, whilst quick actions only perform certain functions

   c. Quick actions are object-specific, while global actions are not

   d. Quick actions run on Lightning, whilst global actions work for both Salesforce Classic and Lightning

5. **When building a custom app from scratch, which of these should you consider?**

   a. The security model will change for each tab or object added

   b. The app will be made available to all users

   c. The app will leverage the same functionality for all the tabs or objects which the user has

   d. The app needs additional configuration for the user's role and profile

6. **In-app guidance is helpful in showing users how to navigate the UI. The following things need to be considered:**

   a. If it is a Single Prompt or walkthrough

   b. The location of the pop-ups

   c. The users and the duration that users will see the in-app guidance

   d. All of the above

7. **Enhance related lists to offer greater functionality of standard related lists by:**

   a. Giving the user additional fields not available through standard related lists

   b. Providing options on how many records to display and easy configuration of field order

   c. Being available for Salesforce mobile as well as desktop

   d. Showing users related information to the fields in the enhanced related list

8. **Can a related list quick link be added to a record detail page?**

   a. True

   b. False

9. **A consideration when using report charts is:**

    a.   They only show the data that the user has access to

    b.   They only work in the Lightning UI

    c.   If the user does not have access to the underlying data, then they will show an insufficient privileges message when they click the report chart

    d.   Report charts can work on standard objects, but custom objects need report charts enabled

10. **A home page has numerous advantages. One of these is:**

    a.   Allowing every user to have the same landing page when they login to Salesforce

    b.   Allowing users to have the same view of company performance

    c.   Providing a convenient screen to show users their most relevant information

    d.   To combine summary information from various objects displayed by each related list

Answers

1	c
2	c
3	e
4	c
5	c
6	d
7	b
8	a
9	c
10	c

Join our Discord space

Join our Discord workspace for latest updates, offers, tech happenings around the world, new releases, and sessions with the authors:

https://discord.bpbonline.com

CHAPTER 4
Creating Object with Custom Fields and Relationships

Introduction

This chapter is about customizing Salesforce by creating custom objects, linking them to existing functionality, and setting Salesforce up so that this new functionality is available to users. It also includes additional information about customization, including how Salesforce can be configured to meet various business needs based on configuration, and not complex customization.

Structure

This chapter covers the following topics:

- Creating custom objects
- Useful field features
- Big objects, external objects, and custom metadata types

Objectives

By the end of this chapter, the reader will be able to add custom objects and build relationships between other standard or custom objects. They will be able to add various fields and also build in sufficient configuration to ensure that the data entered by the user is valid. The user will be also be able to add some standard configuration to track the history of the data stored against fields in an object.

This chapter also includes some additional information about other types of objects, which the reader should be aware of, which may be useful for either projects they are required to work on or provide as an alternative to standard Salesforce objects and fields.

Creating custom objects

Salesforce is not limited to the objects that you are initially given. You can create a custom object to hold specific information. For example, a construction company may wish to have a Project object that allows it to build property for various existing accounts, or a charity may want to have a donation object to store records of donations they have received.

The most important thing to consider before creating an object is how it relates to other objects. This time spent thinking can save many hours for developers trying to code a solution or get a flow to work as intended. If you get the object model right, Salesforce works efficiently. If you get it wrong, getting Salesforce to do what you want is challenging.

Taking the property example above, a property development company might need numerous accounts (i.e., businesses) to invest in the building or be directly involved in the construction. As such, a custom Project object related to accounts is needed. If there is a straightforward relationship between the account and property, then a master-detail or lookup relationship would be fine.

The difference between a lookup relationship and a master-detail is covered in *Chapter 2, Basic Admin Essentials,* but the business has specific requirements outlined in the following sections.

A master-detail would allow roll-up summary fields to capture total expenditure, the number of people working on the project, and more. However, suppose the construction company works on several projects and for different accounts. In that case, a junction object might be more suitable as it would allow for the necessary many-to-many relationship. Ideally, all significant decisions are made as a proof of concept to give a working demonstration to key decision-makers.

There are some considerations when creating custom objects. When adding fields to an object, there can be only two master-detail relationships. This makes the data model manageable and prevents performance issues if Salesforce has to look up records on a related object. This still allows for junction objects, but having more is unnecessary.

Creating custom object

To create a new custom object, go to **Setup | Object Manager** and press **Create**, then **Custom Object**, as shown in the following figure:

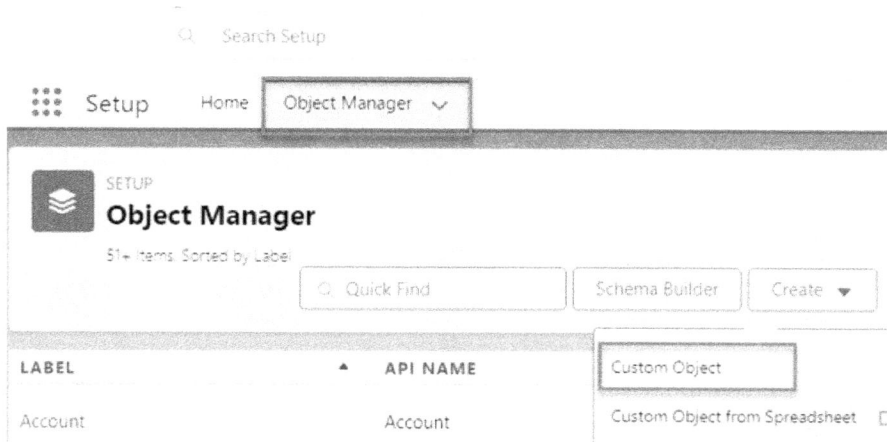

Figure 4.1: *Creating a new Custom Object*

We will use the example of a construction company wanting to create a Project object.

On the first screen, enter the following as shown in the following table:

Item to complete	Value	Description
Label	Project	The name of the object
Plural Label	Projects	Displays a correct name for plurals
Description	Housing or construction projects	Helps other users know what the object is being used for
Record Name	Project name	Shows the name (or number) of the record on the object
Data Type	Auto number	You can enter a name each time, but the auto number is quicker and easier
Display Format	PR-{00000}	Provides a format for the auto number. Putting PR means every project starts with PR, then the number
Starting Number	1	If creating a new object, then let the auto number start at 1.
Allow Reports	Check	Allow reports to be generated from this object
Allow Activities	Check	Track users' activities or allow them to add tasks and events to this object
Track Field History	Check	If a user changes a field value, Salesforce can track who made the change and what was changed.

Item to complete	Value	Description
Allow in Chatter Groups	Check	Records from this new custom object can be shared on Salesforce Chatter (discussed in the following sections).
Allow Search	Check	Make the records available in Salesforce global search.
Add Notes and Attachments related list to default page layout	Check	Allow users to attach files or notes to a record in the new custom object
Launch New Custom Tab Wizard after saving this custom object	Check	This is quite useful. It allows you to create a new tab which displays on the screen. This new tabs wizard will launch after you save the object.

Table 4.1: Values required for the new custom object

If you check the **Launch New Custom Tab Wizard** in the last step above, you will see another screen asking you to choose an icon for the object and add a description. Press **Next**, then **Next**, and then **Save**.

Adding fields to custom object

This has created a new custom object, but it needs to hold information about the projects. Add the following fields as shown in the following table:

Note: **Use the description to populate the Help Text field. This will appear if the user hovers their mouse over the question mark next to the field on the page layout. After entering the first field, press Save and New to go on and enter the next field.**

Refer to the following table:

Field name	Field type	Description
Project Name	Text	When asked, enter length as 255.
Project Description	Text Area (Long)	Leave the default values.
Location	Text	When asked, enter length as 255.
Is Live	Checkbox	Leave the default values.
Start Date	Date	Leave the default values.
Anticipated End Date	Date	Leave the default values.

Field name	Field type	Description
Actual End Date	Date	Leave the default values.
Budget	Currency	There are options for the currency type discussed later.
Actual spend	Currency	There are options for the currency type discussed later.
Project Manager	Lookup relationship (contact object)	Although a project manager is likely to be part of the company, they might not be a user of Salesforce, so the Contact object is used, and they can then be added to Salesforce.
Internal Coordinator	Lookup (user object)	The Salesforce user who will be managing this project information.
Project Type	Picklist	Select the option to enter the values below, with each value separated by a new line. Picklist values of: • Commercial • Residential • Government or local authority • Other
Parent Project	Lookup relationship (Project object)	Salesforce allows objects to look up to the same object. This means a project may have smaller projects as part of a larger project.

Table 4.2: Fields to add to the newly created Project object

NOTE: **When you create a custom object, it is given an API name ending in __c, which is a double underscore and c, likewise, for the fields that have just been created. All custom objects and fields end in __c. Salesforce uses various extensions to help identify various items such as __r (custom relationship) or __mdt (custom metadata type), and more.**

When you have added the fields in the list above, re-arrange the page layout as shown in the following figure. This is done by going to **Object Manager**, selecting the **Project** object, and then **Page Layouts**. Drag the fields on the page into a suitable layout and press **Save**.

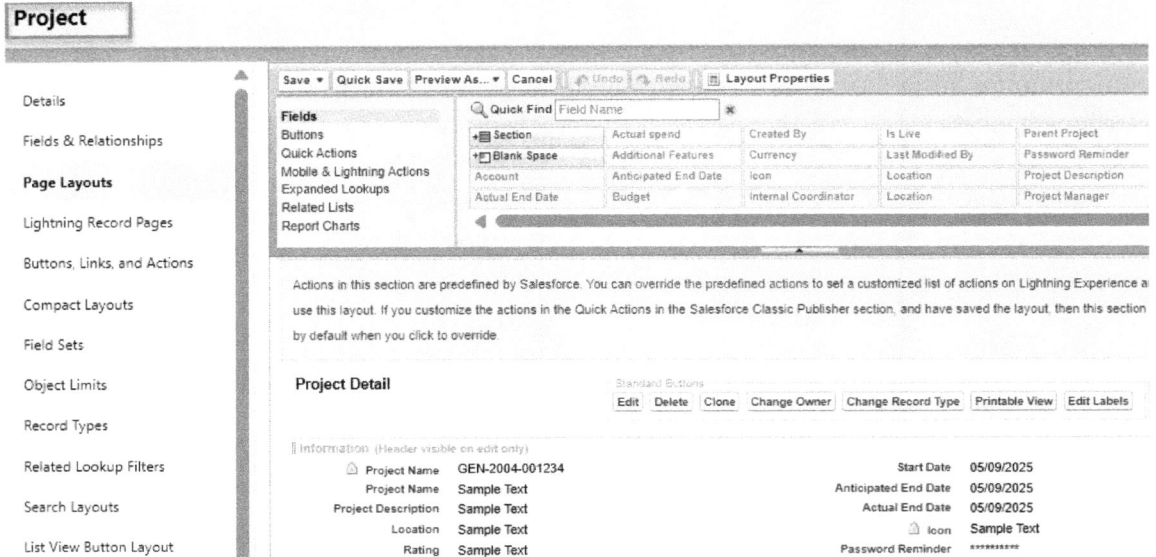

Figure 4.2: *Changing the page layout on the newly created custom object*

If you return to Salesforce as a user (i.e., not while in setup) and refresh the page, you will find a new custom tab based on the new custom object, as shown in the following figure:

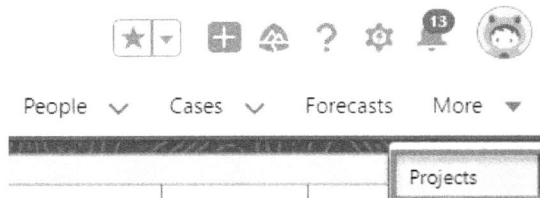

Figure 4.3: *Accessing the newly created custom object*

As this is a new object, it will not contain any data. Press the **New** button to enter information as shown in the following figure:

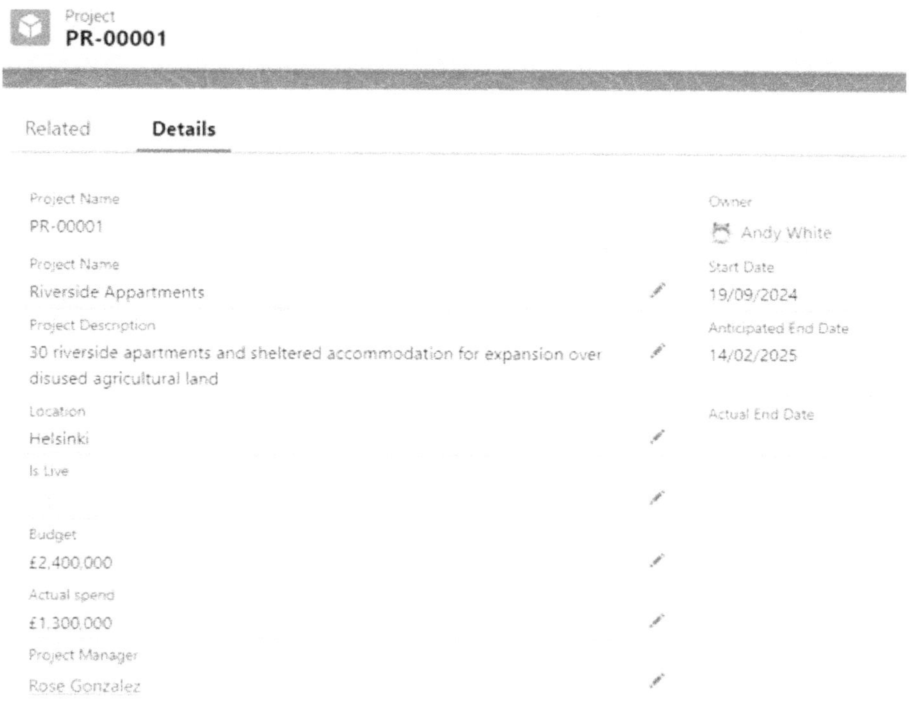

Project
PR-00001

Related | **Details**

Project Name
PR-00001

Owner
Andy White

Project Name
Riverside Appartments

Start Date
19/09/2024

Project Description
30 riverside apartments and sheltered accommodation for expansion over disused agricultural land

Anticipated End Date
14/02/2025

Location
Helsinki

Actual End Date

Is Live

Budget
£2,400,000

Actual spend
£1,300,000

Project Manager
Rose Gonzalez

Figure 4.4: Entering a record into the new custom object

Creating relationship between custom object and standard object

With the new **Project** object, a new requirement has come along that requires all accounts to show which projects belong to them and provide a total amount for the budget allocations to all the projects for each account.

This functionality would require two steps:

1. Add a master-detail field to be created on the **Project** object to have the **Account** object as the master.

2. Add a roll-up summary field to the Account object to summarize the budget amounts.

Adding a master-detail relationship

Adding a master-detail field to an object requires the child object to have no records in it. Since the Project object has very few records in it, you need to delete them first. Otherwise, if the object has many records, you must first create a lookup relationship, populate the lookup field with data from all records, and then change the relationship type to master-detail.

After having deleted any records in the Project object, follow the steps:

1. Add a master-detail field by going to **Setup | Object Manager |** (select **Project** object).

2. Go to **Fields & Relationships** and press the **New** button.

3. Select **Master-Detail Relationship** and then **Next**.

4. For **Related To**, select the **Account** object.

5. Complete the next steps using default values and press **Save**.

6. Optional: If you check the relationship is there, go to **Setup | Schema Builder** and select only the **Account** and **Project** objects to see the new relationship between the objects.

Adding a roll-up summary field

The roll-up summary field needs to be on the **Account** object. This allows the total budget to be calculated for any projects the company is responsible for. To do this, follow these steps:

1. Go to **Setup | Object Manager |** (select the **Account** object).

2. Press **Fields & Relationship** and press **New**.

3. Select **Roll-Up Summary** and then enter the values shown in the following figure.

4. Use the default options for the following screens and press **Save**.

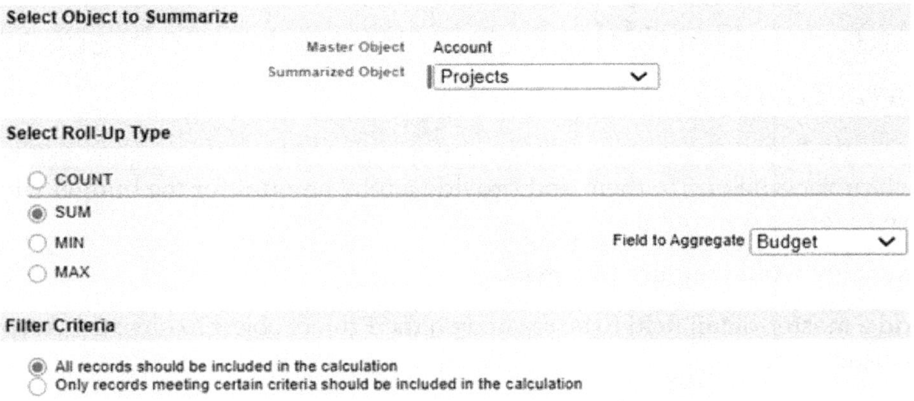

Figure 4.5: Configuring the roll-up summary custom field

5. Notice that there is also a **Filter Criteria** at the bottom of the screen. This could be used to calculate a summary within a time range or other criteria. This could be useful to see the total project budget for the past year.

6. To see the results of this configuration, go to any account record and create a few **Projects** for the account.

7. Once you have added two or three, view the newly created field, which shows the total budget for all projects on that **Account**, as shown in the following figure:

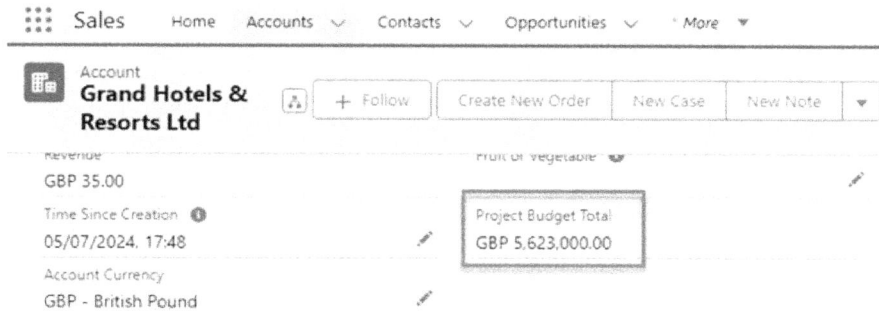

Figure 4.6: Roll-up summary field for total project funding

Although there are many different types of fields in Salesforce, most of them are relatively self-explanatory. Otherwise, Google Salesforce field types. In the upcoming sub-sections, we will look at fields that require more explanation.

Formula fields

The formula field is perhaps the one that requires special attention. Consideration is required before assuming a formula field is needed. Salesforce has to calculate the formula every time the record is viewed. If you have a report with tens of thousands of records, it can become slow to generate, even more so if a dashboard is rendered on top of it. It is worth keeping these to a minimum or not including them in a report if it has several thousand records.

However, formula fields are brilliant and work similarly to *Excel* or *Google Sheets*. A formula always has to return something (i.e., give a value), which means the field is not editable in the user interface. The values a formula field can return:

- **Boolean**: A yes or no. This is useful for decision-making.

- **Currency**: A monetary value, such as a pound, dollar, rupee, or euro.

- **Date**: This can be a day of the year or include 24-hour time. It should be noted that US dates have a different format from many other locals. This can cause problems when loading date information into Salesforce. The best way is to ensure that the local currency is set correctly in the Salesforce org and that settings are also correct when uploading.

- **Date or time**: This includes additional values for the time setting.

- **Number**: This contains a range of values. Typically denoted by the number of decimal points. Salesforce keeps a record of the decimal points, but only shows the user the value on the screen. Hence, if you have a formula field for *1.25 + 1.75*, the screen will show the formula as three, even though both fields will show one and two if they do not have a decimal place.

- **Percent**: Similar to the number field, only a % sign is added at the end of the field.

- **Text**: If you need to concatenate (i.e., stick together) words, a formula field can be added. However, text can also return an image, which is helpful. For example, a small traffic light icon can be displayed, which is included in the examples in the next section.

Formula field examples

There are many Salesforce formula field tutorials online. The following are some to get you started.

Note: **To complete this section, you should first include the Salesforce Graphics Pack outlined in the next section. However, the formula will still work without it.**

For example, if you want to display an icon to represent the status of an opportunity:

1. You must create a picklist with the values **Cold**, **Warm**, and **Hot** and add a formula field to return the image.

2. First, you must add the images as a Static Resource. To do this, go to **Setup | Custom Code | Static Resources**.

3. Each image will have a URL that can be added to the following formula.

4. To create a formula field, click on **Setup | Object Manager |** (select the object) **| Fields & Relationships** and press **New**.

5. Select a field of type **Formula** as shown in the following figure:

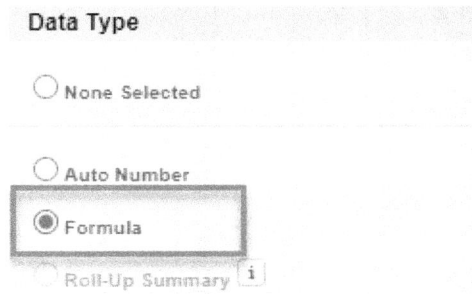

Figure 4.7: Creating a custom formula field

6. Choose type **Text** and select the **Advanced Formula** tab as shown in the following figure:

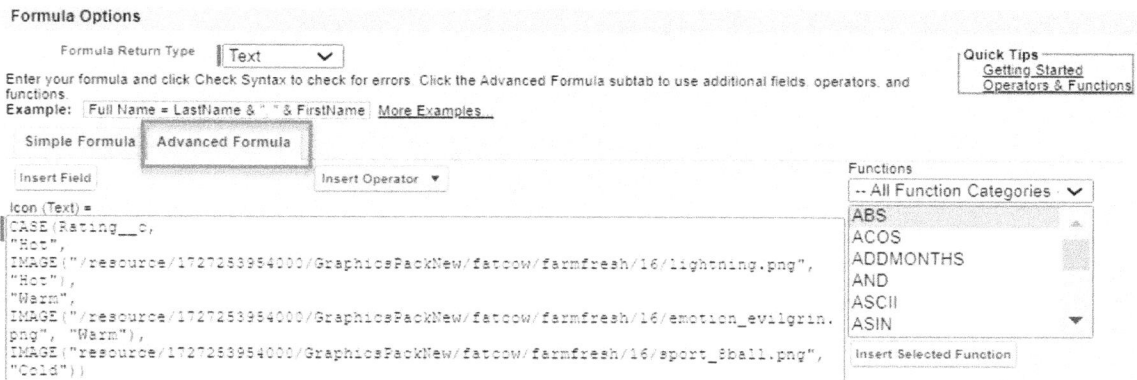

Figure 4.8: Entering a formula into a custom formula field

7. Enter the following formula. Note that this formula references icons installed by the Salesforce Graphics Pack in the next section. Errors will display red text below the formula editor. If you are building complicated formulas, press the **Check Syntax** link below the editor to check if the formula can work. There is additional help with Einstein for Formulas as part of a recent addition to writing or fixing formulas.

CASE(Rating__c,

"Hot", IMAGE("/resource/1727253954000/GraphicsPackNew/fatcow/ farmfresh/16/lightning.png", "Hot"),

"Warm", IMAGE("/resource/1727253954000/GraphicsPackNew/fatcow/ farmfresh/16/emotion_evilgrin.png", "Warm"),

IMAGE("resource/1727253954000/GraphicsPackNew/fatcow/farmfresh/16/ sport_8ball.png", "Cold"))

8. Once saved, if you change the picklist value for the custom **Rating** field, the **Icon** will update accordingly, as shown in the following figure:

Figure 4.9: Displaying an icon from the newly created custom formula field

9. Images also show up in list views, as shown in the following figure:

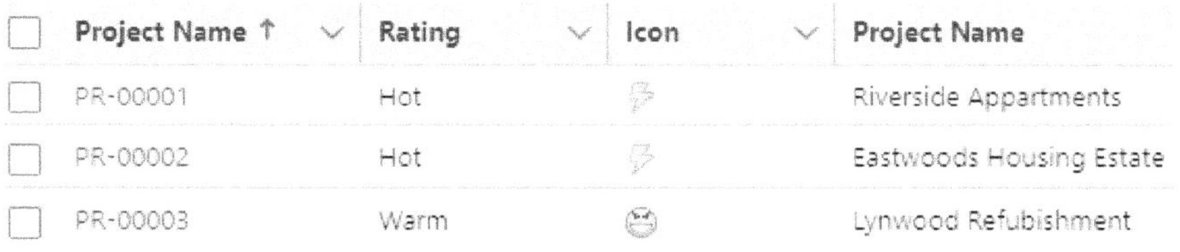

Figure 4.10: Displaying icon values in the list view

Salesforce Graphics Pack on AppExchange

If you want to add many icons, **Salesforce Labs** offers the **Graphics Pack** for free.

To find it, visit the Salesforce AppExchange at **https://appexchange.salesforce.com/** and search for **Graphics Pack**. Refer to the following figure:

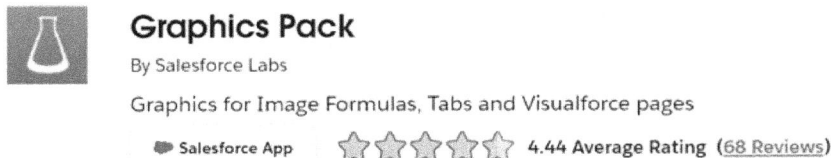

Graphics Pack
By Salesforce Labs

Graphics for Image Formulas, Tabs and Visualforce pages

Salesforce App   ⭐⭐⭐⭐⭐ 4.44 Average Rating (68 Reviews)

Figure 4.11: Adding Salesforce Graphics Pack

Follow these steps to install the Graphics Pack from the Salesforce AppExchange:

1. Select the app on the AppExchange and press the **Get It Now** button.

2. Select the **Login** button, typically with the **Login with Trailblazer.me** button.

3. Select **Salesforce** and no other authentication options, such as Google, MuleSoft, or others.

4. Login to your Salesforce account, which should be the Developer Edition org that you have been working in.

5. Select the environment that will be installed in production.

6. Press **Confirm and Install**.

7. Select the **Terms and Conditions** tick box.

8. You should receive an email confirming the successful installation.

9. Once done, go to the **App Launcher** in the top left-hand side of the screen and select **Graphics Pack** to give you the screen as shown in the following figure:

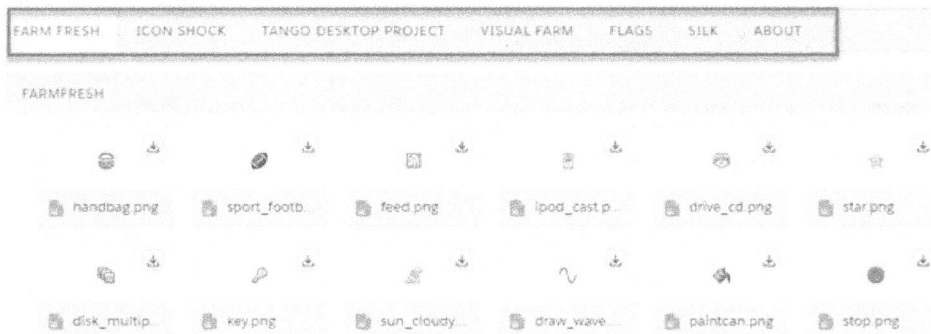

Figure 4.12: Installed Graphics Pack in your Salesforce environment

One of the most valuable features is using the **IF** statement to do conditional formulas. For example, **IF** an opportunity is above a certain amount, then set the opportunity commission to 15%; otherwise, the base commission of 10% is used. For example, refer to the following command:

```
IF(Amount < 100000, Amount * 0.10, Amount * 0.15)
```

If you need to refer to a picklist value, then the **ISPICKVAL** function is used. For example, refer to the following code:

```
(IF( AnnualRevenue = 0, 0, 10)) +
(IF(ISPICKVAL(Industry, "Finance") , 0, 10)) +
(IF( Phone = "", 0, 10)) +
(IF(NumberOfEmployees > 1000,100,10)) /*increase anticipated revenue
based on company size */
```

Note: A comment using /* syntax was added to the final line to show what the formula is intended for. In the following, there is another example of ISPICKVAL, where a five percent commission is calculated for an opportunity with a stage of Closed Won.

For example, refer to the following code:

```
IF(ISPICKVAL(StageName, "Closed Won"),
  ROUND(Amount *0.05, 2), 0)
```

Dependent picklists

Picklists are useful for ensuring data consistency in Salesforce. Dependent picklists allow one picklist to control what values are available in a second picklist.

For example, you may have a picklist for job roles, where an executive will only have specific job titles, whilst those in sales or marketing may have different job titles.

To make a dependent picklist, follow these steps:

1. Go to **Setup** | **Object Manager** | (select the object) | **Fields & Relationships** and press **New**.

2. Create two picklists, one for **Food Types** and the other with a list of different foods, as shown in the following figure:

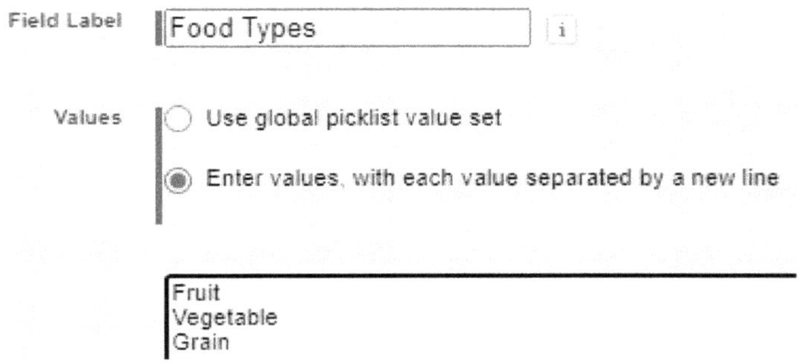

| Field Label | Food Types | i |

Values

    ◯ Use global picklist value set

    ◉ Enter values, with each value separated by a new line

    Fruit
    Vegetable
    Grain

Figure 4.13: Creating a custom picklist field

3. Return to the object by going to **Setup** | (select the object) | **Fields & Relationships** and press the **Field Dependencies** button at the top of the screen, then press the **New** button.

Refer to the following figure:

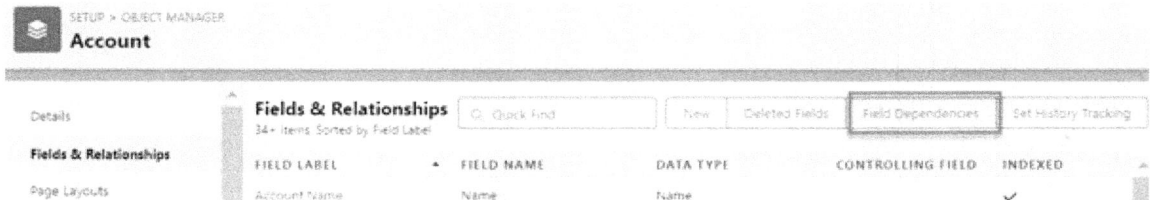

SETUP > OBJECT MANAGER
Account

Details	**Fields & Relationships**	Q Quick Find	New	Deleted Fields	Field Dependencies	Set History Tracking
Fields & Relationships	34+ items. Sorted by Field Label					
Page Layouts	FIELD LABEL ▲	FIELD NAME	DATA TYPE		CONTROLLING FIELD	INDEXED ▲
	Account Name	Name	Name			✓

Figure 4.14: Creating a dependency between picklist fields

4. You will then select which field is the **Controlling Field** and what field is the **Dependent Field**. Refer to the following figure:

Continue   Cancel

| Controlling Field | Food Types ⌄ |
| Dependent Field | Fruit or Vegetable ⌄ |

Continue   Cancel

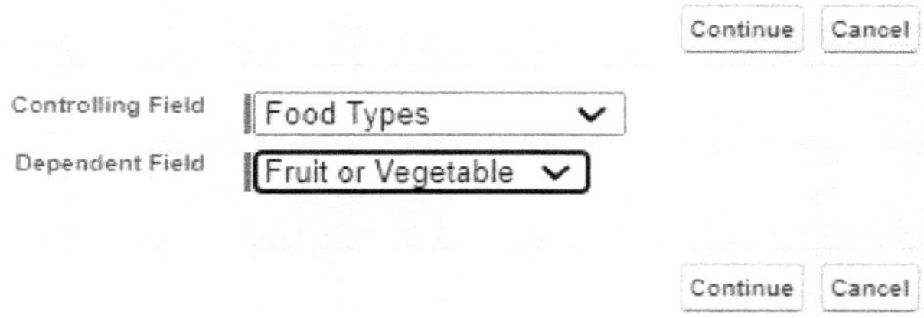

Figure 4.15: Selecting the Dependent Field

5. Hold the *ctrl* button (PC) or the *cmd* key (Mac) to do multi-select.

6. When selected, the cells turn purple. Press the **Include Values** button to save the configuration, and the cells will then turn yellow.

Refer to the following figure:

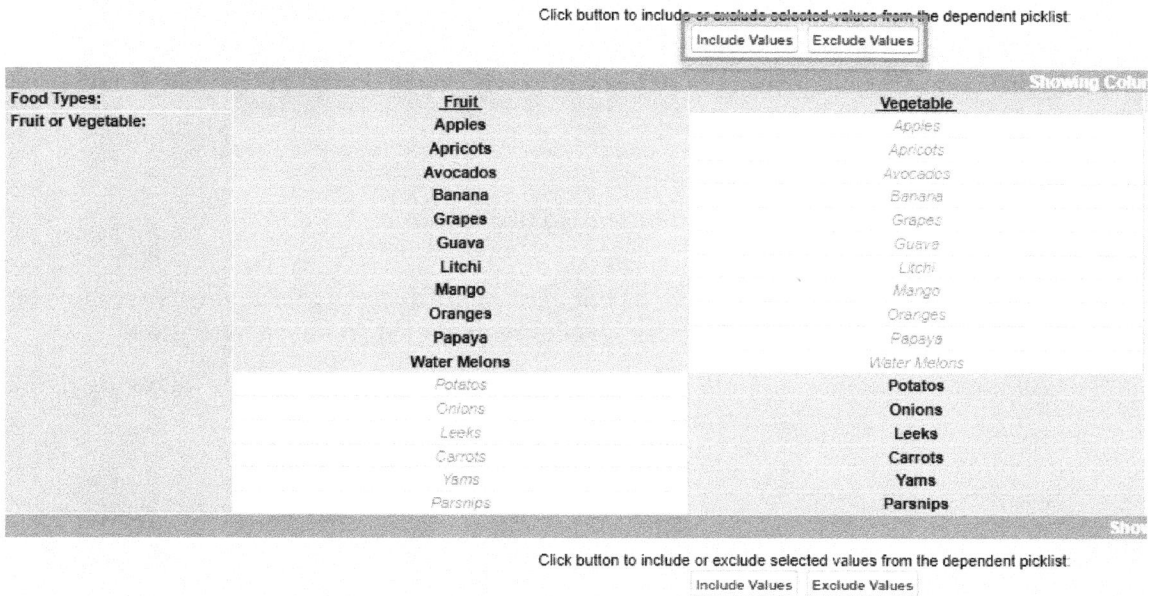

Figure 4.16: *Selecting the options for which fields are displayed on the dependent picklist*

7. Press **Save**. Now, when you turn to the record, you can control which fields are available, as shown in the following figure:

Figure 4.17: *The results of configuring a dependent picklist*

8. It is worth noting that you can chain picklists together to have a third or fourth picklist with dependencies between them.

9. Another feature of picklists is to make them available on all objects. This could be useful for a list of countries or similar. To do this, press the **Edit** button next to the picklist and then the **Promote to Global Value Set**, as shown in the following figure:

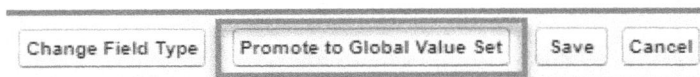

Figure 4.18: Creating a Global Value Set

> **Note** that field dependency can be between many different field types. For example, you may have a different service level agreement (SLA) based on region.

10. As such, a dependency could be made for these fields, as shown in the following figure:

Click button to include or exclude selected values from the dependent picklist:

Include Values   Exclude Values

Region:	Albania	Brazil	Carribean	Denmark	England
SLA:	Gold	Gold	Gold	Gold	Gold
	Silver	Silver	Silver	Silver	Silver
	Platinum	Platinum	Platinum	Platinum	Platinum
	Bronze	Bronze	Bronze	Bronze	Bronze

Showing Columns: 1 - 5 (of 13) < Previous | Next > View All

Click button to include or exclude selected values from the dependent picklist:

Include Values   Exclude Values

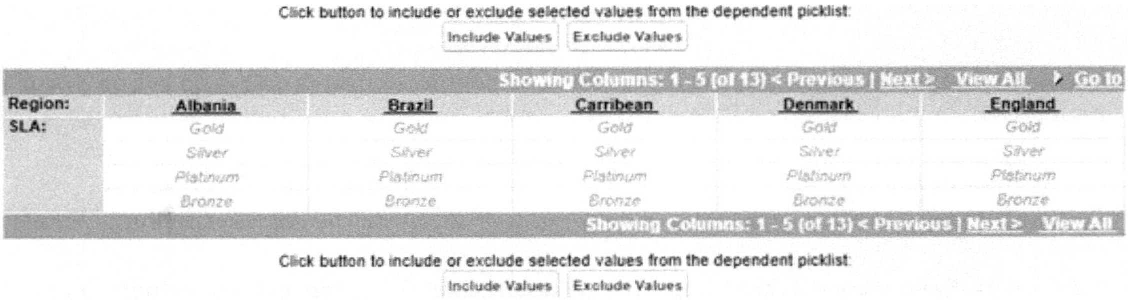

Figure 4.19: Example of a different dependent picklist configuration

Rich text

Often overlooked, rich text fields can help when an object may need to add very different fields in each detail record. For example, an equipment manufacturer may have a vast product catalogue. Some fields will be common, such as the name or part number, but there may be features unique to each product. In this case, rich text is very useful to avoid adding too many fields to the object.

The following example shows how a catalogue entry could easily be made with one rich text field, which is still searchable in the global search feature, but note, only the first 255 characters of the rich text field are indexed and searchable, so make sure this contains the most important information:

Additional Features ⓘ

The platform will consist of 12- and 16-cylinder configurations, with a maximum-rated power of 1865 kW (2500 hp) and 2500 kW (3350 hp) respectively. The design will meet the emission standards for both the European Union's Stage 3 A/B and the International Union of Railways' UIC Stage 1/2. The engine is ideal for shunter and light-weight locomotive

Figure 4.20: Example of a rich text field

The example above was used in conjunction with standard fields for all the items the company sold, so the additional information in the rich text field kept the object clean. The rich text is still available in the global search, saving a lot of unnecessary configurations.

Text encrypted

Suppose you want to secure the data so it cannot be easily read elsewhere in Salesforce (for example, on a report). In that case, the text encrypted field allows only users in the record to view it, and that is if they have the necessary permission.

The following is an example that shows a field that uses special characters to mask the field from other users seeing the value in it:

Figure 4.21: Example of an encrypted text field

Now follow these steps:

1. You have a choice of the field size (up to **175** characters) and the type of mask and characters you wish to display.

2. Press **Save** and notice that even if you type a value in, once the record is saved, the text is masked out, as shown in the following figure:

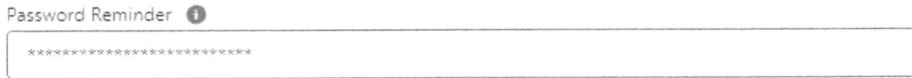

Figure 4.22: Text masked in the user interface

3. To view the data, you need the View Encrypted Data permission.

4. You create a new permission set (assigning a Salesforce license) and add the permission from System Settings at the bottom of the screen, as shown in the following figure:

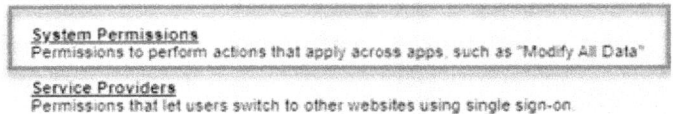

Figure 4.23: Including the permission for viewing encrypted data

5. Once created, assign the new permission set to yourself. If you refresh the page with the record on it, the masked text has been replaced by the original text.

Geolocation

It is becoming increasingly important, particularly for companies that wish to send field agents who go out of the office to visit a customer or install equipment. It integrates with *Google Maps* or an established **geographic information system (GIS)** software (such as *Esri* or *MapInfo*).

It is not necessary to populate this field, as various apps on the AppExchange, such as *Geopointe*, *Map Plotter*, and more, will do this for you.

> Note: **If you are using Google Maps, you can only make a certain number of calls before you need to buy a license or use an alternative tool such as Salesforce MapAnything.**

If you need to get geolocation values, right-click on Google Maps, which will give the value. For example, refer to the following figure:

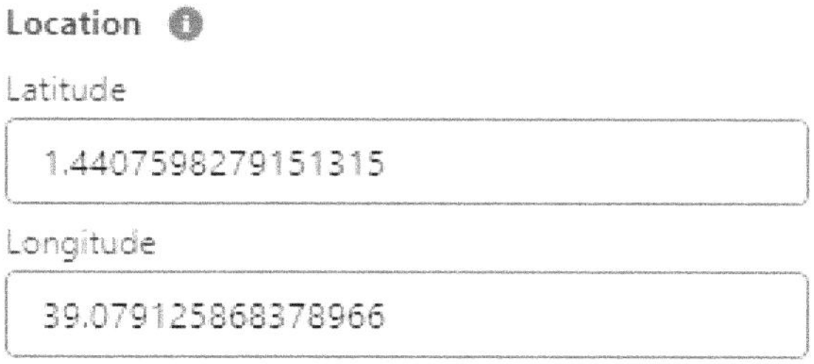

Figure 4.24: *Getting geolocation values from Google Maps*

Chapter 11, Basics of Apex and Lightning Web Components, includes a Google Maps example. Enabling **Field Service**, as shown in the following figure, can add more advanced mapping functionality:

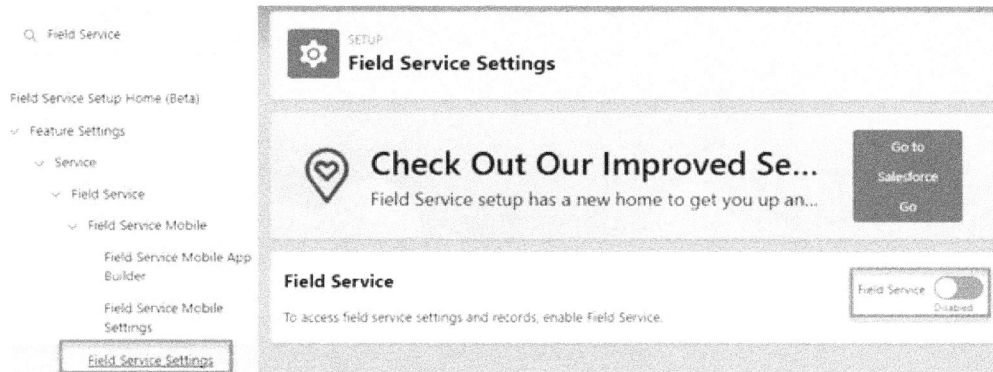

Figure 4.25: *Enabling Field Service in Salesforce*

Useful field features

The following sections are not about creating fields but rather about features in Salesforce to help audit changes in field values or how to check that the data being entered is valid. This can help to maintain the integrity of the data so it meets business requirements, or check on previous values of a field. Both field history tracking and validation rules help ensure the data in your Salesforce org is fit for purpose and can be audited to see which user changed an important field value. More details are given in the following section, but since they are configured on a field-level and not an org wide level, they are included in this chapter for completeness.

Field history tracking

Salesforce can store historical values for fields. It shows who changed the field and when. To setup field history tracking, follow these steps:

1. Go to **Setup** | **Object Manager** | (select the object) | **Fields & Relationships**, then press the **Set History Tracking** button at the top of the screen, as shown in the following figure:

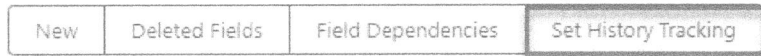

New	Deleted Fields	Field Dependencies	Set History Tracking

Figure 4.26: Setting field history tracking

2. If this is the first time you have setup field history tracking, press the **Enable Account History** checkbox.

    The following example is for the **Account** object. Select up to 20 fields that you wish to track. Refer to the following figure:

Account Field History

☑ Enable Account History

This page allows you to select the fields you want to track on the Account History related list. Whenever a user mod picklist and large text field values are tracked as edited: their old and new field values are not recorded.

Save   Cancel

Deselect all fields

Track old and new values

Account Name	☑
Account Owner	☑
Account Source	☐
Annual Revenue	☑
Clean Status	☐
D&B Company	☐

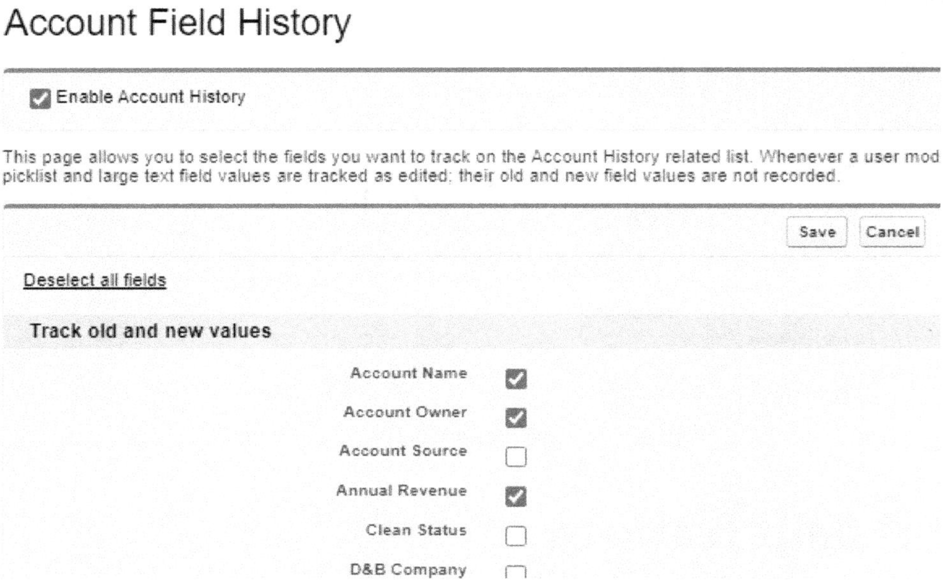

Figure 4.27: Selecting which fields to include in field history tracking

3. Once enabled, the history-related list needs to be added to the page layout.

4. Go to **Setup** | **Object Manager** | (select the object) | **Page Layouts** | (select the layout) and go to the **Related Lists** section in the page layout editor, drag the **Activity History** related list onto the page, and press **Save**.

    Refer to the following figure:

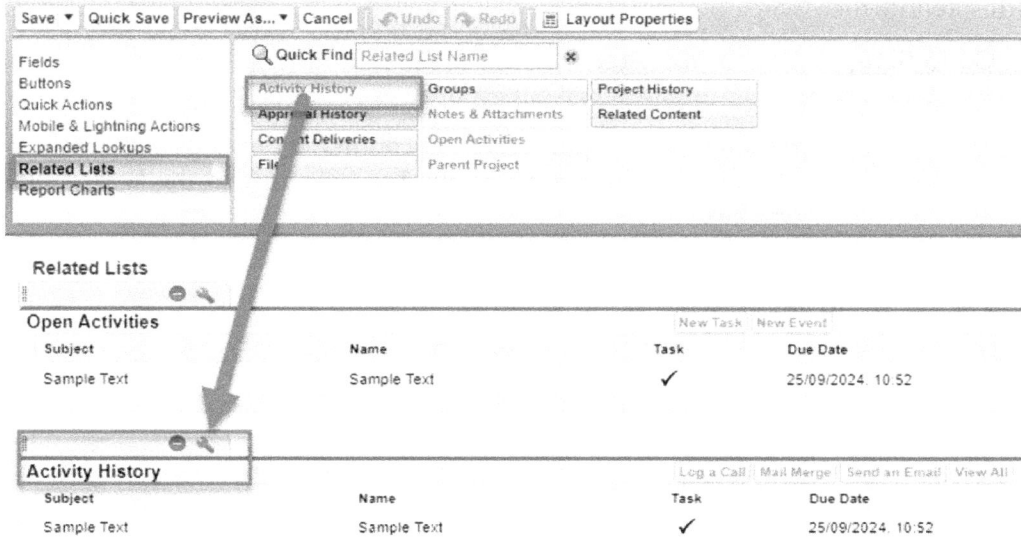

Figure 4.28: Adding field history to the page layout

5. Save the new page layout, visit a page, and change the field's value. In the following example, the name of the account was changed, as shown in the following figure:

Figure 4.29: Results of adding field history tracking on the Account object

Validation rules

Salesforce validation rules use a combination of various fields on an object to help enforce data integrity. They help enforce business rules at the field or record level by evaluating logical expressions and displaying custom error messages when the rules are not met. This ensures that only accurate and meaningful data is entered into the system. They can compare the field being entered and other fields on the same or parent object, and can be applied selectively to a user profile or record type, meaning that the validation rule does not have to be enforced on all users.

There are many examples online, but a simple validation rule for the Project object created previously could be to ensure that the **Actual End Date** field is completed if the **Budget spend** equals the **Actual spend**.

To do this, follow these steps:

1. Go to **Setup** | **Object Manager** | (select the object, in this example, it is project) | **Validation Rules**.

2. The next screen resembles the formula editor encountered previously. Enter the details as shown in the following example, including the following in the **Error Condition Formula**, and press **Save**.

   ```
   Budget__c = Actual_spend__c && ISNULL(Anticipated_End_Date__c)
   ```

   Refer to the following figure:

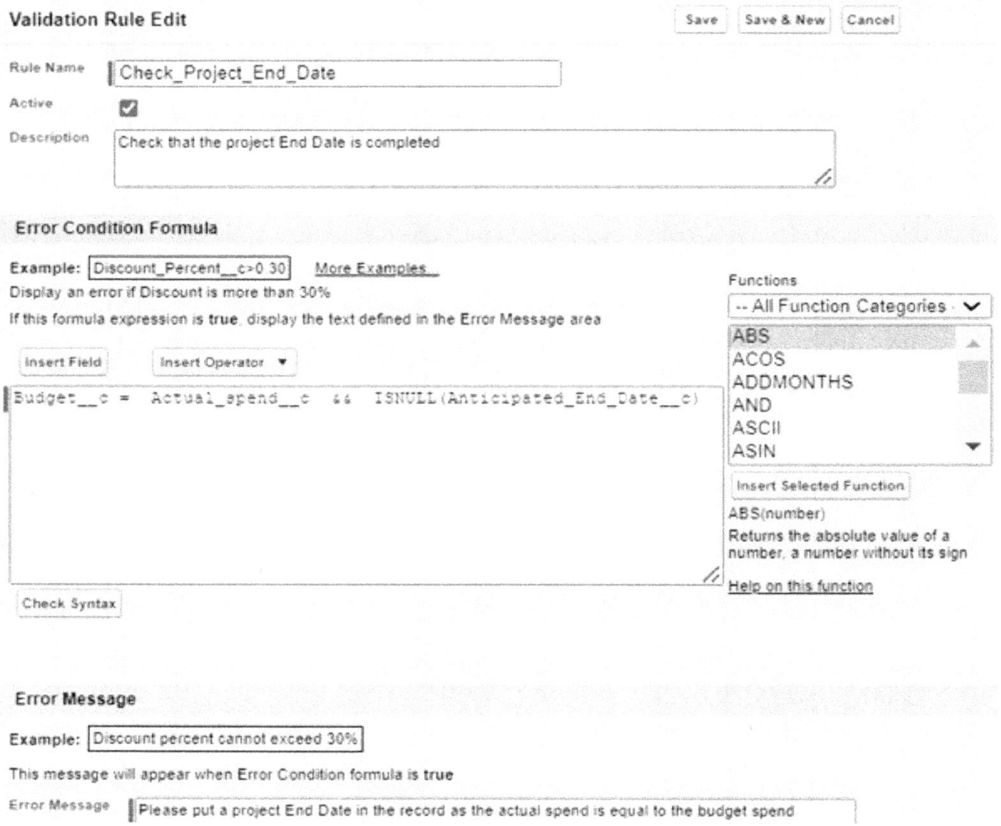

Figure 4.30: Adding a formula to a validation rule

Return to a Project record and enter the same amount in the **Budget** and **Actual spend** fields. If the **Anticipated End Date** field is not completed, you get a helpful error message, as shown in the following figure:

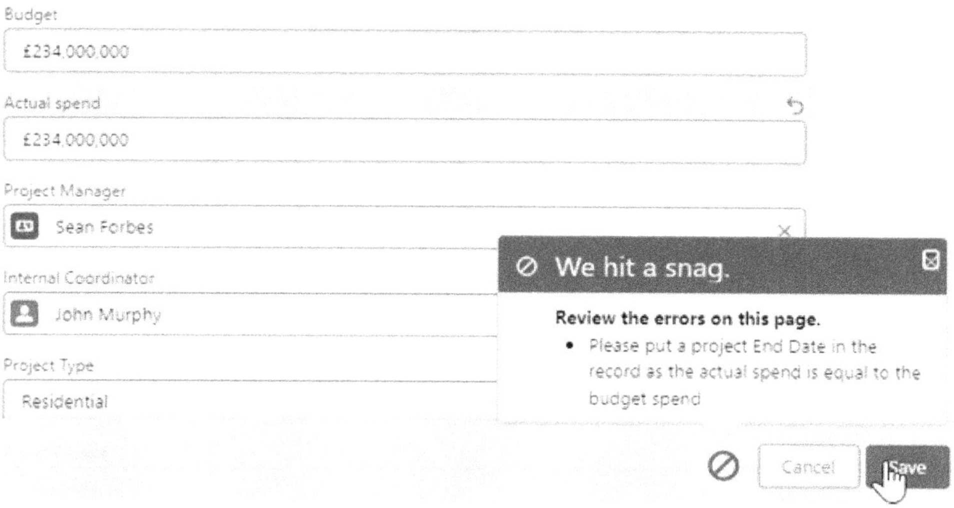

Figure 4.31: Validation rule providing an error message to the user

Approval processes

Salesforce has approval processes so users can submit records, such as a high-value opportunity, a discount, or an expense. These processes allow other users to accept or reject the request.

Approval processes can be configured so that only one person can approve, or a group can approve with either unanimous approval or a single person from the group.

The following steps are required when setting up an approval process:

1. Define who is going to do the approval.

2. Setup a queue.

3. Create an email template.

4. Setup the actual approval process.

To get to the approval processes, go to **Setup | Approval Processes |** select the object from the picklist.

Select **Opportunity** and **Use Jump Start Wizard** for the following example, as it is a lot quicker. Refer to the following figure:

Manage Approval Processes For: Opportunity ⌄

A listing of both active and inactive approval processes for Opportunities is displayed below. To create a new approval process, click then select Use Jump Start Wizard to set up your approval process in a few short steps. Or, select Use Standard Wizard to configure

Create New Approval Process ▼
Use Jump Start Wizard
Use Standard Setup Wizard

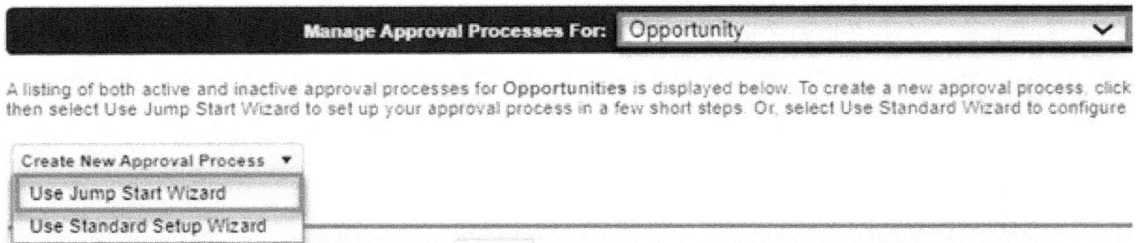

Figure 4.32: Creating an approval process using the jump start wizard

For this approval process, the manager needs to be notified if someone closes an opportunity with an amount over £ 1 million and either a Closed Win or a Closed Loss:

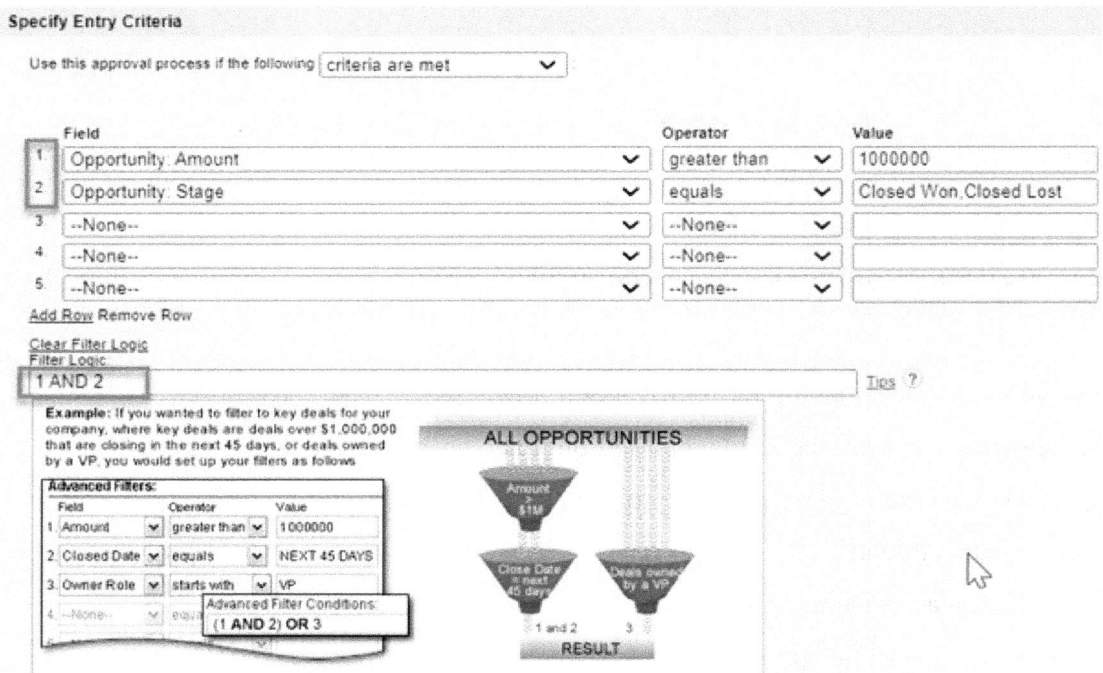

Specify Entry Criteria

Use this approval process if the following | criteria are met ⌄

	Field	Operator	Value
1	Opportunity: Amount ⌄	greater than ⌄	1000000
2	Opportunity: Stage ⌄	equals ⌄	Closed Won,Closed Lost
3	--None-- ⌄	--None-- ⌄	
4	--None-- ⌄	--None-- ⌄	
5	--None-- ⌄	--None-- ⌄	

Add Row Remove Row

Clear Filter Logic
Filter Logic:
1 AND 2   Tips ?

Example: If you wanted to filter to key deals for your company, where key deals are deals over $1,000,000 that are closing in the next 45 days, or deals owned by a VP, you would set up your filters as follows

Advanced Filters:

	Field	Operator	Value
1	Amount ⌄	greater than ⌄	1000000
2	Closed Date ⌄	equals ⌄	NEXT 45 DAYS
3	Owner Role ⌄	starts with ⌄	VP
4	--None-- ⌄	equa	

Advanced Filter Conditions:
(1 AND 2) OR 3

ALL OPPORTUNITIES
Amount > $1M
Close Date = next 45 days
Deals owned by a VP
1 and 2   3
RESULT

Figure 4.33: Adding filter logic to the approval process

In the preceding figure, we have said that **1 AND 2** must be met, but Salesforce also allows **OR** logic.

Salesforce has two types of settings:

- **criteria are met**: Using field value combinations.

- **formula evaluates to true**: Giving a range of functions that can be used, as shown in the following figure:

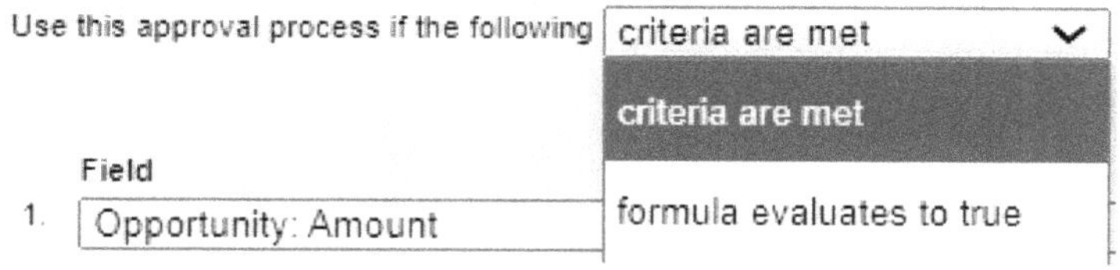

Figure 4.34: *Selecting the logic for the Approval Process*

In the following steps, we will assign the approval process to the correct users.

The following figure defines who is notified and whether they can edit the record:

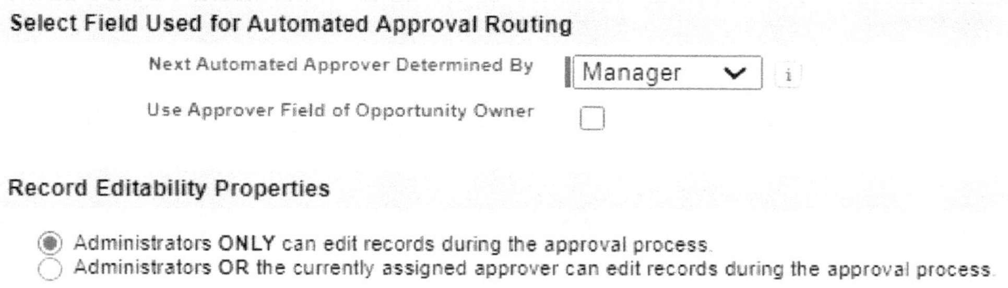

Figure 4.35: *Assigning the approval process*

1. For the following steps, use default values. For example, select any from the list since we have not designed a suitable email.

2. For any remaining steps, choose the default options. You will end up with an approval process like the following figure.

3. Finally, make the approval process active by pressing the **Activate** button, as shown in the following figure:

Approval Processes
Opportunity: Big Deal Approval
« Back to Approval Process List

Process Definition Detail   Edit ▼   Clone   Delete   Activate

Process Name	Big Deal Approval
Unique Name	Big_Deal_Approval
Description	
Entry Criteria	(Opportunity: Amount GREATER THAN "GBP 1,000,000") AND (Opportunity: Stage EQUALS Closed Won,Closed Lost)
Record Editability	Administrator ONLY
Approval Assignment Email Template	Appointment for Unauthenticated User using Appointment Types - For Amazon Chime
Initial Submitters	Opportunity Owner
Created By	Andy White, 25/09/2024, 18:04

Active

Next Automated Approver Determined By   Manager of Record Submitter

Allow Submitters to Recall Approval   ✓
Requests

Modified By   Andy White, 05/09/2025, 12:1

Initial Submission Actions ℹ   Add Existing   Add New ▼

Action	Type	Description
	Record Lock	Lock the record from being edited

Approval Steps ℹ

Action	Step Number	Name	Description	Criteria	Assigned Approver
Show Actions | Edit	1	Step 1			Manager

Final Approval Actions ℹ   Add Existing   Add New ▼

Action	Type	Description
Edit	Record Lock	Lock the record from being edited
Edit | Remove	Email Alert	Send Opportunity Closed email

Figure 4.36: Activating the approval process

4. Finally, test the approval process by going to an opportunity record. In the **Amount field**, enter **5m** (shorthand for five million) and mark the stage as **Closed Won**.

5. Approval processes can do a lot more, such as field updates and allowing for email approval, but these are covered in the Trailhead courses.

Big objects, external objects, and custom metadata types

This section provides a simple overview and supplementary information. While it is unlikely that you will be asked to work on projects requiring in-depth knowledge, it is helpful to know that Salesforce offers additional types of objects needed in some instances. Let us understand this in detail:

- Big objects are similar to custom objects but can store vast amounts of data which is useful for data such as survey results or imports from external systems. They behave slightly differently to custom objects since they have a limited number of field types, including no master-detail relationship. In some ways they are identical to a flat file, like a CSV file although they do support lookup relationships.

Unlike a relational database, database, where objects all relate to each other, big objects rely on the data to be suitable for use in analysis or reports. At the time of writing, big objects are used in many legacy orgs, but Data Cloud would provide a more flexible solution.

- External objects allow Salesforce to reference data from an external system. They use an external lookup relationship field, which can be added to any object under **Fields & Relationships**. Since it is not possible to do a walkthrough in this guide without setting up an external system, it is recommended that you do the Trailhead tutorial titled *Create an External Lookup Relationship*, which guides you through the process.

- Custom metadata types these create an object which stores information about the fields in another object called a **custom metadata object**. If this sounds confusing then consider the following figure:

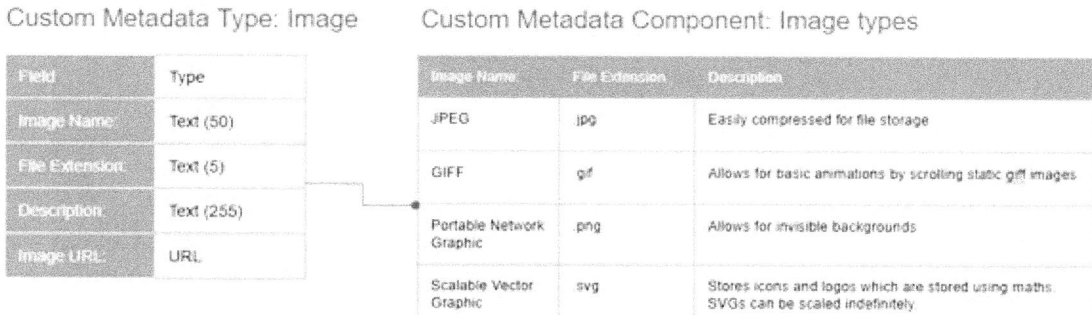

Custom Metadata Type: Image   Custom Metadata Component: Image types

Field	Type
Image Name	Text (50)
File Extension	Text (5)
Description	Text (255)
Image URL	URL

Image Name	File Extension	Description
JPEG	jpg	Easily compressed for file storage
GIFF	gif	Allows for basic animations by scrolling static gif images
Portable Network Graphic	png	Allows for invisible backgrounds
Scalable Vector Graphic	svg	Stores icons and logos which are stored using maths. SVGs can be scaled indefinitely

Figure 4.37: Illustration of custom metadata types being used for a custom metadata object

Setting up Salesforce big objects

To complete the big object setup, you must add a custom field on the newly created custom object and make it required. You are not expected to complete this exercise, but knowing the process is beneficial. Having created a big object and configured the indexing then, the results are shown in the following figure:

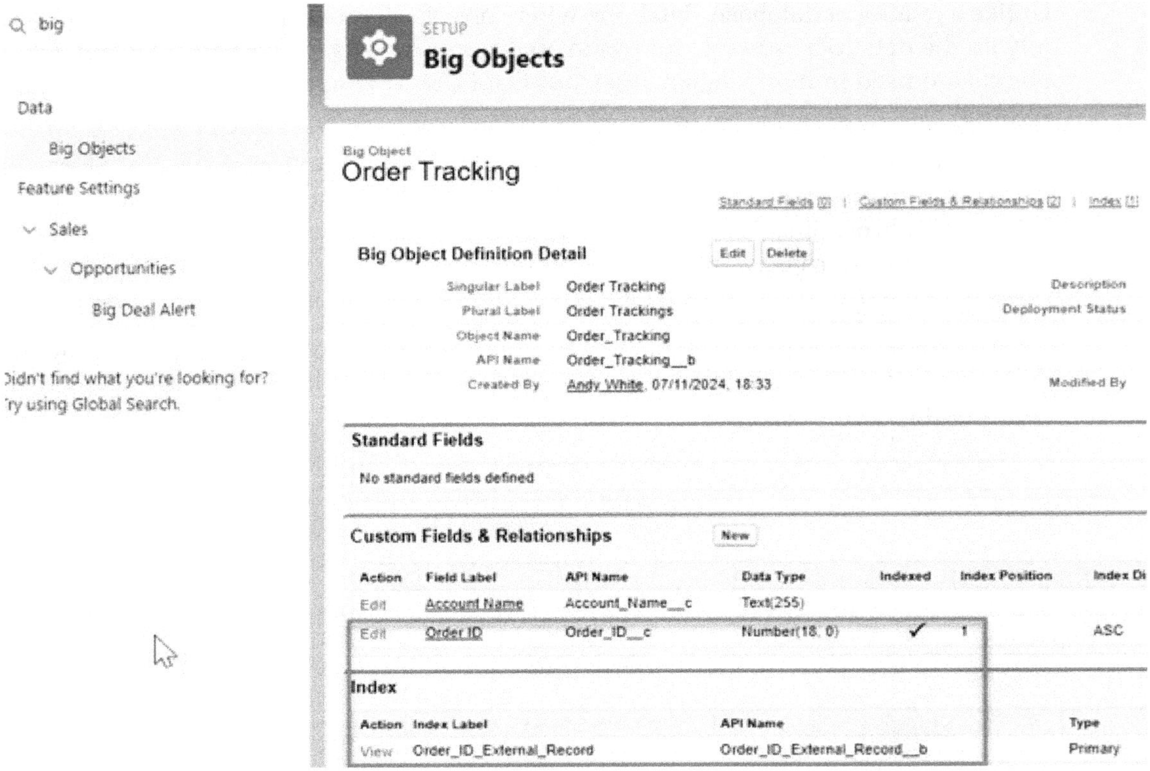

Figure 4.38: Adding a big object and assigning an index record

This section is included to inform you of the requirements associated with significant objects, or big data, as it is also called. This knowledge is sound when working in other areas, such as Data Cloud or external systems requiring skinny tables or custom indexing.

Setting up custom metadata types

Here is an overview of custom metadata types:

- If you installed the Graphics Pack earlier, go to **Setup | Custom Metadata Types**, and you will see the image in the following figure.

- If you select **Manage Records**, you will see information about the various icons in the package, including their locations.

- **Custom Metadata Types** make building the app in Salesforce much easier, as you can reference information about a record or groups of records.

- You will also notice that **Custom Metadata Types** have an additional level. To get further information, go into **Manage Records** and press **Edit** next to the record, as shown in the following figure:

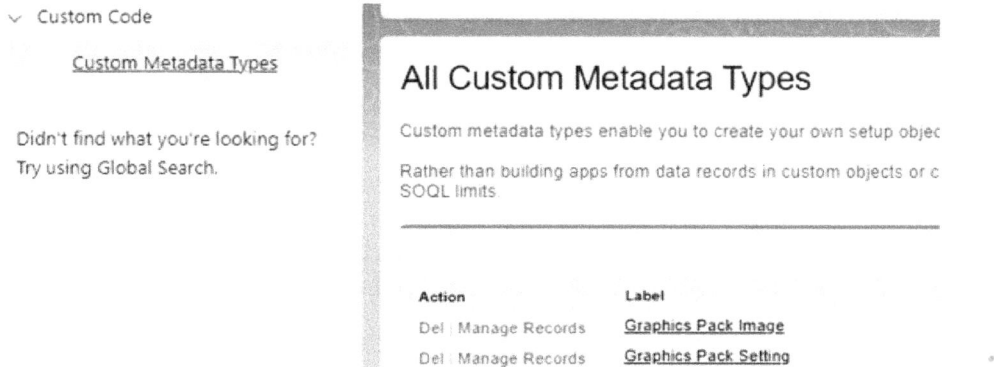

Figure 4.39: Custom metadata types used for installing the Graphics Pack

Chapter 10, Various Salesforce Features, provides more information about custom metadata objects and types. However, they are generally used in conjunction with programmatic development, which is also covered in *Chapter 11, Basics of Apex and Lightning Web Components.*

Conclusion

This chapter has provided insights into creating custom objects with various fields. In particular, we have covered master-detail and use it for doing roll-up summary records. Additionally, we have looked at some custom fields, such as formulas for displaying icons and calculating values based on other fields or rich-text fields, which can save a lot of complexity when used correctly. We have also looked at fields that require more consideration, such as encrypted fields.

This chapter also includes ways to ensure the data's reliability, such as adding field history tracking or validation rules. Finally, we learned more complex object types, such as external objects, significant objects, or custom metadata types. These were included for completeness but generally require much further knowledge outside this book's scope.

Multiple choice questions

1. **All objects can support master-detail and lookup relationships. When considering a master-detail relationship, what considerations are important?**

   a. A master-detail relationship is a strongly bound relationship, meaning the parent record has security and access over the child record

   b. There can be only two master-detail relationships when adding fields to an object

   c. Master-detail relationships allow for roll-up summary fields on the parent object

   d. All of the above

2. **How many fields can have field history enabled on an object?**

   a. 20

   b. 30

   c. 50

   d. 100

3. **You can have picklist fields on the main picklist, which determine fields available on a dependent picklist. Which statement below is true?**

   a. You can multi-select a picklist value as the main picklist, which shows available options on the dependent picklist

   b. You can have several picklists, each with its own dependencies

   c. The central picklist values must be added before the dependent picklist

   d. Picklist values need to be of the same data type, such as text, numbers, etc

4. **What is the best way to do this when adding several fields to an object?**

   a. Upload the fields from a CSV file with the correct field mapping

   b. Add the field, and at the end, press the Save and New button

   c. Add multiple fields of the same type

   d. Use the page layout and press the New Field button

5. **When adding field history tracking, what is tracked?**

   a. Field name, record owner, and original value

   b. Original field value, time, date, and who made the change

   c. New value, original value, who made the change, and when it was done

   d. New value, who made the change, and when it was done

6. **Validation rules are useful for?**

   a. Ensure the data is correct and valid for other users

   b. Ensure the data is saved before the record is updated in related records

   c. Ensure the data meets criteria-based on other fields on the same object

   d. Ensure data is validated against the filters defined on the object

7. **An approval process must be assigned to?**

   a. Managers or people above the user in the role hierarchy

   b. Internal or external users who have been assigned to the approval process

c. Users, groups, or administrators

d. Users, groups, or anyone added during the approval configuration

8. **Salesforce has the option of using big objects for storing vast amounts of data. Big objects are not similar to custom objects since:**

a. The data is unstructured, meaning it combines records

b. The data is unstructured, meaning it does not have relationships with other Salesforce objects

c. The data can store images and video, making it suitable for storing large volumes of data

d. The data is not searchable by the Salesforce Global Search function

9. **Salesforce custom metadata types are objects that store what type of information:**

a. Data about customer settings, which can be used to record customer information

b. Data about the Salesforce org can be used to assist in administration

c. Data about application settings, such as field types and configuration

d. Data about related file information, which is used in custom configuration

10. **External objects refer to what type of functionality:**

a. Adding data into your Salesforce org from an external system

b. Referencing data from an external system by adding a field of type external lookup relationship

c. Being able to update data in an external system when a user modifies a record in Salesforce

d. Embedding an external system's user interface into the Salesforce page layout

Answers

1	**d**
2	**a**
3	**b**
4	**b**
5	**c**
6	**c**
7	**d**
8	**b**
9	**c**
10	**b**

Join our Discord space

Join our Discord workspace for latest updates, offers, tech happenings around the world, new releases, and sessions with the authors:

https://discord.bpbonline.com

CHAPTER 5

Adding Users and Assigning Correct Access Levels

Introduction

Every organization using Salesforce needs to have the right information available to the right people. This begins with the fundamental task of adding users to Salesforce and assigning them the appropriate access levels.

This is important because Salesforce is much more than just a database. It is a dynamic platform that supports collaboration, drives productivity, and protects sensitive business data. When users are properly added and configured, teams can work efficiently, and processes run smoothly. Likewise, when they are not, then the opposite can happen.

This chapter will guide you through the essential concepts and practical steps involved in managing users and providing the correct access to Salesforce. It will cover the ways to add new users and to troubleshoot common issues.

Structure

This chapter covers the following topics:

- Adding new users to Salesforce
- Troubleshooting user issues

Objectives

By the end of this chapter, readers will be able to add users to Salesforce and ensure they have access to the features they require. The aim is that you are confident that features such as the role hierarchy, profiles, and permission sets are configured correctly. One of the key objectives is to be able to login as a user and test functionality. This is required many times throughout this book since features are often built in Salesforce for specific users and not for the entire organization.

Adding new users to Salesforce

Let us start with two scenarios:

- You have a new joiner to the company, and you need to give them access to Salesforce.

- You have 100 new joiners to the company; they work for different departments and need access to different parts of Salesforce.

Both scenarios are essential, and the required thought is very similar. However, adding 100 new users to Salesforce would be very time-consuming and would prove complicated to undo if it were wrong.

Adding single user to Salesforce

The best way to setup a single user is to ensure the correct profile, permission sets, and role are determined first.

To add a single user to Salesforce, go to **Setup | Users | Users**. You will see the list of users in your Salesforce org. Some of the features are shown in the following figure:

Figure 5.1: Accessing user records in Salesforce

Let us break down the preceding figure:

- You can view users by filtering using a view. Use the **Create New View** option to build lists based on your chosen criteria, such as **Role**, **Profile**, or other criteria.

- Select the letter of the alphabet for the last name of the user.

- Add a **New User** or **Add Multiple Users** as required.

Note: **In a Salesforce Developer Edition org, the limit for adding new users is two. As such, you have already reached the limit. This means the following steps would not work since a Salesforce license will not be available to add a new user.**

To free up a license, make the user *John Murphy* inactive. To do this, press the **Edit** link next to **Murphy John** and deselect the **Active** checkbox, as shown in the following figure:

Role	<None Specified> ∨
User License	Salesforce ∨
Profile	Standard User ∨ i
Active	☐

Figure 5.2: Making users active

You may be asked to remove them from various groups and reassign the records they own, in which case, accept the default.

Steps for adding new user

Adding a new user requires the following fields to be entered. Follow these steps:

1. From **Setup | Users | Users** press the **New** button.

2. Enter **First Name** and **Last Name**.

3. Change this to something the user would recognize.

4. This is essential as the user will receive a **Welcome to Salesforce** email, which has the user activation instructions in the email provided.

5. Username in the form of an email. It is recommended to make this different from the email address used above, as it cannot be used in other Salesforce organizations. Typically, usernames should follow the same format as those of other users.

6. Nickname change to a similar format to other users, such as initials or last name.

7. Role requires careful consideration. Role hierarchy determines what users can see in Salesforce based on role hierarchy. However, it can be left empty, restricting the visibility of that user.

8. Profile will depend on what permissions must be assigned to the user. For example, the standard user has access to basic Salesforce functionality, whilst the marketing user will have additional access to campaigns and various marketing tools.

9. User license is typically Salesforce, but it depends on what is already installed in your Salesforce org.

Other user records to check or include on the user's profile are:

- Time zone, locale, and language settings
- Permission set assignments

Towards the bottom of the page, you will see a tick box for **Generate new password and notify user immediately**, which should be ticked before pressing **Save**:

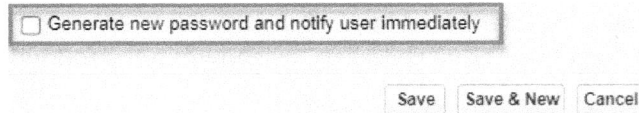

Figure 5.3: Generating a new password for a user

Adding multiple users

As with everything, getting it right the first time is better. For this reason, you can practice in a Developer Org or a Salesforce Sandbox.

To add multiple users, go to **Setup | Users | Users**. You will see a button for **Add Multiple Users**, as shown in the following figure:

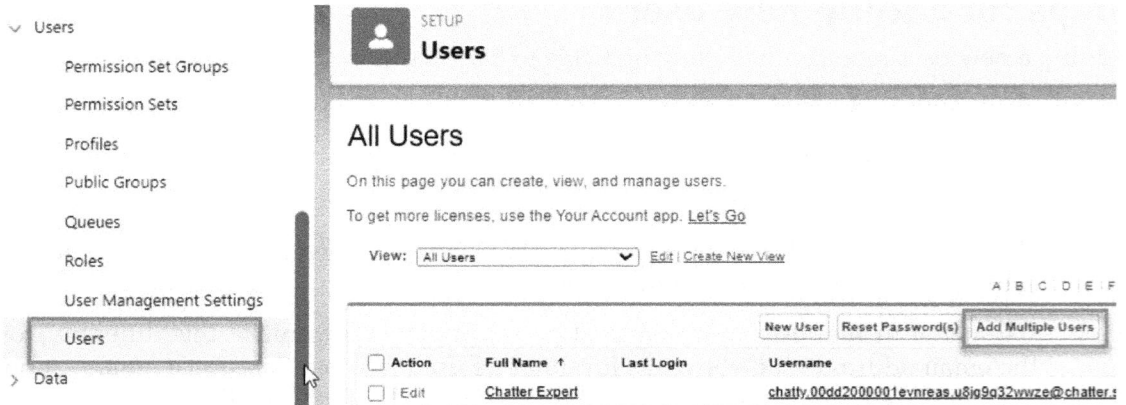

Figure 5.4: Adding multiple users

The process is similar to adding one user, with a limit of adding up to 10 users at a time. This can be done multiple times and broken down into various roles and profiles. For example, if you have 20 standard users, you will do this twice, then add five marketing users only once.

If you have to load a large number of users, for example, 500, it is better to break them into identical groups of users by the required role and profile. This can be done in various ways, but Data Loader will allow you to export a typical user record as a CSV file, which can then be used as a template. This can then be populated and loaded back into Salesforce. This is covered in *Chapter 9, Various Salesforce Tools*.

Understanding role hierarchy

Salesforce grants users access via profiles and roles, which are ordered logically in the role hierarchy. To view the role hierarchy, follow these steps:

1. Go to **Setup | Users | Roles**.

2. You will first see a splash screen explaining different ways to configure the roles according to the type of business using Salesforce.

3. Since roles are crucial to how users use Salesforce, it is worth looking at the examples illustrated in the following figure:

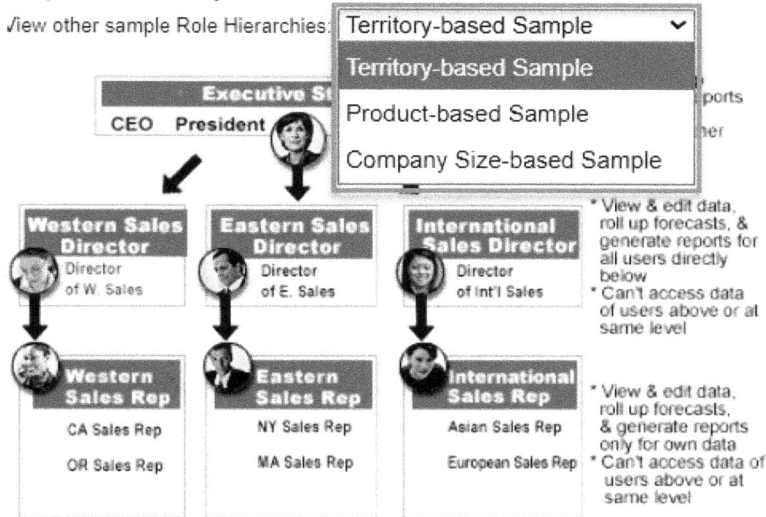

Figure 5.5: Instructions when first going to the role hierarchy

Press the **Setup Roles,** and you will see something like the following.

If it is very compact, press the + or – buttons next to each branch of the hierarchy to expand or contract the nodes, as shown in the following figure:

Your Organization's Role Hierarchy

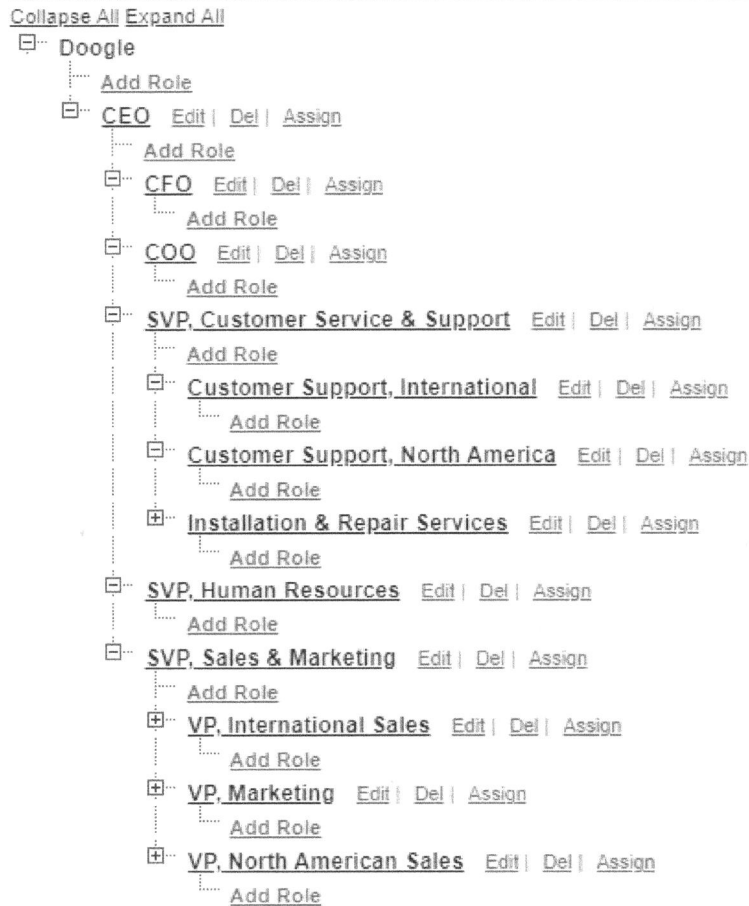

Collapse All Expand All

```
⊟ Doogle
    ├ Add Role
    ⊟ CEO   Edit | Del | Assign
        ├ Add Role
        ⊟ CFO   Edit | Del | Assign
            └ Add Role
        ⊟ COO   Edit | Del | Assign
            └ Add Role
        ⊟ SVP, Customer Service & Support   Edit | Del | Assign
            ├ Add Role
            ⊟ Customer Support, International   Edit | Del | Assign
                └ Add Role
            ⊟ Customer Support, North America   Edit | Del | Assign
                └ Add Role
            ⊞ Installation & Repair Services   Edit | Del | Assign
                └ Add Role
        ⊟ SVP, Human Resources   Edit | Del | Assign
            └ Add Role
        ⊟ SVP, Sales & Marketing   Edit | Del | Assign
            ├ Add Role
            ⊞ VP, International Sales   Edit | Del | Assign
                └ Add Role
            ⊞ VP, Marketing   Edit | Del | Assign
                └ Add Role
            ⊞ VP, North American Sales   Edit | Del | Assign
                └ Add Role
```

Figure 5.6: Expanding the role hierarchy

The above is the role hierarchy that came with the Developer Edition Salesforce org. It will likely be much more significant if you work in an existing corporate Salesforce instance.

Standard objects all have the setting **Grant Access Using Hierarchies**, which is optional for custom objects. This means owners can see or edit their own records, as can the users above them in the role hierarchy.

Role hierarchy works by using the level of visibility set by the **Org Wide Defaults** (**OWDs**). These are given in more detail in *Chapter 7, Salesforce Security Model,* but are summarized in the following.

The OWD defines the level of access to an object across Salesforce. These can be either of the following:

- **Private**: means only the record owner or anyone above them in the role hierarchy can see or edit their own record.

- **Public Read Only**: means everyone can see all the records on an object, but only the owner or someone above them in the role hierarchy can edit it.

- **Public Read/Write**: means all records are available on the object to all users.

These three are the most common settings in Salesforce OWDs. Other settings are controlled by the parent when a child object inherits the OWDs from the parent via a master-detail relationship. Finally, Public Read/Write/Transfer is useful for objects such as cases or leads where the current owner can change the record's ownership.

The role hierarchy can be easily configured by pressing the **Edit** link next to a role and assigning it the correct position in the hierarchy. Likewise, press the **Add Role** link to create new roles in the hierarchy.

Troubleshooting user issues

Users may have various issues with Salesforce as part of being a system administrator. The following tasks are performed by an administrator to check the user record and ensure that they have access to Salesforce.

Checking user records and resetting the password

The most common issue is not being able to access Salesforce. As an administrator, you should first check that they exist in Salesforce, either by using the global search or going to **Setup | Users | Users** and checking their basic settings, such as whether they are active and have any login history, which can be seen at the bottom of the user record.

If this is all correct, press the **Reset Password** button at the top of the page, as shown in the following figure, and out of courtesy, they gain access:

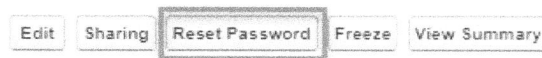

Figure 5.7: Resetting a user's password

For other common issues, they typically fall into two categories:

- The user is not using Salesforce correctly which may be a training issue such as not using the search feature to find records, not understanding required fields or entering duplicate records.

- There is a genuine issue with their Salesforce setup. In that case, it is worth ensuring the problem is understood and not just based on a rough description.

In both cases, if it is impossible to screen-share or sit with the user, they should be able to describe the problem and grant you login access. Follow the steps:

1. Go to their profile and select **Settings**.
2. On the left-hand menu under **My Personal Information**, select **Grant Account Login Access**.
3. Ask them to grant **Your Company's Administrator** access for three days.
4. You can then login to resolve the issue they have previously described.

    Refer to the following figure:

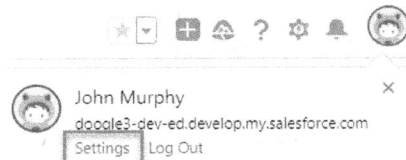

Figure 5.8: Accessing users' settings

Under **Grant Account Login Access**, set the support for **Your Company's Administrator** to **1 Year**, as shown in the following figure, and press **Save**.

Note: **There is also the option to grant Salesforce.com Support login access if you need support from them.**

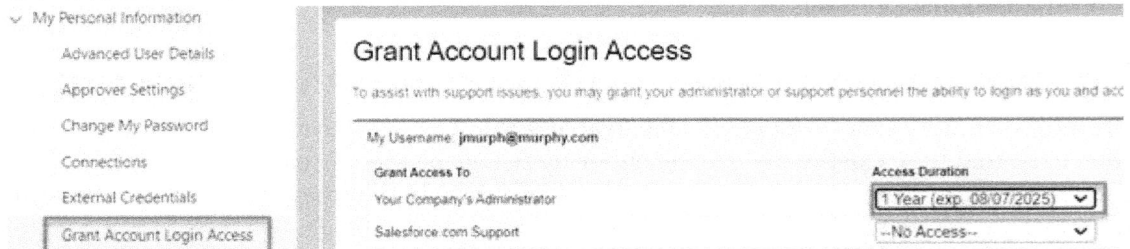

Figure 5.9: Granting account login access

For the next step to work, you may have to log out of Salesforce and log back in again.

Return to the user's page, and you will now see the new user with the **Login** option next to their record. Click the **Login** link, as shown in the following figure:

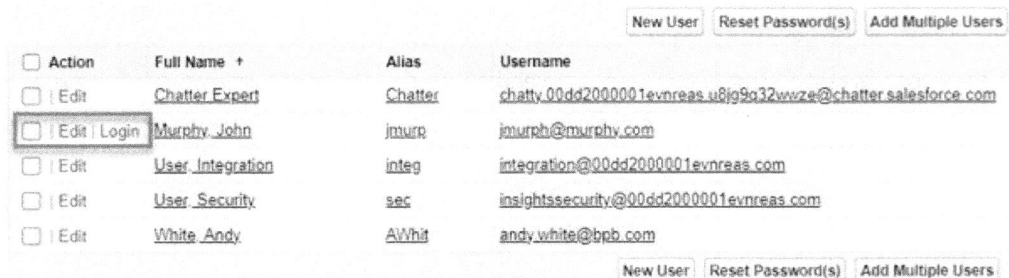

Figure 5.10: Having access to login as another user

You will now see that at the top of the screen, it says **Logged in as (name)** with the option to **Log out as (name)**.

You can now browse Salesforce as another user. This is useful throughout this book to check if the security is set correctly and working:

Figure 5.11: *Screen displaying that you have logged in as another user*

Grant login access to all users

Since being able to login as other users is very helpful, you can enable this feature for the entire Salesforce org.

To do this, follow these steps:

1. Go to **Setup | Security | Login Access Policies**.

2. Select the option for **Administrators Can Login as Any User**, as shown in the following figure:

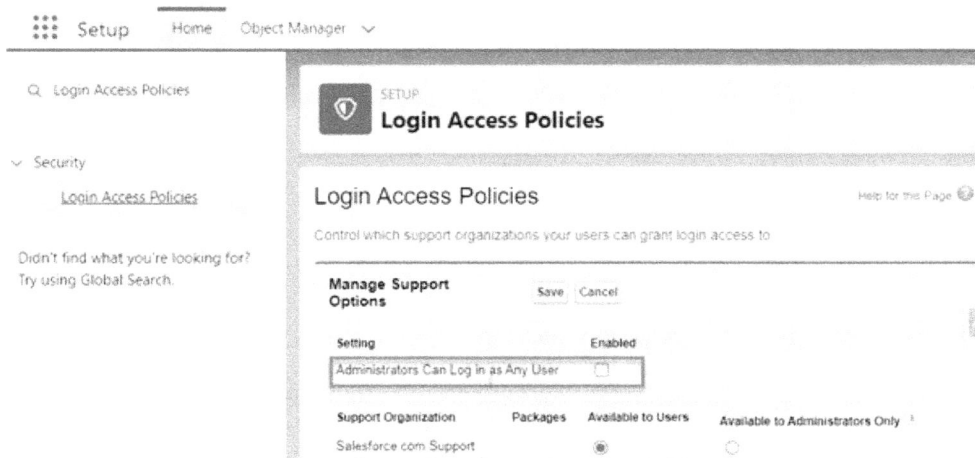

Figure 5.12: *Granting administrator access as any user*

Troubleshooting for group of users

One of the key areas to check for users is access to an object. If you have already checked the OWD, then the next area is to check the field-level security, as outlined in the following.

To check field-level security, do the following:

1. Go to **Setup | Object Manager |** (select the object) and **Set Field-Level Security** and **View Field Accessibility**, as shown in the following figure:

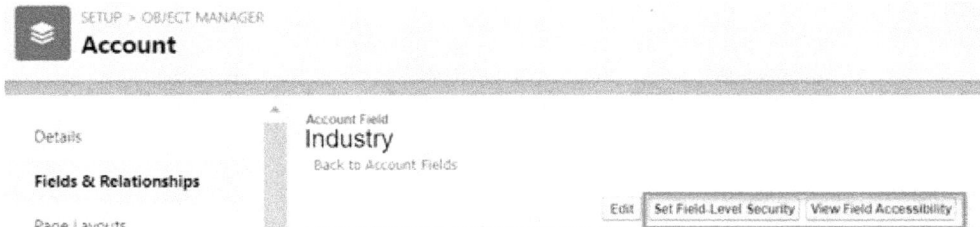

Figure 5.13: Checking field accessibility

The options shown above are for the **Account** object.

2. Another, more generic way to view all the objects can be done by going to **Setup | Security | Field Accessibility** and selecting the object you wish to view, as shown in the following figure:

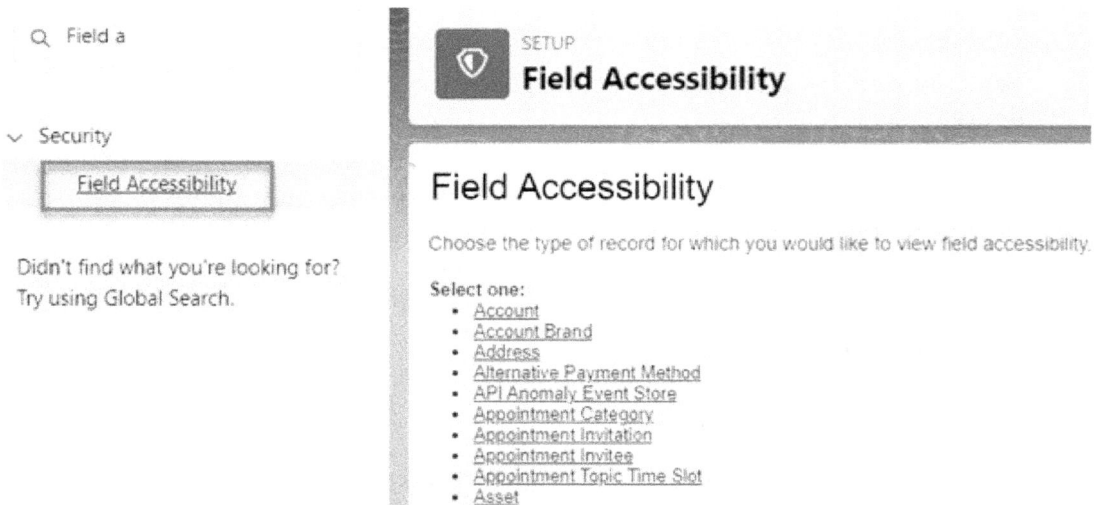

Figure 5.14: Field Accessibility to various objects

3. Although both methods provide visibility into who can see what, both are useful for troubleshooting user access to specific records on a specific object.

4. Once you have ensured the user (or profile) has access to the field they wish, if the problem persists, numerous areas exist to check, including page layout assignment or record types covered in more detail in *Chapter 7, Salesforce Security Model*.

5. However, logging in as the user is the best way to guarantee the problem is resolved.

Troubleshooting user with too many privileges

On the other hand, it is possible to give users too much freedom in Salesforce, and this can be harder to resolve since users tend not to report an issue that could lead to a security breach. The following are typical issues that can go unnoticed:

- **Too many sharing rules**: Sharing rules are discussed in *Chapter 7, Salesforce Security Model*, but they give users access to records outside the sharing model used in your Salesforce org. They are best done by sharing with groups where users can be added or removed.

  To see the sharing rules in your Salesforce org, go to **Setup | Security | Sharing Settings** and scroll right down to the bottom of the page. The number will depend on the size of the Salesforce org, but typically, there may be 10 sharing rules per object. If there are many more, compare them to see if the role hierarchy could be improved.

- **Too many administrators**: Although there will always need to be one system administrator (i.e., you), having more than one can help when the Salesforce org is significant. However, if you have (for example) 1000 users in your Salesforce org and you see 50 system administrators, then it becomes hard to manage configuration, deployments, and security. To check all the system administrators in your org:

  1. Go to **Setup | Users | Users**.

  2. Select the view **System Administrator** as shown in the following figure:

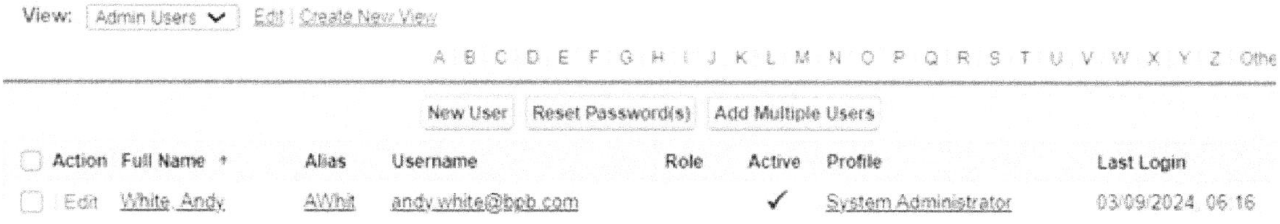

Figure 5.15: Checking administrator users

Note: The Last login field has been added to this view, which will indicate whether this user deserves to be a System Administrator. If they have not logged in for some time, then it is worth checking if they need the license, in which case they can be deactivated, as covered in the following section.

If a user should not have the system administrator's profile, they should be assigned one corresponding to their responsibilities, which is more suitable.

Deactivating users

Deactivating users is required if they no longer need access to Salesforce, but it will also make their user license available to another legitimate user. There is a similar option to **Freeze** a user, which prevents the user from accessing Salesforce, but this does not make their license available until they are inactive.

In most cases, deactivating a user is done by unchecking the **Active** option in their user record, and best practice would be to transfer record ownership as part of user deactivation. However, there are some cases where you cannot immediately deactivate a user, for example, if they are part of lead assignment rules, a customer portal admin, or the sole recipient of an email alert.

The **Freeze** and **Active** options are found on the user record, as shown in the following figure:

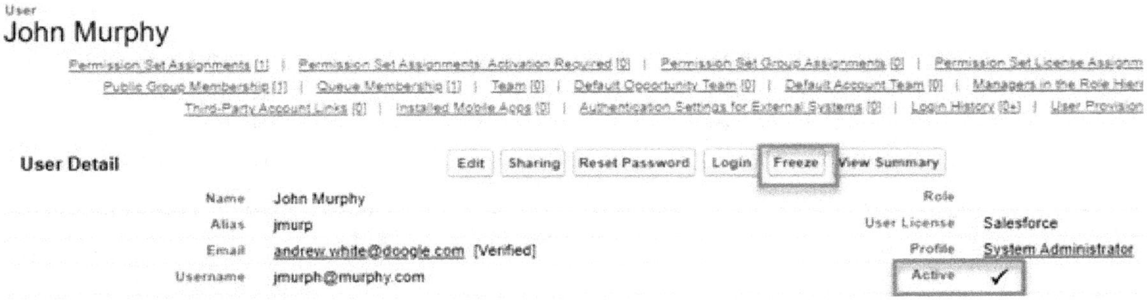

Figure 5.16: Freeze and Active options

Although you can deactivate users, you cannot delete them outright. Deleting a user can result in orphaned records and the loss of critical business information. If you visit a record previously owned by an inactive user, it simply says **User Inactive** in the record owner field.

Checking user activity

A similar task can be done by creating a view on the user record to show, which users have not logged in for a long time.

An example is shown in the following figure, for users who have not logged in for 30 days, but it will depend on the size of your Salesforce org:

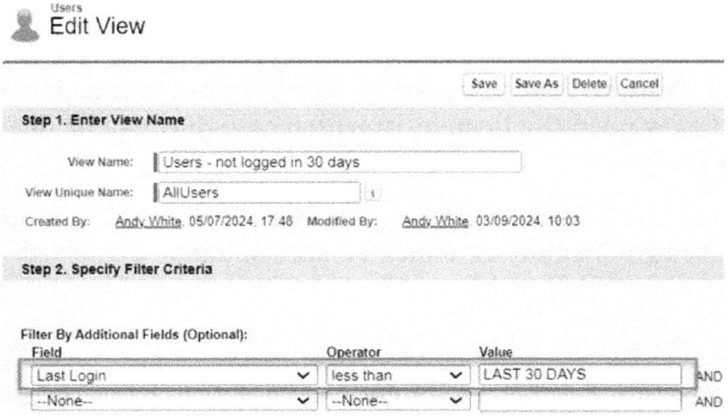

Figure 5.17: Custom view on Last Login date

If someone has not logged in (and therefore is not using Salesforce), their user account can be made inactive or frozen, as explained previously.

Adoption dashboards

It is important to track how users are engaging with their use of Salesforce. Adoption dashboards help administrators or managers gauge users' use of Salesforce, including:

- **Login frequency**: How regularly are users logging in, and are some users rarely or never logging in?

- **Record creation**: What users are creating records important to the organization, such as new leads, converted opportunities, cases closed, etc.

- **Task and event tracking**: How are users using Salesforce to manage their workload?

- **Key metrics and KPIs**: Such are opportunities closed by the opportunity owner.

These dashboards are important to help drive user adoption or possibly identify training needs. They also help to provide a measure of the return on investment the organization is making with its Salesforce system.

Various dashboards are available for administrators, as discussed in *Chapter 9, Various Salesforce Tools*. The Salesforce AppExchange has a free app called **Salesforce Adoption Dashboards**, which contains many reports and dashboards useful for viewing users' activity in your Salesforce org. Refer to the following figure:

Figure 5.18: Salesforce Adoption Dashboards from the AppExchange

Understanding permission sets

Two permissions should not be given to users unless they need them. These are listed here:

- Modify All Data
- View All Data

These permissions should not be assigned to general Salesforce users. Still, they may have been added unwittingly, for example, by a system administrator who cannot resolve an issue with sharing or visibility.

To see where these permissions are used, go to **Setup | Users | Permission Sets** and create a view for `Modify All Data` as shown in the following figure:

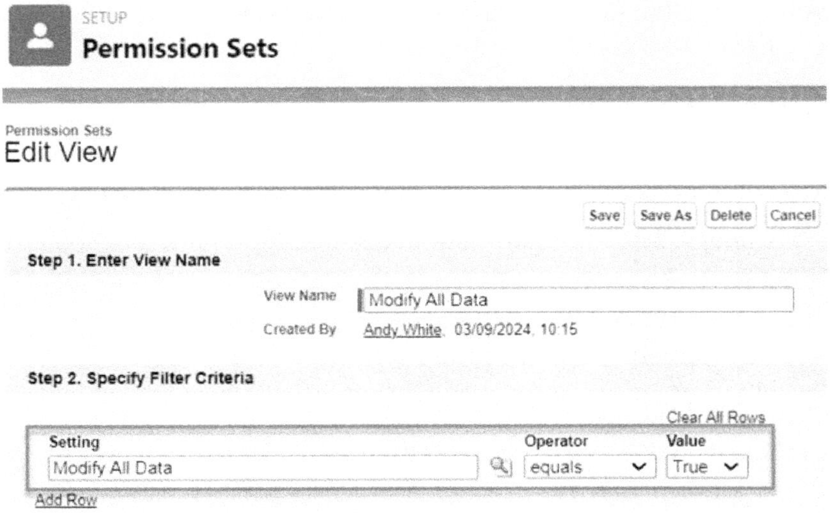

Figure 5.19: *Checking permission sets with Modify All Data*

This will list permission sets with the `Modify All Data` capability. The ability to refine **Permission Sets**, **Profiles**, and **Groups** is outlined in the following sections.

Profiles, permission sets, and permission set groups

Profiles assign permissions for what you can do in Salesforce. The best practice is to have as few profiles as possible and keep them bare, then use permission sets to add the necessary permissions. Since you will end up with many permission sets, these can be grouped logically into permission set groups, as illustrated in the following figure:

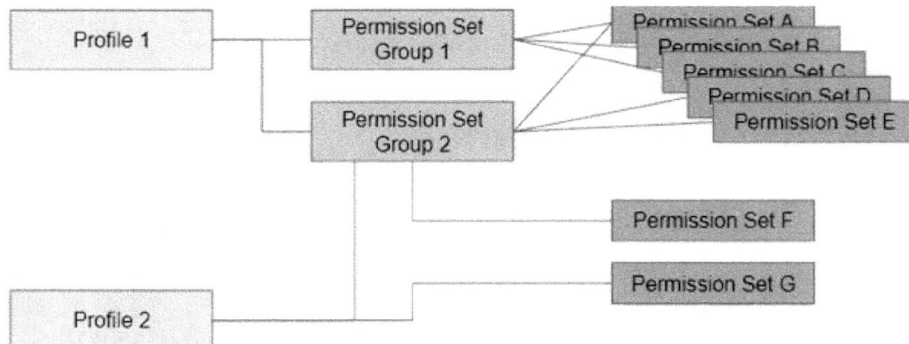

Figure 5.20: *Profiles, permission set groups, and permission sets*

The preceding figure may look complicated, but it shows how flexible and configurable Salesforce profiles are when using permission sets and permission set groups.

In Salesforce, every user must be assigned one profile. In the illustration, there are two profiles, two permission set groups, and seven permission sets. permission sets can be assigned to both permission set groups and directly to a profile.

However, permission sets can also be added to more than one permission set group and assigned to multiple profiles. This means it is easy to configure permission sets for a profile directly or by adding a permission set group.

To view this configuration, you can either:

- Start with **Permission Sets** to see where they have been added. Go to **Setup | Permission Sets** and view **Permission Set Assignments**.

- Start with **Profiles** and see the **Permission Set Groups** or **Permission Sets** added to them. To do this, go to **Setup | Users | Permission Set Groups** and see the **Permission Sets in Group**, as shown in the following figure:

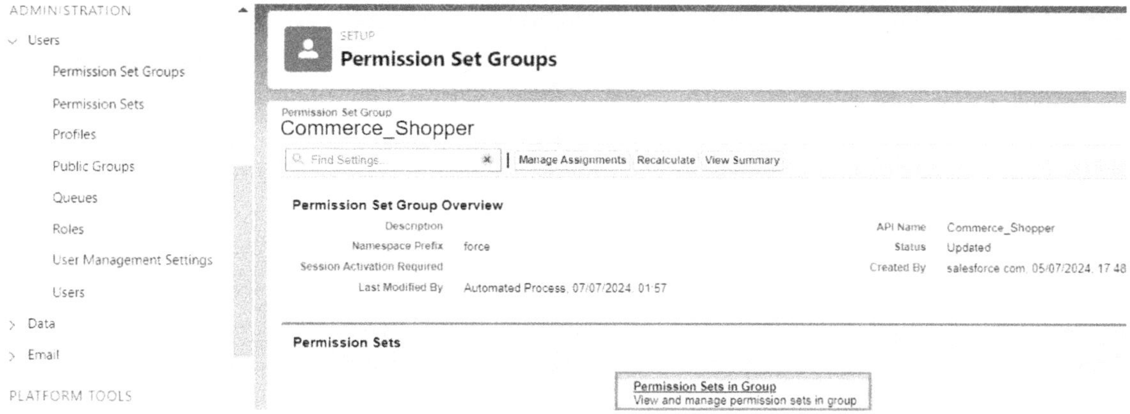

Figure 5.21: *Permission Set Groups*

There are additional features to **Permission Sets** and **Permission Set Groups**, such as **Session Activation Required**, but it is better to gain an understanding of how to use the basics first.

Salesforce license types

Salesforce has various licenses that grant users access. These are assigned to users against their user records.

To view which users have a specific license, go to **Setup | Users | Users** and select a user. The licenses available in the Salesforce Developer Edition are shown in the following figure:

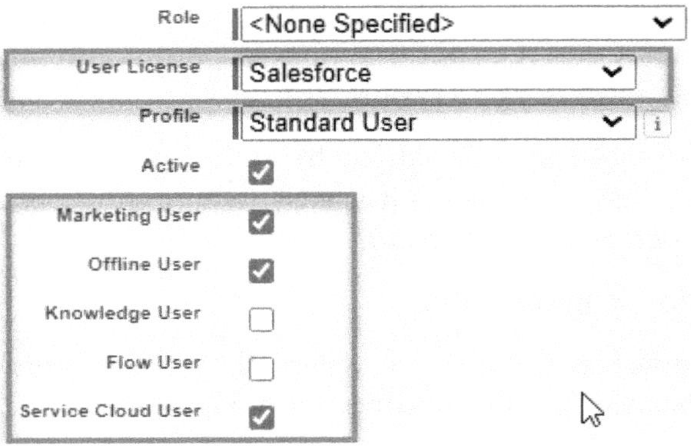

Figure 5.22: Salesforce license types

Many users will have a Salesforce license. A user can only have one license assigned to them. Here are some Salesforce licenses to be aware of:

- **Platform license**: This cheaper license gives access to Salesforce objects but with many limits. It is mainly used for building custom apps without leveraging Salesforce Sales and Service functionality.

- **Experience licenses (or community licenses)**: It is for external users accessing Experience Cloud, typically for customers or suppliers.

- **Einstein licenses**: Used for adding AI capabilities to Salesforce.

In addition, there are also Salesforce feature licenses, which are used when the company uses additional Salesforce features such as Marketing Cloud or Service Cloud, as highlighted above. If the company using Salesforce buys additional products, then there is also a section on the user record for adding **Permission Set License Assignments**, as shown in the following figure:

Figure 5.23: Salesforce Permission Set License Assignments

Since there are many Salesforce products and, therefore, many additional feature licenses available, an administrator's role is to be aware of where to find the permits and what each one does.

Conclusion

This chapter is part of the day-to-day life of a Salesforce Administrator, but it is also essential for configuring Salesforce, as any configuration must always be done within the context of its intended purpose for users.

As a Salesforce Administrator, the key is to ensure that people love using Salesforce, and there are many features that you can configure to enable this. However, if users are not able to access the features, then your efforts may not be appreciated.

This chapter aims to ensure that you view Salesforce from the user's perspective. You can login as them and make sure they are able to do what they need to do.

In the next chapter, we will explore automating business processes with Salesforce Flow.

Multiple choice questions

1. **Users in Salesforce need a profile but do not necessarily need a role. Is this true or false?**
   a. True
   b. False

2. **Grant Access Using Hierarchies is the default for standard objects, but not necessarily required for custom objects. Is this true or false?**
   a. True
   b. False

3. **Which permission set setting should not be granted to users without careful consideration? (choose two)**
   a. Modify All Data
   b. Access All Data
   c. View All Data
   d. Delete All Data

4. **A permission set can belong to a permission set group or a profile, but not both. Is this true or false?**
   a. True
   b. False

5. **In the role hierarchy, users can see records belonging to other users who:**
   a. Share the same profile
   b. Are below them in the role hierarchy
   c. Have the same permission set(s) assigned
   d. Own the same account

6. **A record in Salesforce is private if the object's OWD is set to Private, and it is only visible to the record owner and those above them in the role hierarchy. Is this true or false?**

    a. True

    b. False

7. **You can check who has access to a record by going to its sharing settings and pressing the View Field Accessibility button. Is this true or false?**

    a. True

    b. False

8. **If a user is no longer required in Salesforce, the best way to prevent them from having access is to:**

    a. Delete the user record

    b. Make them inactive

    c. Change their license to expired

    d. Reassign all their records to the general user

9. **Deleting a profile will automatically make all users with that profile inactive. Is this true or false?**

    a. True

    b. False

10. **To check users who have not logged into Salesforce for 30 days, you can: (choose two answers)**

    a. View all users and sort by Last Login

    b. Check users with View All Data less than 30 days

    c. Create a custom view on users with Last Login less than last 30 days

    d. Check user profiles with Last Login less than last 30 days

Answers

1	**a**
2	**a**
3	**a, c**
4	**b**
5	**b**
6	**a**
7	**a**
8	**b**
9	**b**
10	**a, c**

CHAPTER 6

Automating Salesforce with Flows

Introduction

Salesforce Flows are powerful automation tools that automate complex business processes without the need for code. Flows offer a drag-and-drop interface that allows users to define logic to make decisions and perform actions such as creating or updating records, sending emails, or integrating with external systems.

In this chapter, we will learn about how to build flows, and key features of Salesforce Flows include the ability to provide various types of flows. There are several types of flows, each serving different purposes. Screen flows are perhaps the most common, offering a user interface that allows users to enter or retrieve data through guided, screen-based logic. Auto-launched flows can be triggered automatically by record changes, schedules, platform events, or user actions, and they do not require user interaction. Triggered flows are a subset of auto-launched flows that specifically respond to changes in data or events, also running without any user input. Lastly, scheduled flows are time-based automations set to run at specific times or intervals, executing independently of user interaction.

Flows are ideal when automation requires interaction with the user, complex branching logic, or multi-step workflows that span different objects.

We will also cover some best practices for building flows, as well as how to test and debug flows.

Structure

In this chapter, we will cover the following topics:

- Introduction to Salesforce Flows
- Getting Started with Flows
- Einstein for Flows
- Best and worst practices for Flows

Objectives

The objective of this chapter is to get you familiar with the Flow Builder interface. There are some examples of exercises with step-by-step instructions on building a flow. The subject of flows is very large, so the aim of this chapter is to get you started with flows and some resources that are available online that can go into more depth in particular areas.

By the end of this chapter, you should be confident in building out flows, be able to test and debug them, and be familiar with Einstein for Flows.

Introduction to Salesforce Flows

Historically, Salesforce used to have a few automation tools, such as workflow rules and Process Builder, but these were all superseded by Flows, which have the following advantages:

- Automations can be kept in one place.
- Automations can be linked or have subflows.
- They have a huge range of possibilities, from building screen flows to integrations.
- They have an intuitive interface, making it easy to follow the logic.

They also do not generally rely on code, although Apex can be invoked if needed. Typically, Apex is used for doing large data processing or jobs that flows are less suited to. Flows are generally used to automate anything that can be done in the user interface or logical business processes.

Salesforce Flows is a fundamental tool for building automations in Salesforce, such as:

- Automating business processes, such as providing users with options for entering data based on criteria.
- Automating the creation, editing, and deleting of records based on defined criteria.
- Sending emails or other communications, such as custom notifications.

- Connecting to external systems using various methods, such as an HTTP callout or invoking Apex.

- Flows can run on a schedule, a platform event, or via user interaction.

- Flows can be extended by adding Lightning components or calling Apex classes.

- Einstein for Flows allows you to create flows based on entering Einstein prompts.

Overview

This chapter will give you a basic introduction to flows, but it is meant to be hands-on. Flows are a big subject, and this chapter is to give you an introduction. There are many resources, such as *Trailhead, Automation Champion, Apex Hours, Salesforce Ben,* as well as various *YouTube channels,* such as *Salesforce Cafe.* For each resource, use the search bar to find examples of flows.

These have many step-by-step tutorials to help you go from beginner to expert. As such, this chapter is to help you get started and build your confidence with Salesforce Flows.

In this chapter, we will:

- Give some basic flow examples of how to do field updates on the same object. This is to get us used to the Flow Builder.

- Do some further examples to bridge functionality that was not available in previous chapters.

- Give an overview of more advanced examples to guide you in the best way that flows can meet various business scenarios.

- Look at Einstein for Flows, which is a generative AI feature relatively new to Salesforce.

The chapter will also end with the flows' best practices to avoid common pitfalls or areas that may need further consideration. This will assist when using Einstein for Flows, which may seem to make learning flows unnecessary. However, it is important to have a good working knowledge of how to create and test flows so an AI-generated flow can be understood and tested properly.

Getting started with flows

Flows are very intuitive and rewarding. The best way to start with flows is to sketch them out and check that the automation can also be performed manually. These two steps help you to design the flow when the objective is clearly defined and to avoid any complexity if there are other features built into Salesforce that might interfere with the building process.

Assigning flow user permission

When you first access Salesforce, the ability to build flows is restricted. Although flows can be used by all Salesforce users, the ability to build them requires an update to your user details. The first step is to ensure that you have access to flows. Go to **Setup | Users** and on your user profile, check that the **Flow User** is enabled and press **Save** as shown in the following figure:

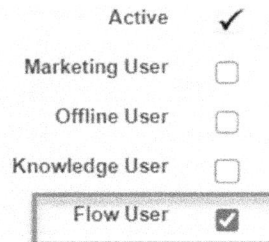

Figure 6.1: *Granting flow user permission*

Accessing flows

Your Salesforce org will come with some flows already included. To access them, go to **Setup | Flows**, and you will see various flows as well as a column showing the **Process Type**, as shown in *Figure 6.2*.

A flow is a highly visible representation of an automation you want to do in Salesforce. They are built in Flow Builder. To go to Flow Builder, go to **Setup | Flows**, as shown in the following figure:

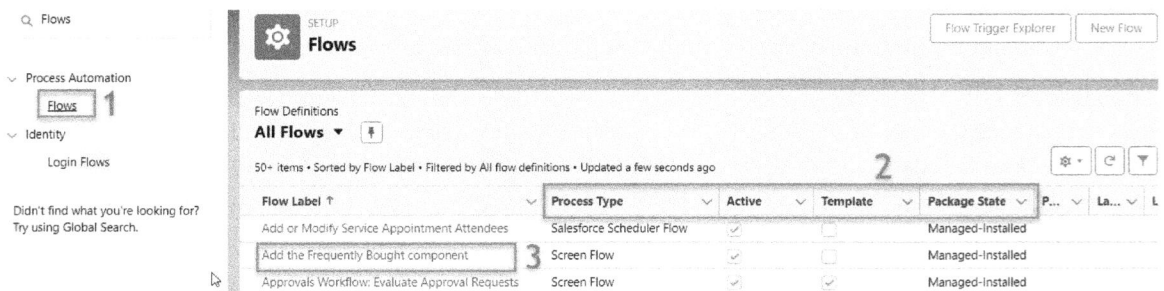

Figure 6.2: *Accessing flows*

In the above figure:

- Flows is the menu item to access all flows.

- The column headers are:

    o **Process Type**: When a flow is created, you have to choose what process type you wish to use. This will be discussed later.

- o **Active**: A flow can be active or inactive. Flows always have a version associated with them. There can be many versions, but only one version can be active.

- o **Template**: If the flow is based on a template with predefined steps and field mappings

- o **Package State**: If a flow is included as part of an application from the AppExchange or a default Salesforce Flow. If the flow is from an unmanaged package, then it is editable; if it is from a managed package, then it cannot be changed.

- To open a flow, simply press the **Flow Label**.

Open a flow, such as **Create a Case**, and review the general layout of flows, as shown in the following figure:

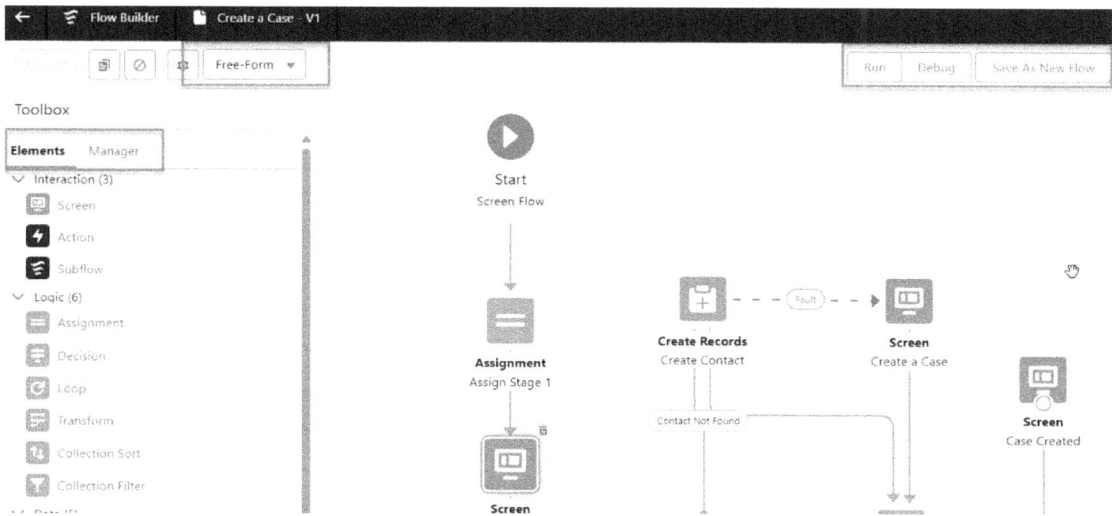

Figure 6.3: Flow Builder overview

There are a few areas highlighted in the illustration above, namely:

- There is a menu on the left showing components that can be added, and listing out the variables used in the flow.

- The top left-hand corner has a slider to show the menu, which has the option to have the flow builder automatically arrange the components or let you arrange them as you prefer.

- The top right-hand corner allows you to save a new version of the flow. This is required to make changes to the flow. The flow automatically stores previous versions. You will also regularly save and debug a flow. Debugging runs the flow where you will be asked to enter any variables that are needed, and then you are provided a list of steps conducted as the flow ran with successes and errors.

The large area of the screen is the flow canvas where elements are connected and configured. You will simply drag elements from the toolbox onto the canvas and configure them as needed.

Flow development

When flows first came out, there were only a few types of flow. Although this number has grown, they still fall into two basic categories:

- Screen flow, which appears on the screen, typically allows the user to interact with Salesforce, such as entering data or selecting options on the screen. This can be multiple screens to give a wizard-type feel to interacting with Salesforce.

- Event-driven flow, which happens behind the scenes. The number of flow types has grown considerably over the past few years. To see a full list with description, go to **Setup | Flows** and press **New Flow**, then **Start from Scratch**. The most commonly used flows are:

  o **Record-triggered flow**: Runs when a record is created, updated, or deleted.

  o **Schedule-triggered flow**: Runs at a time and can be repeated.

  o **Platform event triggered flow**: Runs when you need to automate real-time responses to system events that are published either within Salesforce or from external systems.

Remember the following:

- With all flows, it might sound unnecessary, but flows can get complicated, and it helps to simply draw out the flow on a whiteboard or any diagram tool. This can help to keep the context of the overall design while you work on specific areas during configuration. In the design, list out variables that you might need and keep a list of where they are either created or used.

- Before you start to design the flow, if the process can be done manually, then do it once or twice, logging in as different users. For example, if updating an opportunity, then do the steps manually. You may find there are validation rules or required fields that need consideration in the flow. This will help ensure the flow does not encounter errors, which can be time-consuming to debug if you are not aware of them beforehand.

As an example, go to an existing flow by going to **Setup | Flows** and select one. The following is an example of the flow **Approve a Deal**. Change the option near the top of the screen from **Auto-Layout** to **Free-Form**, as shown in the following figure:

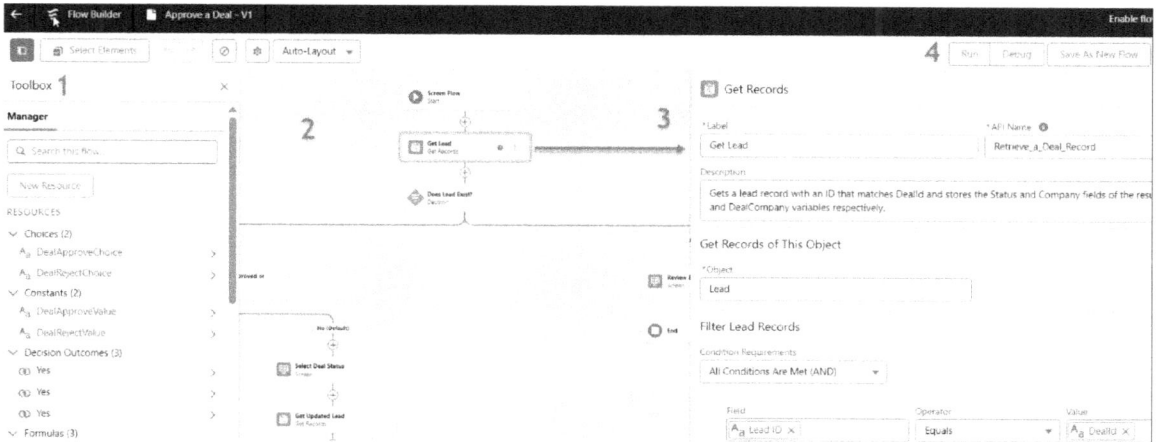

Figure 6.4: Flow Builder features

In *Figure 6.4*, we have the following features numbered as described in the following:

1. The **Toolbox**, which contains **Elements** and a **Manager**:

   a. **Elements** show components that can be added to the flow.

   b. The **Manager** shows variables and configurations already in the existing flow and where they are used.

2. The canvas (which is also known as the **flow visualizer**) displays the elements or components of the flow. Flows are built using elements, connectors, and resources. Elements perform logical actions; connectors determine which element leads to which, and resources, which are the variables or containers that are available.

3. The properties for each element in the flow. If you do not see the area on the right-hand side, it may also display as a pop-up if you click on a component in the flow.

4. The ability to save, run, or activate the flow.

Note: Once a flow is activated, you need to save it to a new version of the flow if you wish to modify it. This is very useful for rewinding to previous versions of the flow or seeing how it has been modified over time.

It should be noted that the flow above is installed by Salesforce, so you will not be able to modify the flow since it is a managed package. A managed package means that the configuration and setup are part of a custom application, which you do not have the ability to modify. This is typically a flow included by default with Salesforce or as part of adding an app from the AppExchange.

Flow elements

Flow elements are also frequently called **components**. They are the building blocks of flows. They are the various icons that are shown on the Flow Builder canvas. These are simply dragged from the **Elements** menu on the left-hand side of the screen onto the canvas. Refer to the following figure:

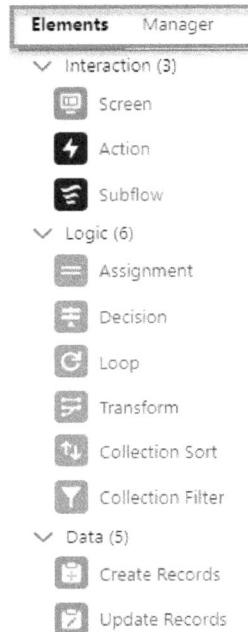

Figure 6.5: The element toolbox

Rather than going through every element in this book, you can hover your mouse over the element for a quick overview. The elements that are most used are:

- **Screen**: This creates a screen for the user to be able to see or edit records.
- **Decision**: Creates logic in the flow, which provides a branch to guide the flow.
- **Loop**: Allows a process to be repeated with exit criteria.
- **Create, update, get, and delete records**: These are used to retrieve and modify the data in Salesforce.

However, there are many more that will be useful depending on what you are trying to achieve.

Creating flow from scratch

To get used to the flow interface, we will create a flow that will not be saved. To do this, do the following steps:

1. **Setup | Flows** and press the **New Flow** button on the top right-hand side.
2. Select **Start from Scratch** and **Next**.
3. Select **Screen Flow** and **Create**.
4. Change the option in the top menu from **Auto-Layout** to **Free-Form**.
5. In the **Toolbox** on the left, under the **Elements** tab, select **Decision** and drag it onto the node below the **Start** icon.
6. You will have to give the **Decision** a label, such as **My First Decision**, and an outcome. For the resource, enter `Running User IsActive equals True`.
7. Press **Done**.
8. Drag the small circular node below the **Start** icon onto the **Decision** element to create a connector between the two elements.

You should see a screen like the one in the following figure:

Figure 6.6: Connecting elements in a flow

Clicking on the **Decision** element shows the values you entered in the previous step. For now, either close the browser window or press the back arrow in the top-left corner of the screen to exit the flow. You will be prompted that your changes will not be saved, which is fine.

Auto-layout or free-form

For familiarity, repeat the exercise, but rather than doing the step above where you change the option in the top menu from **Auto-Layout** to **Free-Form**, try simply pressing the + button between the **Screen Flow Start** and the **End** components, as shown in the following figure. This achieves the same as the exercise detailed above, and some users may prefer this method.

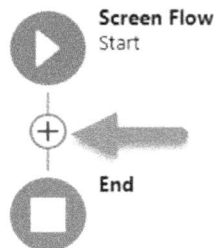

Figure 6.7: Auto-layout vs. free-form

It is worth becoming familiar with the two ways of working with flows. They do the same thing, but auto-layout allows Salesforce to position the components, whilst free-form allows the user to position the components.

Auto-layout and free-form have subtle differences in where the properties and the toolbox are positioned. You might find it easier to use free-form since the toolbox is displayed by default with **Elements** and **Manager**. The **Manager** can be shown in the **Auto-Layout** setting by pressing the small slider icon, but this does not show the **Elements** tab since elements are accessed using the + icon between other elements. This has the advantage of only providing elements compatible with each adjoining element. The choice is yours.

Hands-on example, updating record

The following flow example is very simple and only updates a field based on another field. Although this could be done using a simple formula field, this exercise is to gain experience with flows. In addition, a formula fields need to be calculated every time the record is accessed and if you have many formula fields and need to produce a report with many thousands, or even millions of records then it can possibly slow performance down whilst a flow gives much more control as to when it is used with a much greater control of the logic required.

The following example simply gives a date for renewing the membership and is unlikely to change. Using a flow here allows you to build additional functionality if needed.

In this example, we will make a flow to update a field on the **Contact** object for **Membership**. We will assume Salesforce is being used for contacts who require membership and have an annual renewal date.

We will create two new fields on the **Contact** object. To do this, go to **Setup | Object Manager** and select the **Contact** object and then the menu option for **Fields & Relationships**. Press the **New** button. One field will be **Joining Date**, and the other will be **Renewal Date** as described in the following table:

Object	Field label	Field API name	Type
Contact	Joining Date	`Joining_Date__c`	Date
Contact	Renewal Date	`Renewal_Date__c`	Date

Table 6.1: Configuration values required for two custom fields

Once done, feel free to adjust the page layout; it will not affect the flow, but it will make the screen easier to read. In *Figure 6.8*, drag a new section of the page layout builder to allow you to easily group the fields into a logical section.

A **Section** can be found in the page layout and simply dragged onto the page. Refer to the following figure:

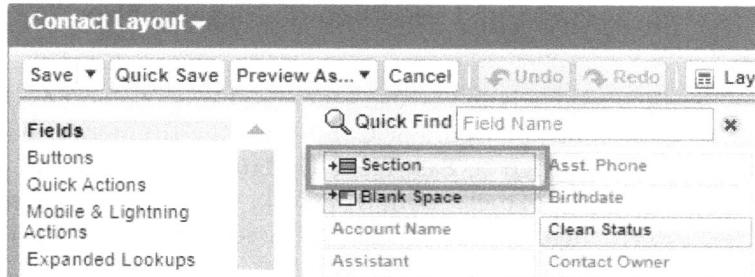

Figure 6.8: Adding a section to the page layout

When the section is added, you will have a dedicated area on the screen to display your records as shown in the following figure:

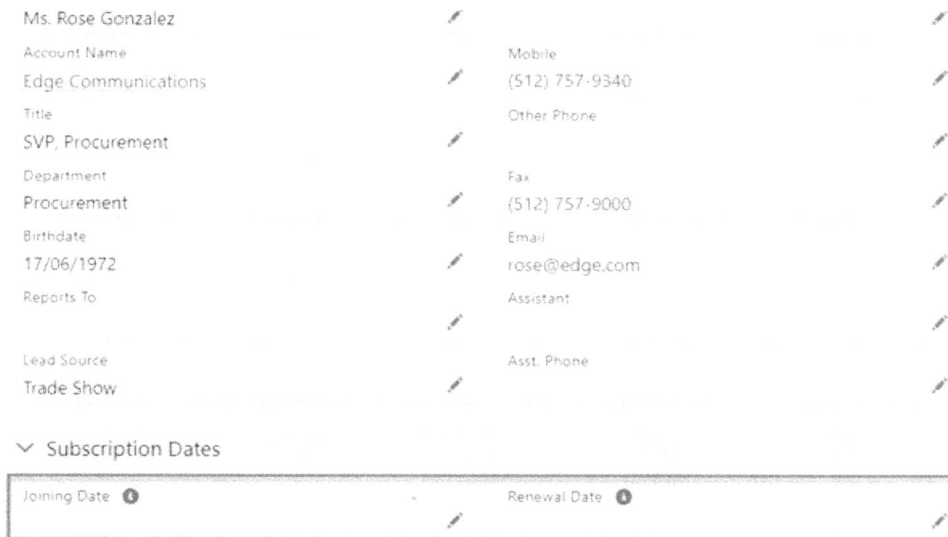

Figure 6.9: Custom fields to be updated by a flow

The two new fields only contain dates. We want the renewal date to be a year after their joining date.

To do this, create a flow by going to **Setup | Flows** and pressing the **New Flow** button, as shown in the following figure:

Figure 6.10: Creating a new flow

Select **Start from Scratch**, then next, and select **Record-Triggered Flow**. This basically means a change in a record fires the flow.

You will see the following screen, where you can select the **Contact** object as well as the option for an **A record to be created or updated**. For **Condition Requirements**, leave this as **None**. Other options include features such as **Fast Field Updates**, or **Action and Related records** have explanations. Choose either of these; both will work, but if you want to send out an email after saving a contact record, then you should choose the second option. Refer to the following figure:

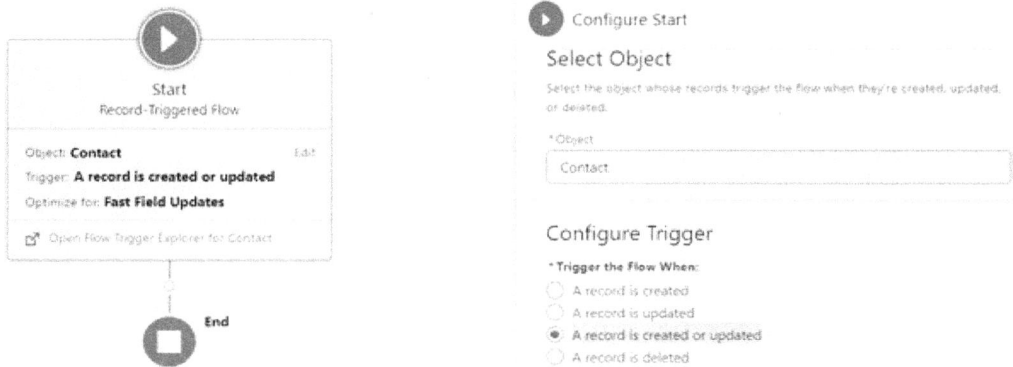

Figure 6.11: Options for creating a record

Next, you need to update the contact record. There are two pieces to this:

- Create the formula for adding 12 months to the **Renewal Date** based on the **Joining Date** fields.

- Adding an update record element to the flow.

To create the formula, reveal the **Toolbox** by clicking the small icon at the top left-hand side of the screen, then add a **New Resource**. Refer to the following figure:

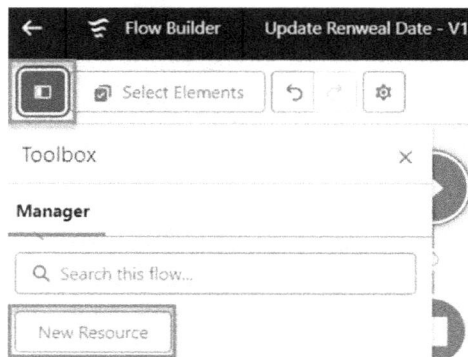

Figure 6.12: Adding a new resource to a flow

Select a resource of type **Formula** and enter the information shown in the following table:

Resource Type	Formula
API Name	`MembershipRenewalDate`
Description	`Setting the membership renewal date`
Data Type	`Date`
Formula	`ADDMONTHS({!$Record.Joining_Date__c},12)`

Table 6.2: Setting up the formula resource to be used in the flow

This will show the screen, as shown in the following figure:

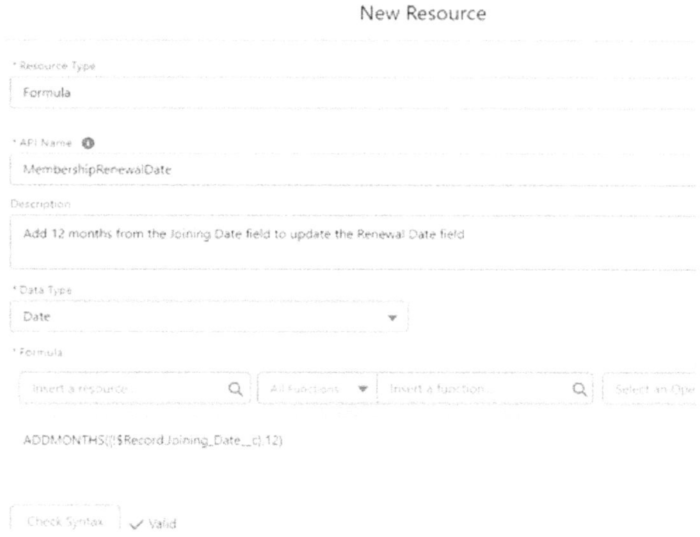

Figure 6.13: Configuring the new resource

Once the information is entered, press **Done**.

To add an **Update Records** element to the flow, click the + button between the **Start** and **End** elements, as shown in the following figure:

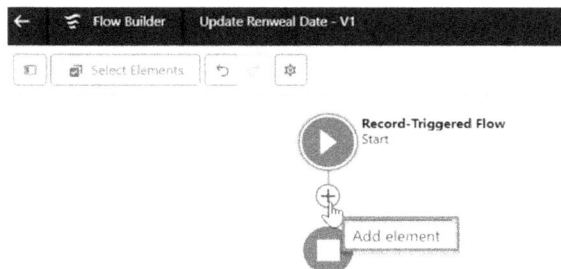

Figure 6.14: Adding a new element to a flow

Select the **Update Records** element to display the options available.

Label it `Update Membership` and give a **Description** of your choice. Choose **Use the contact record that triggered the flow** and then in the **Set Field Values for the Contact Record** option choose the **Renewal_Date__c** to have the value created in the formula field **MembershipRenewalDate**, as shown in the following figure:

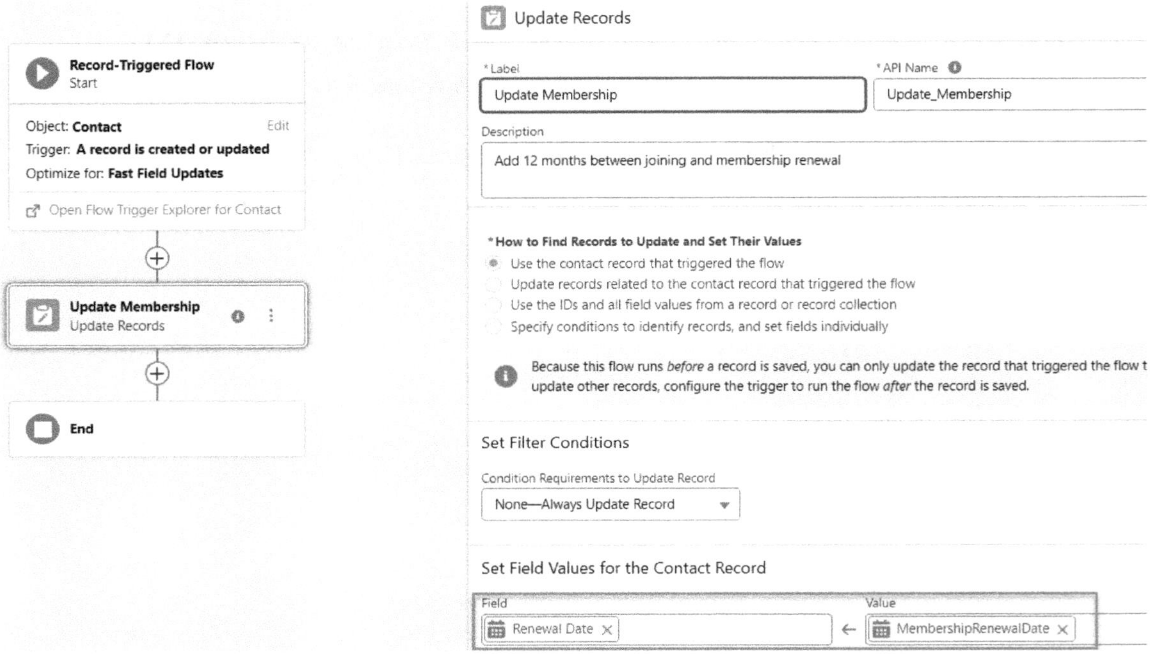

Figure 6.15: Configuring an Update Records element

Finally, press **Save** for the entire flow and **Activate** it, as shown in the following figure:

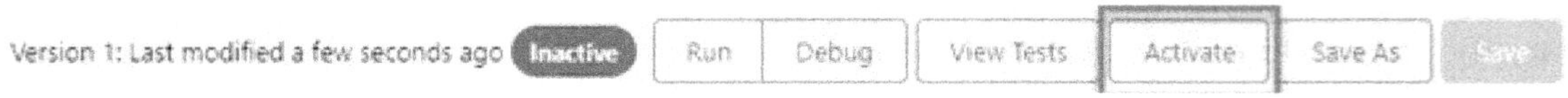

Figure 6.16: Activating a flow

Now, when you visit a contact record and enter a **Joining Date**, press **Save**, and the **Renewal Date** is automatically populated to be a year afterwards, as shown in the following:

Figure 6.17: Results of a working flow

Hands-on example, getting related records

In this example, we are going to collect related records and loop through them, performing an update. Prior to building a flow, write out the logical steps that need to be done. In this example:

- Find the related objects, such as accounts and tasks.

- Query the records based on the requirement (task status).

- Use a loop to go through the records.

- Update the records.

Consider a scenario, accounts are accumulating too many tasks, which need to be updated based on their due date, as shown in the following figure:

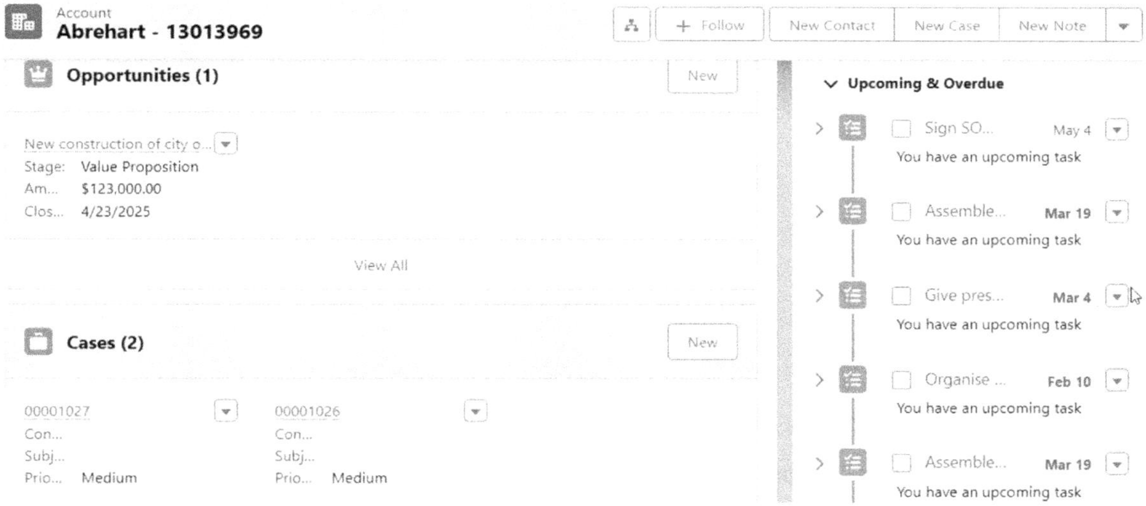

Figure 6.18: Showing an account with many related tasks

Building flow

Start by creating a screen flow from **Setup | Flows | New Flow | Start from Scratch | Screen Flow**.

We need to store the account ID. To do this, create a resource in the **Toolbox** by going to the. **Manager** tab and pressing the **New Resource** button.

Give it the following values:

- **Resource Type**: **Variable**

- **API Name**: `AccountRecordID`

- **Data Type: Text**

- **Available for input**: Checked

This will give you the screen shown in the following figure. Press **Done**.

New Resource

* Resource Type

Variable ▾

* API Name ❶

AccountRecordID

Description

Storing the Account ID as a text variable for input

* Data Type

Text ▾   ☐ Allow multiple values (collection) ❶

Default Value

Enter value or search resources... 🔍

Availability Outside the Flow
☑ Available for input
☐ Available for output

Figure 6.19: Resource configuration

Next, drag a **Get Records** element onto the canvas. Complete the values, namely:

- **Label: `Get Account`**

- **API Name: `Get_Account`**

- **Object: `Account`**

- **Condition Requirements: All Conditions Are Met (AND)**

- **Field: `Id`**

- **Operator: `Equals`** (variable)

- **Value: `{!AccountRecordID}`**

- **How many records to store: Only the first record**

- **How to store record data: Automatically store all the fields**

You should see the screen shown below. One completed press **Done**. Now is a good time to save the flow. Refer to the following figure:

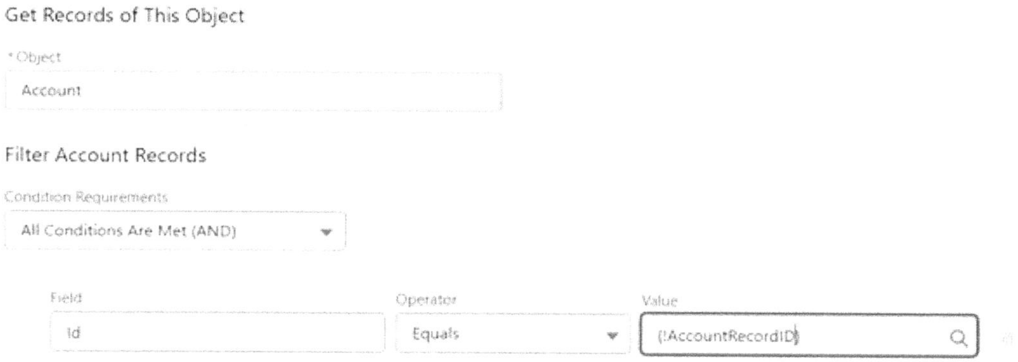

Get Records of This Object

*Object

Account

Filter Account Records

Condition Requirements

All Conditions Are Met (AND)

Field	Operator	Value
Id	Equals	{!AccountRecordID}

Figure 6.20: Configuration of a Get Records element

The above was done as it is a screen flow. So, when this flow runs on the screen on the **Account** object, it will use the current account record to store the variable as well as the fields on that **Account** record. It could be done using a flow of type **Record-Triggered Flow**, which would take the account ID off the record that fired the flow. There are different ways to do many things in flows that users should be aware of.

The next step is relating the tasks to the account. Salesforce has master-detail and lookups. Tasks use a related-to relationship since tasks can be related to many objects.

Drag a **Get Records** element onto the canvas and add the following information:

- **Label**: `Get Related Tasks`
- **Object**: `Task`
- **Condition Requirement**: **All Conditions Are Met (AND)**
- **Field**: `WhatId`
- **Operator**: `Equals`
- **Value**: `AccountRecordID`
- **How many records to store**: **All Records (since an account may have many tasks)**
- **How to store record data**: **Automatically store all fields**

This will give you the screen as shown in the following figure. Press **Done** and connect the element to the previous one. Press **Save the Flow**.

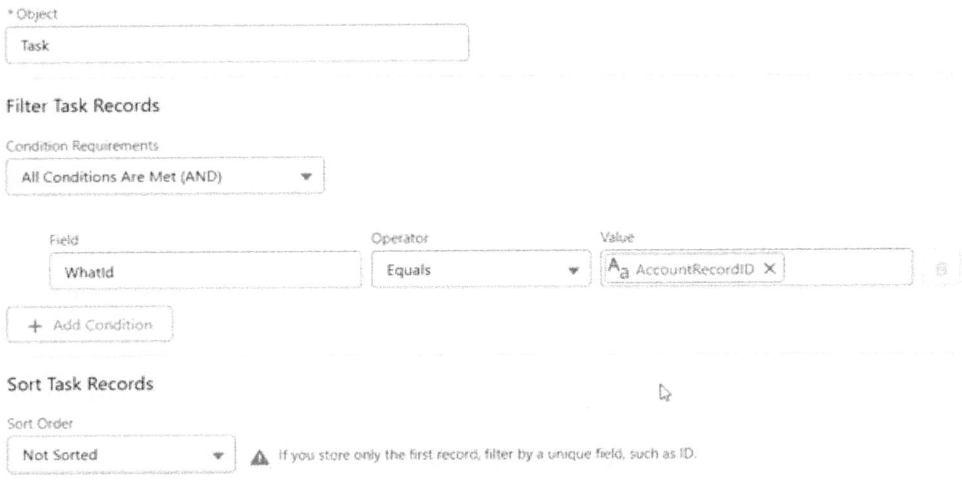

* Object

Task

Filter Task Records

Condition Requirements

All Conditions Are Met (AND) ▼

Field	Operator	Value
WhatId	Equals ▼	Aa AccountRecordID ✕

+ Add Condition

Sort Task Records

Sort Order

Not Sorted ▼   ⚠ If you store only the first record, filter by a unique field, such as ID.

Figure 6.21: Configuration of the second Get Records element

We now need to loop through the tasks to be able to update them. However, to store the task data, we need to create a collection, which is a collection of variables. It will store the updated tasks before we save them to Salesforce.

To do this, go to the **Toolbox** and the **Manager** tab and press **New Resource**.

- **Resource Type**: **Variable**
- **API Name**: `UpdatedTaskCollection`
- **Data Type**: **Record (so it is holding the entire Task record)**
- **Object**: **Task**
- **Allow multiple values (collection)**: Tick this

Press **Done** and **Save the Flow**.

Next, drag a **Loop** element to the canvas. Enter the following:

- **Label**: `Loop Through Tasks`
- **Collection variable**: `Tasks from Get Related Tasks`

Drag an **Assignment** element to the canvas and enter the following:

- **Label**: `Change Task Status`
- **Record Fields**: `{!Loop_through_tasks.Status}`
- **Operator**: `Equals`
- **Value**: `Completed`

The last step is a variable created by Salesforce when you added the **Loop** element, which is used to hold a single record and update the **Status** field to **Completed**, as shown in the following figure:

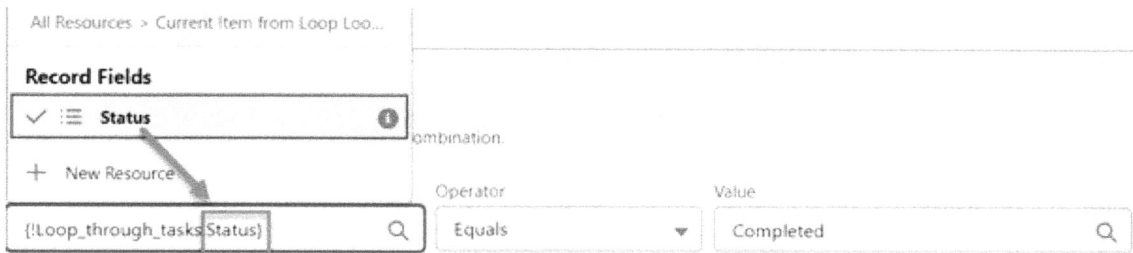

Figure 6.22: Configuring the assign element

Add a second **Assignment** element to the canvas and enter the following:

- Label: `Add to Update Collection`
- Variable: `UpdatedTaskCollection`
- Operator: `Add`
- Value: `Current Item from Loop Loop through tasks`

Press **Done**, as shown in the following figure:

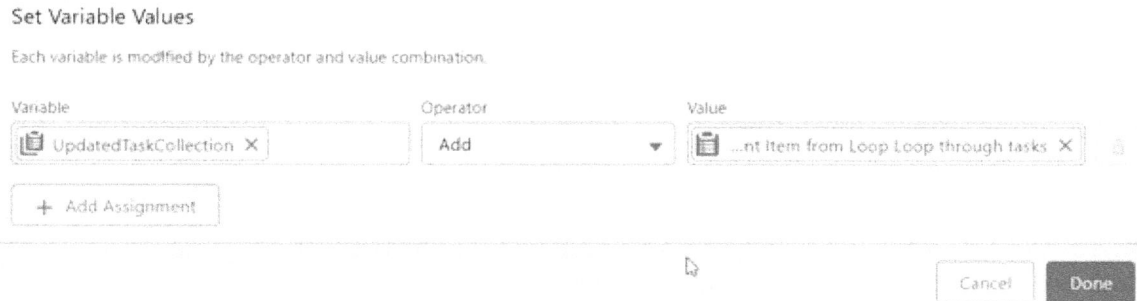

Figure 6.23: Configuring the assign element

Note: **By doing updates on all the records and storing them in a collection, we can update them all at once. This is known as bulkification, which avoids doing unnecessary callouts to Salesforce, or in simple terms, rather than updating one record at a time, update them all at once.**

Finally, add an **Update Records** element and enter the following:

- Label: `Update Tasks`
- Use the Ids and all field values from a record or record collection: `True`
- Records to Update: `UpdatedTaskCollection`

Note: When you connect the elements, the Loop element will ask you if you want to go through the loop sequentially; in which case, select For each item in the collection. If you revisit the Loop element, you will see that the options are First item to last item or Last item to first item. This can be useful when your collection is based on a date range or opportunity amount, but in this example, it is not important.

Then, press **Done**. The final flow should look like the illustration in the following figure:

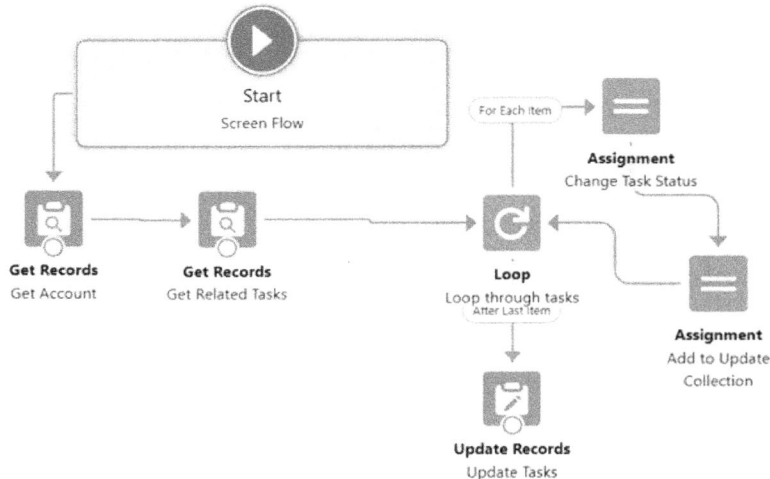

Figure 6.24: The final flow configuration

Testing and debugging flow

To test and debug the flow, first get the account ID from the URL where you want to test the flow. This is found by going to the account record, which had many tasks shown previously in *Figure 6.18* and shown in the following figure:

dev-ed.develop.lightning.force.com/lightning/r/Account/001NS0000185MRYYA2/view

Figure 6.25: Debugging using a test account ID

Press the **Debug** button at the top of the Flow Builder page. Enter the account ID and press **Run**. You will get a debug log window that shows a list of the steps and variable values used in running the flow. Check the values in the actual account record and add the flow to an action to provide users' access as outlined in the section *Triggering flows using buttons*.

Einstein for Flows

Einstein is Salesforce's AI capability. This is covered in more detail in *Chapter 12, Einstein AI*, but a great feature is enabling Einstein for Flows and allowing generative AI to create a flow based on your description. Salesforce provides various examples of prompts that can be used for creating flows at **https://help.salesforce.com/**and type in `Einstein draft flow`.

For this feature to work, you will also need to add either Einstein for Sales or Einstein for Service user licenses to your user profile. However, at the time of writing, Einstein for Flows is not generally available in Developer Edition orgs, but can be found in Salesforce playgrounds.

It might be tempting to think that with the ability to automatically create flows, there is no real need to do it manually. Salesforce is keen to emphasize that there is no guarantee that a flow is generated correctly, so it is important to understand the elements and to go through the configuration. Einstein will do its best based on its interpretation of the prompt provided, but this is no guarantee that it will work as expected.

Einstein for Flows works using Salesforce CodeGen, which allows you to describe your flow in natural language before it is generated. You simply describe your flow requirement in plain words via a natural language prompt. Einstein calls upon CodeGen to interpret the flow and generate the XML/JSON, which is used to create the flow. Refer to the following figure:

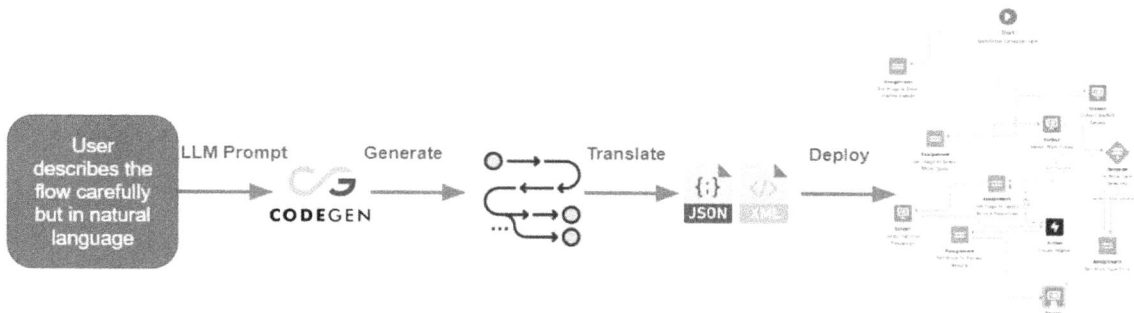

Figure 6.26: *Einstein for Flows overview*

Setting up Einstein for Flows

The first step is to check that Einstein is switched on in your Salesforce org. At the time of writing, the exact configuration has changed several times. The current process for setting the Einstein for Flows is to go to **Setup | Einstein Settings**, as shown in the following figure:

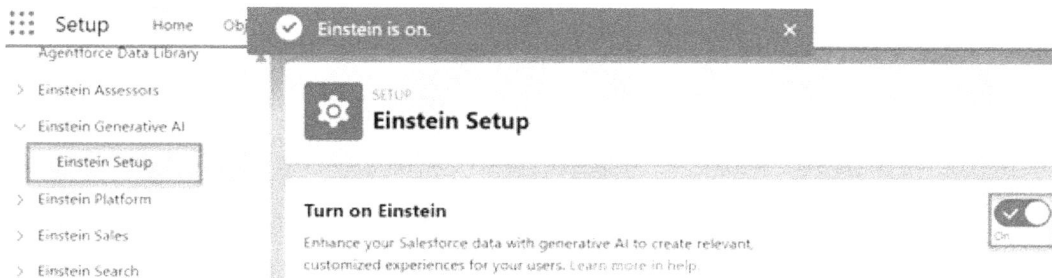

Figure 6.27: *Ensuring Einstein is enabled*

If you do not see this option, then you can get a new Salesforce playground from Trailhead by simply searching for an Einstein Trail with an option to create a new playground.

Note: It can take some time between turning Einstein on and Einstein features being available in Salesforce.

Once Einstein is enabled, create a new flow by going to **Setup** | **Flows** | **New Flow** | **Create from Scratch**.

You should see the screen, as shown in the following figure, which has the Einstein Prompt Builder on the left-hand side of the screen, where you can type instructions for Einstein to create the flow:

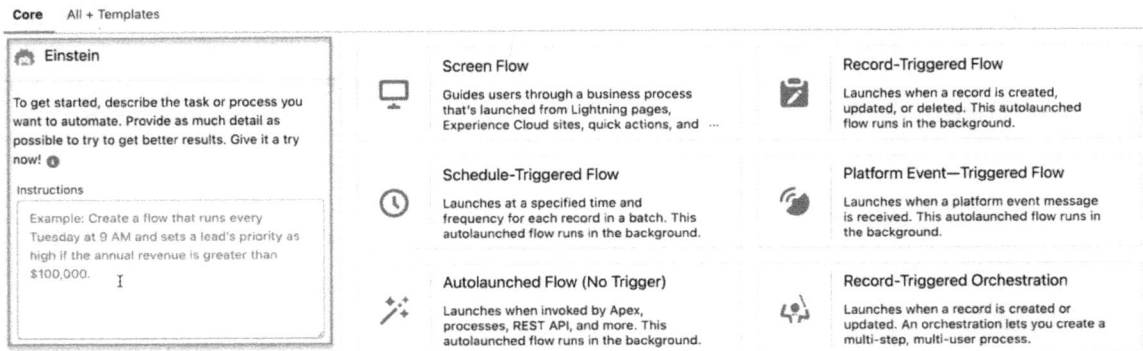

Core   All + Templates

🪶 Einstein

To get started, describe the task or process you want to automate. Provide as much detail as possible to try to get better results. Give it a try now! ❶

Instructions

Example: Create a flow that runs every Tuesday at 9 AM and sets a lead's priority as high if the annual revenue is greater than $100,000.

Screen Flow
Guides users through a business process that's launched from Lightning pages, Experience Cloud sites, quick actions, and ...

Schedule-Triggered Flow
Launches at a specified time and frequency for each record in a batch. This autolaunched flow runs in the background.

Autolaunched Flow (No Trigger)
Launches when invoked by Apex, processes, REST API, and more. This autolaunched flow runs in the background.

Record-Triggered Flow
Launches when a record is created, updated, or deleted. This autolaunched flow runs in the background.

Platform Event—Triggered Flow
Launches when a platform event message is received. This autolaunched flow runs in the background.

Record-Triggered Orchestration
Launches when a record is created or updated. An orchestration lets you create a multi-step, multi-user process.

Figure 6.28: Using Einstein for Flows prompt builder

Triggering flows using buttons

There are two ways to trigger flows from a button:

- Custom button and add the URL associated with the flow

- Quick action and select the flow

From the two methods, quick action is slightly preferable as it opens the screen flow inside the existing user interface, whilst a custom button will open a new screen, which gives a slightly less fluid user experience. It is worth noting that the global actions are found in setup and are available across the entire platform; on the other hand, quick actions are specific to an object.

To launch a flow from a quick action, go to **Setup** | (select the object, for example, **Contact**) | **Quick Actions** and press **New Action** (which is next to the button or link option). Refer to the following figure:

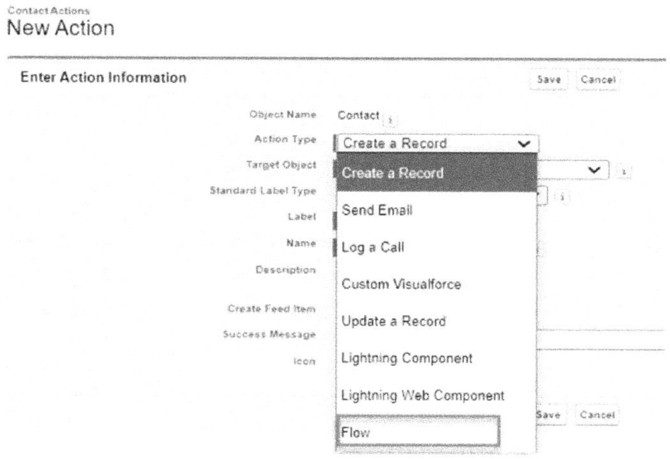

Contact Actions
New Action

Enter Action Information   Save   Cancel

Object Name	Contact
Action Type	Create a Record
Target Object	
Standard Label Type	
Label	
Name	
Description	
Create Feed Item	
Success Message	
Icon	

Create a Record

Send Email

Log a Call

Custom Visualforce

Update a Record

Lightning Component

Lightning Web Component

Flow

Save   Cancel

Figure 6.29: Using quick actions to launch a flow

Select **Flow**, as shown above, and enter the following information (refer to the following figure):

Edit Contact Action
Accept Visit

Enter Action Information   Save   Cancel

Object Name	Contact
Action Type	Flow
Flow	Outbound New Appointment
Standard Label Type	--None--
Label	Crerate Appointment
Name	NewAppointment
Description	Create a new appointment for the Contact
Icon	⚡ Change Icon

Save   Cancel

Figure 6.30: Configuring the quick action for a specific flow

Add the quick action to the page layout by going to **Setup | Object Manager |** (select the object in this example it is the **Contact** object) **| Page Layout** and drag the **Create Appointment** button onto the page layout.

Note: **In the above, if you enter --None-- for the Standard Label Type, then you have the option to give it a custom label which appears on the button. You can also create custom labels by going to Setup | Custom Labels and pressing New.**

The above creates a quick action on the **Contact** record, which fires the flow **Outbound New Appointment** as shown in the following figure:

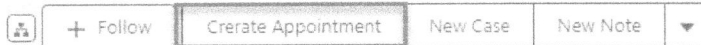

Figure 6.31: The results of adding the quick action to the page layout

Best and worst practice for flows

This book is purely an introduction to Flows and provides an overview of some of the core concepts. However, although it is comparatively easy to build flows, there are some areas that separate out a novice from a professional. In this section, we will cover some of the best and worst things that distinguish a well-built and robust flow from one that is unreliable at best and could cause serious issues at worst.

Best practice

There is an amazing range of functionality with flows, but the following should be used as much as possible:

- **Invoke actions**: As described in *Chapter 3, Customizing User Interface*, flows, such as auto-launched flows, can be run by quick actions, which makes them great for users to simply press a button and have a flow do the processing for them.

- **Subflows**: Rather than having several flows running on the same object, use subflows to manage the order of execution and provide an intuitive way of seeing what happens.

- **Custom metadata-driven logic**: Outside the scope of this book, but in large Salesforce orgs, using custom metadata components can improve scalability, reduce admin time, and also reduce the risk of errors.

- **Fault path**: Flows allow a fault path to be added to assist in debugging flows or cope with unplanned scenarios.

Example of building fault path

There are various ways to debug a flow, but one of the simplest is to add a fault path where there could be an issue. For example, when the flow created as example two had to update the task records, if this had an issue, then simply add a fault path as shown in the following figure:

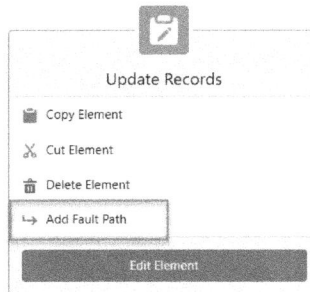

Figure 6.32: Adding a fault path to a flow

If this is a screen flow, then you can add a screen with a **Display Text** element with a text field containing:

```
There was a problem with this flow: {!$Flow.FaultMessage}.
```

The variable **$Flow.FaultMessage** is available by going into the **Display Text** and selecting the **Global Variables | $Flow**, as shown in the following figure:

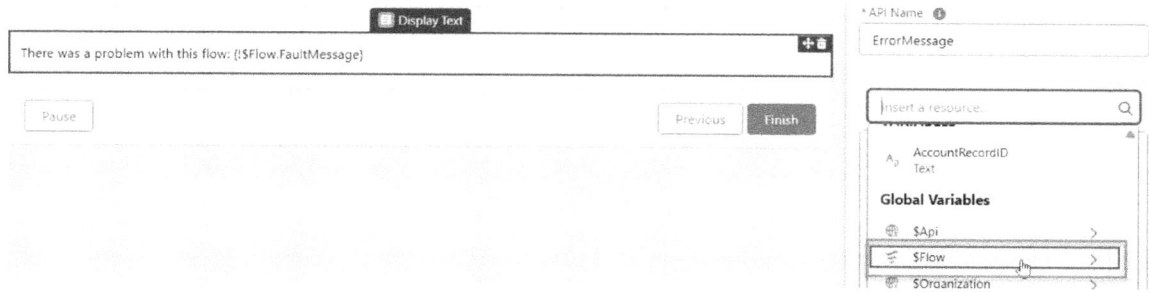

Figure 6.33: Adding the fault variable to a Display Text element

Press **Save**, and this will give a final flow, as shown in the following figure:

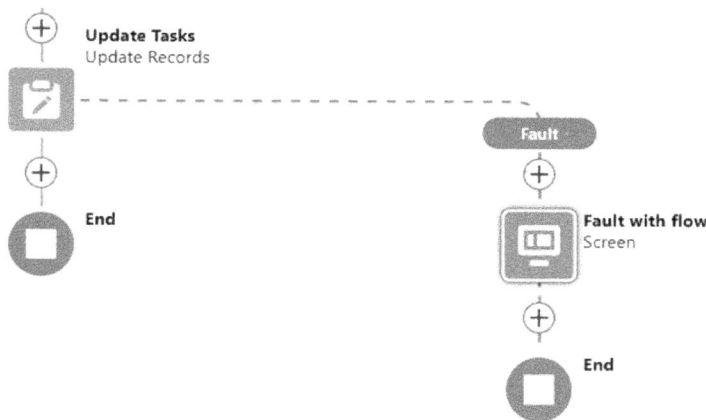

Figure 6.34: The fault path included in the flow

Worst practice

Although flows are a very powerful and versatile tool, there is also room to make mistakes. The following are some common errors:

- **Flow loops without logic gaps**: For example, a decision block may have more options than built into the flow, or variable values could be assumed, whilst others will exist.

- **Large data operations**: Flows are great at automation, but large data volumes are best done using Apex. Typically, more than 100 records in a single transaction are considered a large data set, especially if you are doing **Data Manipulation Language (DML)** or complex processing.

- **Avoid doing any DML**: DML statements in a loop, as this can lead to hitting Salesforce API limits.

Conclusion

In this chapter, you would have learned how to access flows and use the Flow Builder. You would have learned how to access flows in Salesforce by applying the flow user permission. Once access is granted, users can work with flows using the Flow Builder interface. This interface includes a toolbox, which allows users to add elements to their flow, and a manager, which displays the variables used within the flow.

Users can switch between auto-layout and free-form modes depending on their design preferences or project needs.

With Flow Builder, users can start by creating a basic flow, such as one designed to update a record. As skills develop, they can move on to building more advanced flows, such as those that search for related records and update them accordingly.

We have also had an introduction to Einstein for Flows. However, it is important to note that Einstein should be used cautiously. Any flow that incorporates Einstein features should be thoroughly tested before being deployed to a live environment.

This chapter has also provided knowledge about the various ways that flows can be used, but it has not gone into detail about many of the other various flow types possible, because that would be a book in itself. The two most changeable areas of Salesforce currently are flows and Einstein AI, which will be regularly updated by Salesforce. As such, it is not possible to give a detailed guide on these areas since they will change with every Salesforce release.

There are also many more aspects to flows than covered in this chapter, such as Fast Lookups, Fast Create, interacting with external systems, and embedding flows in Experience sites or using flows for advanced approval processes, but this chapter is aimed at giving a good foundation for getting started with Salesforce Flows.

The next chapter goes into deeper knowledge of the Salesforce security model. So far, this book has touched lightly on configuring the security model to give information on what is relevant for each chapter.

Multiple choice questions

1. **What are the three main components of a flow?**

    a. Screen Flows, Actions, and Page Layouts

    b. Resources, Debugs, and Flow Builder

    c.   Elements, Resources, and Connectors

    d.   Flow Builder, Elements, and Variables

2. **What is the reason behind using subflows?**

    a.   They allow different permissions to be used on each subflow.

    b.   They allow a flow to be connected to other objects.

    c.   They perform smaller tasks whilst the main flow is running.

    d.   They allow one main flow to run on an object but can be sequenced to perform separate functions.

3. **Which two methods allow a user to invoke a flow? (choose 2)**

    a.   LWC

    b.   Custom button

    c.   Custom link

    d.   Quick action

4. **When a flow is finished, it is best practice to assign a fault path. Where do you get the variable for adding {!$Flow.FaultMessage}?**

    a.   Global variables

    b.   Screen variables

    c.   Record (single) variables

    d.   Record collection variables

5. **What are the options for working with data using flows?**

    a.   Insert, upsert, create, delete

    b.   Create records, update records, get records, delete records

    c.   Create records, upsert records, put records, delete records

    d.   Update, modify, send, retrieve

6. **One of the main reasons for using collections is:**

    a.   Store similar data in one place

    b.   Allow logical processing of data from different objects

    c.   To bulkify data transactions to Salesforce

    d.   Modify data using formulas or queries

7. **When creating a new flow, you have two options: one is Start from Scratch, whilst the other is:**

    a. Add from the AppExchange

    b. Use a template

    c. Clone

    d. Einstein generates

8. **An important consideration when using Einstein for Flow is:**

    a. To give a precise definition of the flow with logical steps between elements.

    b. To use plain English to describe what you want the flow to do.

    c. To treat the generated flow as a draft and understand every configuration.

    d. To enable Einstein for Flows prior to deployment.

9. **What is the difference between a record-triggered flow and a scheduled flow?**

    a. A record-triggered flow is initiated when an Apex Trigger is fired, whilst a scheduled flow only occurs when a user interacts with the record.

    b. A record-triggered flow occurs when a platform event has happened, whilst a scheduled flow will happen during a specific time interval.

    c. A record-triggered flow will be based on flow logic, whilst a scheduled flow is based on the user's interaction.

    d. A record-triggered flow is initiated when a record changes, whilst a scheduled flow runs at a specified time and frequency.

10. **True or false: Flows observe the roles and the permissions of the user unless they have the flow user permission assigned to them.**

    a. True

    b. False

Answers

1	c
2	d
3	b, d
4	a
5	b
6	c
7	b
8	c
9	d
10	b

CHAPTER 7

Salesforce Security Model

Introduction

We have seen over the past chapters how Salesforce is configured to allow access for different users and how to configure the **user interface** (**UI**) and build out custom objects, fields, and more. We have also seen how to automate Salesforce for routine tasks and some of the more advanced features. However, this has been done using your profiles as a system administrator. As a system administrator, you have privileged rights over what can be seen and done in Salesforce, which obviously should not apply to other users.

This chapter is dedicated to a more detailed view of ensuring Salesforce is correctly configured to provide different users with the necessary access to Salesforce. It covers core concepts for designing the correct level of security in Salesforce. Security can be thought of as ensuring proper data access, which involves several key steps, namely having the correct object-level and field-level permissions, setting up groups or teams to automatically share records, and providing different methods for users to grant access to others, either manually or through carefully predefined roles or permissions.

Structure

This chapter covers the following topics:

- Visibility in Salesforce

- Teams
- Login history

Objectives

By the end of this chapter, readers will be able to configure settings in Salesforce to provide users access to the objects, tabs, and apps they require. You will have gained a good understanding of how to configure user profiles as well as some of the tools Salesforce provides to grant or restrict access.

This chapter also covers some of the additional features for sharing records in Salesforce when the user's setting limit their default access.

This chapter also gives clear advice on how to troubleshoot user access issues and how to test the configuration.

Visibility in Salesforce

Salesforce can be configured to give precise control over who sees what in Salesforce. In general, the Salesforce security model should be setup in the most secure way, and then access added as needed. Simply removing a field from a page layout is not enough to prevent the user from seeing the record elsewhere, for example, in a report.

As such, the sharing model in Salesforce has this golden rule. If someone should not see a record, then the object should be set as private. Then, access should be opened up using the role hierarchy and other methods outlined in this chapter.

If you Google *who sees what in Salesforce,* there are numerous resources, which are summarized in the following sections. As a rule, it is always best to login as a user to check that the configuration is done correctly.

Salesforce security model

As mentioned above, if there is any reason a user in Salesforce should not see a record, then access must be set to private. Object access is found by going to **Setup | Sharing Settings**. This lists out all the standard and custom objects with their security settings. There is also the option to **Grant Access Using Hierarchies**, which means only the person who created a record or users above them in the role hierarchy can see the record. Access to the record is then granted by opening up the visibility in a logical way, as illustrated in the following figure:

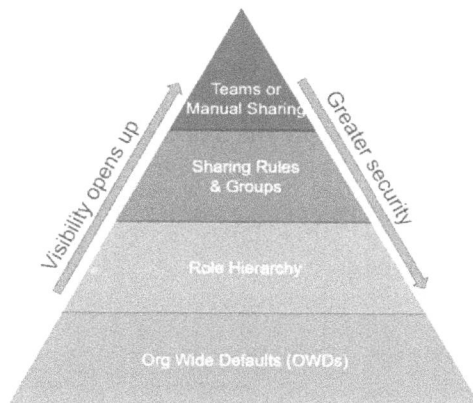

Figure 7.1: *The security structure in Salesforce*

In the preceding figure, the **Org Wide Defaults** (**OWDs**) are the very base of the security model. The different levels show the type of configuration required to open up access. There is always a trade-off between providing users with more visibility and maintaining security.

The following list serves as the basis for this chapter, with further details provided later. Access to records, as illustrated above, is done in the following order:

- **OWDs**: It is the most restrictive setting and forms the base of the pyramid.

- **Role hierarchy**: If the OWD is set to private, then only the record owner or those above them in the role hierarchy have access to the record. However, if the user does not have a role, then they would not get access to the record.

- **Sharing rules**: Most standard and custom objects can have sharing rules that allow records to be shared between users or user groups. To do this, go to the same page as **Sharing Settings** (see above) and scroll down to sharing rules.

- **Groups**: Allow multiple users, users with certain roles, or even other groups to be added to a sharing rule. This provides a broader level of access and is further up the pyramid.

- **Manual sharing**: Allows you to grant individual access to specific records to users or groups who might not otherwise have access based on their default sharing settings. This is done at the discretion of the record owner and is a way to handle situations where standard sharing rules or role hierarchies do not fully address the needed access.

- **Team access**: Sharing can be done between teams. For example, accounts have account sharing teams, which typically are able to see records related to an account. opportunity teams are similar, but only last for the duration of the opportunity. Both features allow users to collaborate on an account or opportunity.

- **Apex sharing**: Allows records to be shared if none of the above methods work. This is a programmatic solution.

Setting up OWDs

To see the OWDs, follow these steps:

Go to **Setup | Sharing Settings** and review the objects OWDs:

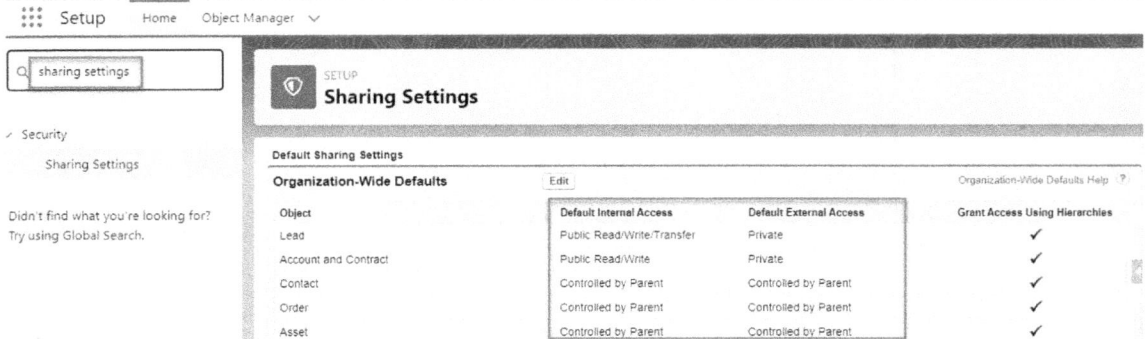

Figure 7.2: *OWDs settings*

This gives the access level or OWDs for the various objects in Salesforce. These can be:

1. **Public Read/Write**, meaning the object is available to all users.

2. **Private** meaning access is limited to the person who created the record and those above them in the role hierarchy if **Grant Access Using Hierarchies** is enabled, as shown in the column on the right-hand side of *Figure 7.2*.

3. **Controlled by Parent**, for example, if you have access to accounts, then you get the same access to contacts since accounts is the parent object of contacts.

There are other options, such as **Public Read/Write/Transfer**, which is useful for leads and cases to allow users to transfer ownership to other users using manual sharing, which is discussed later.

Note: **In Figure 7.2, there are two other columns for providing access to all the objects.**

These two columns are to provide the following access for Salesforce objects, namely:

*   **Default External Access** shows the access when setting up Salesforce Experience Cloud, which is covered in *Chapter 10, Various Salesforce Features*. This setting is generally set to **Private**.

*   **Grant Access Using Hierarchies** means Salesforce will use role hierarchies as described in the following sections. This basically means that users can view records owned by other users below them in the role hierarchy.

Salesforce role hierarchy

A very simplistic rule is that profiles and permission sets control what you can do in Salesforce, whilst roles control what you can see. Roles and profiles combine to provide access to many Salesforce features. In Salesforce, page layouts and record types work together to customize the **user experience** (**UX**) by controlling what information is displayed to different users or groups based on their roles. Profiles then determine which record types and their associated page layouts are available to users.

Page layouts control the presentation of fields, related lists, and buttons. Their visibility is controlled by user profiles and record types. Administrators can create multiple layouts for different user groups and record types to ensure that users see the appropriate information.

When setting up users, you do not need to assign them to a role. If you do not assign a role, they will still have access to Salesforce but will have some limited functionality, such as they will not be able to see their data in displays based on roles. It is generally best practice to assign users to a role; however, before doing so, you must first setup the actual role hierarchy, as shown in the following figure.

Setting up role hierarchy

Roles were briefly covered in *Chapter 5, Adding Users and Assigning Correct Access Levels*. This is done by going to **Setup** | **Users** | **Roles**, which will give you a helpful splash page describing how role hierarchy works, as shown in the following figure:

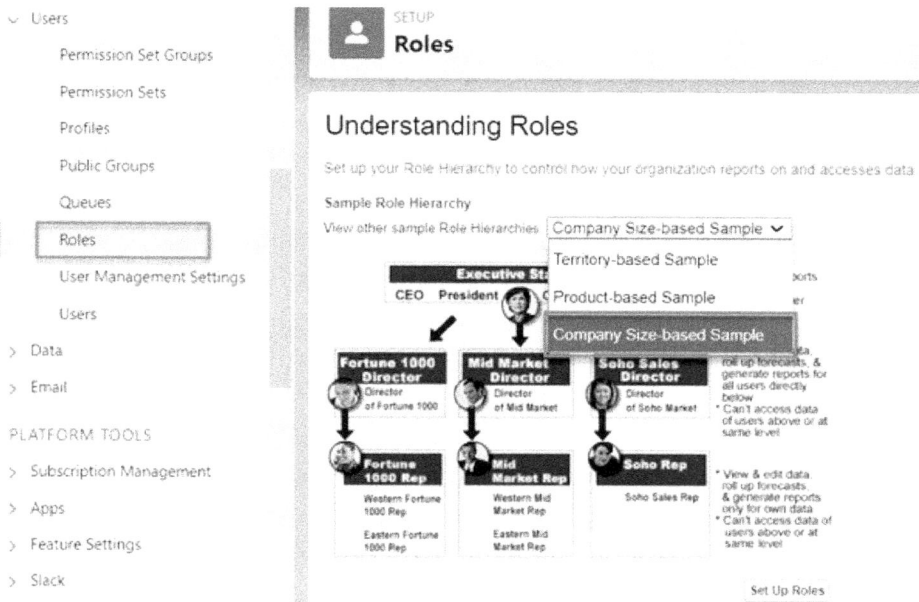

Figure 7.3: Role hierarchy in Salesforce

Press the **Setup Roles** button to see the role hierarchy in your Salesforce org, as shown in the following:

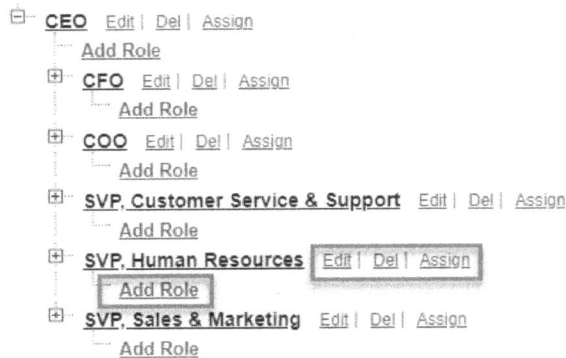

Figure 7.4: Changing the role hierarchy

On each node on the role hierarchy, there are the options to **Edit**, **Del**, **Assign** or **Add Role** to create a new one.

It is important to realize that role hierarchy is not the same as the structure of the organization. It is likely to be similar, but carefully consider if someone in a certain department should see information in a department or person beneath them in the hierarchy.

For example, a team might work on significant investments that are stored on the opportunity object. These contribute to the company's revenue, but people in the sales department should be prevented from seeing these records, even if the company considers investments as part of its sales pipeline.

Role hierarchy is enabled on all standard objects in Salesforce, but can be disabled on custom objects under **Sharing Settings**, which is shown above. If a user is not granted a role in their user profile, then they can only see records they own or those records on an object set to **Public Read Only**.

Considerations when assigning permissions

Although much of the security model is based on the illustration outlined in *Figure 7.1*, profiles can also give users permissions, which can directly impact security. In particular, the following permissions can be added to a permission set or a profile that have strong implications for overriding the security model. They overwrite the security model, but are often assigned as a *quick fix* for a user; however, they should be avoided.

View All Data/Modify All Data: These two permissions override the security model and should be treated with caution. Users with these permissions can **View All Data** or **Modify All Data**.

These are found by going to **Setup | Users** and then checking their profile, as shown in the following:

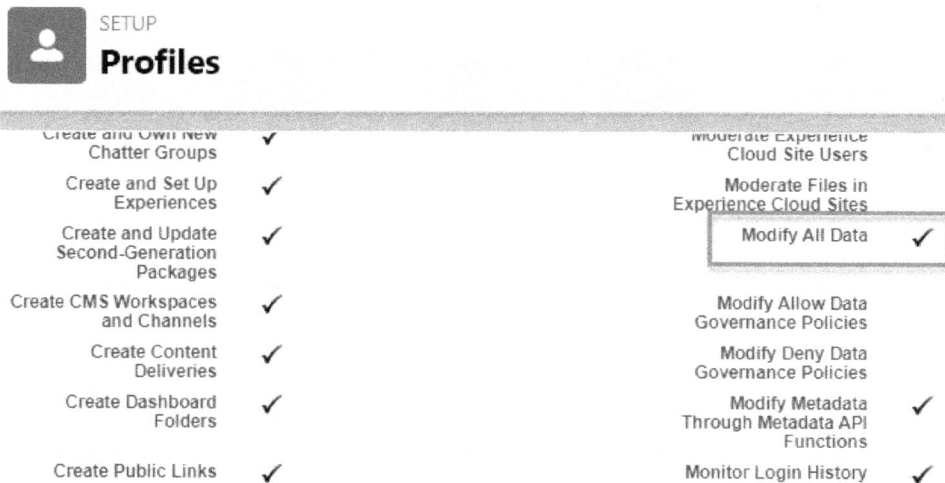

Figure 7.5: *Identifying Modify All Data permission on a profile*

In addition, these permissions can be added using permission sets. To find them, check the permission set and then view the assignments by going **to Setup | Permission Sets** and clicking on the **Manage Assignments**, as shown in the following figure:

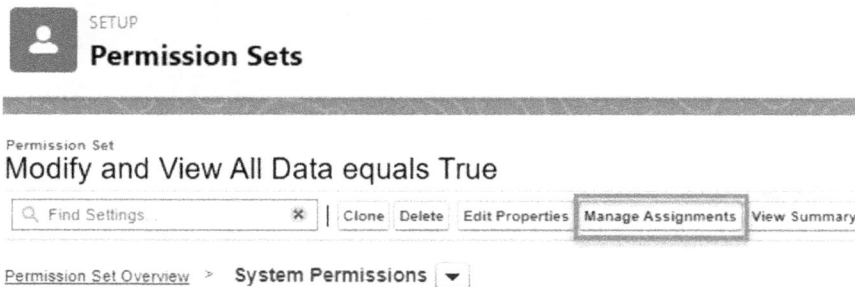

Figure 7.6: *Viewing permission set assignments*

Export Reports permission allows users to generate a report and then export it as either a CSV or Excel file.

Review whether the users should have this level of access to records or be able to export data from a report. If not, then disable them in the profile by unchecking the box next to the permission.

Creating public group

Before setting up a sharing rule in the next section, it is best to have a public group, which is one of the options to share with. Public groups are simply groups of users that can be used in various places around Salesforce, such as sharing rules, Chatter, queues, report and dashboard folders, and more.

To do this, follow these steps:

1. Go to **Setup** | **Public Groups** and press the **New** button as shown in the following figure:

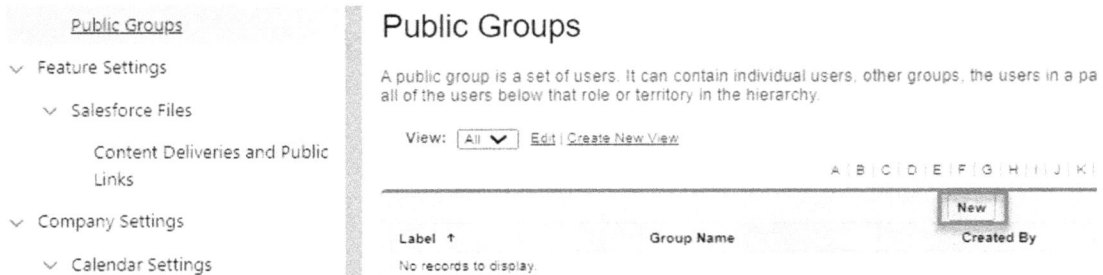

Figure 7.7: *Public Groups*

You then have the option of who you want to add to the public group, which can be other **Public Groups**, **Roles, and Internal Subordinates**, i.e., other users and those below in the role hierarchy, **Roles, Internal, and Portal Subordinates**, i.e., the Experience Cloud website; or just **Users**, as shown in the following figure:

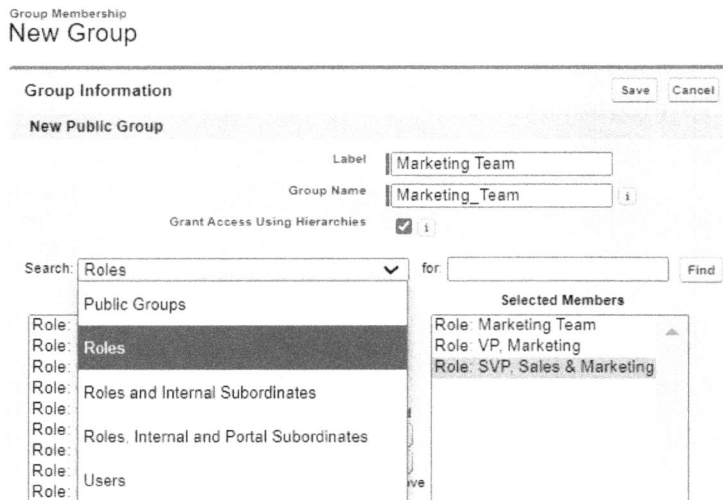

Figure 7.8: *Setting up groups*

2. Press **Save**.

Sharing rules

Sharing rules are the next level up in the security pyramid illustrated in *Figure 7.1*. They give exceptions to the OWDs outside the role hierarchy. They are found on the same page as the OWDs. Go to **Setup** | **Sharing Settings** and scroll to the very bottom of the page.

If you are in a new Salesforce Developer org, then you may not see any sharing rules here. However, it is common to find older Salesforce organizations with many sharing rules. It is worth comparing them since some can be consolidated or not assigned to any users or groups. Generally, keep the number of sharing rules to a minimum and only use them when the role hierarchy is not able to provide the correct level of access.

It is helpful to audit sharing rules periodically by mapping which rules are providing access and if they could be simplified or removed.

Creating sharing rule

There are two types of sharing rules:

- **Owner-based sharing rule**: If you are the owner, then you can share a record.
- **Criteria-based sharing rule**: If the rule matches a criterion, then the record is automatically shared.

To create a sharing rule, follow these steps: Go to **Setup | Sharing Settings**, scroll down to sharing rules, and press the **New** button next to the object you require.

In the following example, the **Account** object is used for creating a new sharing rule. Refer to the following figure:

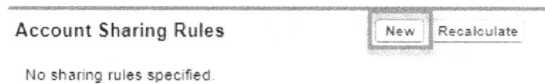

Figure 7.9: Setting up sharing rules

Complete the following as illustrated in the following figure, adding the public group created previously:

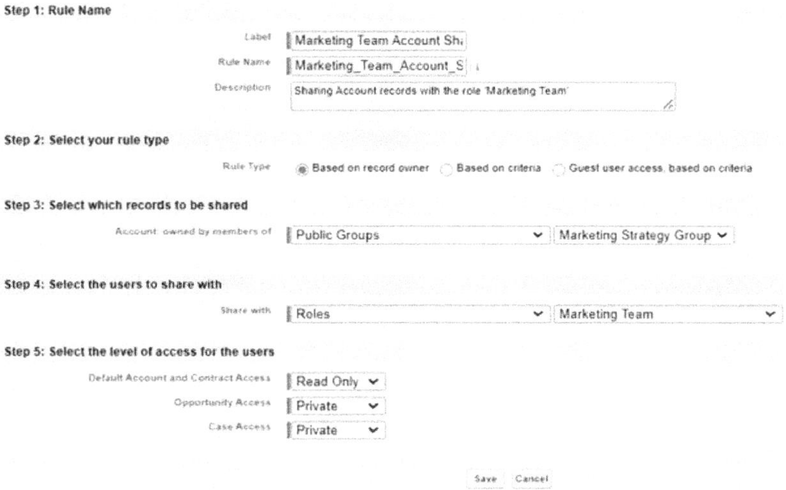

Figure 7.10: Sharing rule settings for a public group

In the preceding figure, we have the following:

- **Step 3**: This simply means share the record with the **Marketing Team** if the user is already a member of the public group.

- **Step 4**: Says that the new record should be shared with the public group.

- **Step 5**: Ask if the account shared should also display related objects, such as contacts, opportunities, and cases. Press **Save**.

The rule above simply shares an account record if the user is part of the **Marketing Strategy Group**; then it shares it with users who have the role **Marketing Team**. If members leave the group, then the account is no longer available to the **Marketing Team**. Salesforce automatically recalculates sharing rules when changes are made to groups, roles, sharing settings, or territories.

Note: **Once the Sharing Rule is saved, steps 3 and 4 are not editable.**

To test the sharing rule, **Login** as a user who is part of the public group, as shown in the following figure:

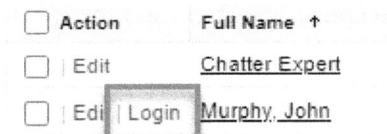

Figure 7.11: Testing the sharing rule

Go to the account records; even though the Account object is set to private, the logged in user can still see the account, but not the opportunities or cases, as per the settings, as shown in *Figure 7.12*:

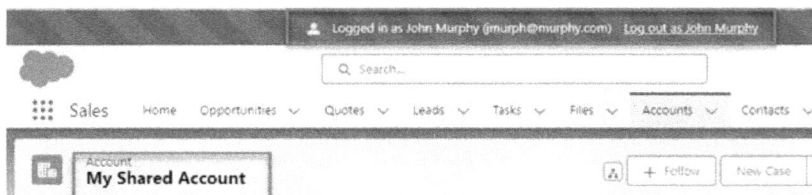

Figure 7.12: Logged in as a user to test the sharing rule

Criteria-based sharing rules

Criteria-based sharing rules are also very useful. Follow the steps above, but make the rule type **Based on criteria**, which means that certain field values can be added to the group (refer to the following figure):

Step 2: Select your rule type

Rule Type   ○ Based on record owner   ◉ Based on criteria   ○ Guest user access, based on criteria

Step 3: Select which records to be shared

Criteria	Field	Operator	Value
1	Billing Country ⌄	equals ⌄	UK
2	Number of Locations ⌄	greater than ⌄	5
3	--None-- ⌄	--None-- ⌄	
4	--None-- ⌄	--None-- ⌄	
5	--None-- ⌄	--None-- ⌄	

Add Row Remove Row

Clear Filter Logic
Filter Logic
1 OR 2

Figure 7.13: Criteria-based sharing settings

In the preceding figure, the sharing rule is applied if the **Billing Country** is the **UK** or the **Number of Locations** is **greater than 5**. The **Filter Logic** was changed from **AND** to **OR**. This could be for a company with a specific geographic focus or a company that may have many subsidiary companies, in which case the account record could be significant for the marketing team group.

Teams

Teams are similar to groups, but Salesforce has specific functionality in teams. There are three types of teams that can be used on the account: opportunity, case, and custom objects. They are designed to allow users to collaborate, but specific roles can be assigned to each team member.

Account teams are typically used to grant users access to account records and their child records, and they remain active as long as the account exists. This is useful for large accounts that may have subsidiary accounts. However, opportunity and case teams are generally short-term to manage collaboration between users until completion of the opportunity or case.

Setting up account teams

To initially setup account teams, you have to enable it first. To do this, go to **Setup | Account Teams** and press the **Enable Account Teams** as shown in the following figure:

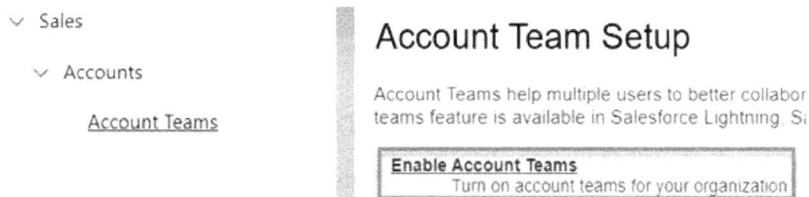

⌄ Sales

  ⌄ Accounts

    Account Teams

Account Team Setup

Account Teams help multiple users to better collabor
teams feature is available in Salesforce Lightning. S:

Enable Account Teams
Turn on account teams for your organization

Figure 7.14: Account Team Setup

Once enabled, you will also be asked for page layout selection, which controls which page layout has the option to use the account team.

For this example, select them all. You will then have options to add or replace team roles. View the default roles with options to rename them, reorder them, replace them, and other functionality.

If you visit an account record, you will notice that there is a related list for the account team with options to **Add Default Team** or **Add Team Members**.

Although the second option works, a default team requires you to add users through their profile settings.

To do this, go to your profile (i.e., the icon on the top right-hand corner, or the screen) and select **Advanced User Details**, as shown in the following figure:

Figure 7.15: Setting up account teams

If you are using the free Developer Edition account, then you will not have sufficient users available to form a working account team, but you can still add yourself.

The following figure shows adding the user to the account team:

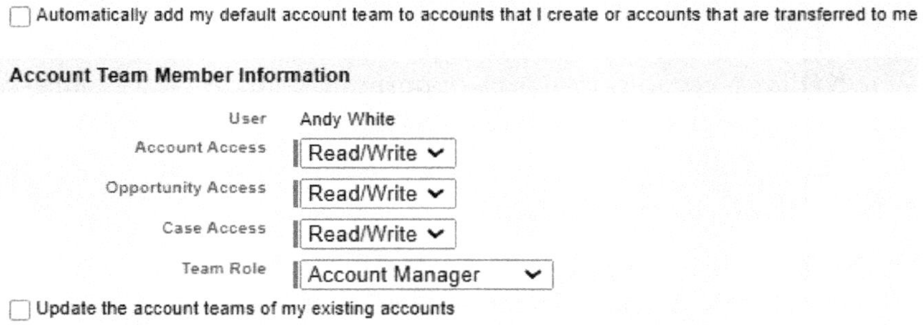

Figure 7.16: Adding a user to an account team

Mass Reassign Account Teams

A useful setting in Salesforce is the ability to **Mass Reassign Account Teams** (with similar functionality for opportunity teams), which allows you to add, remove, or reassign a team member to multiple accounts. To do this, go to **Setup | Mass Account Team Reassign**, as shown in the following figure:

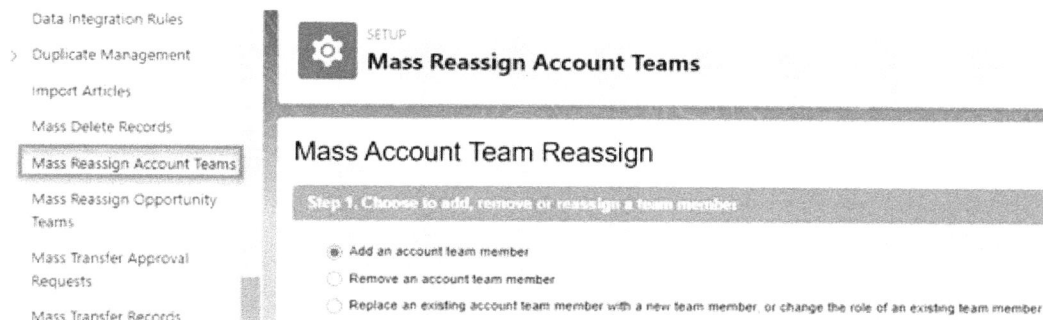

Figure 7.17: *Mass Account Team Reassign*

Select if you choose to add, remove, or reassign a team member, and filter for the various accounts to add the team member.

The final step requests you to select the user and assign them an account team role, as shown in the following figure:

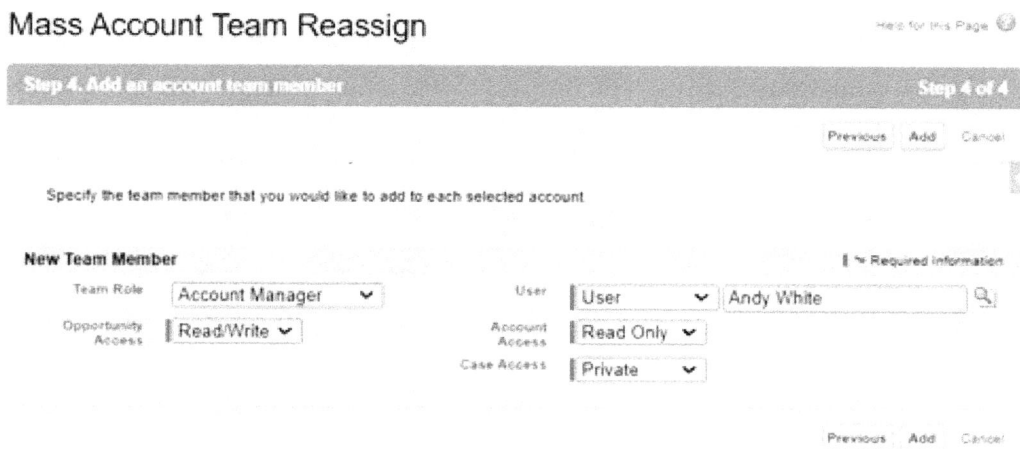

Figure 7.18: *Adding a user via Mass Account Team Reassign*

Setting up opportunity teams

Opportunity teams are similar to account teams, but the team exists for the duration of the opportunity. This is also a good time to consider using opportunity splits, which assign different ratios of commissions for the opportunity to different team members.

To setup opportunity teams, you first need to enable team selling by going to **Setup** | **Opportunity Team Settings**, as shown in the following figure:

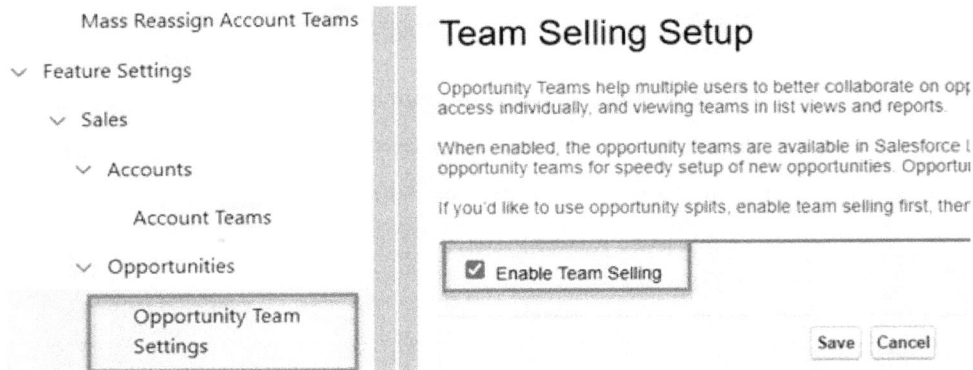

Figure 7.19: Setting up opportunity teams

Press **Save**, and then also add the opportunity teams related list to the various page layouts. In a Developer Edition org, there will be only four.

In the same way as account teams were setup, you will need to visit your user record and add users to the **Default Opportunity Team** as shown in the following figure:

Figure 7.20: Adding users to the Default Opportunity Team

Visit an opportunity record to see the opportunity team-related list. To create opportunity splits, first go to **Setup | Opportunity Split Settings** and enable it. There are two types of opportunity split:

- **Revenue split**: Where 100% of the commission is allocated to sales reps in the team.

- **Overlay split**: Is more flexible but allows additional contributors to get a percentage of the deal.

Manual sharing

Manual sharing allows users to grant access to a specific record and is done manually. They are useful when exceptions are needed that are not covered by features such as the role hierarchy or sharing rules. It is available if the OWDs for the object are set to private or read only. This will provide a **Share** button on the record where a user can select another user to own the record. The user can specify the level of access, such as **Read Only** or **Read/Write**, but sharing cannot be restrictive than the default OWD setting. Salesforce follows a most permissive wins model, which means access to records is granted, not revoked. Refer to the following figure:

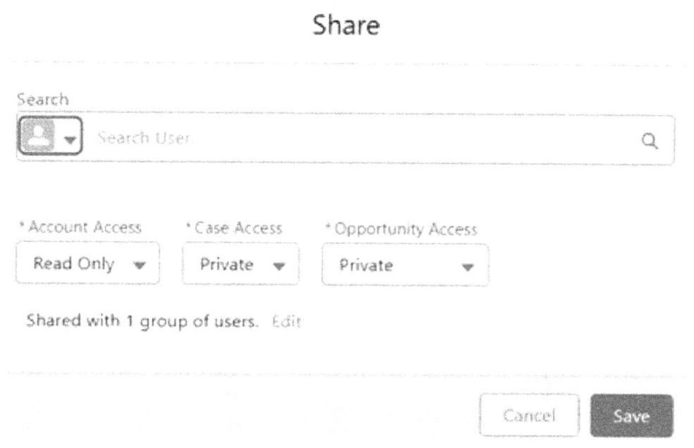

Figure 7.21: Manually sharing a record

Scoping rules

Scoping rules apply only in the Lightning UI but allow a filter to be applied to users or groups so that only records that match the criteria are shown. This is useful for users or groups that are only concerned with a certain subset of larger data records. To set scoping rules, go to **Setup | Object Manager** and select the object.

The following example creates a new scoping rule on the **Account** object:

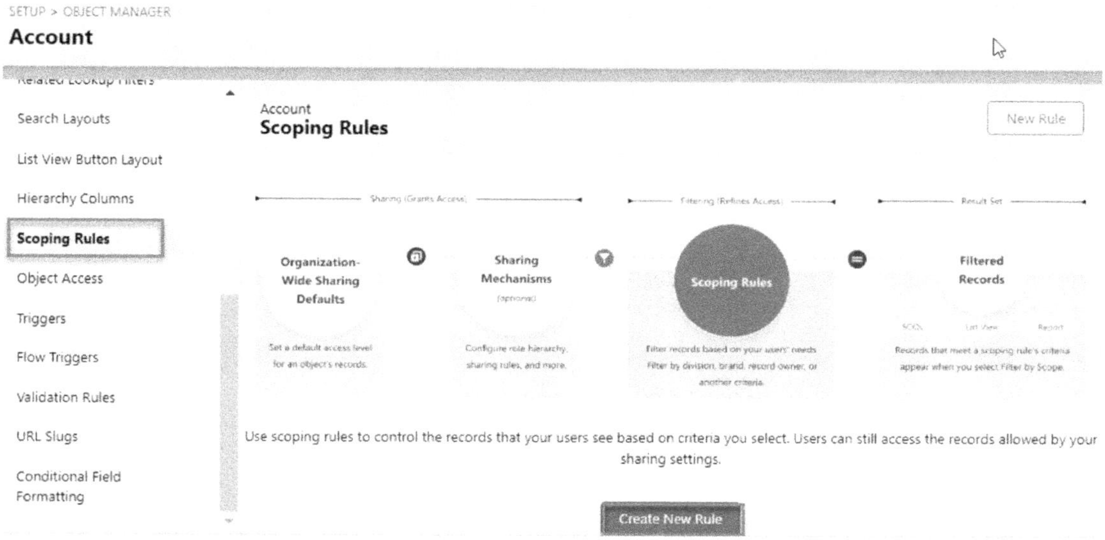

Figure 7.22: Setting up scoping rules

The scoping rule has user-based criteria set, so if the user's department is finance, then only accounts with an industry type of finance or banking are shown.

To apply the scoping rule, ensure that your department is set to finance on your user record and then apply the scoping rule to the list view of all accounts as shown in the following figure:

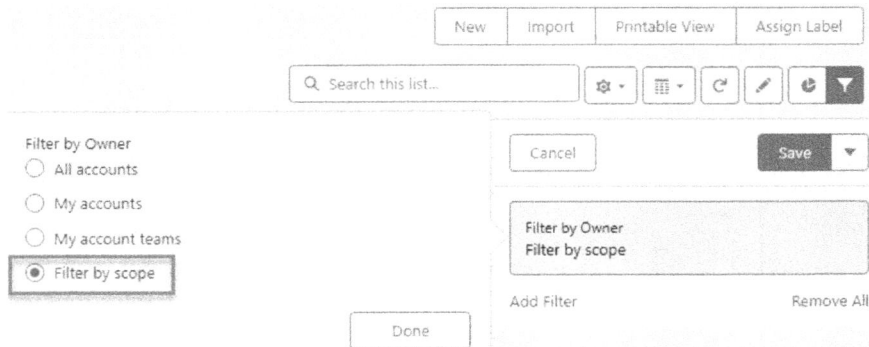

Figure 7.23: Applying scoping rules to accounts

Salesforce also offers **Restriction Rules**, which prevent users from accessing records they should not. They have various limits on which objects they can use and how many rules can be used, which will depend on your edition of Salesforce. There is a good article on *Salesforce Ben* found at: **https://www.salesforceben.com/salesforce-restriction-rules/**. If you navigate to **Setup | Object Manager** and select a custom object or those outlined in the article link above, then you will see an illustration of how **Restriction Rules** work, which is shown in the following figure:

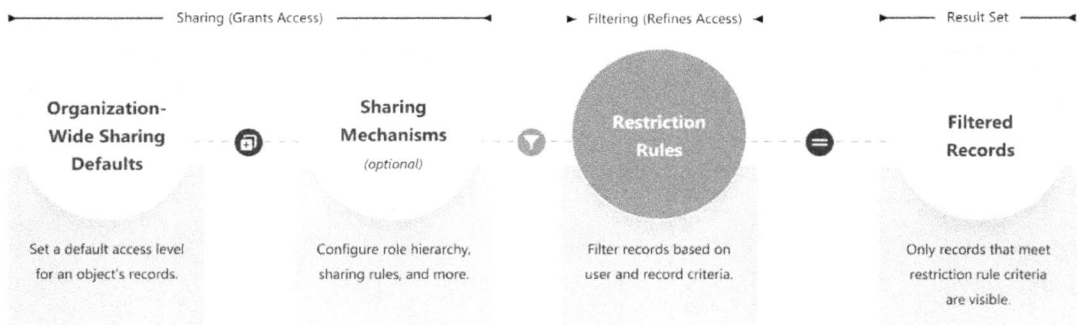

Figure 7.24: Restriction Rules illustration

Data security

Data is the lifeblood of many businesses. It is important that the business is a responsible steward of their data, not only for the business benefit but also for the records of individuals' information stored in Salesforce. Data security in Salesforce is crucial because it ensures the confidentiality, integrity, and availability of sensitive business and customer information. Some of the key reasons why data security is important are:

- **Ensuring customer trust**: Salesforce stores personal and financial customer data. Data breaches can damage a company's reputation and undermine customer trust.

- **Regulatory compliance**: Many businesses must follow regulations like the *General Data Protection Regulation (GDPR)*, the *Health Insurance Portability and Accountability Act (HIPAA), or the California Consumer Privacy Act (CCPA)*. Failure to comply with this legislation can incur legal penalties.

- **Preventing data leaks**: Strong security controls protect against unauthorized access, accidental data loss, or intentional data theft from both users and customers, such as via Experience Cloud.

- **Ensuring appropriate access controls**: Using the security controls outlined in this book, ensure that users only access the data they need.

- **API security**: Many companies integrate Salesforce with other systems. Securing these connections is vital to preventing data breaches.

The best approach is to ensure data cannot leave Salesforce unless required. Admittedly, it is hard to stop users from taking a photo of their laptop screen or dragging a mouse over a report and dishonestly taking the data. Outside the security model, there are a number of ways to make this as hard as possible.

The tightest Salesforce can go is platform encryption using Salesforce Shield. Another feature is utilizing the individual object to enforce legislative data security. Other methods can include field history tracking, where a field will store historical data for previous values and who changed them. These are discussed in the following sections.

Another best practice is to avoid using Salesforce for sending and receiving emails, as, by definition, they are handled outside of Salesforce. Although it is fine to send email notifications, they should not contain any personal or sensitive data. A better solution is to use Experience Cloud to provide updates on cases or orders and customer details. This way, it can be controlled in a more professional and secure manner.

Sensitive data and individual object

In many cases, a company will have to be very careful about the data stored in Salesforce. There are numerous legislations that are both relevant to the country and the type of industry. For example, the *US* has HIPAA for health care, whilst many *European* countries require GDPR to be implemented so that information about individuals is not used outside the intended purpose.

However, it is important to realize that legislation also applies to companies outside the country where this data is handled. Other types of legislation include payment security, welfare or disabilities, **personally identifiable information** (**PII**), etc.

For this reason, Salesforce comes with various features so that fields that contain sensitive data are separated out. Salesforce data classification allows admins to highlight key fields that contain sensitive data.

When you access any record in Salesforce and then click the **Edit** link, you will find data classification options that should be utilized. For example, a contact with a first name, last name, and email address should be highlighted as fields associated with GDPR legislation, as shown in the following figure:

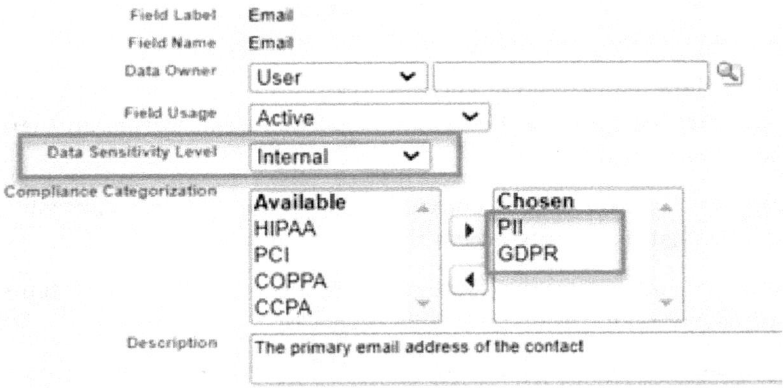

Figure 7.25: Salesforce data classification field-level settings

Salesforce includes the individual object, which separates data privacy records. The individual object is useful for storing an individual's contact preferences and contains fields used in both the account and contact objects, as well as being linked to numerous objects used for consent management. The object is not populated by default, but it is related to the following:

- **Consent**: For contact type, for example, when a new lead comes in
- **Subscription**: Maintaining the channel and frequency of communications
- **Authorization**: Such as text to inform the customer of the type of content or further terms and conditions

For example, if a contact exists as both a contact and a lead, then the individual object gives a central record to give a single view of the customer.

Field history tracking

Salesforce can track the history of up to 20 fields per object. This means that the field can have the old and new values, as well as who changed it and when the change occurred.

To do this, follow these steps:

1. First, check that **Field History Tracking** is enabled by going to **Setup | Field History Tracking** and selecting the object; in this example, the **Contact** object is selected.

2. Select the **Enable Contact History** checkbox and select the fields you wish to track, as shown in the following figure:

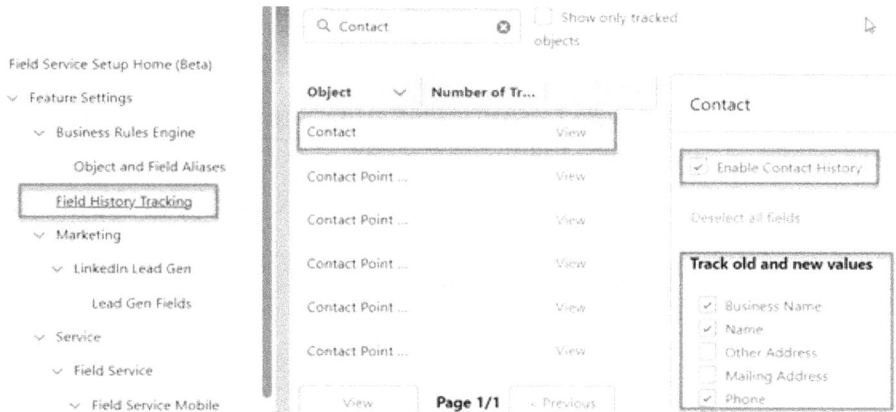
Figure 7.26: Enabling Field History Tracking on the Contact object

3. Once selected, press **Save**.

4. Finally, add the field history-related list to the page layout either on the classic page layout editor or on the Lightning record page. It is generally easier to do this in the Classic page layout editor as shown in the following figure, whilst you can add related lists directly onto a Lightning record page using either the **Dynamic Related List–Single** component, which allows you to add filters and customize the fields displayed:

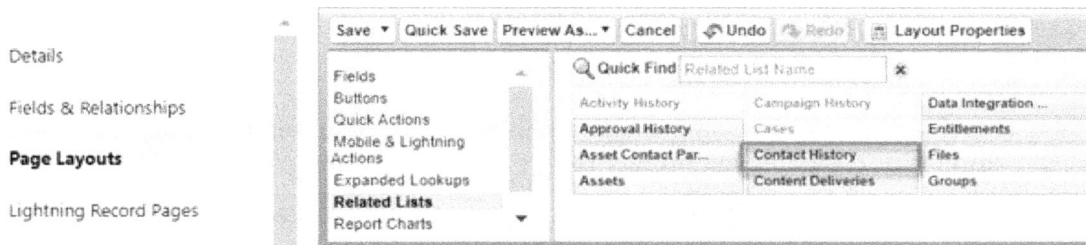
Figure 7.27: Adding field history tracking to the contact page layout

5. In the preceding example, return to a contact record and change the **Account Name** and **Email** fields to a different value and press **Save**.

6. The record now has a related list for the old and new values with information about who changed them and when, as shown in the following figure:

Contact History (2)

Date	Field	User	Original Value	New Value
04/01/2025, 00:33	Account Name	Andy White	United Oil & Gas Co...	Burlington Textiles ...
04/01/2025, 00:33	Email	Andy White	spavlova@uog.com	spavlova@acme.com

Figure 7.28: Displaying the field history to the user

External users

The first part of this chapter started with the OWDs, which give the core security settings per object. Revisit the page by going to **Setup | Sharing Settings**, and there is a column for **Default External Access** (refer to the following figure):

Default Sharing Settings

Organization-Wide Defaults   Edit   Organization-Wide Defaults Help ?

Object	Default Internal Access	Default External Access	Grant Access Using Hierarchies
Lead	Public Read/Write/Transfer	Private	✓
Account and Contract	Public Read/Write	Private	✓
Contact	Controlled by Parent	Controlled by Parent	✓
Order	Controlled by Parent	Controlled by Parent	✓
Asset	Controlled by Parent	Controlled by Parent	✓
Opportunity	Public Read/Write	Private	✓

Figure 7.29: External access settings

External access is for users of Experience Cloud. Experience Cloud is essentially a website or portal that you can build using Salesforce, which can be a standalone website or embedded into an existing, larger website if needed. Experience Cloud is introduced in *Chapter 10, Various Salesforce Features*.

Although the basic principles are the same as for internal access, there are some considerations for granting external access to Salesforce, such as:

- External access cannot be more open than internal users

- There are various licensing models depending on requirements such as customer community, customer community plus, partner community, and more

For external access, there are two types of users: authenticated and unauthenticated. Authenticated users login to the site using one of the licenses above, whereas unauthenticated users are often referred to as **guest users** and have limited public access to features in Experience Cloud.

Best practice would always be to make external access for objects set to private unless the object contains data, which would pose no harm in being publicly available. This is because it is possible for external users to manipulate the URL to gain access to records that they should not have access to, as internal users may store information on an object without knowing it is publicly available.

Data encryption

Salesforce has an additional layer of protection for data to encrypt it. The Shield is an additional license feature, but it is useful for ensuring data is encrypted in Salesforce, making it hard to export or use outside of Salesforce.

The simplest way to think of Shield is like laptop encryption. You may have experienced a laptop or Mac that requires an additional login, such as BitLocker for a Windows laptop or FileVault for a Mac. Once you have logged on, the laptop behaves exactly the same, but if someone tries to retrieve data from the hard drive, then it would be meaningless.

When Salesforce has Shield enabled, the data is encrypted at the platform level, meaning it cannot be accessed maliciously. An example of this is using Shield for securing data used in external systems. By encrypting the data, it cannot be used by the external system since it is tokenized, meaning that a key is generated by Salesforce and used by the hosting service to interpret the data before being encrypted again and returned to Salesforce, which can then unencrypt it.

However, for this to work, you must first activate Shield, enable it on the objects and fields you wish to encrypt, and if the data is to be used by an external system, then the encryption key must be provided to that system.

Setting up Shield

The steps to setup Shield are as follows:

1. Create a permission set with **Manage Encryption Key** and **Customize Application**, and assign the permission set to yourself.

2. To do this, go to **Setup | Permission Sets** and press **New**. Give it a name such as **Shield Encryption**, assign a Salesforce license, and press **Save**.

3. Scroll down the following screen to **System Permissions**, add the **Manage Encryption Keys** permission, **Customize Application**, and press **Save**.

4. If asked for confirmation, accept the changes.

5. This should return you to the permission set page. Press the **Manage Assignments** button at the top of the screen.

6. Press the **Add Assignment** button.

7. Select yourself as the user and press **Next**, then **Assign**.

Generate a tenant secret, which is a text file that is needed to encrypt the data. For this example, it is simply to activate the Shield, but in a real-life scenario, the tenant's secret can be used by external systems to decrypt the data.

To do this, follow these steps:

1. Go to **Setup | Platform Encryption | Key Management**.

2. Select **Generate Tenant Secret** from the options under the **Fields and Files (Probabilistic)** tab.

3. Press **Export** to keep a local copy of the key. This will be a small text file that you would normally keep in a very safe place.

Using Shield example

Now that Shield is setup, it can be applied to fields on objects of your choice. For example, if certain fields on the Contact object were considered to be confidential, then they should be encrypted using the following steps:

1. Go to **Setup | Platform Encryption | Encryption Settings**.

    Scroll down to the **Advanced Encryption Settings** section. On the **Encrypt Standard Fields** row, press the **Select Fields** button as in the following figure:

Figure 7.30: Adding platform encryption

2. Return to this screen after completing the next steps and select the **Encrypt Files and Attachments** if you wish to encrypt these, too.

    On the new screen, press **Edit** and select the fields to encrypt. Choose various ones, but in the example, the following were selected:

    a. **Account**: Description

    b. **Contact**: Phone, mobile, email, description

3. Press **Save**.

4. You should get an email confirming if the encryption of the fields has been successful.

Note: **Shield encryption only works on records created or updated after encryption has been enabled. It would not apply to existing records in Salesforce.**

Monitoring and auditing

Salesforce offers various monitoring and auditing tools to help ensure Salesforce and users are behaving as expected. It is worth noting that the word *event* can mean many different things to business users, Salesforce users, and Salesforce developers. As such, this book will cover the basics of monitoring and auditing Salesforce events.

Setup Audit Trail

All configurations done in Salesforce by users such as system admins, developers, and users with certain rights are recorded in the Audit Trail. To view this, follow these steps:

1. Go to **Setup | View Setup Audit Trail**.

2. If you are doing this in your Salesforce development environment, then you will see a list of everything you have done so far, as shown in the following figure:

View Setup Audit Trail

The last 20 entries for your organization are listed below. You can download your organization's setup audit trail for the last six months (Excel .csv file).

View Setup Audit Trail

Date	User	Source Namespace Prefix	Action	Section
05/01/2025, 23:12:40 GMT	andy.white@bpb.com		Changed Account page layout Account Layout	Customize Accounts
05/01/2025, 23:12:40 GMT	andy.white@bpb.com		Changed Account page layout Account (Support) Layout	Customize Accounts
05/01/2025, 23:12:40 GMT	andy.white@bpb.com		Changed Account page layout Account (Sales) Layout	Customize Accounts
05/01/2025, 23:12:40 GMT	andy.white@bpb.com		Changed Account page layout Account (Marketing) Layout	Customize Accounts

Figure 7.31: Setup Audit Trail

The Audit Trail only shows the action that was done in a particular area of Salesforce, but does not provide very detailed information. It will include other practical details such as:

- Details on which object the change occurred

- Change of a formula field details flows, or automations

- Changes to user details

- Changes to any configuration in setup

The Audit Trail covers a six-month period, so it should be exported within this time if a company wishes to keep a strict record of what has been done in their Salesforce org.

Event Monitoring

In this context, an event is concerned with events occurring on the Lightning platform. This is separate from the Setup Audit Trail in the previous section. To view this, go to **Setup | Security | Event Monitoring | Event Monitoring Settings** and enable **Generate event log files**, as shown in the following figure:

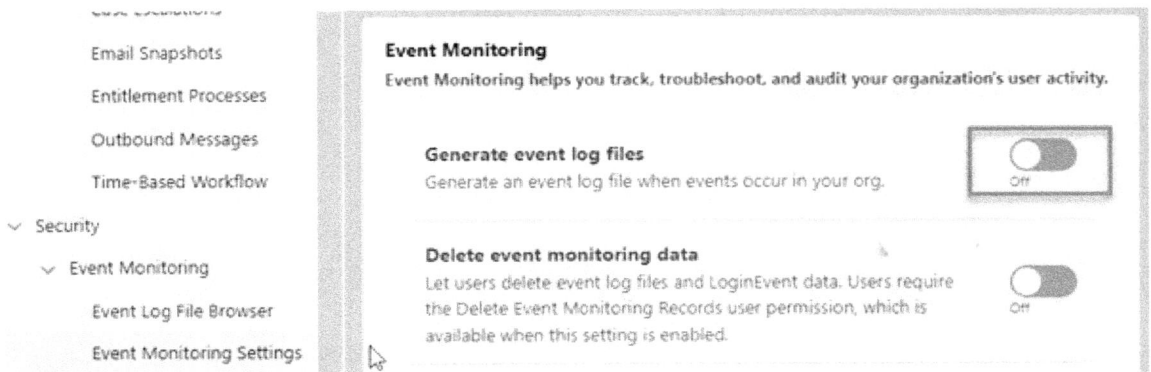

Figure 7.32: Setting up Event Monitoring

Event logs are generated hourly, so you will have to wait until they are generated. Once available, you can view the event logs as shown in the following figure:

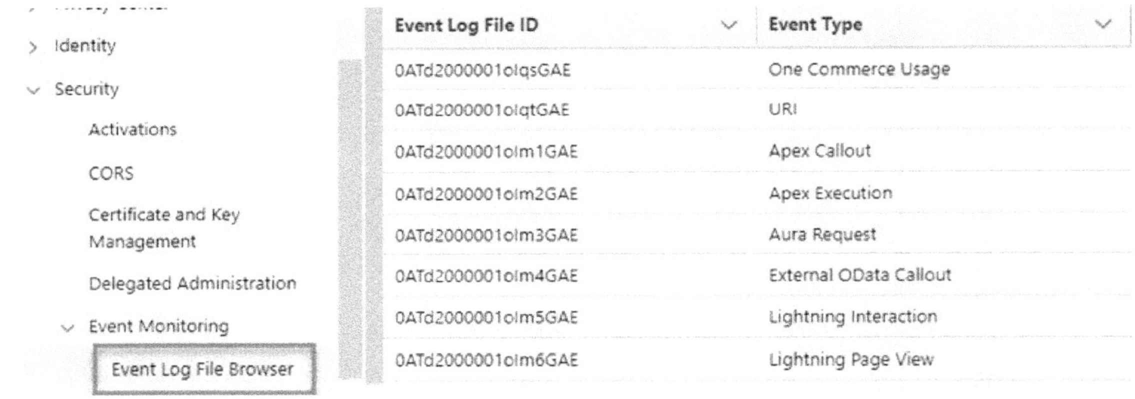

Figure 7.33: Viewing event log files

To get more details on the event log, select the down arrow at the end of each row, which will generate a small CSV file with further details.

Login history

To view a record of all logins performed by users, including other types of logins, such as those via API or Outlook integration. It also includes information about what was used to login, such as a mobile device or browser information. This can be useful for seeing how users access Salesforce.

To view the **Login History**, go to **Setup | Identity | Login History**, as shown in the following figure:

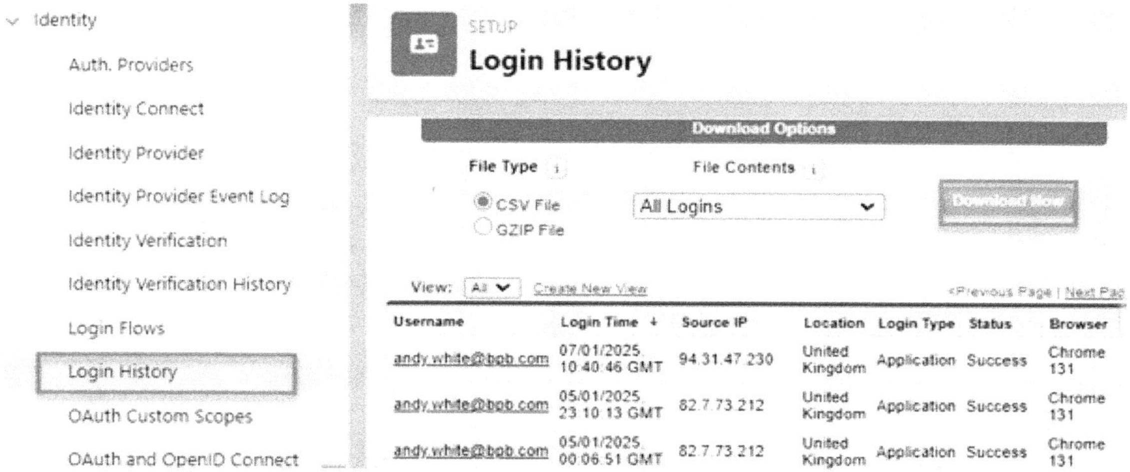

Figure 7.34: Viewing users Login History

AppExchange

For specific requirements, it is worth starting with the Salesforce AppExchange and researching available tools which are available. For example, entering Event Monitoring into the AppExchange provides various apps available to view, with an example, as shown in the following figure:

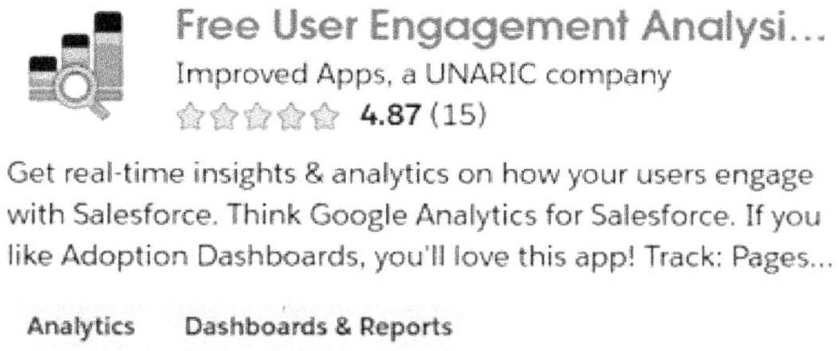

Figure 7.35: Example of monitoring apps from the AppExchange

The app you select will depend on your requirements. However, always try out an app in a sandbox, or if you are in your Salesforce Developer org, you can delete the app afterward by going to **Setup | Installed Packages** and selecting the **Uninstall** link next to the app that has been installed.

Advanced monitoring

There is a very useful monitoring tool available through GitHub, found at: **https://github.com/seamusocionnaigh/eventmonitoringplus**

However, this implementation is outside the scope of this book, unless you spend some time on *Chapter 9, Various Salesforce Tools*, which provides advanced monitoring for system performance, errors, components, and more. Refer to the following figure:

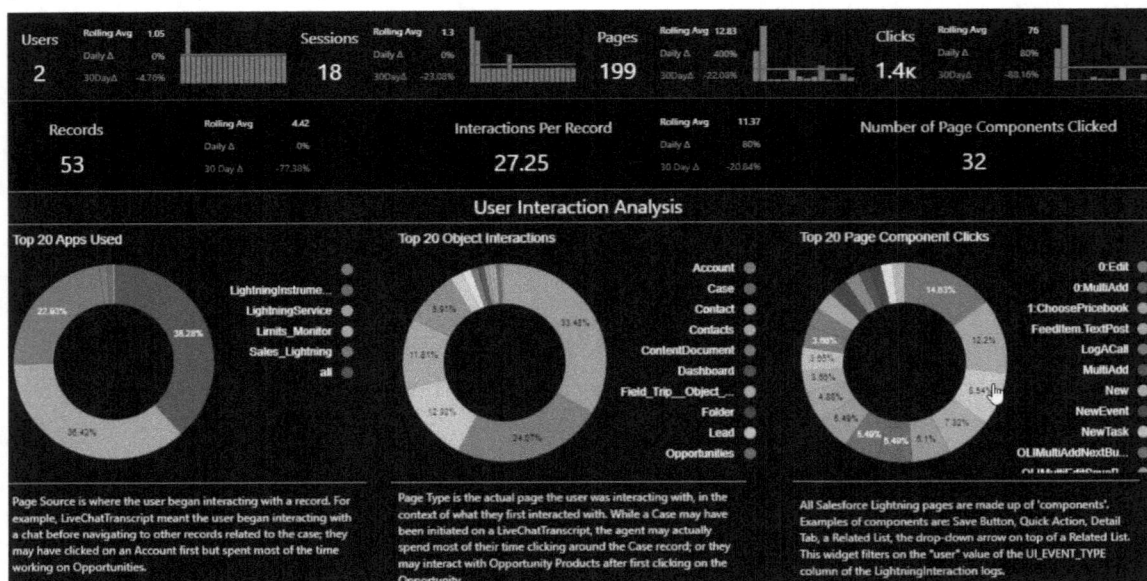

Figure 7.36: Sample dashboard of advanced monitoring tools

Advanced security configurations

Outside of setting objects to private and using the security model, you have also seen how to track field history and implement Salesforce Shield. You have also seen how to use various monitoring tools for different types of events in Salesforce.

Other features include controlling how users login to Salesforce in the first place. So far, we have only used a login and a password, which is the lowest level of security. Password policies can be controlled by going to **Setup | Password Policies**. This gives the following options for:

- How long before the password needs to be reset?

- Whether historic passwords are allowed

- The length and complexity of the password

- How many attempts are permitted, and the lockout period when the number of attempts has been exceeded?

These settings apply to all users of the org, so they need careful consideration. Typical values are shown in the following figure:

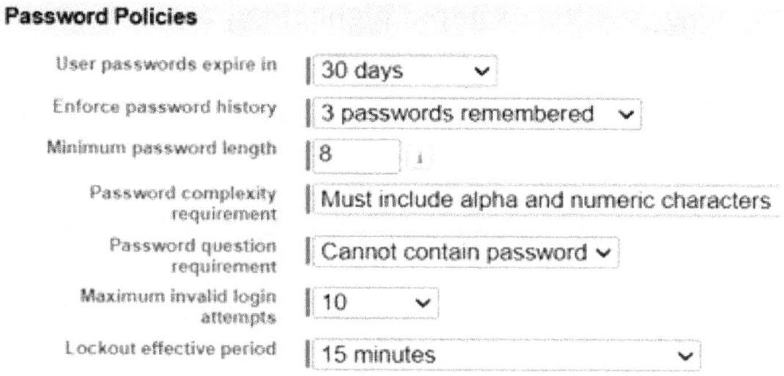

Password Policies

User passwords expire in	30 days ⌄
Enforce password history	3 passwords remembered ⌄
Minimum password length	8 ℹ
Password complexity requirement	Must include alpha and numeric characters
Password question requirement	Cannot contain password ⌄
Maximum invalid login attempts	10 ⌄
Lockout effective period	15 minutes ⌄

Figure 7.37: Setting up password policies

Multi-factor authentication

Multi-factor authentication (**MFA**) builds on **two-factor authentication** (**2FA**), which is outlined here:

- 2FA is a combination of something you know, such as your username and password, and something you have, such as a mobile phone.

- MFA builds on 2FA but may include visible steps such as biometrics or invisible steps such as location or change of device.

Enabling two-factor authentication in Salesforce

You may have noticed that Salesforce gives you the option to authenticate using your mobile phone as standard when you first register for a Developer Edition account. You may have chosen to ignore this option, and it no longer appears. However, as a system admin, you can enforce this by going to **Setup | Identity | Identity Verification** and choosing one of the options shown in the following figure:

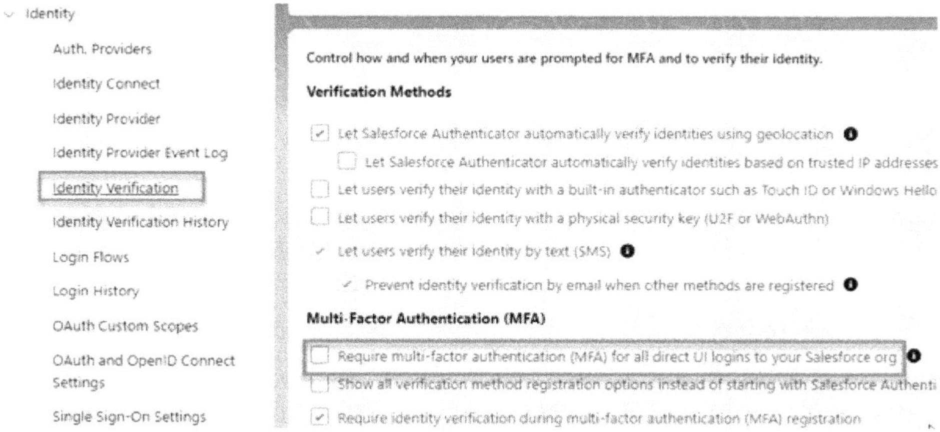

⌄ Identity

Auth. Providers

Identity Connect

Identity Provider

Identity Provider Event Log

Identity Verification

Identity Verification History

Login Flows

Login History

OAuth Custom Scopes

OAuth and OpenID Connect Settings

Single Sign-On Settings

Control how and when your users are prompted for MFA and to verify their identity.

Verification Methods

☑ Let Salesforce Authenticator automatically verify identities using geolocation ❶

☐ Let Salesforce Authenticator automatically verify identities based on trusted IP addresses

☐ Let users verify their identity with a built-in authenticator such as Touch ID or Windows Hello

☐ Let users verify their identity with a physical security key (U2F or WebAuthn)

✓ Let users verify their identity by text (SMS) ❶

✓ Prevent identity verification by email when other methods are registered ❶

Multi-Factor Authentication (MFA)

☐ Require multi-factor authentication (MFA) for all direct UI logins to your Salesforce org ❶

☐ Show all verification method registration options instead of starting with Salesforce Authenti

☑ Require identity verification during multi-factor authentication (MFA) registration

Figure 7.38: Enabling MFA in Salesforce

There are various options, but the example highlighted above requires the user to install *Salesforce Authenticator* from *Google Play* or the *Mac App Store*. If you select this option, then next time you login, you will see the following:

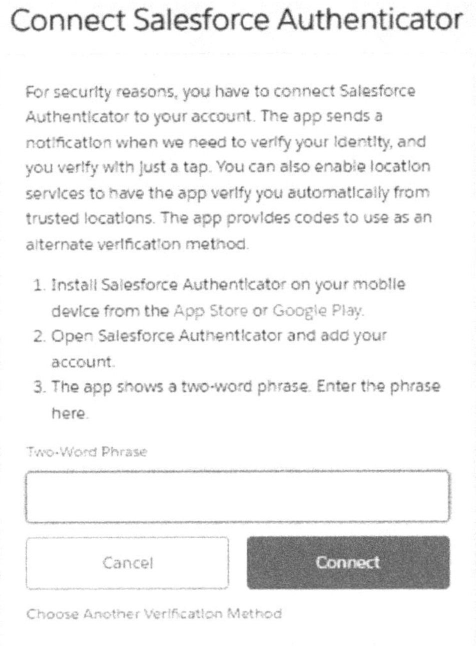

Connect Salesforce Authenticator

For security reasons, you have to connect Salesforce Authenticator to your account. The app sends a notification when we need to verify your identity, and you verify with just a tap. You can also enable location services to have the app verify you automatically from trusted locations. The app provides codes to use as an alternate verification method.

1. Install Salesforce Authenticator on your mobile device from the App Store or Google Play.
2. Open Salesforce Authenticator and add your account.
3. The app shows a two-word phrase. Enter the phrase here.

Two-Word Phrase

Cancel Connect

Choose Another Verification Method

Figure 7.39: Salesforce Authenticator app used in conjunction with your phone

Enabling MFA in Salesforce

MFA depends on the requirements of the business. As such, it is typically built upon 2FA but has an additional layer of security such as device type, location, biometrics, login flow, and social login via *Google*, *Facebook*, and more. As such, a detailed example is outside the scope of this book; however, a common method is **single sign-on** (**SSO**), as outlined in the upcoming sections.

Single sign-on

SSO is used extensively in most corporate Salesforce instances. Additional security can be added using MFA, for example, when a user first accesses a Salesforce page, and the Salesforce Authenticator app will provide an additional level of verification.

There are a few different types of SSO; the most common are described in the following:

- **Enterprise SSO**: Based on the fact that you are already logged into your laptop, authentication is provided against your company's Active Directory, which is a list of employees, their details, and the systems to which they have access.

- **Federation ID**: Access is provided using SAML 2.0 to authenticate against existing company systems.

- **Social SSO**: Based on social media accounts and other sources, authentication is performed via providers such as Okta to authenticate you into Salesforce.

Typically, SSO works in the following way (refer to the following figure):

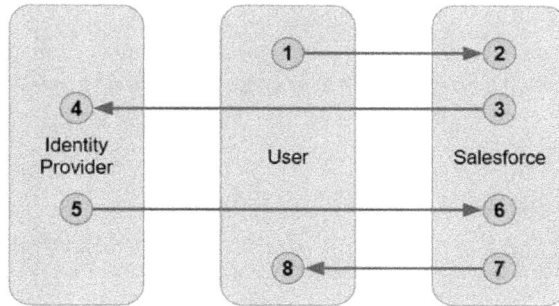

Figure 7.40: SSO authentication overview

In the preceding example:

1. The user tries to access Salesforce.
2. Salesforce is configured to know the identity provider, such as Azure Active Directory, Google, etc.
3. Salesforce generates an SAML 2.0 message to send to the identity provider.
4. The identity provider verifies that the message is correct.
5. A SAML 2.0 response is generated and sent to Salesforce.
6. Salesforce verifies the SAML 2.0 response.
7. Salesforce completes the user's sign-in.
8. The user has access to Salesforce.

Setting up SSO involves working with the identity provider, such as the company's Active Directory team, Google, or Okta. If you are using this book with the stand-alone Developer Edition, then it is not possible to demonstrate. However, to be aware of the settings, go to: **Setup | Single Sign-On Settings** and press **New**. You will see various settings that are used by Salesforce to manage the flow outlined above.

Best practices for security

The best practice depends on avoiding the worst-case scenario. Even if you have an open-sharing model, a business should consider the consequences of what would happen if the data were to be made publicly available.

Best practice is to observe the golden rule for security: is there any person who should never see a particular record? If the answer is *yes*, then you need to set the object to private and then open up the access and visibility using the methods outlined in this chapter. As with everything in Salesforce, the best practice is to build the solution out in a sandbox and thoroughly test it before implementing it in the live environment.

Conclusion

In this chapter, the Salesforce security model is explained, along with practical examples of its implementation. Security can be considered on a data or user level, which means data must be secure as well as only available to users who genuinely need access to it.

Security in Salesforce is built using OWDs to control user access to an object, roles that provide access based on the role hierarchy, and sharing rules and groups that organize users for sharing rules. Permission sets should be used with caution, and sets like View All Data, Modify All Data, and Export Reports should be avoided as they can override security settings and allow users to export large amounts of data.

Salesforce offers several tools to enhance user access security, including MFA, Shield encryption, and more. An administrator should be aware of the benefits these can bring to a company and ensure that the company is compliant with data regulations regarding the data it stores or uses.

Multiple choice questions

1. **If an object security model is 'Controlled by Parent' then: (choose 2)**
    a. The parent is set to private, meaning all related objects are also set to private
    b. The child object inherits the same security settings as the parent
    c. The child object cannot be seen by users lower in the role hierarchy
    d. There is a master-detail relationship between the parent and child object

2. **Page layout is controlled by which two Salesforce features:**
    a. Permission sets and profiles
    b. Users and profiles
    c. Roles and profiles
    d. Roles and permission sets

3. **Three permissions which should be treated with caution are:**
    a. Summarize All Data, Export All Data, View All Data
    b. View All Data, Modify All Data, Delete All Data

    c.   Export Reports, View All Data, Export All Data

    d.   View All Data, Modify All Data, Export Reports

4. **Criteria-based sharing rules can be based on which two options?**

    a.   Based on the record owner

    b.   Based on profile

    c.   Based on role

    d.   Based on criteria using AND or OR logic

5. **Field history tracking stores which values?**

    a.   The new value, previous value, and when it was changed

    b.   The new value, the previous value, when it was changed, and who changed it

    c.   The new value, the date it was changed, and who changed it

    d.   The old value, the date it was changed, who changed it, and the reason why

6. **When you export a report from Salesforce with Shield enabled, you will not see the data in the report. Is it true or false:**

    a.   True

    b.   False

7. **External users are:**

    a.   Users who do not belong to your company

    b.   Users who work remotely

    c.   Users gaining access via Experience Cloud

    d.   Users who are not using Salesforce

8. **Setup Audit Trail is useful for:**

    a.   Seeing configuration changes in Salesforce

    b.   Measuring compliance with regulations about the data in Salesforce

    c.   Ensuring that the configurations are done correctly

    d.   Auditing data in Salesforce

9. **The golden rule for security: Is there any person who should never see a particular record? Is it true or false:**

    a.   True

    b.   False

10. **MFA can use the following methods to provide access to Salesforce. (choose any three)**

    a. Username, password, biometrics

    b. Social account login details, government ID, employment status

    c. Active Directory, location, device type, mobile phone number

    d. Authentication apps such as Salesforce Authenticator

    e. Username, security token, laptop ID

Answers

1	**b, d**
2	**c**
3	**d**
4	**a, d**
5	**b**
6	**b**
7	**c**
8	**a**
9	**a**
10	**a, c, d**

Join our Discord space

Join our Discord workspace for latest updates, offers, tech happenings around the world, new releases, and sessions with the authors:

https://discord.bpbonline.com

CHAPTER 8
Reports, Dashboards, and Basic Tableau

Introduction

Reports in Salesforce enable users to view data across different objects easily, summarizing the information in a clear and easy-to-understand format. Reports are often requested for Salesforce Administrators to build, so a good working knowledge is useful daily.

Reports are also the basis of building dashboards, which are graphical summaries of the report. Dashboards are always based on a report, so you will first need to know how to build reports before you can build dashboards.

There is a golden rule for reports and dashboards: If the data underlying the report or dashboard is of poor quality, then the report or dashboard will be inaccurate and can lead to poor decision-making. This is one of the reasons that the ongoing role of an administrator is to ensure that the data in Salesforce is accurate and reliable. Data quality is covered in *Chapter 9, Various Salesforce Tools*.

You can build many types of charts on a report, such as funnel, scatter, donut, and more. The basic requirement of building most of the dashboard charts is that the underlying report is grouped by a field. This means that a specific field should be chosen as the basis for the report or dashboard. These are typically fields such as country, industry, opportunity stage, or a field that covers a much larger subset of data.

You can also add a dashboard of simple tabular data based on a report if the report is not grouped.

Structure

This chapter covers the following topics:

- Introduction to Salesforce reports

- Creating summary and matrix reports

- Dashboards

- Introduction to Tableau

Objectives

By the end of this chapter, readers will be able to ensure they have the necessary permissions to create reports and dashboards and understand the four main report types, their differences, and uses. Additionally, they will learn to customize reports to meet different business requirements, optimize report performance, and create custom report types if Salesforce does not provide a report that is required.

Introduction to Salesforce reports

Having said that, an administrator is often requested to build a report; any user can create their own reports if they have the correct permissions. The permission required is **Create and Customize Reports**, which could be added directly to the profile if you want all users with the profile to be able to create reports, or done via a permission set and permission set groups. Both methods are outlined here:

- **Method 1**: To add to a profile: Go to **Setup | Users | Profiles**, select the profile associated with the users, and press **Edit**. Scroll down the page and select the **Create and Customize Reports** permission. Press **Save**.

- **Method 2**: To add to a permission set: Go to **Setup | Users | Permission Set** and press **New** or find an existing permission set if you can see one already assigned to the same users or groups. Name the permission set **Create and Customize Reports** and give it a description and a license of type **Salesforce**. Press **Save**.

  o On the next page, scroll down to the **System** section and select **System Permissions**. Press **Edit** and select the **Create and Customize Reports** option and press **Save** (and then **Save** again).

  o Finally, add the newly created permission set to the users you wish by pressing the **Manage Assignments** button at the top of the page. Press **Add Assignments** and select the users. Press **Next**, select **No expiration date**, and press **Assign**.

The following figure shows the newly created permission set being added to users as required:

Figure 8.1: Adding the permission set to the required users

Quick tour of Salesforce reports

To access Salesforce reports, go to an app such as Sales or Service or simply select **Reports** from the **App Launcher**. Select the reports tab as shown in the following figure:

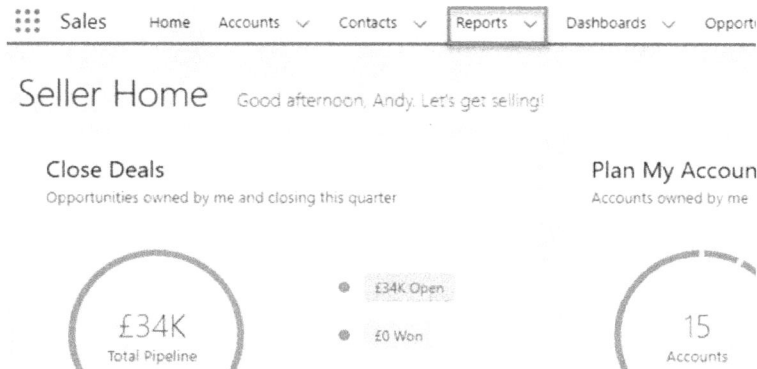

Figure 8.2: Accessing Salesforce reports

After pressing the **Reports** tab, you will notice a list of recent reports, which may be empty if it is your first visit to the reports feature in Salesforce, as well as a menu on the left that will show various report folders; these can be:

- **Public**: reports accessible to all users
- **Private**: generally, the reports that are only visible to the user who created them
- **Shared with me**: Private reports shared with you directly or via groups

Note: **The menu is split between reports and folders, which share the same logic.**

If you are using the Salesforce Developer Edition org, then many of the reports will not contain meaningful information. However, to quickly review a finished report, use the search bar to find the report titled **Opportunities by Value**.

This will bring up the report shown in the following figure:

Figure 8.3: *A typical Salesforce report with a report chart added*

The preceding figure is numbered as follows:

1. **Edit the report**: This allows you to add or remove fields, apply groups and sub-groups, order and filter the data, and more

2. **Change the report chart**: Report charts are like mini dashboards that display the data graphically in the report. You can toggle the report chart on or off by pressing the small setting icon at the top of the report.

3. **Toggle**: The level of detail required on the report for totals, subtotals, and line details

Press **Edit** and the controls, but do not press **Save**. Building reports is covered in the following sections of this chapter.

Salesforce report types

There are various report types in Salesforce. The simplest is a tabular report, which is a display of the fields and filtered to only show the records of interest. Details of the report types are outlined in the following:

- **Tabular reports**: These are the simplest reports for displaying information. They can be displayed on a dashboard, but they are limited to simply displaying the data, which may be useful in some instances. However, when you go to add the widget, you will find the other report types greyed out as shown in the following figure:

Report

Opportunities Report ⊗

☐ Use chart settings from report ⓘ

Display As

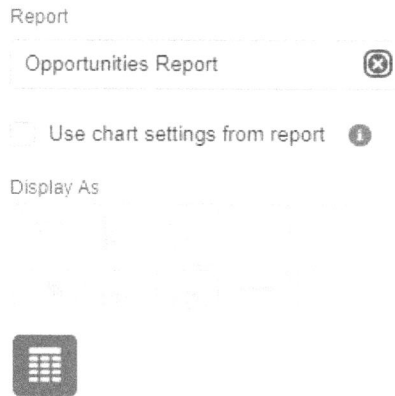

Figure 8.4: *Adding a tabular report to a dashboard*

If you need to group data or base dashboards on it, then you cannot use tabular reports. Instead, you will need the following report types:

- **Summary reports**: Including cross summaries are like tabular reports, only you can group the report by a field. For example, contacts grouped by age or accounts grouped by country.

- **Matrix reports**: Like summary reports, but you can group by both row and column. For example, you could show opportunities by type and summary values for their expected revenue.

- **Joined reports**: Typically, reports are for an object with options for related objects. However, if the relationship can be across multiple objects with the same parent, then a joined report allows you to combine other reports, even if they are different report types. For example, accounts have both opportunities and cases as child objects. A joint report could be used to show how the opportunity's expected revenue could be impacted by the number of cases associated with the account.

Here are some additional features:

- **Buckets**: Allow you to categorize data by creating a bucket and not using a field on the object.

- **Themes and conditional formatting**: Provide additional formatting to highlight cells in colors or to add extra emphasis to the key metrics.

These features are covered in the following sections.

Creating basic tabular report

A tabular report is the most basic report type. To do this, go to:

1. The **Reports** tab and press **New Report** as shown in the following figure:

Figure 8.5: Creating a new report

2. This will give you a list of available report types. If you do not see the report type that you want, refer to **Custom Report Types** as shown in *Figure 8.6*.

3. For now, select the **Category | Opportunities**, select **Opportunities with Products**, and press the **Start Report** button:

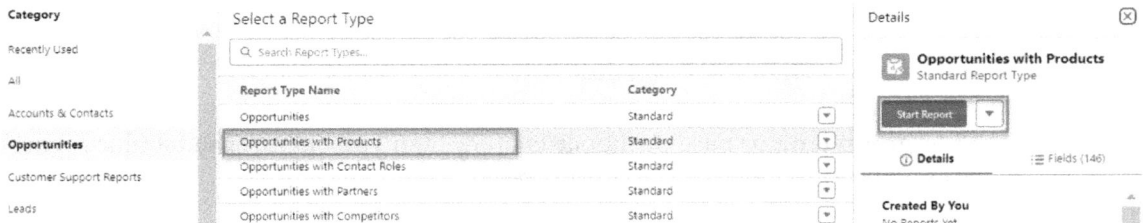

Figure 8.6: Selecting a report type

4. This will bring up the report builder, as shown in the following figure:

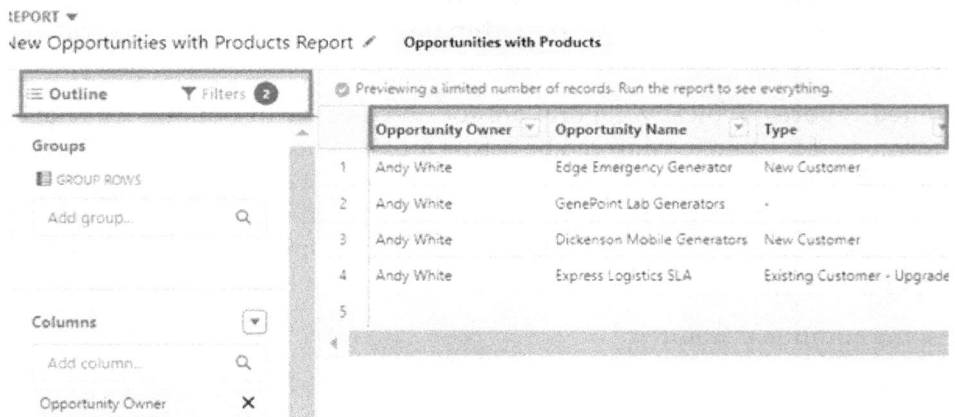

Figure 8.7: Report builder showing the report outline, filters and fields displayed

5. To the left-hand side, there is the **Outline** tab to give the ability to add or group fields. This is to add fields to the report layout and group them. Grouping is crucial for more advanced report types and is necessary if you want to create a dashboard from the report. A group is essentially a field that contains many records with that value—for example, group by opportunity stage is the foundation of an opportunity pipeline report. There is also the **Filters** tab, which limits the data displayed, such as within a date range or by opportunity stage.

6. On the right-hand side is the list of fields to display. The small icon above each field allows you to sort the data, group by this field, and perform other options such as bucket (see the following section) or delete the field. Fields can be dragged and dropped into the order you wish.

The following figure shows the options available for ordering a field on a report:

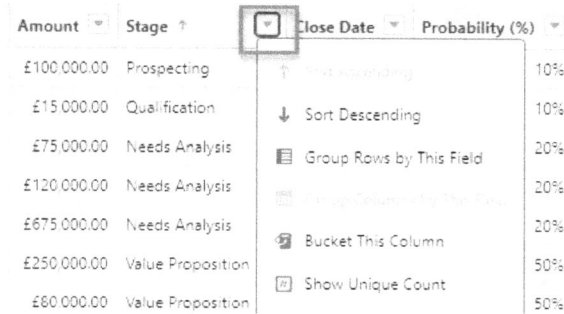

Figure 8.8: Options to order or group a field on a report

Report filters

As mentioned on the left-hand side are the filters for the report. This often includes showing only your data or a specific time range or within criteria such as picklist values or numeric ranges. The following figure shows the filters reset to show all the data:

Figure 8.9: Report filters

When you are satisfied with the report, press either the **Save & Run** or the **Run** button as shown in the following figure:

Figure 8.10: Running a report

Note: When building reports, select the Update Preview Automatically, as it allows you to see changes you make without having to run the report. You might wish to turn these features off if you have large or complicated reports, which might take a while to refresh the page.

Refer to the following figure:

Update Preview Automatically ✓◯

Figure 8.11: *Turning on or off the preview feature in report builder*

Salesforce report features

Many features are useful to know when building Salesforce reports. Reports can be built to show and display a vast range of data, but displaying them in a format that is easy to understand and build dashboards on requires a working knowledge of the various features as described in the following section.

Custom report types

In some cases, Salesforce may not provide the exact type of report you are looking for. When you go to the **Reports** tab and press **New Report**, you may not see the objects you wish to report on or the relationship you want to include. To add a report type, you need to create a custom report type.

If you are reporting on a custom object, first check that the object you wish to report on has been enabled for reporting, and then create a custom report type.

These can be done through the following steps:

1. To check if the custom object has reports enabled, go to **Setup** | **Object Manager** | **Details** and verify that the **Enable Report** option is checked. If it is not, then press **Edit**, and it will allow it. Press **Save**.

2. To create a custom report type, go to **Setup** | **Report Types**, as shown in the following figure:

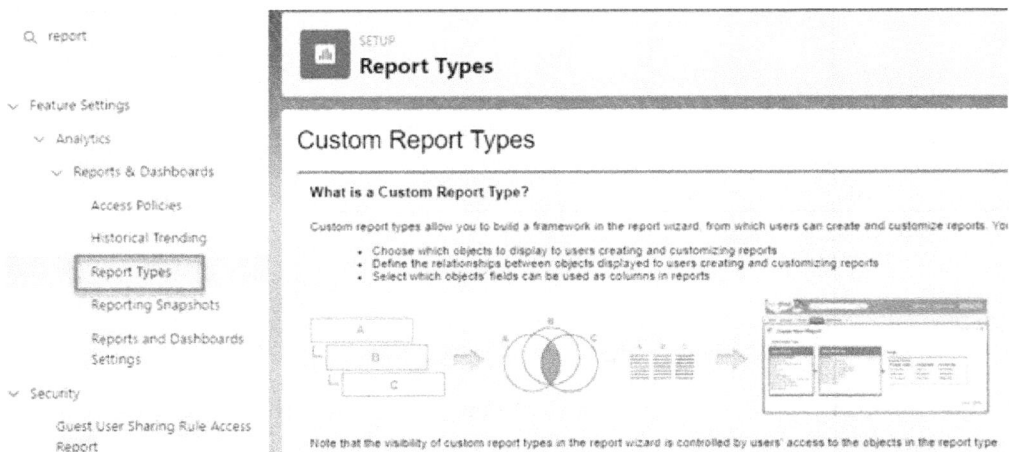

Figure 8.12: *Creating a custom report type*

Note: **Figure 8.12 shows a Venn diagram that helps illustrate the basics of SQL (such as INNER JOIN or OUTER JOIN), which you can research outside the scope of this book. However, it is useful to understand the concepts to create accurate and reliable reports.**

3. Press the **New Custom Report Type** button and select the object you would like to create a new report type for. In the following figure, the custom object **Projects** is selected.

4. It is stored in the **Customer Support Reports** folder since the child object for **Projects with Feedback** is included in the next step.

Report Type Focus

Specify what type of records (rows) will be the focus of reports generated by this report type.
Example: If reporting on "Contacts with Opportunities with Partners," select "Contacts" as the primary object

Primary Object | Projects ⌄

Identification

Report Type Label | Projects with Feedback
Report Type Name | Projects_with_Feedback
Note: Description will be visible to users who create reports
Description | Giving a list of customer feedback on the various projects
Store in Category | Customer Support Reports ⌄

Deployment

A report type with deployed status is available for use in the report wizard. While in development, report types are visible only to authorized administrators and their delegates

Deployment Status | ◯ In Development
                   | ◉ Deployed

Figure 8.13: Adding a custom object to the custom report type

5. Press **Next**, and you will have all the options. In this case, the custom object **Projects with Feedback** has been added.

6. If you toggle the **A to B Relationship**, you will see the Venn diagram changes to illustrate the results, as shown in the following figure:

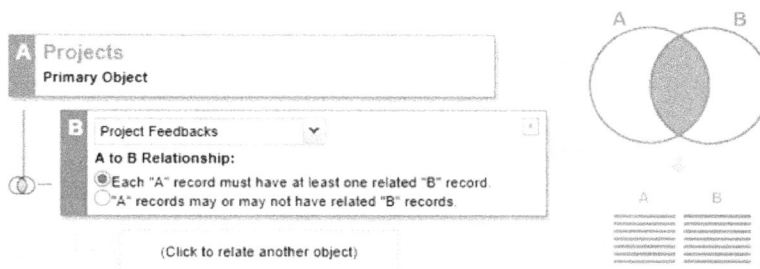

A Projects
Primary Object

B Project Feedbacks ⌄
A to B Relationship:
◉ Each "A" record must have at least one related "B" record.
◯ "A" records may or may not have related "B" records.

(Click to relate another object)

Figure 8.14: Adding a child object to the main object for a custom report type

7. Finally, press **Save**.

If you return to the **Reports** tab in the user interface and create a new report, you will see your new **Custom Report Type** as an option for creating the new report, as shown in the following figure:

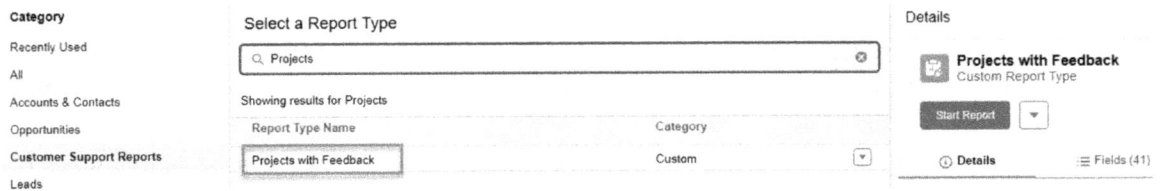

Category	Select a Report Type		Details
Recently Used	🔍 Projects	⊗	**Projects with Feedback**
All			Custom Report Type
Accounts & Contacts	Showing results for Projects		
Opportunities	Report Type Name	Category	Start Report ▾
Customer Support Reports	Projects with Feedback	Custom ▾	ⓘ **Details** ≡ Fields (41)
Leads			

Figure 8.15: Creating a new report based on a custom report type

Viewing reports and dashboards as different users

The data displayed in a dashboard provides summary information, but a user with a specific role may not have access to the underlying data. To observe the security model, Salesforce has the concept of a running user, which means. However, the dashboard can be displayed for summary information. If the user clicks on the dashboard to view the underlying report or data, and if they do not have the necessary privileges, then they are not able to view the underlying data.

For example, senior management may want to showcase new projects or opportunities that are due within the next three months. The report will show for all users, but management might not want to show the data below the summary information.

To set this, follow these steps:

1. Go to the dashboard and press **Edit**.

2. Press the gear icon, which brings up the dashboard properties, as shown in the following figure:

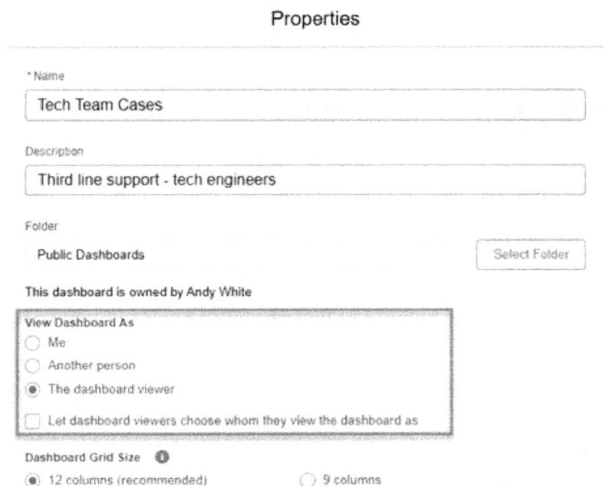

Properties

*Name

Tech Team Cases

Description

Third line support - tech engineers

Folder

Public Dashboards   Select Folder

This dashboard is owned by Andy White

View Dashboard As
○ Me
○ Another person
◉ The dashboard viewer
☐ Let dashboard viewers choose whom they view the dashboard as

Dashboard Grid Size ⓘ
◉ 12 columns (recommended)   ○ 9 columns

Figure 8.16: Access level assigned to a dashboard

3. Here, you can select how the user can view the dashboard.

4. As always, login as the other user to check that the data is displayed correctly.

   If they do not have the necessary privileges, then they will see an insufficient privileges message when they click on the dashboard.

Scheduling report

Reports can be scheduled to run at specific times and then automatically sent to users. This is done by going to the report and selecting the option for **Subscribe**, as shown in the following figure:

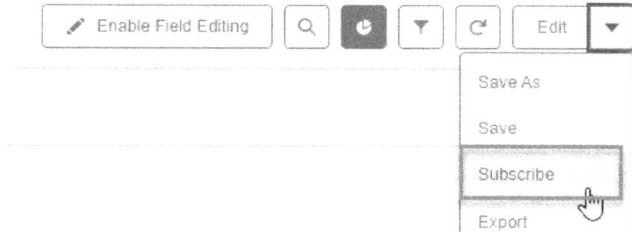

Figure 8.17: Subscribing to a report to allow scheduling

This will bring up the form shown in the following figure, which gives options of when the report is refreshed, who will receive the report notification by email, and also the option to add conditions to be met if the report is to be sent:

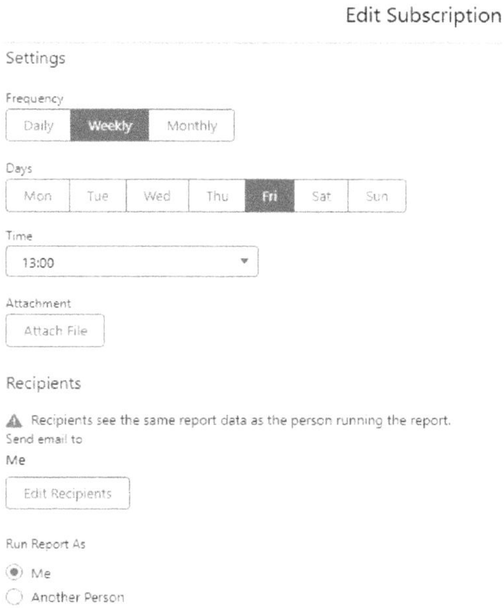

Figure 8.18: Subscription options for scheduling a report

Report folders

Although dashboards are covered later, both reports and dashboards should be stored in folders that accurately reflect the types of reports and dashboards they contain. Folders can be public, private, or shared with certain groups.

Setting up folders for reports and dashboards follows a similar process outlined in the following:

1. Both reports and dashboard folders are created by going into the **Reports** or **Dashboard** tabs, going to the left-hand side menu, selecting **Folders**, and pressing the **New Folder** button, as shown in the following figure:

Figure 8.19: Creating a new dashboard folder

2. When prompted, give the new folder a **Folder Label** (for example, `My Test Reports` and allow Salesforce to complete the **Folder Unique Name**. Press **Save**.

3. We will use this folder for the following examples.

4. Once the folder has been created, check the visibility of the folder by going to the drop-down at the end of the report name and selecting the **Share** option (refer to the following figure):

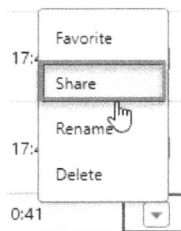

Figure 8.20: Sharing a folder

5. If required, you can make the reports folder available for **Public Groups** as shown in the following figure. Once completed, press **Done**.

Figure 8.21: Sharing settings for a folder

Repeat the above process for the dashboard folder, which will become useful in a later section (optional).

Creating report and dashboard sub-folders

Salesforce supports folders and sub-folders, i.e., folders inside folders. There are a few ways to do this, but by far the easiest is simply to navigate to a folder and then press **New Folder**.

Give it a **Name** and **Description**, and you will see the new sub-folder, as shown in the following figure:

Reports
All Folders > Einstein Bot Reports
1 item

REPORTS	Name	∨
Recent	▨ Einstein Bot Sub-Folder	

Figure 8.22: Creating a sub-folder

Note: **Reordering folders in Salesforce can be done, but there is currently no drag-and-drop functionality. For this reason, it is suggested to plan your folder structure first.**

Creating summary and matrix reports

Having created a basic tabular report above, summary reports are simply tabular reports grouped by a column, i.e., a field, and optionally include additional sub-groups. A matrix report is similar to a summary report, but it can also be grouped by rows. These are not actually different report types but rather use the **GROUP ROWS** or **GROUP COLUMNS**, as shown in the following figure:

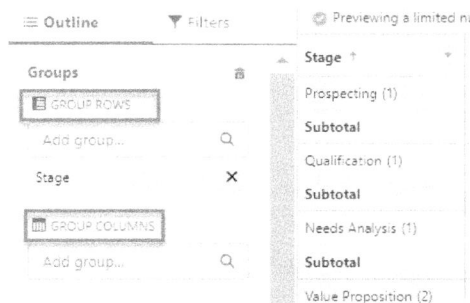

Figure 8.23: Grouping a report to make a summary or matrix report

These two report types also allow you to build a dashboard on top of them, which can, in turn, be added to a user's home page or elsewhere in Salesforce, for example, on the page layout, a **Lightning Web Component** (**LWC**), or even in Experience Cloud for customers to see; for example, show a partner's case statuses grouped by type.

To create a summary report, follow these steps:

1. We will use the example we created earlier. Returning to the report builder, drag the **Stage** field to the far left of the report and select **Group Rows by This Field**, as shown in the following figure:

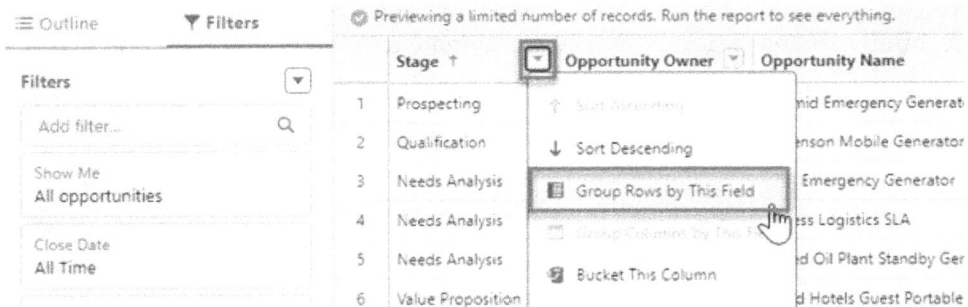

Figure 8.24: Creating a summary report

2. This will produce the report, as shown in the following figure:

Total Records	Total Total Price
39	£6,970,000.00

Stage ↑	Opportunity Name	Amount	Close Date	Created Date
Prospecting (1)	Pyramid Emergency Generators	£100,000.00	10/05/2024	05/07/2024
Subtotal				
Qualification (1)	Dickenson Mobile Generators	£15,000.00	14/11/2024	05/07/2024
Subtotal				
Needs Analysis (3)	United Oil Plant Standby Generators	£675,000.00	26/05/2024	05/07/2024
	Express Logistics SLA	£120,000.00	14/11/2024	05/07/2024
	Edge Emergency Generator	£75,000.00	01/11/2024	05/07/2024

Figure 8.25: Example of opportunities grouped by stage

Conditional formatting

On summary and matrix reports (where there has to be grouping by rows or rows and columns), there is a small **Conditional Formatting** button right on the bottom right of the screen in the utility bar, as shown in the following figure:

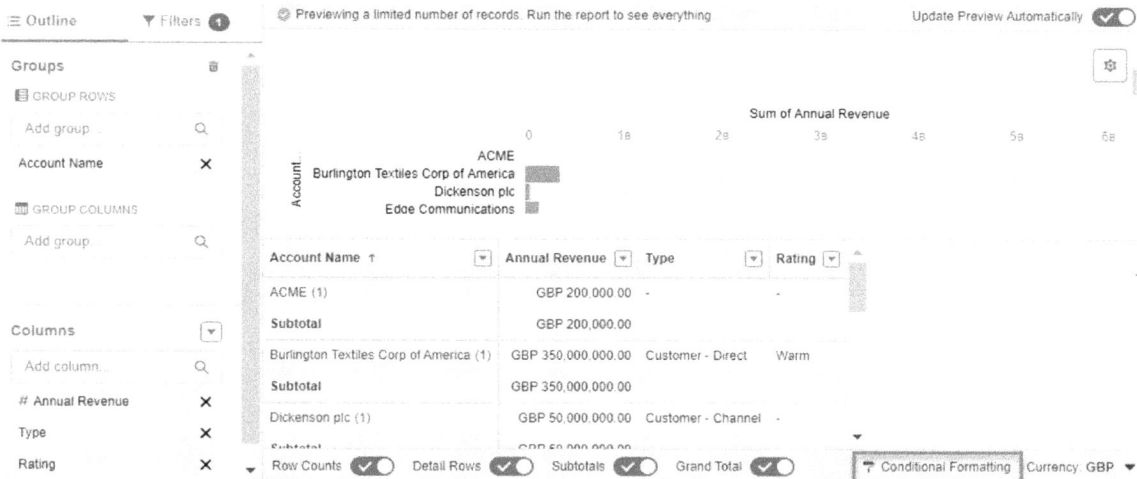

Figure 8.26: *Adding conditional formatting*

Note: **If you do not see the Conditional Formatting option, check that you have at least one summary field, as shown in the following figure:**

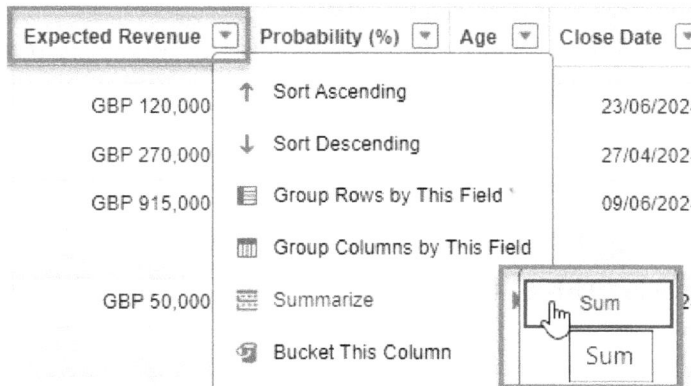

Figure 8.27: *Adding a summary field to allow conditional formatting*

To add conditional formatting, follow these steps:

1. Press the **Conditional Formatting** button and enter the ranges to apply the formatting.

2. Press **Done**, and you will see that the values are now given colors to easily identify which fields are within the specified ranges (refer to the following figure):

	Amount	Close Date	Created Date	Product Name	Quantity	Sales Price	Total Pric

Edit Conditional Formatting Rule

Apply Conditional Formatting to ⓘ

Sum of Total Price ▾

Range		Background Color	
< =	50000	◼ ▾	✕
> 50,000 to	250000	◼ ▾	✕
>	250,000	◼ ▾	✕

Cancel Done

| enerators | £125,000.00 | 02/05/2024 | 05/07/2024 | - | | - | £125,000./ |
| | £270,000.00 | 28/04/2024 | 05/07/2024 | - | | - | £270,000./ |

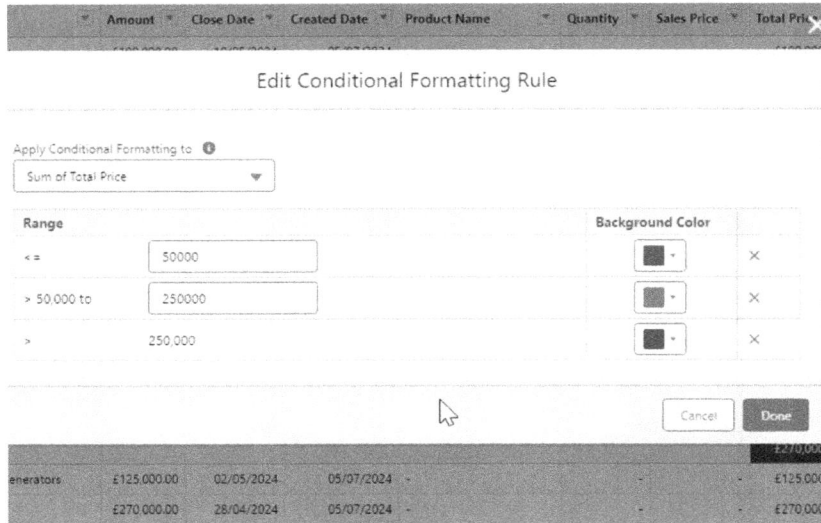

Figure 8.28: Adding ranges to apply conditional formatting

Bucket columns

Bucket columns are a way to group a column by a range of values. If you had a field for **Annual Revenue**, you may wish to bucket them by small, medium, or large.

To do this, follow these steps:

1. Go to the report and press **Edit**.

2. Select the field on the report, such as **Annual Revenue**.

3. Select the **Bucket This Column** option, as shown in the following figure:

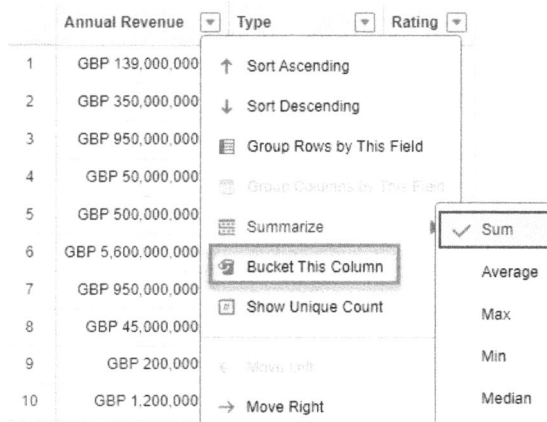

Annual Revenue ▾	Type ▾	Rating ▾
1	GBP 139,000,000	↑ Sort Ascending
2	GBP 350,000,000	↓ Sort Descending
3	GBP 950,000,000	▤ Group Rows by This Field
4	GBP 50,000,000	Group Columns by This Field
5	GBP 500,000,000	▦ Summarize	✓ Sum
6	GBP 5,600,000,000	Bucket This Column	Average
7	GBP 950,000,000	Show Unique Count	Max
8	GBP 45,000,000		Min
9	GBP 200,000	← Move Left	Min
10	GBP 1,200,000	→ Move Right	Median

Figure 8.29: Adding a bucket field to a report

4. This will then ask you to define the ranges to apply to the existing data in the selected field.

5. Press the **Add** button to provide a new range interval, as shown in the following figure.

6. Also, provide a name for each bucket range and a name for the bucket.

Edit Bucket Column

* Field		* Bucket Name	
Annual Revenue	×	Account size by revenue	

	Range		Bucket	
	<= *	100000	* Bucket Name	×
			Small	
Add ▶				
	> 100,000 to *	5000000	* Bucket Name	×
			Medium	
Add ▶				
	>	5,000,000	* Bucket Name	×
			Large	

Figure 8.30: Adding ranges for each bucket

7. Press the **Apply** button to see your data with an additional field displaying the name for each record, categorized according to the bucket name and value.

Note: Different fields have different types of buckets. For example, if you select the Account Name field, then you can bucket by other criteria.

Creating joined reports

Joined reports simply merge two or more existing reports as long as they have a common parent object and a common field on both child objects (refer to the following figure):

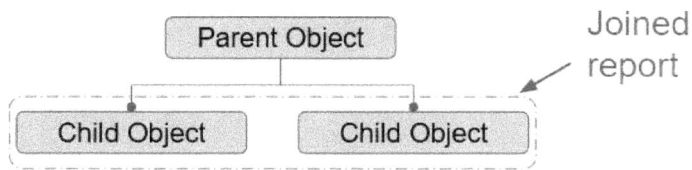

Figure 8.31: Illustration of a joined report

Joined reports work on the principle that a field is standard on both child objects. This allows Salesforce to link both child objects using the relationship to the parent object.

For example, both cases and opportunities have the **Accounts** object as the parent, so a joined report can be shown for cases and opportunities linked by the account.

To create a joint report, follow these steps:

1. Go to **Report Builder**, click the **REPORT** title in the top left corner, and select **Joined Report**. Click **Apply**, as shown in the following figure:

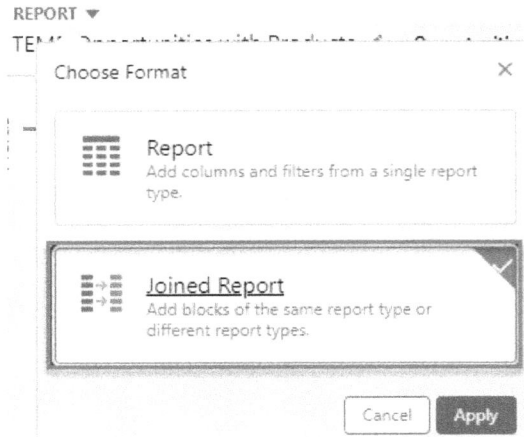

Figure 8.32: Creating a joined report

2. This then gives you an **Add Block** button near the top of the screen (refer to the following figure):

Figure 8.33: Adding blocks to a joined report

3. Select a related object, such as **Accounts**, and press **Add Block**, as shown in the following figure:

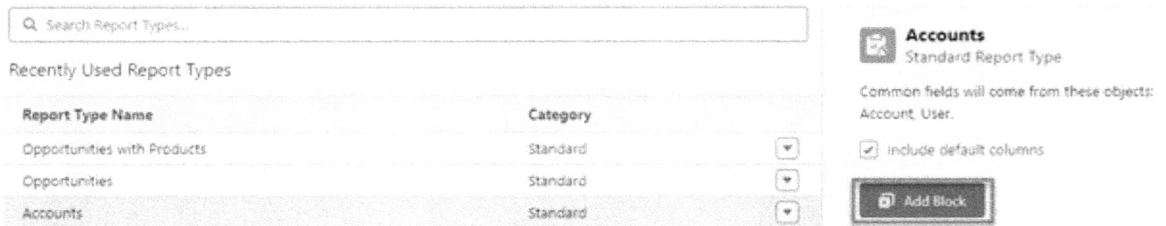

Figure 8.34: Selecting the related object for a joined report

4. Drag the **Account Name** to the far left of the field list and group by **Account Name** to get the following report with **Accounts**, **Opportunities**, and **Products**, all with **Amount** and **Total Amount**:

Refer to the following figure:

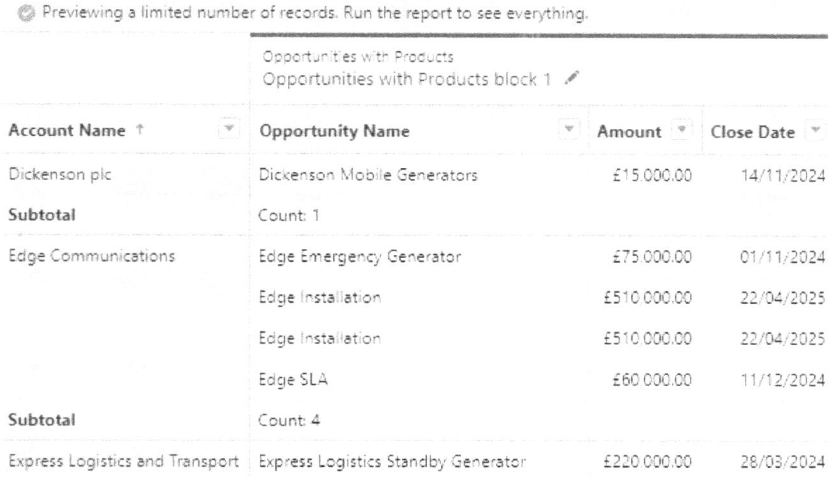

Previewing a limited number of records. Run the report to see everything.
Opportunities with Products
Opportunities with Products block 1
Account Name
Opportunity Name
Amount
Close Date
Dickenson plc
Dickenson Mobile Generators
£15,000.00
14/11/2024
Subtotal
Count: 1
Edge Communications
Edge Emergency Generator
£75,000.00
01/11/2024
Edge Installation
£510,000.00
22/04/2025
Edge Installation
£510,000.00
22/04/2025
Edge SLA
£60,000.00
11/12/2024
Subtotal
Count: 4
Express Logistics and Transport
Express Logistics Standby Generator
£220,000.00
28/03/2024

***Figure 8.35**: A completed joined report*

Report charts

If you have created a summary or matrix report in Salesforce, you can add a simple chart to it, which may help people engage with the content of the report without having to analyze the data.

To perform this, follow these steps:

1. Select the report you wish to add a chart to and press the **Add Chart** button, as shown in the following figure:

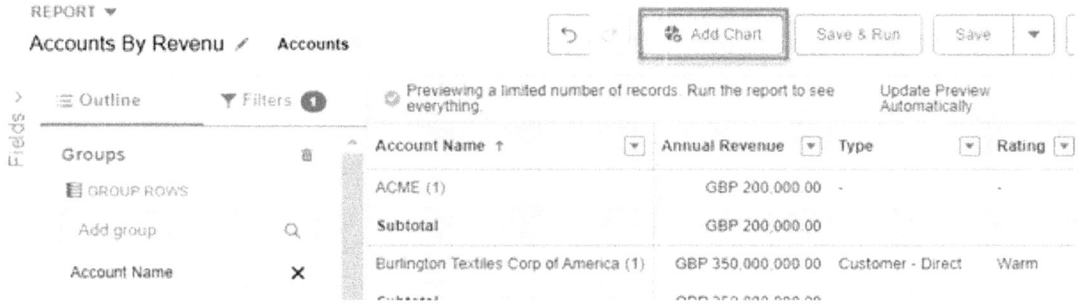

REPORT
Accounts By Revenu
Accounts
Add Chart
Save & Run
Save
Outline
Filters
Fields
Groups
GROUP ROWS
Add group
Account Name
Previewing a limited number of records. Run the report to see everything.
Update Preview Automatically
Account Name
Annual Revenue
Type
Rating
ACME (1)
GBP 200,000.00
Subtotal
GBP 200,000.00
Burlington Textiles Corp of America (1)
GBP 350,000,000.00
Customer - Direct
Warm

***Figure 8.36**: Adding a report chart*

2. This will generate a default chart at the top of the report.
3. Press the small gear icon to the top right of the chart to see the various options available, as shown in the following figure:

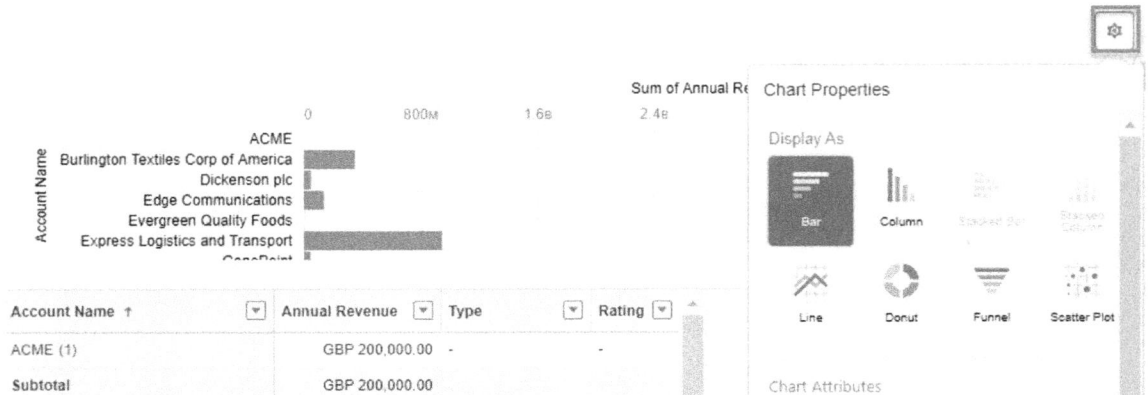

Figure 8.37: Options for the report chart properties

Dashboards

As mentioned, dashboards are built on Salesforce reports. They are similar to report charts, but multiple charts are added to a dashboard to give a complete overview across Salesforce. As such, they are not tied to a specific object but display a lot of information across many objects, which are displayed via widgets.

Creating a dashboard

To create a dashboard, go to the **Dashboards** tab in the user interface and press the **New Dashboard** button, as shown in the following figure:

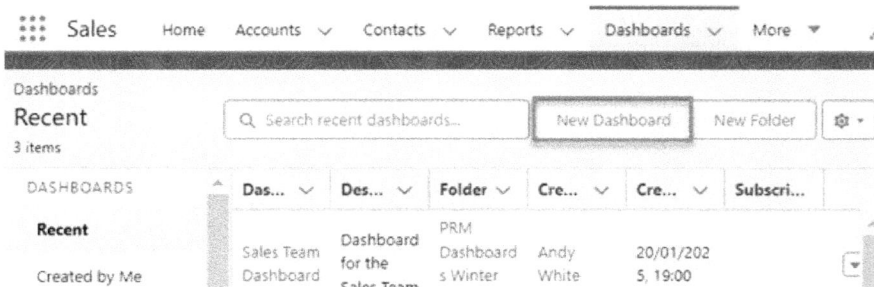

Figure 8.38: Creating a new dashboard

You will first be asked to provide the following information:

- **Name**: `Tech Team Support`
- **Description**: `Third-line support display of incidents and progress`
- **Folder**: Choose either a private folder or one of the public folders if you wish to share the dashboard

The following are the steps you need to take in order to add widgets to your dashboard:

1. This will bring up a blank dashboard with a grid onto which you add widgets.

2. Press the + **Widget** button and select **Chart or Table**, but you also have options to add images or text if needed.

3. You can then choose a report to base your dashboard widget on, as shown in the following figure:

Reports

Recent

Created by Me

Private Reports

Public Reports

All Reports

Folders

Select Report

Q Search Reports and Folders

Opportunities by Value
Andy White   11 May 2025, 00:46   Public Reports

Accounts By Revenue
Andy White   11 May 2025, 00:45   Public Reports

Opportunities Report
Andy White   11 May 2025, 00:05   Private Reports

Figure 8.39: Selecting the report as the basis for the new dashboard widget

4. Choose a report and press **Select**.

5. The next step of the widget wizard gives you options for the type of chart, with a preview and axis options (refer to the following figure):

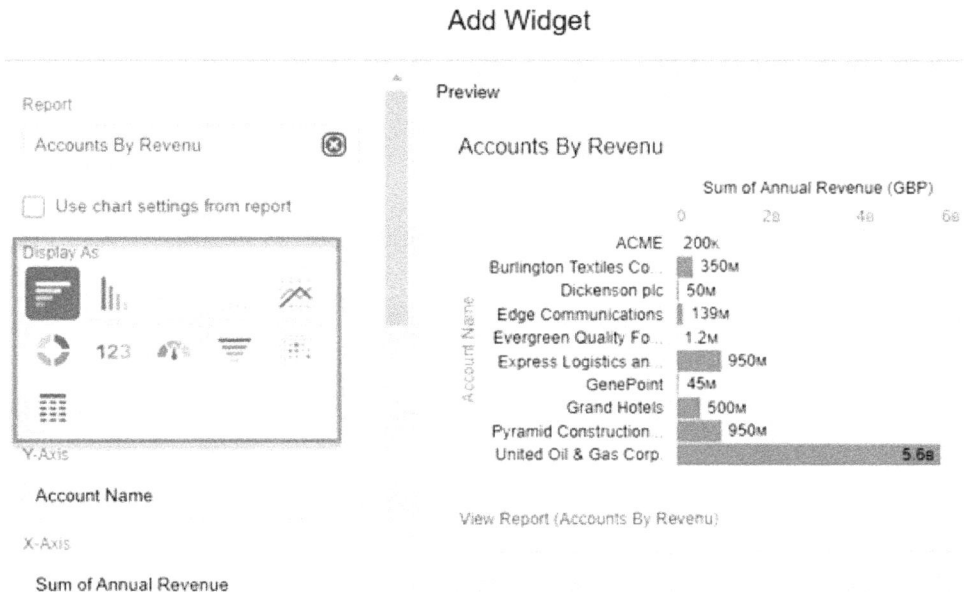

Add Widget

Report

Accounts By Revenu

Use chart settings from report

Display As

123

Y-Axis

Account Name

X-Axis

Sum of Annual Revenue

Preview

Accounts By Revenu

Sum of Annual Revenue (GBP)

Account Name	Value
ACME	200к
Burlington Textiles Co	350м
Dickenson plc	50м
Edge Communications	139м
Evergreen Quality Fo	1.2м
Express Logistics an	950м
GenePoint	45м
Grand Hotels	500м
Pyramid Construction	950м
United Oil & Gas Corp	5.6в

View Report (Accounts By Revenu)

Figure 8.40: Widget options

6. Finally, press **Add** and **Save**. Repeat the process of adding widgets to the dashboard to cover your requirements.

Whilst creating dashboards, it is worth noting the following:

- To edit a widget on a dashboard, check that the dashboard is in edit mode and press the small pencil icon on the widget. This will return you to the image shown above.

- There are various types of charts, such as line, scatter, funnel, etc. It is worth familiarizing yourself with the benefits of each chart type.

Building user home page

If you are using Salesforce Developer Edition and navigate to the **Home** menu item, you will see the **Seller Home** page, containing various dashboard widgets. This feature is enabled by default, but you may want to create a dashboard tailored to different user types.

You first need to disable this feature by following these steps:

1. **Setup** | **Home** and disabling the **Advanced Seller Home** feature, as shown in the following figure:

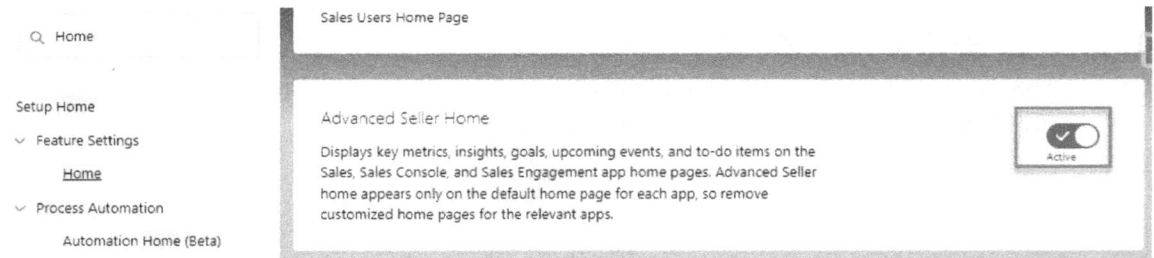

Figure 8.41: Removing the default homepage

2. To create a new custom home page, you need to go to **Setup** | **Lightning App Builder** and press **New**, as shown in the following figure:

Figure 8.42: Creating a new home page from the Lightning App Builder menu

3. In the wizard that appears, select the **Home Page** tab on the left-hand menu and press **Next**. Give the home page a name, such as `Sales Team Home Page`, and press **Next**.

4. Finally, choose the layout you wish, such as **Header and Three Regions**.

5. From here, you can add various components, including dashboards as well as many other types, as shown in the following figure:

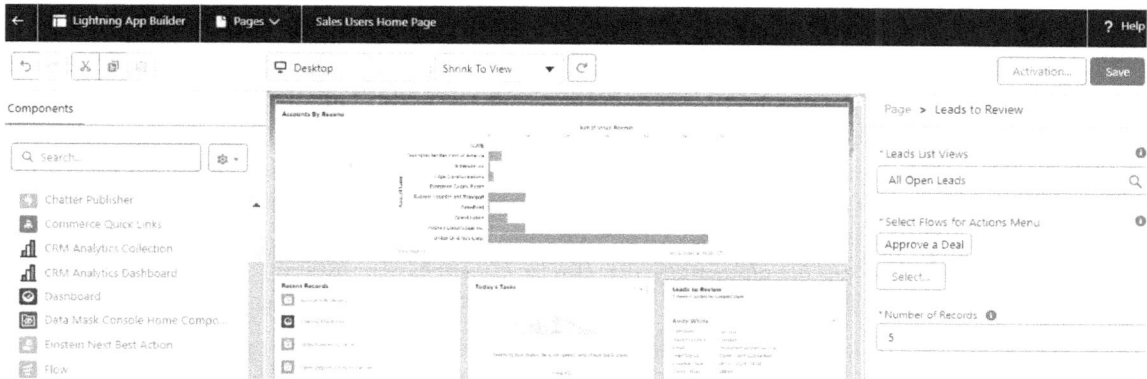

Figure 8.43: Constructing a dashboard with many widgets

Best practice for large reports

Although building reports and dashboards in Salesforce is relatively intuitive, there are a few key considerations to keep in mind, particularly when dealing with large data volumes. A report can be slow to generate if there is a large amount of data. Some areas to consider to speed up extensive reports are:

- Limit the number of formula fields displayed, as these need to be recalculated every time the data is viewed. See if these can be removed or replaced as part of a flow, since the flow will not need to be recalculated to run the report.
- Ensure the date range is relevant and not set for all time.
- Ensure report filters use logic such as equals and not contains.
- Remove unnecessary fields from the report.
- Schedule the report to run out of hours and add recipients to the subscriber list.

If the above remains problematic, custom indexing and skinny tables can be employed; however, this is outside the scope of this book.

Introduction to Tableau

A working knowledge of Tableau is not necessary to be a Salesforce Administrator, nor is it included in standard Salesforce functionality. This is included here to inform you that it is an additional Salesforce product, often included in Salesforce Enterprise or Unlimited Editions.

Note: **If you are not interested in Tableau, you can skip this section.**

Tableau is more than a reporting tool; it is an enterprise-wide **business intelligence (BI)** tool. It is ideal for data visualization, exploration, and collaboration, and can span multiple environments, including several Salesforce organizations and other external systems.

It is included for free on Salesforce Enterprise and Unlimited Editions, but it also comes with the Developer Edition, although it is unlikely that your Developer Edition is connected to other systems, nor will it have large data volumes.

It is worth noting that Tableau Public is a free version of Tableau that you can use with a variety of data sources, including SAP, Excel, and Google Sheets, with a full list available at **https://help.tableau.com/current/pro/desktop/en-us/exampleconnections_overview.htm**. This allows you to practice Tableau without using any corporate or sensitive data. There is also Tableau Exchange **https://exchange.tableau.com/**, which has many prebuilt tools for data analysis and display. You can also integrate *Alteryx* to enhance Tableau with AI capabilities, enabling more advanced data analytics, predictions, and automation.

Tableau has been around for several years and offers three primary versions: Tableau Desktop, Public, and Reader. However, the acquisition by Salesforce has pushed Tableau to be an entirely cloud-based application.

An example of a Tableau report is shown in the following figure:

Figure 8.44: Example Tableau report

Tableau can do many more types of graphs than native Salesforce reports and dashboards. For example, the opportunity pipeline graph (*Figure 8.45*) shows the decline or increase in revenue for the opportunity pipeline in Salesforce.

These charts can then be embedded into Salesforce or any compatible system, including Excel files on a shared drive or on-premises systems using Tableau Bridge:

Rating Correlations by Customer Segment

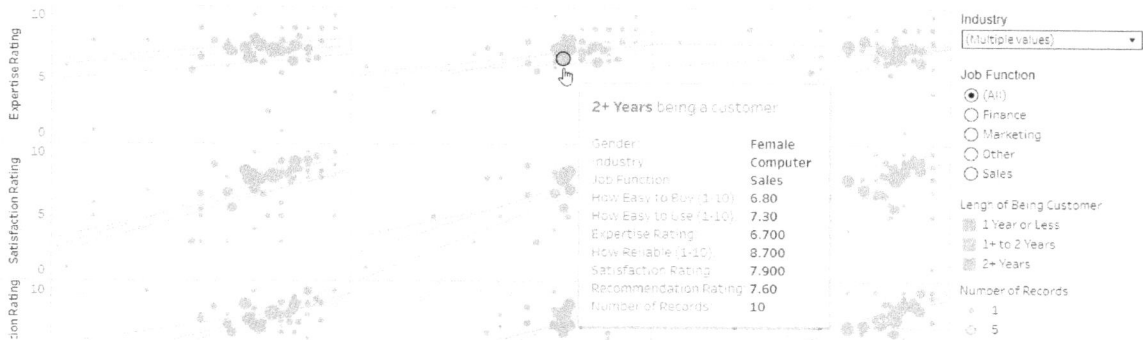

Figure 8.45: Opportunity pipeline shown in Tableau

Tableau comes with over 20 APIs to integrate into the most popular cloud platforms, such as:

- Snowflake
- **Amazon Web Services** (**AWS**)
- DataBricks
- MuleSoft
- Oracle
- SAP
- Cloudera
- **Google Cloud Platform** (**GCP**)

It also enables the construction of purpose-built APIs and numerous public-facing APIs for generic integration, as well as **extract, transform, and load** (**ETL**) functionality, which involves formatting data correctly on the fly.

To understand Tableau, there are a few core concepts, such as:

- **Dimensions**: Columns with values that can be categorized, such as Stage or Region.
- **Measures**: which contain numerical data, which can be summarized or used in calculations.

Both can be filtered, but they also affect the way the final graph is displayed. Tableau also uses a lens, which is a view of the data.

Setting up Tableau in Salesforce

This guide is very brief but enough to get you started. If you have not already, sign up for a free Salesforce Developer Edition account, which is covered in *Chapter 1, Introduction to Salesforce,* of this book and also includes some basic Tableau functionality for embedding Tableau.

To see this, follow these steps:

1. Go to **Setup | Tableau**.

2. To get a complete Salesforce environment with more data and Analytics Studio included, you need to register for a Salesforce playground environment by registering at: **https://trailhead.salesforce.com/promo/orgs/analytics-de**

3. Complete the form in the same way you registered for a standard developer account in *Chapter 1, Introduction to Salesforce.*

4. Once you have access to your new Salesforce Developer Edition account, you will notice that the app **Analytics Studio** is included (refer to the following figure):

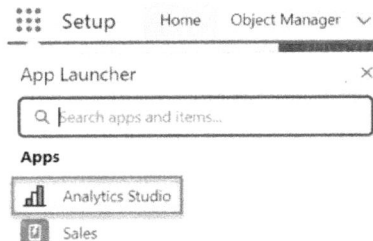

Figure 8.46: Analytics Studio in a dedicated Salesforce playground

5. From here, there are many resources, but a great place to start is with Trailhead, for example: **https://trailhead.salesforce.com/users/00550000007Pk4sAAC/trailmixes/ analytics-studio**.

6. For example, the following figure is from a Trailhead, which requires the user to load a CSV file. Once done, press the **Explore** button, which gives options on how to display the data:

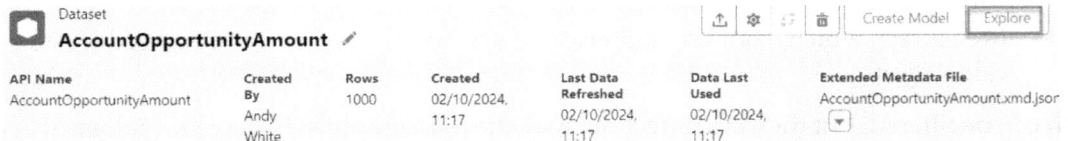

Figure 8.47: Adding a CSV file to the Tableau environment to explore

7. To visually represent the data, you need to create a new lens. For example, the pipeline by revenue and count is shown in the following figure:

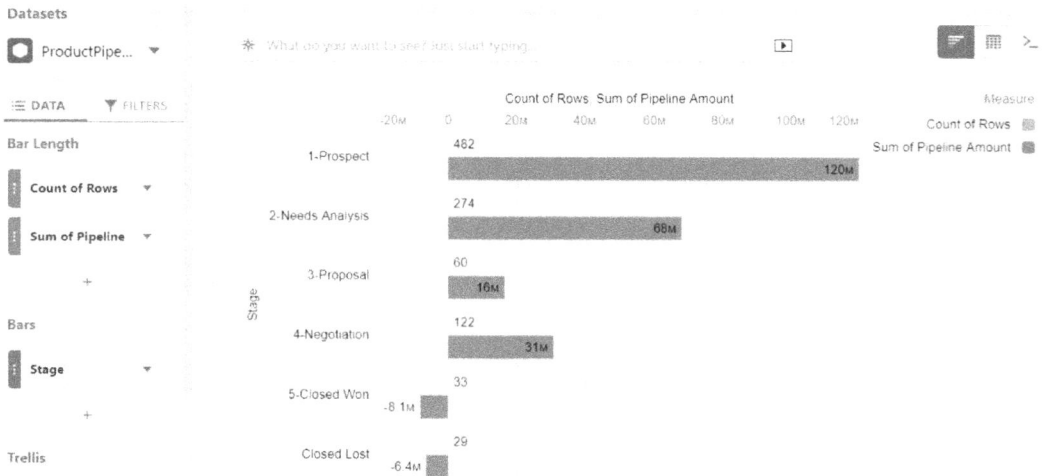

Figure 8.48: Applying a lens in Tableau

8. However, a similar graph to the one shown above is also easily available in Salesforce reports and dashboards.

9. In Tableau, set grouping by **State** and choose a chart type of **Map**, which gives the following view (refer to the following figure):

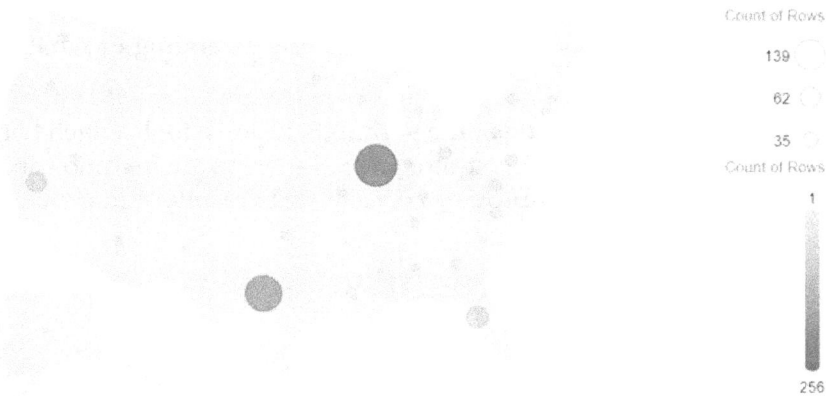

Figure 8.49: Displaying the same data as a map

The above method is significantly more straightforward than the more rigorous way of representing sophisticated maps in Salesforce with Salesforce Maps. This is done by creating the connector in a Tableau flow, selecting Salesforce, and logging into your Salesforce org. The charts can then be built in Tableau before enabling Tableau host mappings to allow the chart to be viewed in Salesforce. This method enables you to combine data from various external data sources outside of Salesforce.

However, having access to your Tableau environment is essential for setting up some of the advanced features, such as Slack integration or Tableau Pulse. Tableau Pulse combines Tableau functionality with AI. It allows AI to provide visible metrics on various data sources. This could be an improvement in **customer satisfaction score (CSAT)** or projected sales revenue by state with the predicted trends based on AI. There are various Trailhead tutorials on Tableau Pulse, but they are outside the scope of this book.

Conclusion

In this chapter, we have explored the core fundamentals of building reports and dashboards in Salesforce. We have seen how to create a basic tabular report and learned how to group it by fields to produce a summary report, as well as how to use rows and columns to create a matrix report. For all the report types, we have seen how filters can be used to focus on certain values or time ranges that are of interest.

We have also seen how to enable users to create their own reports and dashboards and how to share them with other users in the Salesforce org who may have different security settings.

We have also explored some of the more advanced features, such as conditional formatting, bucket columns, and joined reports, which enable further enhancement of reports by making the information more accessible to viewers.

Finally, we explored Tableau, an additional feature in Salesforce that can be used for advanced BI and analytics across Salesforce and other systems. Tableau is not a requirement for becoming a Salesforce professional, but having at least a basic understanding of what it is and how it works is beneficial.

In the next chapter, we will be looking at the various Salesforce tools which help with routine tasks performed by a Salesforce Administrator, many of which are free and can save hundreds of hours, simplifying tasks whilst improving consistency of results or improving performance.

Multiple choice questions

1. **Before you build a dashboard, you have to:**
    a. Create a report to base it on
    b. Enable Create and Customize Reports permission
    c. Add a home page to include the dashboard
    d. Enable dashboards under user settings

2. **True or false: All Salesforce standard objects have reports enabled by default?**
    a. True
    b. False

3. **A joined report must have:**
   a. Two or more child objects
   b. One common field between two child objects
   c. A summary field on both child objects
   d. Be joined by at least one field with a common name

4. **Bucket columns group data into ranges, which must:**
   a. Have at least one related field
   b. Have ranges easy to separate by logic operators or field values
   c. Have data which has been conditionally formatted
   d. Be numeric, currency, percentage, or a date field

5. **Matrix reports are reports that allow you to:**
   a. Group records by group and sub-group
   b. Provide a matrix widget to display data in a grid
   c. Group data by both rows and columns
   d. Show data grouped by common fields

6. **Salesforce folders can be structured with sub-folders by:**
   a. Using folder manager to drag-and-drop them into the right location
   b. Opening the report or dashboard folder and pressing New Folder
   c. Under folder settings, pressing the cog icon
   d. Create a new folder and use the assign to setting

7. **Reports and dashboard had which access settings:**
   a. Private, Group, Draft
   b. Private, Public, or Shared
   c. Public, Read Only, Shared
   d. Private, Shared, Restricted

8. **Subscribing to a report allows the following:**
   a. Setup a schedule to run the report
   b. Assign recipients to receive email notifications of the new report
   c. Filter the report to meet criteria before sending
   d. All of the above

9. **If a user gets access to a dashboard but does not have access to the underlying data, they will:**

   a. Get an error message that they do not have the necessary privileges to see the dashboard

   b. See the dashboard, but only see the data in the report that they are allowed to see

   c. See the dashboard with a warning that it contains confidential information

   d. See the dashboard, but get an error message if they click on it, that they do not have the necessary privileges

10. **Tableau is able to access data from multiple Salesforce orgs. Is it true or false?**

    a. True

    b. False

Answers

1	**a**
2	**a**
3	**a, b**
4	**b**
5	**c**
6	**b**
7	**b**
8	**d**
9	**d**
10	**a**

Join our Discord space

Join our Discord workspace for latest updates, offers, tech happenings around the world, new releases, and sessions with the authors:

https://discord.bpbonline.com

CHAPTER 9
Various Salesforce Tools

Introduction

This chapter is about various tools that a Salesforce Administrator can use to make their life easier. Many are free and used to check that the configuration is done correctly or to simplify complex tasks.

Many tasks can be simplified and improved by using the right tools. They are grouped by similarities, and some tools perform similar functions. For example, Salesforce Org Check is an app available from the AppExchange, while Salesforce already has Optimizer. Likewise, Data Loader is a tool you can download, but it has features like those of a web-based version at **https://dataloader.io/**

Chapter 11, Basics of Apex and Lightning Web Components, includes tools used by developers for simplicity.

Structure

In this chapter, we will cover the following topics:

- Salesforce Inspector Reloaded
- Salesforce Org Check
- Salesforce Optimizer

- Data tools
- Data quality
- Various tools from AppExchange
- Salesforce useful links

Objectives

By the end of this chapter, readers will have learned how to progress their Salesforce experience outside of Salesforce. You would have learned how to ensure your Salesforce org is setup and ready for new users and how to use various tools to make the administration easier. This chapter also includes ways to maintain Salesforce to ensure it is configured optimally, such as data analysis, configuration checking, and ways to get data in and out of Salesforce. By the end of this chapter, you will have gained a broader knowledge of how to keep your Salesforce instance optimized with various free online resources useful for the various tasks required as a Salesforce Administrator.

Salesforce Inspector Reloaded

One of the simplest tools to use as an admin is the Chrome extension called **Salesforce Inspector Reloaded**. It supersedes the original Salesforce Inspector and is the Swiss Army Knife to perform many tasks in Salesforce without navigating the **Setup** menu. If you use Google Chrome, Salesforce Inspector Reloaded, and follow the instructions, you will see a new Arrow on the right-hand side of your screen. Refer to the following figure:

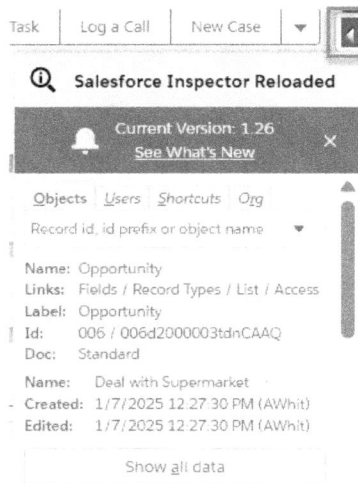

Figure 9.1: Salesforce Inspector with the small arrow highlighted

Salesforce Inspector Reloaded comes with the following features:

- Object and field metadata explorer.

- View all the fields on an object immediately and not just the fields shown on the current **user interface** (**UI**), which includes their API name, data type, labels, and metadata.

- View the fields' field-level security, field definition, such as picklist values, help text, and formulas.

- Easily import and export data via SQL queries, including bulk updates, insert, and upsert with a simple UI.

- View data in real time, including fields not displayed in the UI, and the information about them, such as whether they are system fields, read only fields, or hidden fields.

- Org limits are useful to see how various areas of Salesforce are performing.

There are advanced features for API, Event Monitoring, data migration, and manipulation. The **Options** button at the bottom of Salesforce Inspector Reloaded gives various options for configuring the UI as well as options for each of the main menu settings.

Example of using Salesforce Inspector Reloaded

An example of using Salesforce Inspector Reloaded could be getting multiple records into Salesforce. The steps involved are:

- Export from the object you wish to populate.

- Use the export as a template and include IDs for related records, such as the account ID associated with a contact.

- Populate the template with the data you wish to import.

- Use Salesforce Inspector Reloaded to load the new data.

Some of the key steps are illustrated in the following figure. To export the data, press the **Data Export** button and select the fields you wish to export. Typing the name into the query gives suggestions of fields available, as shown in the following figure:

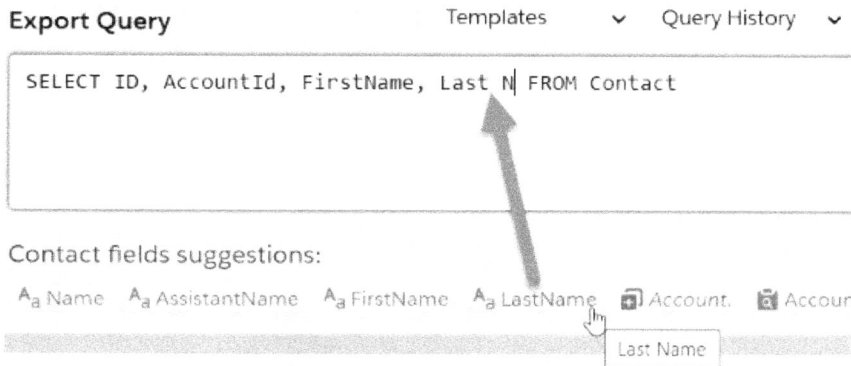

Export Query   Templates   ⌄   Query History   ⌄

SELECT ID, AccountId, FirstName, Last N| FROM Contact

Contact fields suggestions:

A_a Name   A_a AssistantName   A_a FirstName   A_a LastName   ▣ Account.   ▣ Accour

Last Name

Figure 9.2: Building a query in Salesforce Inspector Reloaded

You have a choice of the type of file export, namely CSV, Excel, or JSON. If you simply want to keep the records in your computer's memory, you can also press the **Copy** button and paste them directly into *Excel* or *Google Sheets*.

Add the data you wish to include in Salesforce. If you are updating or upserting, keep the record ID in the file to allow Salesforce to find the matching record. To insert new records, leave the ID record blank.

To import the file, simply paste the data into the data area as illustrated in the following figure, select the **Action**, such as **Insert**, and press the **Run Insert** to insert the data into Salesforce:

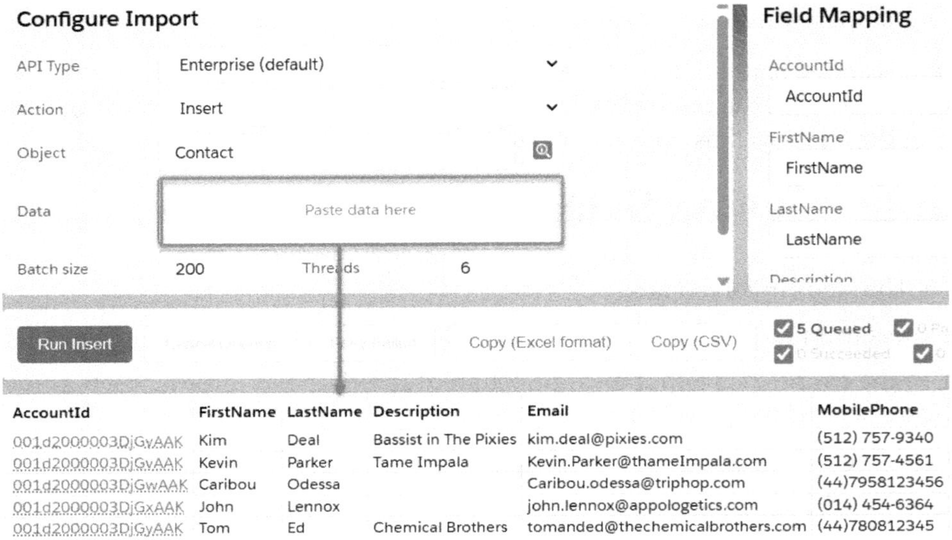

Figure 9.3: *Adding data to Salesforce Inspector Reloaded*

If you get any records that fail to import into Salesforce, you will see the **Failed** checkbox indicating the number of records that failed to import (refer to the following figure):

Figure 9.4: *Failed record import*

If you view the data region of the screen (refer to the following figure), there is an additional column called **__Errors**, which gives the error message. This allows you to then correct the records and try again.

Figure 9.5: *Reviewing the reason for failed data imports*

Other Salesforce Chrome extensions

Google provides other extensions to assist with Salesforce. A few popular ones are listed here:

- **Salesforce advanced Code searcher**: This saves an enormous amount of time when you need to check for a field being used in code. It serves other purposes, but being able to quickly see where a class, trigger, Experience Cloud page, or **Lightning Web Component** (**LWC**) uses fields or other Salesforce features is extremely useful for viewing dependencies between customizations.

- **Salesforce.com Enhanced Formula Editor**: This allows you to build complex formulas but includes functionality such as highlighting syntax, error checking, auto-completion, and more. This requires a subscription.

- **ORGanizer for Salesforce**: Allows you to store your logins across multiple devices as well as direct users to various Salesforce features.

- **Salesforce Change Set Helper**: If you are using change sets for deployment of configuration between sandboxes or production, then you may find the default UI fairly slow and limited in use. Change Set Helper is a Chrome extension designed to address these issues, as well as being suitable for orgs with a lot of configurations. The improved UI includes the ability to filter and search components easily and have a more comprehensive list, which can be filtered, sorted, or highlighted.

There are more tools available depending on your requirements. The AppExchange is your first place to start, but Google Chrome offers a range of Salesforce tools available for your use. Visit **https://chromewebstore.google.com/** and search for Salesforce to see the current list. Familiarizing yourself with these tools can save you many hours, so a little investment in trying them out is well worth it.

Salesforce Org Check

There are various tools for analyzing the health of a Salesforce org. Some of them focus on code, such as CodeScan, SonarQube, or Snapshot, but these require licenses at a cost and also require some in-depth knowledge to analyze the results.

A useful free tool is Salesforce Org Check, which can be found on Salesforce AppExchange.

Simply visit the Salesforce AppExchange and type in Org Check to get the app illustrated.

Refer to the following figure:

Org Check

By Salesforce Labs

Let's have an app to monitor and help reducing technical debt in your org!

Salesforce App   5 Average Rating (16 Reviews)

Figure 9.6: Org Check available on the Salesforce AppExchange

This will analyze your Salesforce org for numerous typical configuration issues, such as security settings, the use of roles, some basic configuration, and more. It is still a basic check, but it can throw light on common issues.

Salesforce Optimizer

Salesforce Optimizer is a great tool to automatically assess the state of your current Salesforce configuration. It highlights many of the typical configuration issues that you may not be aware of. It is included in Salesforce and found by simply going to **Setup | Optimizer**, as shown in the following figure:

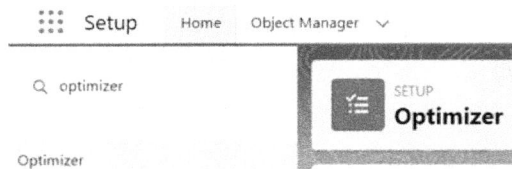

Figure 9.7: *Salesforce Optimizer*

1. Press the blue **Allow Access** button, agree to the terms and conditions, and press **Save & Close**.

2. To initiate a run, press the **Open Optimizer** button, press the **Run Optimizer** button, and wait for a while the **Optimizer** goes through the org and does a series of tests.

3. When complete, you will see a drop-down with the **Edit** option. Select the items you wish to view the results for.

4. The results for **Analytics** are shown in the following figure with the severity highlighted. The list is configurable with options to view the details of each item.

    Refer to the following figure:

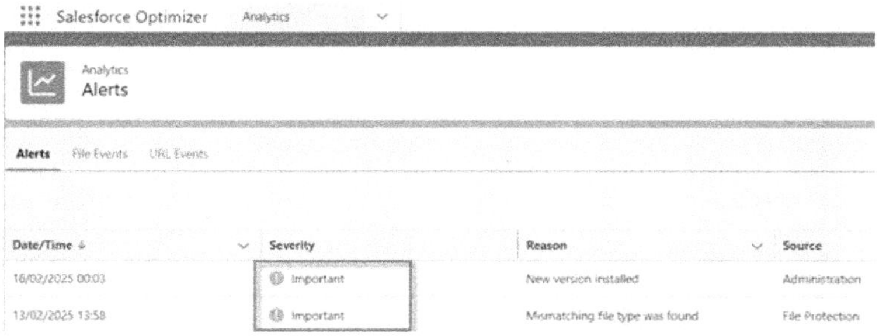

Figure 9.8: *Salesforce Optimizer results*

Note: At the time of writing, Optimizer is undergoing changes in how it is configured and displays the results.

Optimizer can be scheduled to run on a monthly basis. You can return to Optimizer when you need the latest results by visiting the Optimizer app from the **App Launcher**, as shown in the following figure:

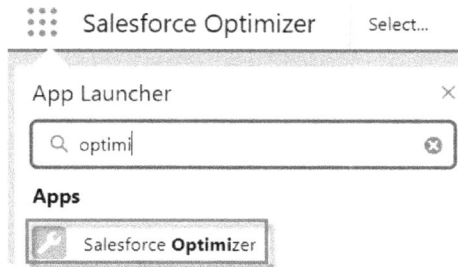

Figure 9.9: Getting Salesforce Optimizer from the App Launcher

Comparing Salesforce Optimizer and Org Check

Initially, it might appear that Org Check and Optimizer are doing the same thing. However, they have a few differences, as outlined in the following table:

Org Check	Optimizer
Easy to use.	Requires more knowledge to know what areas of Salesforce need to be checked.
Provides a wide range of configuration checks, including security overview and generic areas to consider.	Provides an in-depth technical analysis and covers detailed recommendations.
Provides general guidance.	Provides specific links to areas covered in the reports.
Standard reports.	Detailed, customizable reports.
Few options for customization.	Extensive customizations for analysis.

Table 9.1: Comparison of Org Check and Optimizer

Data tools

The following few sections focus on tools to assist with data migration, quality, and usage in Salesforce. As with anything to do with data, the best practice is to back it up and trial any operations in a non-live environment.

Getting data into or out of Salesforce can be done in a few ways. Let us look at them in detail:

- The simplest are data wizards found on the landing page of many objects, such as accounts or contacts.

- One step further are the data tools found in **Setup**, such as **Mass Delete**, **Mass Transfer**, and the **Data Import Wizard**.

- Workbench is a very useful tool for viewing Salesforce data and performing various tasks. With your Developer Edition open, go to a new tab in your browser and visit: **https://workbench.developerforce.com/login.php**

- There are more sophisticated tools, such as Talend or Pentaho, which allow transformation of data, **Extract, Transform and Load** (ETL), and continuous uploading for large data volumes.

Salesforce Data Loader

Salesforce has a specific tool for loading, deleting, or updating data called **Data Loader**, which can be downloaded from **https://developer.salesforce.com/tools/data-loader**. There is also an online version at dataloader.io, which is useful if you do not have the tool on your laptop.

However, dataloader.io has limits on the number of times or the amount of data you can work on before licensing costs are required, so it is recommended to use the official Salesforce Data Loader tool in most circumstances.

To download Data Loader, either search on Google for `Salesforce Data Loader Download` or go to **https://developer.salesforce.com/tools/data-loader**

This will give you the download link. Once installed, you may get various options, as shown in the following figure:

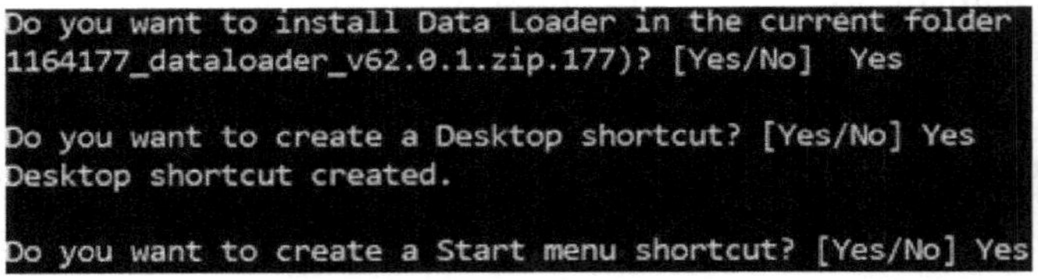

Figure 9.10: Installing Salesforce Data Loader

Once installed, you should see the **data loader**, as shown in the following figure:

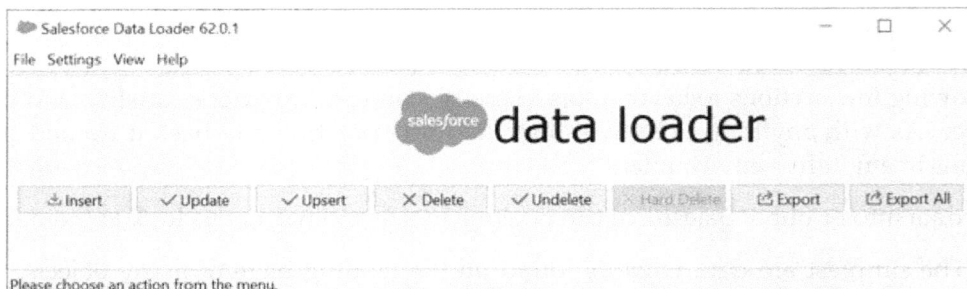

Figure 9.11: Salesforce Data Loader menu options

Instructions are available online. However, there is always a need to ensure that a record matches any parent record. This means you cannot load contacts unless you know the account they belong to, and you cannot load accounts unless you know who owns them (i.e., the user record).

To get these, you first need to export the records (using Data Loader) and match the records together using the record ID. There is not only one way to do this, but the key is to match the Salesforce ID in a format compatible for uploading.

The general order to do this is as follows:

- Export users. You need to do this, as every record will have an owner.

- Export Profiles and roles.

- Export accounts, contacts, and any other objects you wish to update or load.

- Match the accounts and contacts with the user ID, role, or profile.

- Load or upsert the data.

For example, you cannot load a contact into an account if you do not know the account ID. This requires a bit of practice to know which objects are child or parent (refer to *Chapter 2, Basic Admin Essentials*). To manipulate the data into the right format often requires Excel or Google Sheets and the use of the VLOOKUP formula. This formula matches a certain record of one format with another record of a different format.

Note: **Many of the more sophisticated tools avoid needing to map fields by ID since this is done by the tool for you.**

Understanding VLOOKUP

VLOOKUP is a formula that maps one field to another. For example, the contact record only has the account ID, but you need to map the data in the contact record to an account. An example is shown in the following figure:

	A	B	C
fx =vlookup(,Accounts!$A$2:$D$16,4,FALSE)			
	Contact ID	Account ID	VLOOKUP
	003d2000000imH3AAI	001d2000003DjGvAAK	Edge Communications
	003d2000000imH4AAI	001d2000003DjGvAAK	Edge Communications
	003d2000000imH5AAI	001d2000003DjGwAAK	Burlington Textiles Corp of Am
	003d2000000imH6AAI	001d2000003DjGxAAK	Pyramid Construction Inc
	003d2000000imH7AAI	001d2000003DjGyAAK	Dickenson plc
	003d2000000imH8AAI	001d2000003DiGzAAK	Grand Hotels & Resorts Ltd

Figure 9.12: Example of using VLOOKUP in Excel or Google Sheets

In the above illustration, accounts and contacts have been exported out of the Salesforce Developer Edition Org. A new field has been added called **VLOOKUP**, and the following formula can be entered into the first cell:

`=vlookup(B2,Accounts!$A$2:$D$16,4,FALSE)`

There is plenty of documentation on **VLOOKUP**, but in short-hand, this is saying to **VLOOKUP** the cell **B2** (which has Salesforce account ID as **001d2000003DjGvAAK**), go to the accounts sheet and look in the range **A2** to **D16** (where **$** is used to freeze the data range).

Go along 4 columns until you get to the **Account Name**, and if it is a match, then put the **Account Name** value in this cell (refer to the following figure):

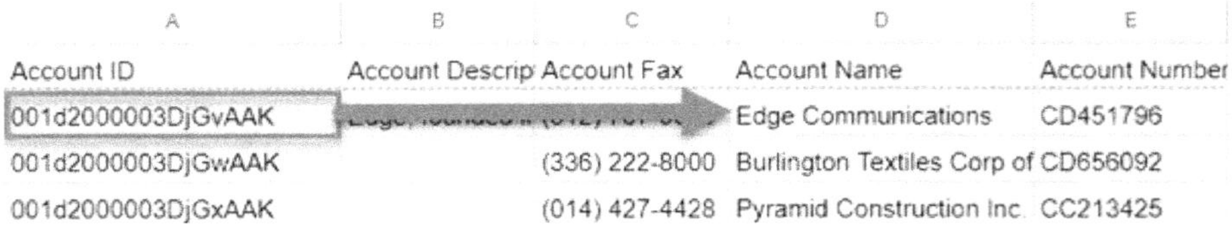

Figure 9.13: VLOOKUP comparing Account ID for Account Name

Complete the remaining missing cells and populate with new data as required, then either press the **Update** or **Upsert** buttons on Data Loader. **Upsert** will either update an existing record if the record ID is the same or insert a new record if no match can be found.

dataloader.io

Being able to modify Salesforce data is a regular task for administrators. Although it is often best to have the Data Loader tool, it is often helpful to have an online version, which can be used without adding the tool to your laptop. dataloader.io is a Salesforce web-based version of Data Loader. Simply login, go to dataloader.io, and use your Salesforce credentials (refer to the following figure):

Figure 9.14: dataloader.io

Although this requires less initial setup than Data Loader, it is quite limited for use for free. The pricing menu gives you a breakdown of the various pricing options.

Once logged in, press the **NEW TASK** button and select from importing, exporting, or deleting data, as shown in the following figure:

Figure 9.15: *Creating a new task in dataloader.io*

Data quality

There is the phrase *garbage in, garbage out* which basically means if your Salesforce org is full of junk data, then reports, Einstein AI, and linking meaningful information together get to be a pointless task. Or to look at it more positively, if you have good data in your Salesforce Org, then you can do insightful reports and great marketing activities.

There are two main areas where data can go wrong in your Salesforce instance:

- Duplicate data so there is more than one record of the same thing.

- Redundant or replicated fields in your Salesforce org that add complexity when trying to analyze it.

These two areas are addressed in the following sections.

Duplicate rules

Users of Salesforce often enter information that may already exist, or load data that creates existing records; either way, you may end up with multiple accounts, contacts, or other records. This can cause problems across Salesforce, from automations and code to reports and dashboards. The simplest way to resolve this is by training the user to search for a record before entering it, but duplicate rules mean this can be prevented.

To prevent this, Salesforce has duplicate rules that can do any of the following:

- Block a record from being entered that already exists.

- Provide a report of all duplicate records that need to be sorted out.

- Let the user know the record already exists, but save the record regardless.

Duplicate rules are found by going to **Setup | Duplicate Management**, where you will see both:

- **Duplicate rules**: Work with matching rules to say what action needs to be taken.

- **Matching rules**: The logic used to identify a duplicate.

If you are only reporting on duplicate records, then the results can be found from **Setup |
Duplicate Error Logs**. You can also build duplicate reports by going to **Setup | Duplicate
Management** and selecting a **Duplicate Rule**. If you allow a duplicate to be created, then you
have the option to report on it as shown in the following figure:

Figure 9.16: Allowing reports on duplicate rules

To create duplicate reports, you first need to create a custom report type by going to **Setup |
Report Types** and searching for the **Duplicate Record Sets** object, as shown in the following
figure:

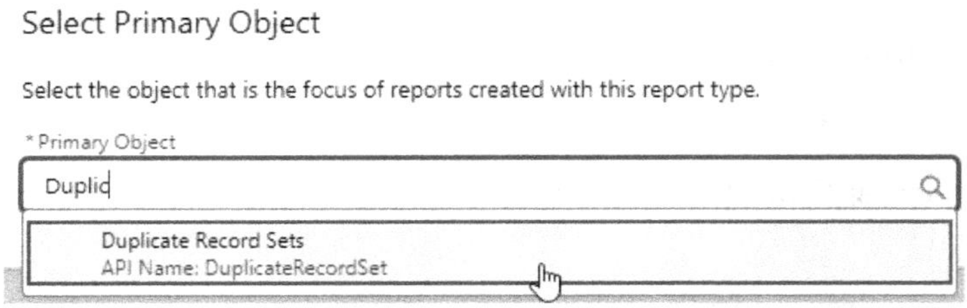

Figure 9.17: Creating a customer report type for duplicate records

Store it in the category **Administrative Reports** and set the availability as **Deployed**. Press **Save**
and **Save** again. Use the report creation capabilities outlined in *Chapter 8, Reports, Dashboards,
and basic Tableau,* but base the report on the report type created in the previous step.

Various apps are available on the AppExchange for duplicate and data management.
The selection will depend on requirements, but popular ones are Apsona, DataGroomr,
DemandTools, and Plauti. Cloudingo is a well-established tool for more complicated duplicate
management, including de-duping existing records in Salesforce across related objects and
highly configurable logic. This can be done for an existing org with a lot of existing duplicated
data, essentially cleaning up your Salesforce org and maintaining the data integrity.

Field Trip

Over time, your Salesforce org will have data issues, and it is all too easy to add fields that
are not used. This can have an impact on reporting and dashboards for the use of Agentforce.
One of the common issues is redundant fields, which are not even visible on the page layout.
These can be hard to identify. A very useful tool is Field Trip, as described in this section.
However, at the time of writing, Field Trip has been removed from the AppExchange, possibly
due to having an out-of-date API. It may be available soon once it has been updated. A very

good alternative is *Cuneiform* by *PeerNova*, available on the AppExchange as illustrated in the following figure:

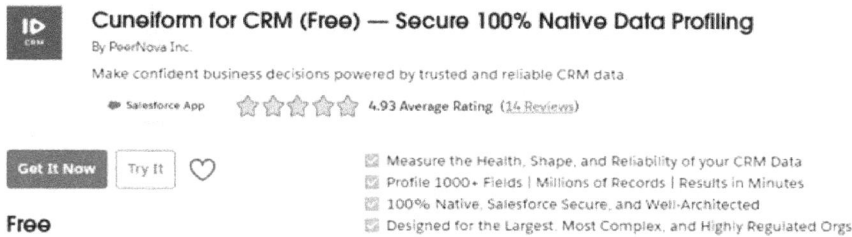

Figure 9.18: *Cuneiform on the Salesforce AppExchange*

Ideally, every field on an object is useful, but often, fields are added to an object and never get used. Sometimes, they are not added to the page layout or included in configuration, leaving them empty. If a Salesforce org is several years old, then these fields tend to be ignored, but serve no purpose.

Various apps can easily find these fields on the AppExchange, but a simple-to-use one is Field Trip (refer to the following figure):

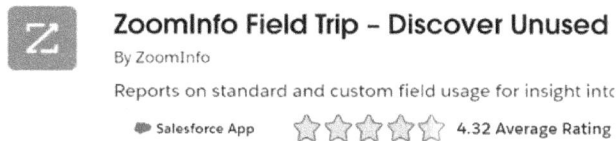

Figure 9.19: *Getting ZoomInfo Field Trip from AppExchange*

The basic process is as follows:

1. Install it (for admins only).

2. Go to the Field Trip app and create a new Field Trip.

3. Select the object to analyze and wait for it to run. Depending on the size of the org, it can be quite a while.

4. When you get a confirmation email, revisit the Field Trip app and go to the analysis link.

5. On the related list, you have the fields on the object with the number of records and the percentage populated. For example, a created date field will be 100% populated, whilst there will be some fields that are mostly populated, but quite often a large number of fields are unpopulated.

    a. The role of an admin would be to assess whether these are needed at all. Generally, do not just delete a field, but rename the API name to start with an **X__**. This means the field cannot be referenced elsewhere in Salesforce or be part of an external system.

    b. If there are no unforeseen problems, the field can be deleted. If there are any problems, then it can be quickly renamed.

Field Trip example

An example of a Field Trip report is shown in the following figure. It shows a large number of fields in an old Salesforce org that are never used. To the right of the graph are fields completely unpopulated, while to the left, you can see fields populated up to 100%.

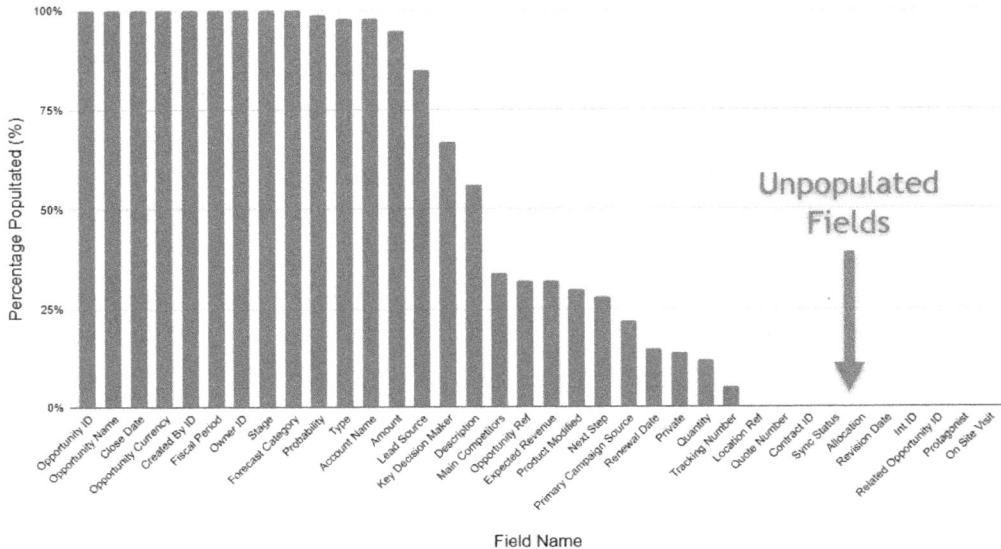

Figure 9.20: Example results from Field Trip

In the above example, fields with no data can be removed. Salesforce allows a limit of 500 fields on an object. In the preceding figure, many fields are not being used. This slows down performance and also causes issues with users and administrators.

Data backup

Many companies are required to back up their own data. This is typically for legal or disaster-recovery purposes. This can be done by Salesforce's own process or using a third-party tool such as **https://www.owndata.com/**. Many companies are legally obliged to keep records of their data for auditing purposes. However, although the likelihood of this is remote, it is important to prepare for the scenario. Fortunately, Salesforce comes with data backup tools that can be easily configured for the organization's requirements.

Backing up data in Salesforce

To back up data on a regular basis, go to **Setup | Data Export** and set a schedule, as shown in the following figure.

The backup file does not contribute to your Salesforce storage limits and is saved as a zip file.

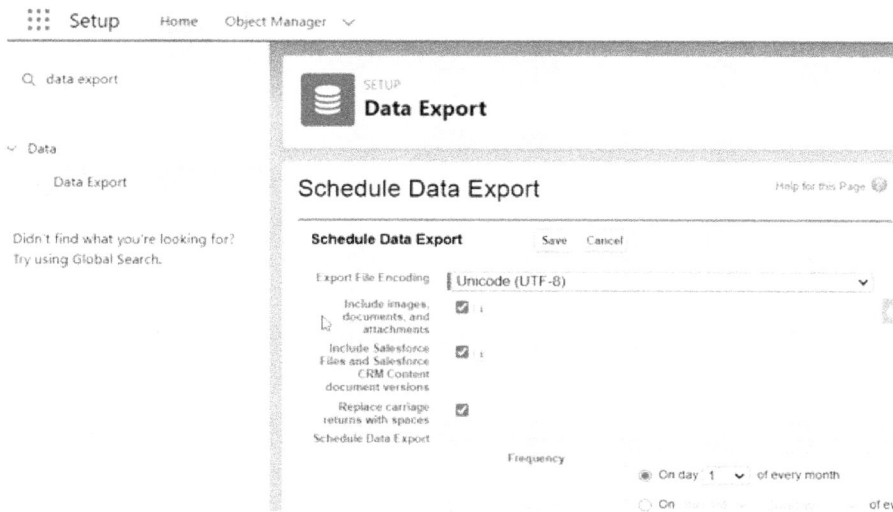

Figure 9.21: Setting up Data Export

Date deletion, Recycle Bin

Salesforce has a Recycle Bin, which is available to all users. This can be deleted automatically or manually. This can also be done by individual users or by a system administrator to remove all items in the Recycle Bin.

The **Recycle Bin** can be found on the **App Launcher**, as shown in the following figure:

Figure 9.22: Salesforce Recycle Bin

Various tools from AppExchange

With thousands of apps on the AppExchange, the selection would depend on the business requirements and budget. Salesforce provides an app leaderboard so you can see the most popular apps by various categories for all admins, found at: **https://appexchange.salesforce. com/mktcollections/curated/adminmusthaves**

A short list of some of the better-known ones is provided here:

- **Clone this user**: Take the trouble out of adding new users by simply cloning an existing one.

- **DLRS: Declarative Lookup Rollup Summaries (DLRS)** allows you to do various summary functions from a child object if a lookup relationship exists. There is growing popularity for Apex Rollup, which performs a similar function.

- **Timewarp**: Provides a timeline of key objects as to when the record was created.

- **Eposly**: It is a great tool for managing intuitive payment options to complete the order process.

- **FieldSpy**: Although similar to Field Trip, it offers some further analysis to assist in deleting unwanted fields.

- **Inspire planner**: A highly acclaimed paid-for app to assist with project management.

- **Flexpricer**: A simplified but less costly version of **configure, price, quote (CPQ)**.

- **SMS-Magic**: There are several SMS apps on the AppExchange. SMS-Magic is easy to configure and inexpensive to run.

There are many more apps available, such as eSignature, document generation, social media integration, and more, some of which are covered by Salesforce Ben at: **https://www.salesforceben.com/best-salesforce-apps/**

Salesforce useful links

Although not a tool as such, Salesforce offers complete visibility into the past performance of your Salesforce instance or any planned future maintenance. For example, any service outages, performance issues, or future planned maintenance.

To get this information, visit **https://trust.salesforce.com/** and either take the server instance name from your Salesforce instance. To find out which Salesforce server the instance is on, go to **Setup | Company Information** and see the server instance, as shown in the following figure:

Figure 9.23: Getting your Salesforce instance ID for use with Salesforce Trust

As shown in the following figure, the server instance name is **SWE126**, which is not to be confused with the organization ID. Return to **https://trust.salesforce.com/** and select **Sales and Service** Cloud, and select the instance to see the performance and any future maintenance or previous issues:

Figure 9.24: Entering the instance ID into Salesforce Trust

Salesforce Architects

When having to work on large projects, it can be very helpful to realize that someone has been there before. Salesforce Architects is a group dedicated to providing free online resources to assist. Visit: **https://architect.salesforce.com/** to get free templates and resources, as shown in the following figure:

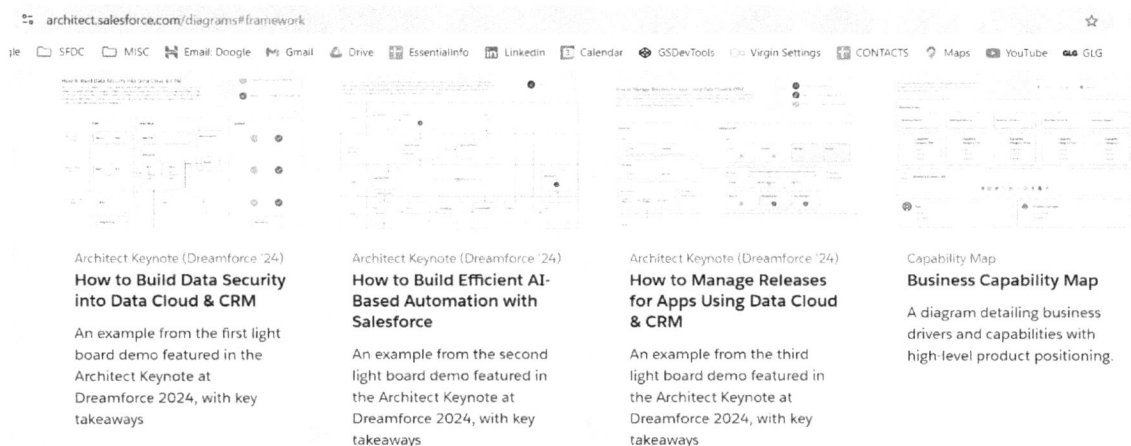

Figure 9.25: Examples of architecture solutions on Salesforce Architects

The site is dedicated to designing system architecture that has been proven to work and adopts the best practices for implementing Salesforce and related products. For example, the design of including Heroku with Salesforce Mobile SDK gives a design template that can be used for steering design decisions.

Conclusion

This chapter has covered a range of useful tools for Salesforce Administrators to keep on top of their organization. There are many more, but these are the tools used widely by Salesforce Administrators. The tools listed here are generally free, but some have additional features for paid licenses.

This chapter has covered the core basic areas required, while there are tools dedicated to specific requirements, such as Salesforce Page Analyzer, or tools useful for other Salesforce products. As a general rule, if doing something is tedious and time-consuming, then generally, someone has thought of a tool to do it.

In the next chapter, we will be looking at various Salesforce features that all administrators should be aware of, such as multi-currency, advanced currency management, and multi-lingual Salesforce Orgs. Setting up such features can really help us use Salesforce to make users' experience a pleasure.

Multiple choice questions

1. **Data export is used to back up your Salesforce org. This can be scheduled:**

    a. Daily

    b. Weekly

    c. Monthly

    d. Dates from the company calendar

2. **Many of the tools can be found at which two places:**

    a. Google Play

    b. The AppExchange

    c. The Chrome Webstore

    d. Apple App Store

3. **Duplicate rules can do which of the following (choose three):**

    a. Prevent the record from being saved

    b. Alert the user that an existing record already exists

    c. Do nothing but save the duplicate record in Duplicate Error Logs

    d. Provide administrators with an email to notify them of the duplicate record

4. **When using upsert for importing data, it will:**

    a. Import all the records, but alert if a duplicate record has been created

    b. Update all matching records and prevent new records from being created

    c. Update an existing record or create a new one if it does not exist

    d. Create duplicate records if they already exist, and insert records if no existing record can be found

5. **To use Salesforce Trust, you first need to have what information?**

    a. The Salesforce org instance ID

    b. Your username and password

    c. The Salesforce org instance name

    d. The Salesforce org company name

6. **Salesforce Architects is:**

    a. An online forum to showcase new ways of configuring Salesforce

    b. A service offered by Salesforce to improve your Salesforce ecosystem

    c. A resource for various templates and decision guides to assist you in architectural decisions

    d. Available on the AppExchange to assess the architecture of your Salesforce environment

7. **Excel and Google Sheets use the VLOOKUP function to**

    a. Match a record based on criteria to find the value in a range and display it

    b. Look at the records in a data range and replace them with a specific value

    c. Check that the ID of one record matches the ID of another record

    d. Check that a value in a formula matches the value in a sheet

8. **Field Trip is an App that is useful for:**

    a. Ensuring data is unique in each record in Salesforce

    b. Identifying which objects are the least used in Salesforce

    c. Assisting with populating empty fields

    d. Identifying the percentage used of a field on an object

9. **Which of the following statements is true about dataloader.io:**

    a. DataLoader can do the upsert command, whilst dataloader.io cannot

    b. It requires you to import the data before using

    c. dataloader.io requires a subscription to use; Data Loader does not

    d. dataloader.io requires the Chrome plugin to work with Salesforce

10. **What is the difference between Salesforce Optimizer and Org Check?**

   a. OrgCheck is available in Salesforce, whilst Optimizer needs to be installed

   b. Optimizer is for optimizing data, whilst Org Check is about checking the configuration

   c. Org Check is simple and broad, whilst Optimizer is detailed but specific

   d. Optimizer is for checking the configuration, whilst Org Check is about security and visibility

Answers

1	**c**
2	**b, c**
3	**a, b, c**
4	**c**
5	**c**
6	**c**
7	**a**
8	**d**
9	**a**
10	**c**

Join our Discord space

Join our Discord workspace for latest updates, offers, tech happenings around the world, new releases, and sessions with the authors:

https://discord.bpbonline.com

CHAPTER 10
Various Salesforce Features

Introduction

This chapter is dedicated to various Salesforce features that can be used in many places, which is known as a **Salesforce Administrator**. These often enhance standard functionality, but since they are frequently used, knowing that these features exist can help with configuring Salesforce correctly.

The sections are ordered in a sequence to group them together, but a brief overview of each feature and enough information to get you started is provided. However, there will be more documentation online, such as *Salesforce Trailhead*, *Salesforce Ben*, *Apex Hours*, or similar.

Since many of the features have various capabilities, they are grouped into sections with functionality that will be useful in similar situations. Some features, such as Experience Cloud, are a subject in themselves, while others are just useful to know that they exist, but if not given some reasonable mention, they would otherwise go unnoticed.

Structure

In this chapter, we will cover the following topics:

- Across org Salesforce features
- Salesforce features

- Salesforce configuration features
- Other Salesforce features

Objectives

By the end of this chapter, readers will have learned about features in Salesforce that can be applied across the org. These features are generic but very useful, such as making your Salesforce org multi-currency or suitable for users who speak another language. Salesforce also has some simple but powerful features, such as Web-to-Lead, which make getting data from outside of Salesforce easy. Other features are simply to make your Salesforce instance look brilliant and include some standard functionality that the users will love. This chapter is to make you aware of what Salesforce could be if you were aware of what is available, as well as some tips on how to include additional functionality, which is nice to have.

Across org Salesforce features

The following features span Salesforce and are useful for increasing functionality in many areas. They should also be used in the context of business requirements and not necessarily added simply because they are available. These features can be used in various places or across the entire Salesforce system, which means they do not fit neatly into a particular section. They can also be used in different ways to enhance the user experience with Salesforce. This builds on knowledge gained from previous chapters. For example, building out a complicated path on an opportunity may be suitable for sales reps but not for senior management, and as such, the Salesforce security model covered in *Chapter 7, Salesforce Security Model*, would require you to ensure the design was suitable for both types of users. However, many of the sections in this chapter give good advice on how to take your Salesforce org to the next level.

Person accounts

Salesforce is generally used for businesses to work with other companies. This is called a **business to business** (**B2B**) model. As a result, the Account object is used to store business information, with contacts often belonging to an account.

However, it might be that the business only really does business with customers. This is called a **business to customer** (**B2C**) model; as such, Salesforce has person accounts, which allow the business to work directly with the customer.

Salesforce allows person accounts to provide a B2C model and claims various benefits such as:

- Simplification of contact management by combining accounts and contacts into one record.
- A more personalized experience for end users since they are not associated with an account.
- Suitable for some industries such as insurance and the public sector.

However, admins should be aware of the following points:

- Once person accounts are enabled, they cannot be turned off. As such, always trial person accounts in a test sandbox first.

- Person accounts generate more data storage in Salesforce. A typical contact record in Salesforce without person accounts is 1 KB; when person accounts are enabled, contacts combined with an account are 2 to 4 KB. Although this is tiny, if you have many thousands or millions of records, then it can add considerably to data storage.

- Although the data model is meant to be simplified, some might consider it harder to conceptualize since the B2B model has a clear definition of what an account and contact are.

Whether you like them or not, they are popular or required under certain situations, and an administrator should be aware of them. There have been some organizations that end up running two Salesforce environments, one for B2B and the other for B2C, so they can concentrate on both sides of their business.

To enable person accounts, go to **Setup | Person Accounts** as shown in the following figure:

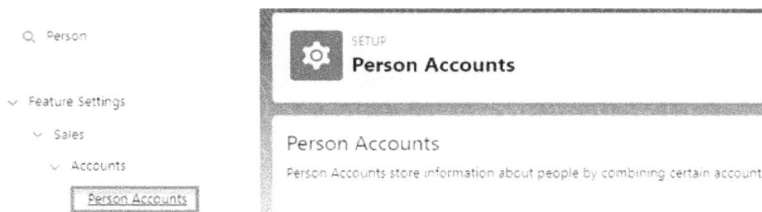

Figure 10.1: Setting up Person accounts

Note: **That since person accounts cannot be turned off, it is recommended to trial this feature in a separate environment, either a new Developer Edition account or a separate sandbox.**

You will first be asked to complete a checklist including:

- **View Org Impacts**: Accepting the terms and conditions of using person accounts.

- **Create a record type of accounts**: Press the **Setup** button and add the following record types:
  - **Existing Record Type**: **Master**
  - **Record Type Label**: `Person Accounts`
  - **Record Type Name**: (let it automatically populate)
  - **Description**: `Account record type used for person accounts`
  - Press **Next** and select the **Page Layout**
  - Press **Save**

- **Setup**: Once completed, press the **Check Readiness** button at the top of the page or simply press the **Enable Person Accounts** button. You will be asked again for confirmation, and then the option to turn on the **Reports to field on Person Account**, which has a description of the functionality, as shown in the following figure:

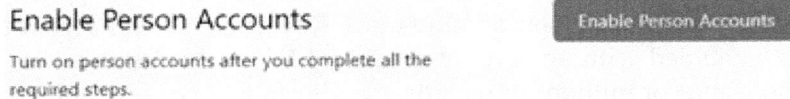

Figure 10.2: Enabling Person Accounts

Complete the steps above. It can take a short while for person accounts to become active, and you will be sent an email to confirm that it was successful. To check if they are go to **Setup | Person Accounts** and you will see that they are enabled, as shown in the following figure:

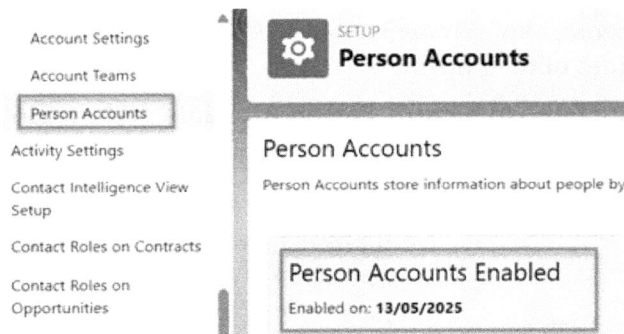

Figure 10.3: Activating Person Accounts in Setup

Chatter

Chatter is a Salesforce collaboration tool with features similar to popular social media messaging apps. Chatter is often overlooked and often discounted from the outset, as it can create more noise than meaningful collaboration. However, this is not to say it is not useful if setup correctly and has a few very useful features, such as the ability for users to collaborate internally with colleagues and externally with customers.

There are many online articles about setting up and using Chatter, which focus on basic functionality such as:

- Posting to groups or against records and being able to add files, links, or @mentions.
- Having polls for group decision-making.
- Being able to like or use emojis in messages.

Possibly one of the more useful features of Chatter is to be able to collaborate outside the user base of Salesforce.

To allow this, follow these steps:

1. Go to the **Chatter** tab (found in various apps) or simply open Chatter from the **App Launcher**.

2. Setup a Chatter Group by pressing the + icon next to existing groups and include the option for **Allow customers**, as shown in the following figure:

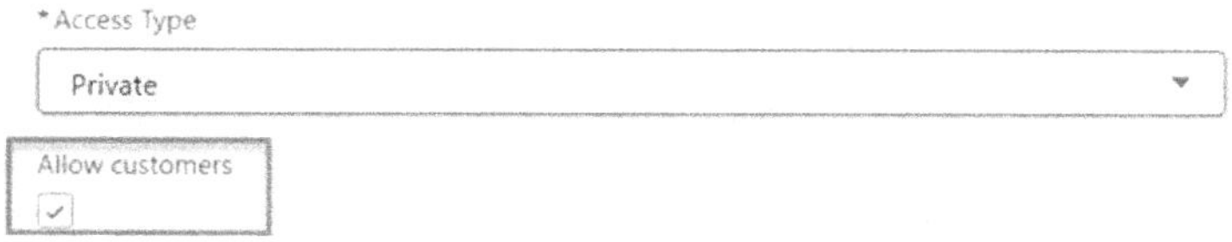

Figure 10.4: Allowing Chatter to be available for customers

To complete the group setup, add an icon or photo and select the users to add.

Note: Public groups cannot be used with customers since any Chatter Feeds might not be appropriate for the broader audience.

Chatter Settings and configuration

Chatter also has many settings that you should be aware of. These are found in **Setup | Chatter | Chatter Settings**.

Chatter can be added to a page layout. It is often referred to as a **feed** in Salesforce. To check if Chatter can be added to a page, first check that it is enabled for that object.

To do this, go to **Setup | Feed Tracking** and enable it.

Select the object you wish to add Chatter to and then the fields to track, as shown in the following figure, and press **Save**:

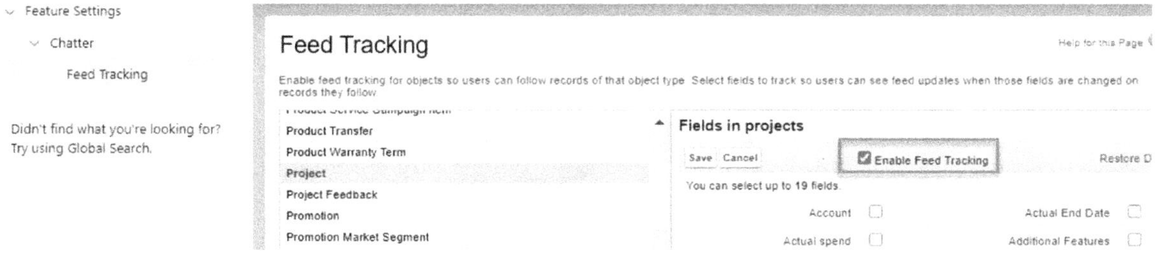

Figure 10.5: Adding Chatter Feed to an object

The best way to add Chatter to a page is by going to the page you wish to see Chatter on and selecting **Setup | Edit Page**, as shown in the following figure:

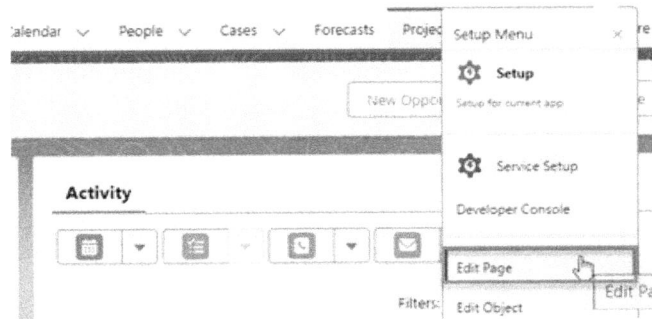

Figure 10.6: *Adding Chatter to a page layout*

From here, simply drag the Chatter Feed component to the relevant part of the page layout as shown in *Figure 10.7* and press **Save**.

Chatter Feed is specific to the object, whilst Chatter is the broader collaboration across the Salesforce environment. For this example, you want Chatter Feed:

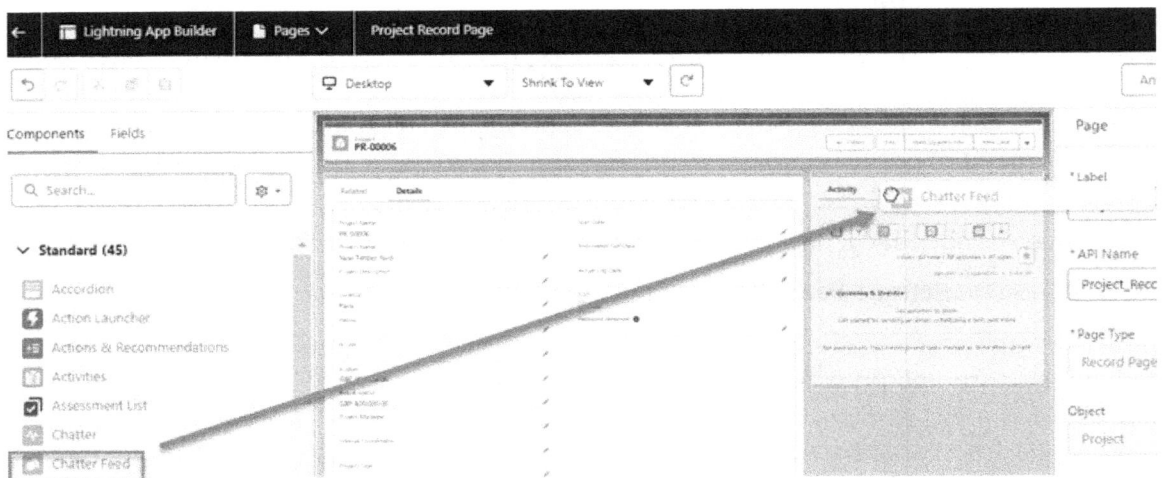

Figure 10.7: *Placing Chatter Feed on a page layout*

Salesforce Go

Salesforce Go is a new feature to provide easy configuration for common business goals such as pipeline management or opportunity scoring. It is found on the main Setup menu by going to **Setup | Salesforce Go**. Salesforce Administrators are often aware of new features in Salesforce, but implementing them can be difficult and time-consuming. Salesforce Go is a single resource to help turn new features on and monitor adoption and usage in a centralized way. Salesforce Go displays various tiles, which will vary depending on your Salesforce org and the most recent Salesforce release. Each tile will provide a suggested configuration that an administrator should be aware of, which will also include the necessary training and documentation to implement the feature.

Calendar

The calendar feature is handy as it allows you to see your tasks or events in one place. The calendar can be private, public, or shared and synced with your own work calendar.

Although users would generally want all their meetings in one place, a good use of the calendar is to share a company view on significant events. To do this, go to **Setup | Public Calendars and Resources** and then set it for a specific group to add events to the calendar as shown in the following figure:

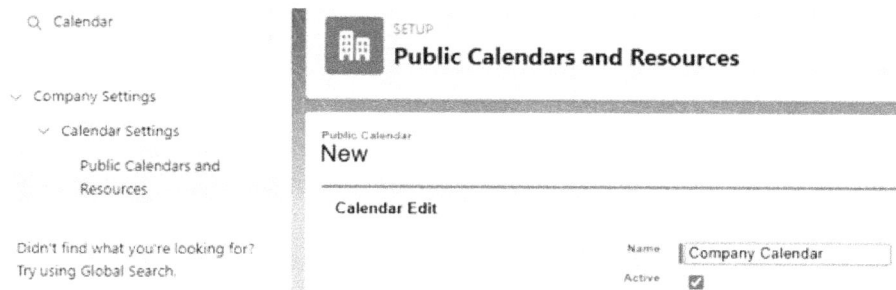

Figure 10.8: Creating a new public calendar

Calendars can be synced with Salesforce objects such as:

- Opportunity Close Date
- Open Cases with SLA agreement dates
- Campaign launch date

To do this, follow these steps:

1. You need to create a calendar based on an object. To do this, go to the **App Launcher** and select **Calendar**, as shown in the following figure:

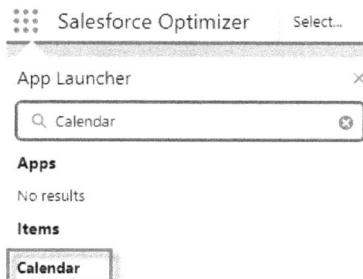

Figure 10.9: Accessing the Calendar app

2. On the far-right hand side of the screen, press the gear icon and select the **New Calendar** button, which will ask you for the object to base the calendar on and what is required to make an entry to the calendar, as shown in the following figure:

Create Calendar
Step 2 of 2

* Calendar Name

Opportunities Close Date

Start and Duration of Calendar Items ⓘ

* Field for Start ⓘ

Close Date (Date)   ▾

Field for End ⓘ

Close Date (Date)   ▾

Apply a Filter ⓘ

All Opportunities   ▾

* Field Name to Display ⓘ

Description   ▾

Back   Save

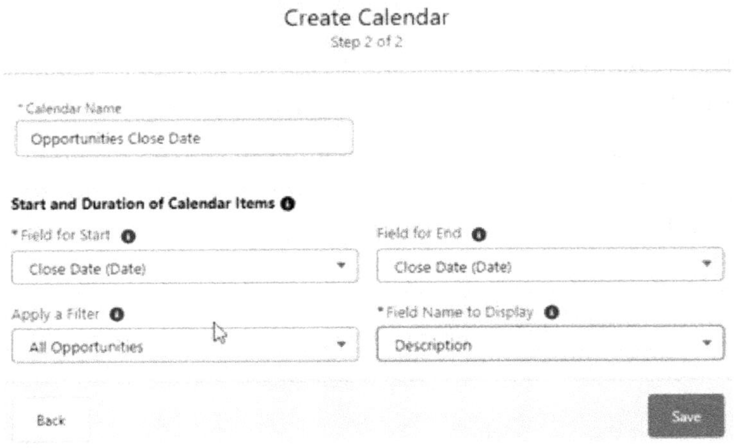

Figure 10.10: Creating a calendar

3. The calendar can then be shared under the same menu by assigning groups to the calendar, as shown in the following figure:

Public Calendars

Action	Name
Edit ¦ Del ｜Sharing	Company Calendar

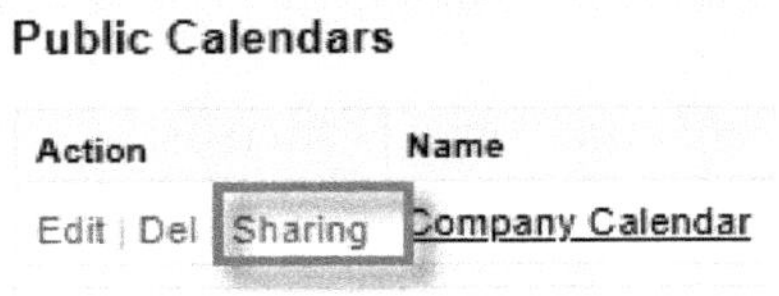

Figure 10.11: Sharing a calendar

4. In the sharing settings, you can assign different access levels to the calendar, such as to just show the details or add events.

Campaigns

Campaigns are a central feature of Salesforce, but are often used in conjunction with dedicated marketing platforms such as Marketing Cloud or **Marketing Cloud Account Engagement** (**MCAE**). This is because Salesforce CRM is used to keep a single record about the campaign, whilst using more sophisticated functionality about the campaign in the chosen marketing platform.

Campaigns can be organized into hierarchies, so you may have a campaign for a new product launch with regional campaigns based on tradeshows or the social media used to pilot the product launch. This also helps with summary reporting and high-level campaign performance analysis.

Campaigns are also linked to the lead and opportunity object, which means that they can be used to nurture a Lead into an opportunity. This is typically done using **Campaign Members**, which allows users to track member status where they might engage in a campaign. This could be if they were sent an email, responded, and attended an event such as a webinar or trade show. This helps **Campaign Members** understand engagement on an individual level. To do this, go to a **Campaign Members** related list and press the **Add Leads** button, as shown in the following figure:

Figure 10.12: Adding Campaign Members to a Campaign

Campaigns also try to give a measure of **return on investment** (**ROI**) by linking the field Primary Campaign Source on the opportunity record, which allows the opportunity value to be summarized against a campaign. This is referred to as **Campaign Influence**, which simply means marketers are able to see which campaigns led to an opportunity if it was won. This also allows for data-driven decision-making since campaign reports can track cost per lead, ROI, or other useful engagement statistics.

Although many companies prefer to do highly targeted marketing using Salesforce Marketing Cloud, it is still important to keep the success of these campaigns in a single place to keep a 360^0 view of the customer. As a result, campaigns are an important part of building a successful marketing strategy.

Knowledge and articles

Salesforce Knowledge allows you to provide useful documentation to users on a particular subject. The more recent Lightning Knowledge also has capabilities to work with Agentforce to give AI-generated information for agents. An example of this could be in a call center where a high-value customer calls in, and Agentforce can augment the customer's query with AI, as well as a suitable Knowledge article. This can assist the agent, give first-class customer service, and be tracked in case of history.

Other scenarios where Salesforce Knowledge is used could be to assist users in having relevant information or to display articles through Experience Cloud to allow customers to find answers to questions about the company's products or services. This can reduce the number of customers who need to contact the company, which reduces the cost of running a call center or support service. For example, the customer might have a query about a particular product or service and is able to find the answer online using the Knowledge exposed on Experience Cloud on the company's website.

There is also the older Salesforce Classic Knowledge, which should be migrated to the more recent Lightning Knowledge, which includes better features such as version control and publishing approval. This section is about Lightning Knowledge.

Salesforce Knowledge is a paid feature license. If you go to your Developer Edition account and go to **Setup | Company Information,** you will see the number of Knowledge licenses assigned, as shown in the following figure:

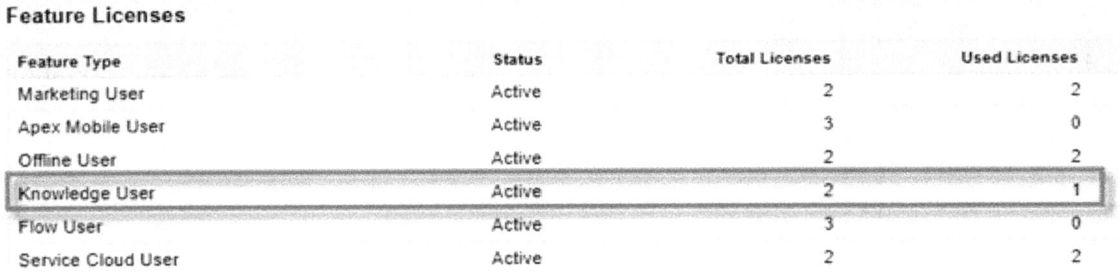

Feature Licenses

Feature Type	Status	Total Licenses	Used Licenses
Marketing User	Active	2	2
Apex Mobile User	Active	3	0
Offline User	Active	2	2
Knowledge User	Active	2	1
Flow User	Active	3	0
Service Cloud User	Active	2	2

Figure 10.13: Checking if the org has available Knowledge licenses

Check that the license is also assigned to you under your user profile settings, as shown in the following figure:

Email	andrew white@doogle.com	Active	✓
Username	andy white@bpb.com	Marketing User	☑
Nickname	andy white	Offline User	☑
Title		Knowledge User	☑

Figure 10.14: Checking a user profile to see if a Knowledge license is assigned to them

Setting up Salesforce Knowledge

Setting up Knowledge is a big subject with plenty of online tutorials. However, some key concepts in setting up Salesforce Knowledge are mentioned here:

- **Data categories**: Provide a hierarchical view of your knowledge articles and visibility into the articles via data category visibility.

- **Data category groups**: Provide a way of keeping data categories in related groups.

- **Topics**: These are like tags, which contain words that are key to users or customers searching for a knowledge article.

Setting up Lightning Knowledge is best done by going to **Setup | Service Setup Assistant** and pressing the **Service Setup Assistant** slider.

This may take some time, but when complete, press the **Knowledge Setup** wizard, which will allow you to select authors, data categories, and more. Note that there are some limitations if you are using the Developer Edition account, such as data and file storage, and the use of Knowledge with Einstein.

To continue the configuration, go to **Service Setup**, as shown in the following figure:

Figure 10.15: Using Service Setup to configure Knowledge

To setup **Data Categories** and **Category Groups**, go to **Setup | Data Categories** and add the appropriate details, as shown in the following figure:

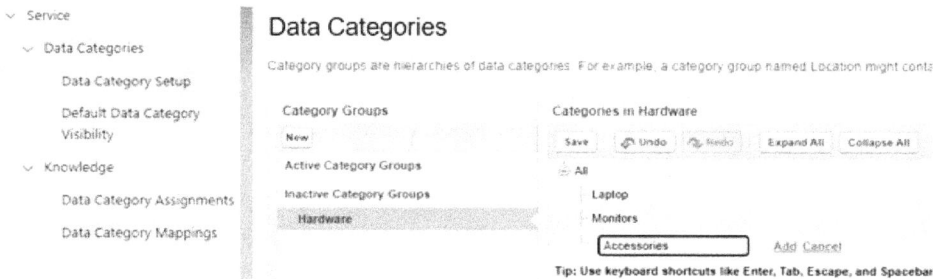

Figure 10.16: Defining Data Categories

You will need to make each category group active before it can be used with Knowledge articles.

To actually see Knowledge working, go to **App Launcher** and type `Knowledge`.

This will bring you into the **Knowledge** app, where you can create a new article, publish it, and see the versioning, as shown in the following figure:

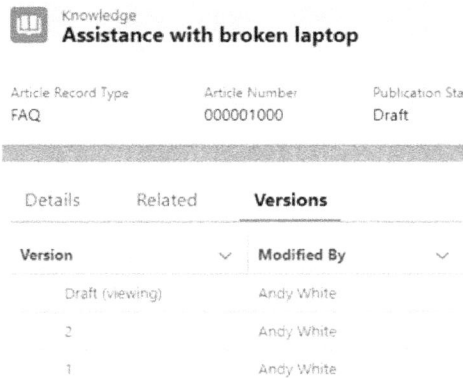

Figure 10.17: Viewing a Knowledge article

Macros

Macros are useful for automating repetitive tasks. These can be made available for all users and are available on the utility bar at the very bottom of the screen.

To create a macro, follow these steps:

1. Go to **Setup | App Manager** and search for the app you want the macro to appear on.

2. For this example, select **Service Console** and use the drop-down arrow on the right-hand side of the screen and press **Edit**.

3. Under **Utility Items (Desktop Only)**, press the **Add Utility Item** button, as shown in the following figure:

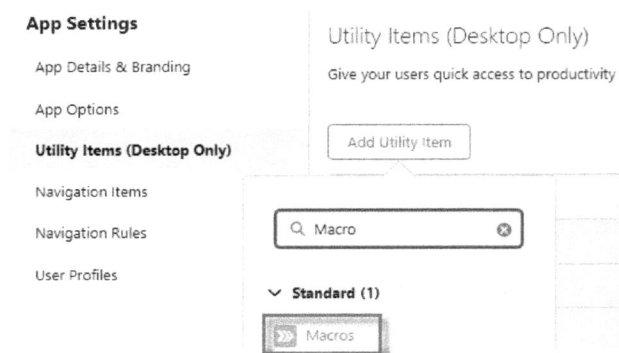

Figure 10.18: Creating a macro as a new utility item

4. Select **Macros** and press **Save**.

5. Then go to the **Service Console**, and you will see the **Macro** option in the utility bar at the very bottom left-hand side of the screen.

6. Press **Macro** and then add a new macro as shown in the following figure:

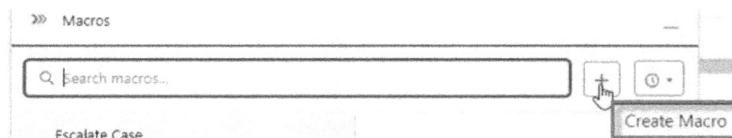

Figure 10.19: Adding a macro from the utility bar

7. Give the macro a name such as **Create Email** and select the object it needs to apply to, for example, the case object.

8. Press **Save**, and you will see a new macro but with no functionality behind it. To do this, press the **Edit Instructions** button, as shown in the following figure:

Figure 10.20: Editing a macro to provide the functionality

9. The next window has various options on how to pre-populate the email, including an email template or add further instructions or logic, as shown in the following figure:

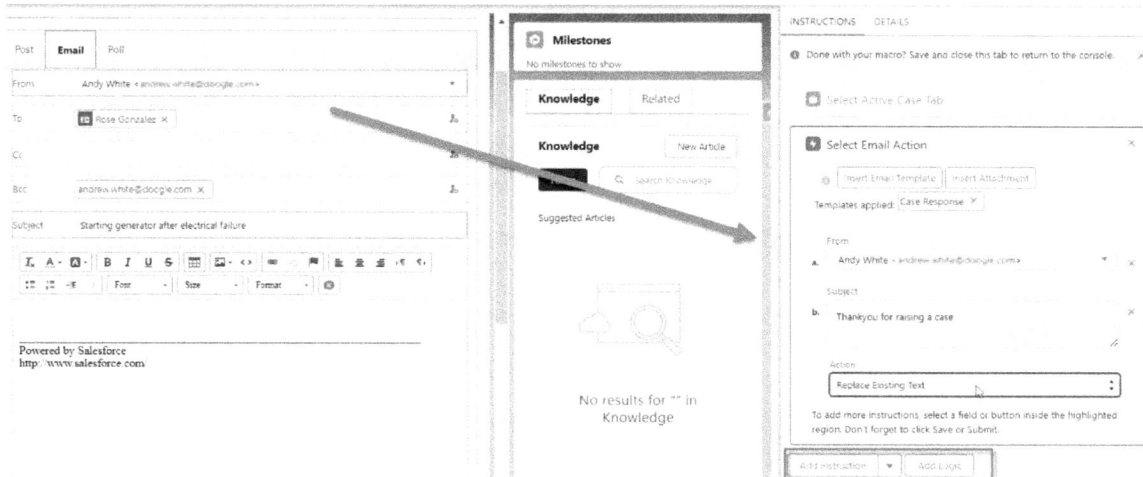

Figure 10.21: Adding instructions to the macro

Experience Cloud

Experience Cloud is a public facing front-end to your Salesforce org. It can only be summarized here, as it has many features worthy of a book in itself. Salesforce can put a customer-facing website on top of the instance to provide public access or limit access to specific users who are typically from companies that you need to work with. Salesforce Experience Cloud is often used to give customers access to their records, submit cases, or engage directly with the business.

The level of access depends on further configuration, but to build Experience Cloud, go to **Setup | Digital Experiences** and **Enable Digital Experiences**. Press **Save**, as shown in the following figure:

Einstein is building your prediction...

It can take anywhere from half an hour to 24 hours to build your prediction depending on your data and settings. The notification bell tells you when building has finished.

Go to the list view in Setup to review your scorecard and prediction quality.

Go to Setup

Figure 10.22: Enabling Digital Experiences

On the next page, press **New** and select the type of website you are looking to build. There are several to choose from. Note that you can build one from scratch, and some are **Lightning Web Runtime (LWR)**, which is the latest Salesforce Experience Cloud technology, relying on **Lightning Web Components (LWC)**, which is covered later in *Chapter 11, Basics of Apex and Lightning Web Components*.

In this example, we will be using the **Customer Service** template, but you may choose one you feel is more suitable for your needs (refer to the following figure):

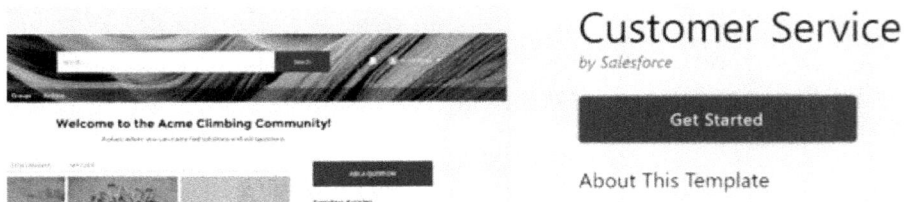

Figure 10.23: Example of an Experience Cloud template

Follow the steps and wait for Salesforce to setup your new Experience Cloud. The commonly used area is **Builder**, but for initial setup, it often uses the **Guided Setup**, as shown in the following figure:

My Workspaces

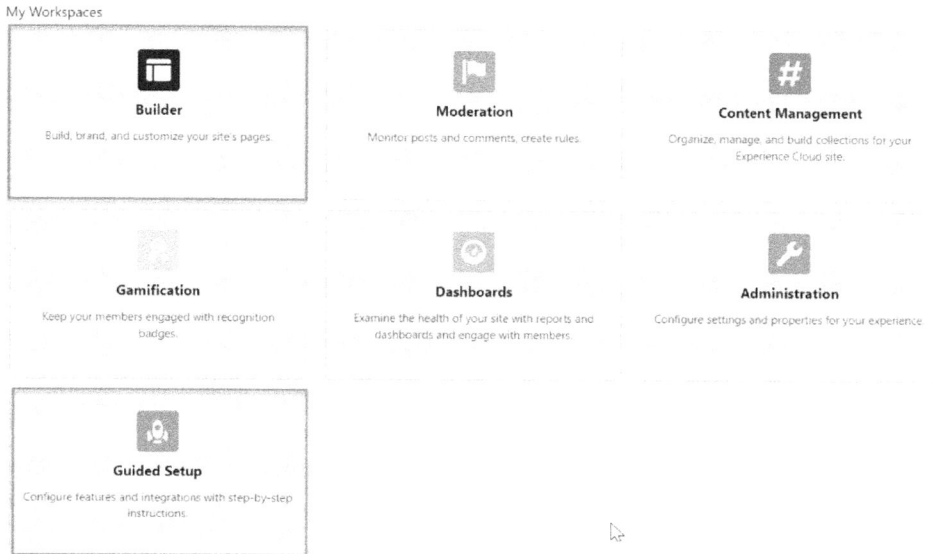

Figure 10.24: Exploring options for building Experience Cloud

Before you start modifying your newly built Experience Cloud, you can see what it looks like by going to the **Builder** option above and pressing the **Preview** button, as shown in the following figure:

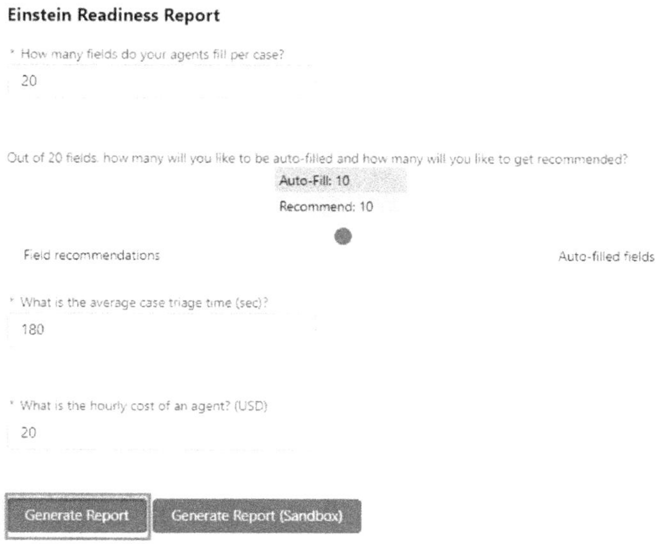

Figure 10.25: Preview of a blank Experience Cloud template

Press the **Back to Builder** button to return to editing mode. The menu has the following functionality, as shown in the following table:

Icon	Description of functionality
	Settings to allow you to go straight to other areas of the configuration, as well as jump to other Experience Cloud sites you may have.
	Add various components, grouped by functionality: analytics, content, feeds, etc.
	Change the look and feel across the Experience Cloud, for example, include corporate colors to standardize the Experience Cloud site for your business.
	Change the page structure by saying what components you want in which particular area of the site.
	General settings such as the language, security settings, and theme. The theme still keeps the same functionality and data of the website, but gives you many options for how the website will look. Try a few out, and revert back if it is not suitable.

Table 10.1: Options available in the Experience Cloud Builder

Salesforce features

There are various ways to use Salesforce data and easily merge the functionality with other systems or devices. This can go from the relatively simple, such as using the mobile app, to embedding complicated visual flows on external systems using OmniOut (which is outside the scope of this book). The following are just two examples of using Salesforce externally but independently of core functionality. As such, they can be used independently with other technologies to achieve functionality from other technologies or systems.

Salesforce mobile app

Your instance of Salesforce is available for all users on a mobile app. This can be found on the *Apple App Store* or *Google Play*. Search for Salesforce and install the app, as shown in the following figure:

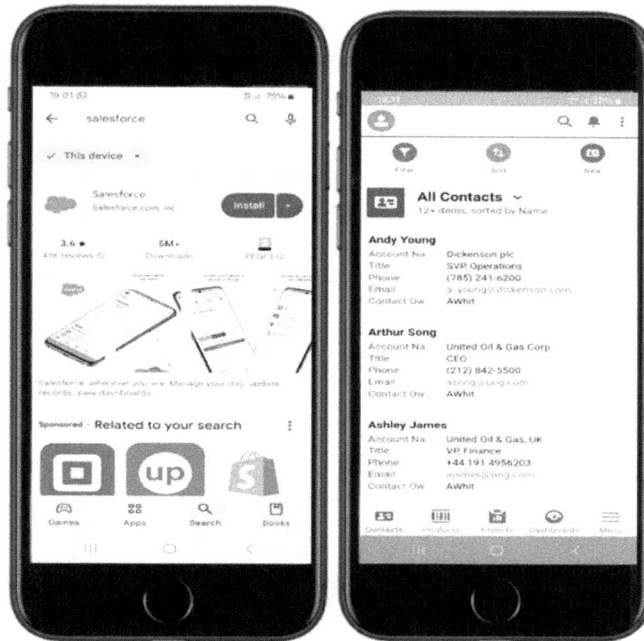

Figure 10.26: Installing and accessing Salesforce on mobile devices

Once installed, open the Salesforce app and complete the login steps, which may include the following:

- **Using a custom domain**: If you are using a Developer Edition account or a corporate account, it is the URL you have on your screen whilst using Salesforce, right up to the `.com`

- Depending on the authentication, you may be asked to use other methods such as Salesforce Authenticator or biometrics

When you have gained access, you will see your Salesforce instance on your mobile phone as shown in the figure above on the right-hand side.

Note: **Using the Salesforce app is not the same as building a custom mobile app based on Salesforce. This can be done by building a mobile app that can be installed from the Apple Store or Google Play. This involves using Salesforce Mobile SDK and typically an external supporting system to manage data volumes or content, such as Heroku, Render, or a range of alternatives. Since Heroku is a Salesforce product, a system design is covered in Chapter 14, Broader Salesforce Ecosystem.**

WhatsApp for Salesforce

To use Salesforce with WhatsApp, you will need a WhatsApp Business account. However, in your Developer Edition account, you can still activate this feature. To do this, go to **Setup |**

Messaging Settings and press the **Messaging** slider. Press the **New Channel** button, and you will get a multi-stage wizard with the option to select **WhatsApp**, as shown in the following figure:

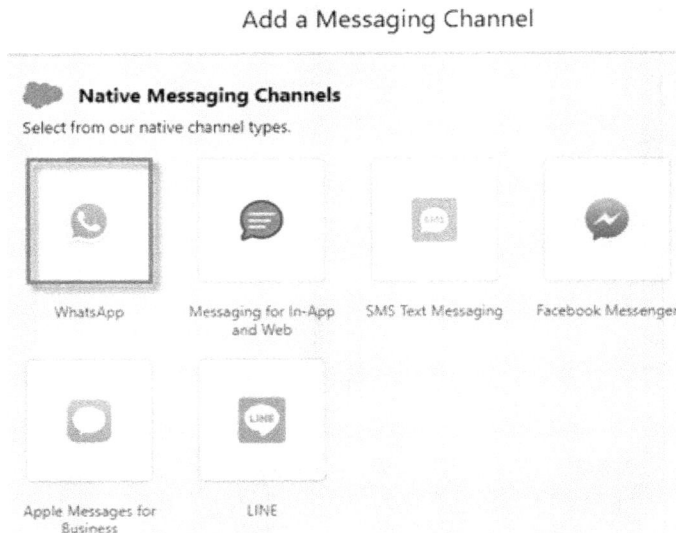

Figure 10.27: Selecting WhatsApp as a messaging channel

This will then require you to perform the following steps:

1. Turn off two-step verification.

2. Enter your **Facebook login** credentials and select a **Meta Business account**.

3. Select a **WhatsApp Business account** and **Business Profile**.

4. Verify your business phone number.

5. Further configurations are required depending on your business requirements, such as adding it to the Service Console, including it in Marketing Cloud, and more.

Salesforce configuration features

Many of the features covered in this book are generic Salesforce configurations. However, it is useful to be aware of other features that work across the entire Salesforce environment. These features provide functionality to all users, so it is best to know they are available and when to use them. They are also often configured incorrectly, so this guide is an experience-based approach to implementing them. For example, implementing omni-channel is also combined when setting up Service Cloud Voice, but it is important that the user understands why omni-channel offers certain advantages compared with Service Cloud Voice. This chapter is meant to give the user a good understanding of various Salesforce features that can be used when necessary.

Translation Workbench

Salesforce supports multiple languages, and users can login and select their preferred language. This can be done in a few ways:

- By the user when they register or edit their profile by going to **View Profile** | **Settings** | **Language & Time Zone**.

- Set by the administrator by editing the user record under **Setup** | **Users** | **Users** and selecting **Edit** next to the user record.

- On a company level, by selecting the language of the organization by going to **Setup** | **Company Information** | **Default Language**.

An example is shown in the following figure to setup the Sales app with the language set to *Danish*:

Figure 10.28: Salesforce with a different language on the user interface

However, there will be various words Salesforce would not recognize, such as custom fields you have added or a custom object. In this case, Salesforce offers the Translation Workbench to provide a translation.

To do this, go to **Setup** | **Translation Workbench** and press the **Enable** button.

Once enabled, select the language you wish to translate into and also the Salesforce component requiring the translation, for example, a field as shown in the following figure:

Figure 10.29: Translation Workbench with custom words added as required

It is not possible to translate the name of custom objects using **Translation Workbench**. Instead, this is done using **Setup | Rename Tabs and Labels**, then selecting the language and renaming accordingly. For example, the custom object Projects is renamed to Project for French users. When the user selects their preferred language, Salesforce will reference the name of the field and replace it with the user's language instead.

Multi-currency and advanced currency management

Salesforce caters to various currencies in your Salesforce org. It could be the business sells products to various countries or the sales team is dealing with customers based in different countries. The primary advantage of using multiple currencies is to allow exchange rates between currencies.

Although this is great, the currency exchange rate is set manually and applies to all the currencies in your org. It is best to include advanced currency management, as this allows you to give a date range in which currency exchange rates apply, which is useful for seeing the value of opportunities, quotes, and invoices at the time they were created, since they will remain the same. Advanced currency management is shown later in this section.

Currency is often linked to your company's location, both of which are found in **Company Information**. To do this, go to **Setup | Company Information** and look for **Default Locale** and **Currency Locale**, but they work independently. If you change the default currency, then it affects the entire Salesforce org.

To setup multi-currency, follow these steps:

1. Go to your **Company Information** (as shown above), press **Edit**, and tick the **Activate Multiple Currencies** checkbox as shown in the following figure:

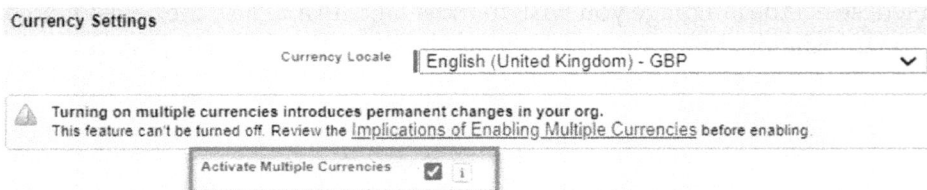

Figure 10.30: Activating multiple currencies

2. There are warnings that, once enabled, you cannot turn them off. Do read the article behind the link for **Implications of Enabling Multiple Currencies**, as there are a lot of considerations, and always make any significant changes first in a test sandbox to test the implications.

3. Assuming you proceed with activating multiple currencies, you will see a button at the top of the same page saying **Currency Setup**.

4. Press this to get the following figure, which should reflect on the screen:

Currency

Use this page to define all the currencies used by your organization. Corporate Currency should be set to the currency in which your corpora corporate, all conversion rates will be modified to reflect the change

Advanced Currency Management is not enabled
   Allows you to manage dated exchange rates that map a currency conversion rate to a specific date range. For more information, see Understanding (

Enable

Parenthetical Currency Conversion is enabled
   In multi-currency organizations, Salesforce displays converted currency amounts to users whose personal currency is different from the currency of tt
   disable this feature, currency fields display only the currency of the record.

Disable

Active Currencies   New   Edit Rates   Change Corporate

Action	Currency Code	Currency Name	Corporate	Conversion Rate
Edit Deactivate	GBP	British Pound	✓	1.000000

Figure 10.31: *Enabling advanced currency management*

5. The preceding figure has the **Enable** button for advanced currency management, which we will do shortly.

6. For now, press the **New** button to enter a new currency.

7. Enter the currencies you wish to include in multi-currencies, as shown in the following figure:

Active Currencies   New   Edit Rates   Change Corporate

Action	Currency Code	Currency Name	Corporate	Conversion Rate	Decimal Places
Edit Deactivate	AUD	Australian Dollar		0.510000	2
Edit Deactivate	GBP	British Pound	✓	1.000000	2
Edit Deactivate	INR	Indian Rupee		0.009100	4
Edit Deactivate	JPY	Japanese Yen		0.005100	4
Edit Deactivate	USD	U.S. Dollar		0.770000	2

Figure 10.32: *Setting the primary corporate currency*

There is still some work to go into setting up multi-currencies, such as price books, products, and opportunity currency, but this is covered in Trailhead and often depends on the business scenario required.

Setting up advanced currency management

Advanced currency management allows you to give a date range over which an exchange rate applies. This is useful for freezing quotes and order amounts based on when they apply. The most recent date range does not have to have an end date, which means it is the current currency exchange rate.

To do this, go to:

1. **Setup | Company Information** and press the **Currency Setup** button.

2. Then press the **Enable** button for advanced currency management and accept the checkbox for **Yes, I want to enable Advanced Currency Management**.

Three similar-sounding features

The following are grouped together, although they sound similar, they perform very different tasks:

- **Custom labels**: These are simple text values that can be stored and then referenced elsewhere. These can be included in formula fields, flows, LWC, Apex, email templates, and within custom fields labels, help text, and error messages. To view them, go to **Setup | Custom Labels**.

- **Custom settings**: These turn features and permissions on and off for various things. Use custom settings to create and manage custom data at the organization, profile, and user levels. Custom settings data is stored in the application cache. This helps the user experience of Salesforce be efficient, without repeated calls between the browser and Salesforce. Custom settings can be used by formula fields, LWC, Apex, and the Web Services API. To view them, go to **Setup | Custom Settings**.

- **Custom metadata**: There are custom metadata types that are used to make custom metadata components. These are used for storing tables of data for automations, which can query and return values. These are found under **Setup | Custom Metadata Types**. These were described in *Chapter 4, Creating Objects with Custom Fields and Relationships*.

Contact roles

Salesforce also caters to the situation where a contact could work for more than one company. For example, a health care professional may work for a hospital as well as a local doctor and also assist at a range of pharmacies. In this case, neither the B2B nor the B2C model works. Salesforce has contact roles that work with both standard Salesforce B2B and Salesforce B2C with person accounts.

Contact roles are available for accounts, cases, contracts, or the opportunity object and effectively provide a many-to-many relationship between these objects.

To setup contract roles, go to **Setup | Contact Roles** and select the appropriate object. Contact roles are a related list on each object that needs to be added to the page layout.

Omni-channel

Salesforce has a specific feature to allow a business to manage customer interactions across multiple channels, such as email or web. Omni-channel works for accounts, leads, orders, cases, and custom objects.

For example, a new lead has been generated from an email campaign and comes into Salesforce. It can then be routed to the appropriate user, queue, or group based on omni-channel rules, such as the agent's skills and availability. This can also be given a scoring criterion and be combined with other Salesforce functionality, such as an Agentforce-driven chatbot or creating a case. The following figure shows a high-level configuration of omni-channel, where various agents have different language skill-sets and an AI bot is able to deal with calls that do not fit the routing rules. A case can be created if the agents cannot answer the request. This is illustrated in the following figure showing how leads are assigned to an agent based on their skills, availability, and current workload.

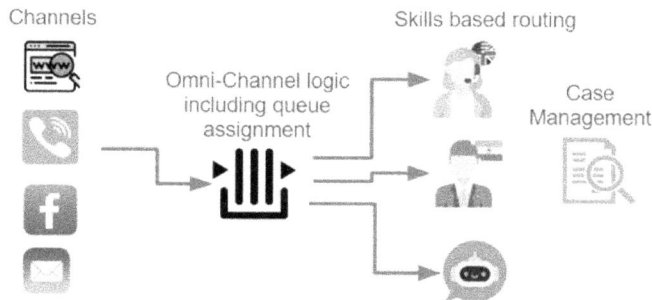

Figure 10.33: Omni-channel basic overview

Setting up omni-channel

Setting up omni-channel is a fairly complicated task. It is best done by drawing out the exact process that you wish to configure first. As such, the following is only a high-level guide on getting started.

Setting up omni-channel can be done in a few different ways, but the best way to get started is by going to **Setup | Service Setup Assistant** and pressing the **Omni Channel Setup** button, as shown in the following figure:

Omni Channel Setup
Automatically route cases to your agents.

Figure 10.34: Using the Omni Channel Setup button

This will then give you a two-step wizard to perform the following:

- Choose or create a queue
- Assign work item size and agent capacity

To setup omni-channel further, go to **Setup | Omni-Channel Home,** where you will see a screen for the three main areas to configure, as shown in the following figure:

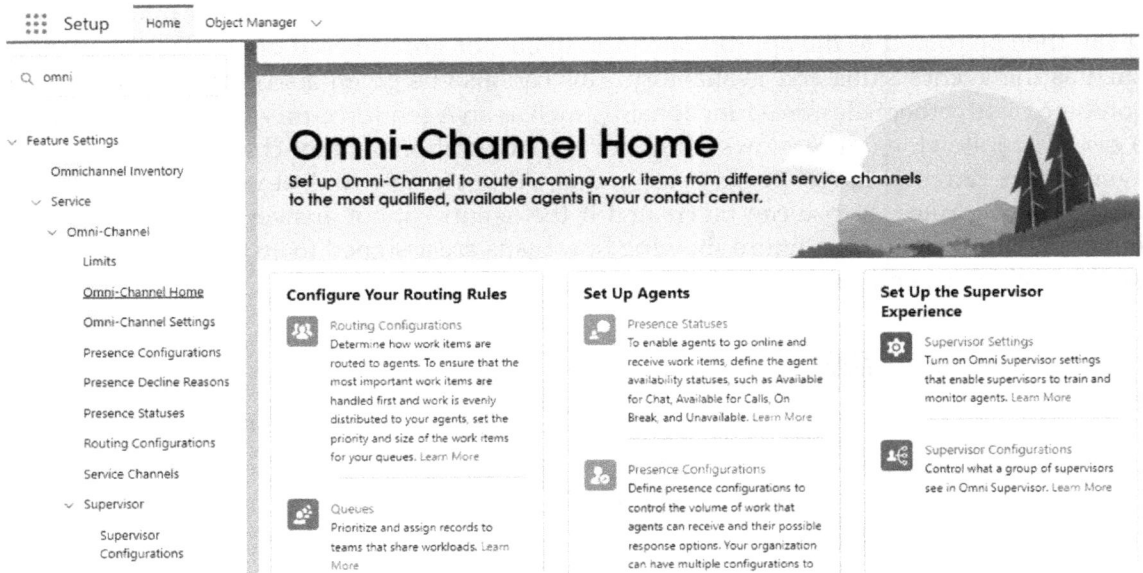

Figure 10.35: Omni-channel setup home page

The three areas are described in the sections. Each one has a series of steps to configure. Follow the links from left to right to setup omni-channel.

Social media

As mentioned in the previous sections, Salesforce can be used in a variety of ways to manage accounts and contacts. These will likely have some presence on social media such as *Facebook*, *Twitter (X)*, *LinkedIn*, and others. It is best to use a dedicated product such as Marketing Cloud to engage in social media. There is no automatic way of linking a social account to Salesforce since you cannot be sure if the social account is the exact one. Also, these platforms are dedicated to social media, so it is best to use them and use Salesforce as the single record for customer information.

For this and many other reasons, Salesforce has retired the direct integration with social media platforms and products like Social Customer Service Starter Pack, which are no longer available. As such, it is often easier to simply create a custom field of type URL and give it the appropriate label for which social media platform it is, and then let the users of Salesforce populate the record themselves. Automating social media records is best done using integration with Marketing Cloud, but this can still be an arduous process.

There are numerous apps on the AppExchange for adding social media functionality to a Salesforce org, but these tend to rely on their own configuration and are outside the scope of this book (refer to the following figure):

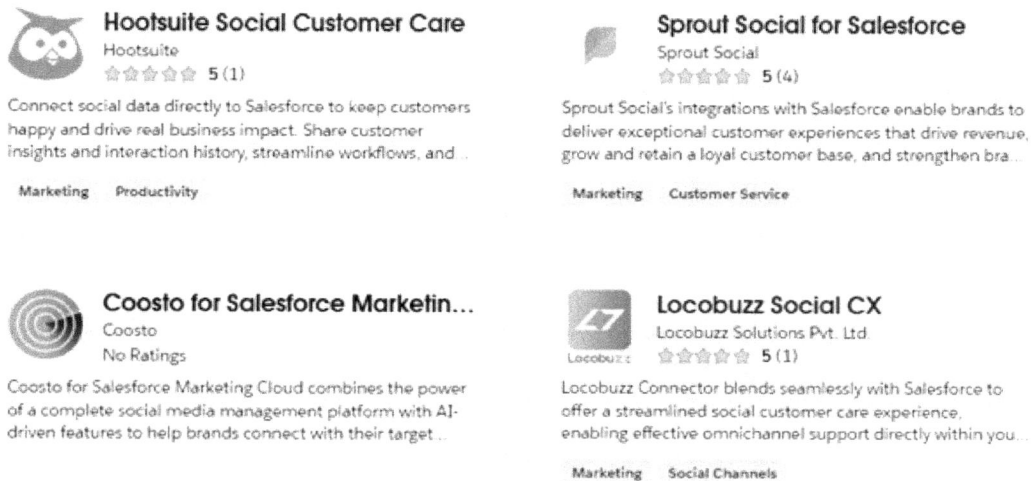

Figure 10.36: *Social media apps from the AppExchange*

Web-to-Lead and Web-to-Case

If you want to put a page on your website to capture some basic information but not build a whole webpage from Experience Cloud, then the code can be generated automatically for you. The code is simple HTML, which you can give to the website team to build into a page and work with their existing website platform.

There are two existing options:

- **Web-to-Lead**: Builds a form for submitting new inquiries on your website to the lead object.

- **Web-to-Case**: Likewise, to get a form to submit to the case object.

Fortunately, Salesforce is able to generate all the code for you, which you only have to provide to your company's website design department. As an example, you can test the code out yourself as shown in the following:

1. In **Setup** type `Web-to-Lead` or `Web-to-Case` and press the **Create Web-to-Lead** (or **Create Web-to-Case**) button.

2. The following screen lists fields you can put on the webpage. Use the **Add/Remove** buttons to select which fields you want to display, then order them using the **Up/Down** buttons:

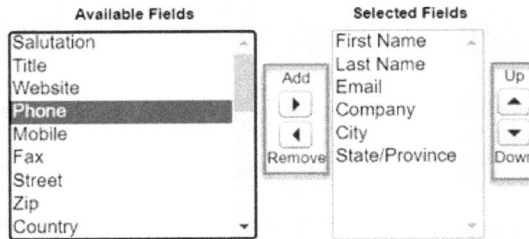

Figure 10.37: Selecting fields to add to the Web-to-Case or Web-to-Lead form

3. The return URL is the webpage you want the person to see once they have submitted the form. Un-tick the **Include reCAPTCHA in HTML** for now, although you might want to include this feature in real life.

4. Now, press the **Generate** button to get the code. Save the code in *Notepad, Apple Notes,* or similar and change the file extension to `.html`.

5. Open the file, which will give a very simple form, as shown in the following figure:

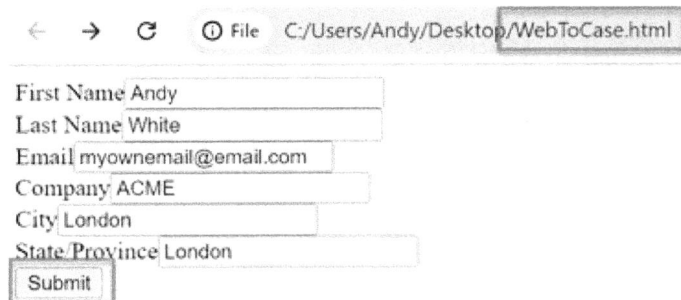

Figure 10.38: The exported html for a Web-to-Case or Web-to-Lead form

6. Press **Submit,** and you will have created a new record in Salesforce. To see the record, simply go to the case or lead object to see the newly created record.

Email-to-Case

Salesforce also offers similar functionality using Email-to-Case by going to **Setup | Email-to-Case**. However, although this is conceptually simple, this book avoids many Salesforce email configurations since they are often error-prone due to the unpredictability of sending emails outside of Salesforce and hoping for a meaningful response when Salesforce offers many alternative features. However, Email-to-Case has a good way of getting cases raised, but it is far better to use the initial enquiry via other channels.

If you choose to use Email-to-Case, then you also need to setup the routing addresses, which may take conversations with your email provider or internal email team using *Exchange, Outlook, Microsoft 365,* or *Google*.

Paths

Salesforce paths are simply the chevron area, which can be seen at the top of many records in Salesforce. For example, the opportunity object has the following opportunity path displayed at the top of an opportunity record:

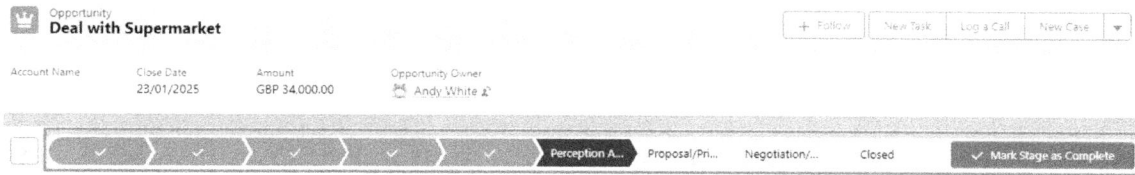

Figure 10.39: Example of a Salesforce path

All paths are fundamentally driven by one field. For example, the opportunity path illustrated above is driven by the Stage field. If you change the value of this field, then the path changes, and likewise, if you select a chevron on the opportunity path, then the field updates to reflect the change.

Creating a path for an object

To create a path for an object, go to **Setup | Path Settings** and press the **New Path** button.

A three-step wizard helps you build the path.

1. The following screen will appear (refer to the following figure), where you need to select the object and a picklist field to control the path:

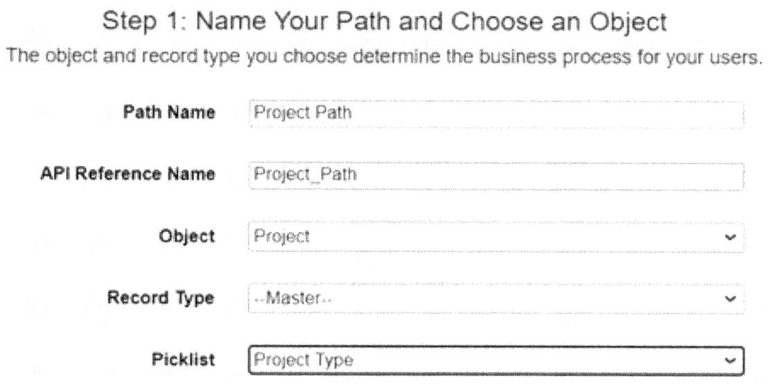

Figure 10.40: Salesforce path configuration options

2. Update fields on the record automatically if the stage on the path changes, or give a description to assist users if needed (Optional).

3. Activate the path and feel free to add a confetti shower. This means that when a stage of the path is reached, the user sees confetti falling across the screen. For example,

this could be when an opportunity is won. Set the **Celebration Frequency** to **Always**. Check that your path is **Active**, as shown in the following figure:

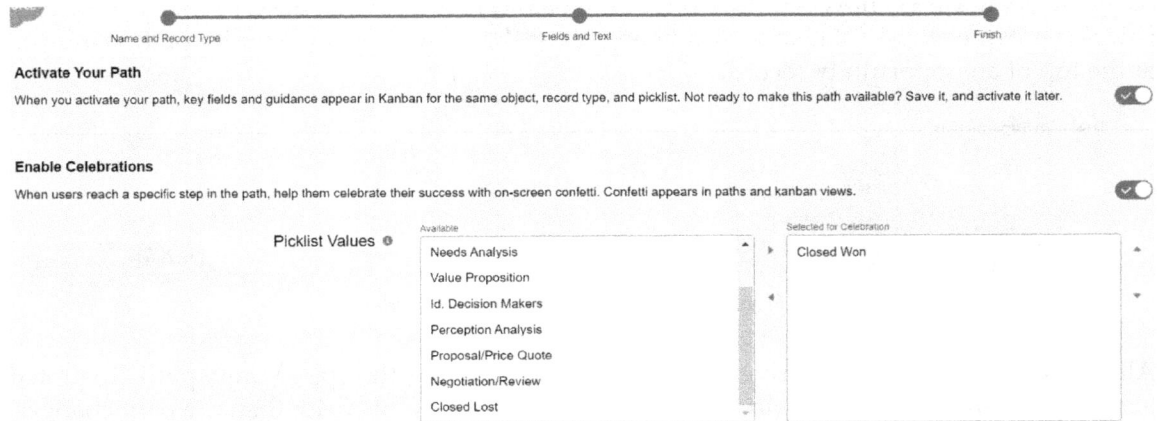

Figure 10.41: Adding a confetti shower to a Salesforce path

Note: **If the confetti shower frequency is set to Always and users typically work in Kanban view, then it could become challenging.**

4. The final step is to add the path to the page layout. To do this, go to the page you want to see the path on and drag it onto the page header, as shown in the following figure:

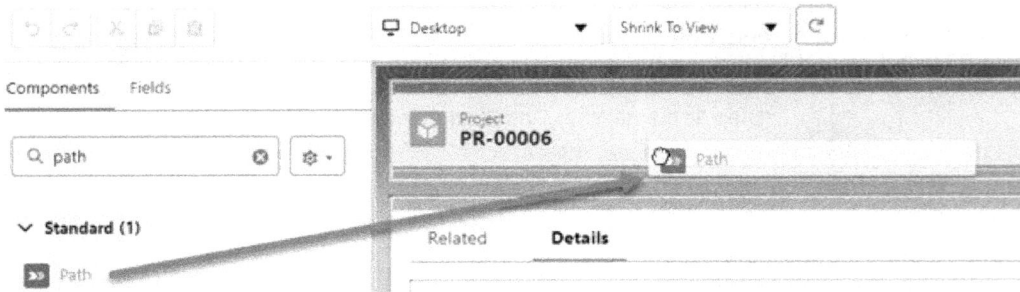

Figure 10.42: Adding the path to a page layout

5. Press **Save** on the new page layout, and visit a record from the object to which you added the path.

6. Change a stage in the path and press **Save**.

7. The screen is showered with confetti, as shown in the following figure:

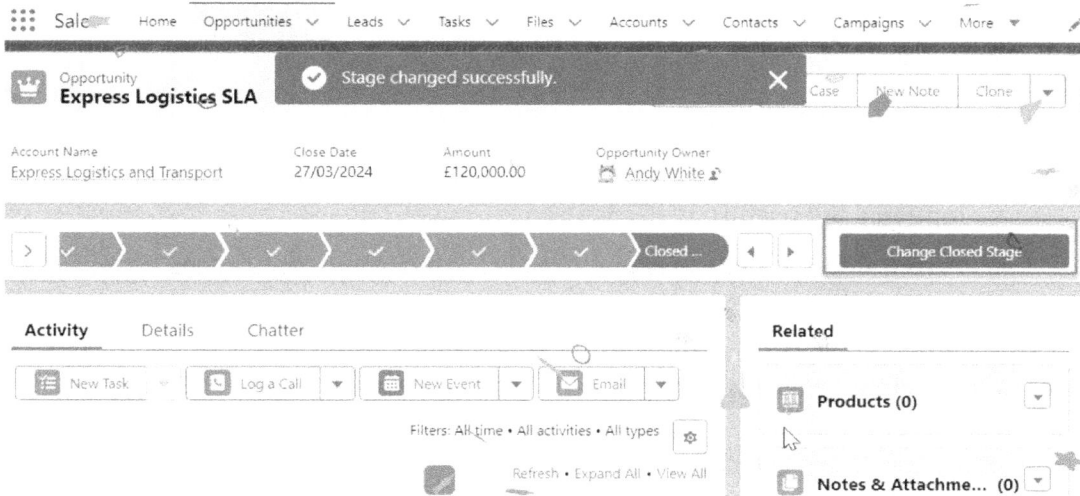

Figure 10.43: Screen displaying a confetti shower when an opportunity is Closed Won

Email templates

Emails can be sent from Salesforce, but the best practice is not to rely on emails for two-way communications; but, use channels such as Experience Cloud, Chatter for customers, OmniOut, or whichever product best suits your needs. Having said that, sending out a confirmation email with an order number or confirmation of case details is perfectly reasonable. However, receiving a plain-text email is a missed opportunity to show company branding or attention to detail.

Salesforce comes with Lightning Email Templates, which are reusable for sending out emails that are well formatted but contain the text applicable to the recipient. This can be their name in the subject line and pre-header text. Marketing material can be embedded as well as links in the footer to promote social media and more.

Once created, an email can be used in campaigns or flows, as part of a quick action, or elsewhere.

Initial configuration for Lightning Email Templates

To create a Lightning Email Template, there are two main steps:

1. Enable them by going to **Setup | Lightning Email Templates** and pressing the slider for **Folders and Enhanced Sharing**.

2. Create a permission set with a system permission of `Access Drag-and-Drop Content Builder`. You may need to log back into Salesforce for this permission set to take effect. This provides a button called **Edit in Builder** on the email template. Details of this setup are described in the following section..

3. Go to **Setup | Permission Set** and create a new one. Call it **Lightning Email Builder**. To the bottom of the screen, find **System Permissions** and add the following permissions:

    a. **Permission set name**: `Access Drag-and-Drop Content Builder` (required to make a Lightning template)

    b. **Permission set name**: `Create Folders for Lightning Email Templates` (optional but useful)

    c. **Permission set name**: `Manage Public Lightning Email Templates` (optional but useful)

Finally, assign the permission set to yourself or other users using the **Manage Assignments** button, as shown in the following figure:

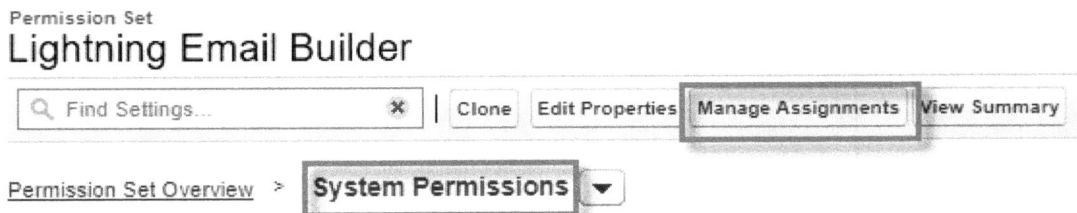

Figure 10.44: Adding the required permission set to users

Creating Lightning Email Templates

Go to the **App Launcher** and find email templates. Press the **New Email Template** button and complete the basic information. This is not the actual email itself, but it helps to store information about the email to assist in keeping email templates ordered. Enter the information, such as the **Email Template Name**, **Description**, and **Folder**. The **Relevant Entity Type** is the object you may wish to use data from to help personalize the email. For example, this could be the case object if the email was in response to a case being raised.

The following screen has the **Edit in Builder** button, which was the result of adding the permission set in the previous steps. Press the **Edit in Builder** button, as shown in the following figure:

Figure 10.45: The Edit in Builder option for Lightning Email Templates

This will display the following on your screen:

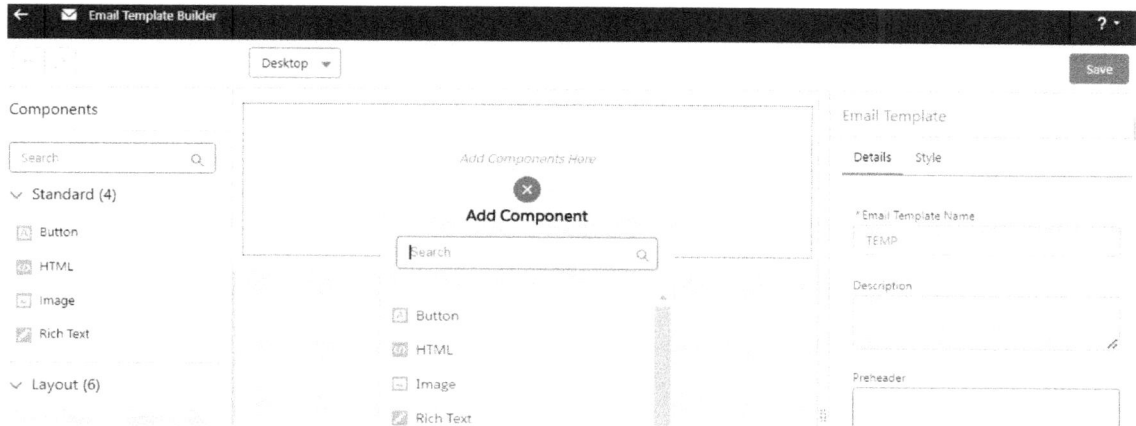

Figure 10.46: Using the Lightning Email Template Builder

In the above:

- On the left are the email template components.

- In the center is the canvas, which is where you create the template.

- On the right is the property panel with tabs and sections depending on which component you have selected.

Note: Salesforce comes with various Lightning Email Templates but the Edit in Builder button is only for emails created by you or by the company. It does not apply to sample email templates.

Lightning Email Templates have the following features:

- Pre-header so the email has a message to the recipient without having to open it.

- Content from either a content management system or Salesforce Files.

- Use alt-text to provide additional information.

- Dynamic text such as **First Name**, depending on which object was selected in the **Relevant Entity Type** previously.

- Add various call-to-action features, such as **Press here to get your discount code**.

- Preview the email for either a desktop or phone.

- Embed html to add a wide variety of functionality.

Other Salesforce features

If you are using a Salesforce Developer Edition org, then there are two Salesforce features you should be aware of that are not included, but used extensively in Salesforce environments used by most companies they are sandboxes and change sets, as detailed in the following two sections.

Sandbox environments

Sandbox environments are copies of other Salesforce environments that allow administrators and developers to make updates to Salesforce in a safe space, allowing you to have multiple, isolated environments for development, testing, and other purposes. They are not available in a Developer Edition of Salesforce. The number of sandboxes you can have would depend on which edition of Salesforce you have.

Sandboxes are typically created in one of two ways:

1. A copy of the live production environment, which means the configuration will match the live environment.

2. By cloning an existing sandbox. This process copies the data and metadata from the source sandbox to a new one.

There are a few different types of sandboxes, which are listed out here:

*   **Developer**: A basic copy of production without data, but can be refreshed daily and only allows 200 MB of data storage.

*   **Developer Pro**: As above, but with an increase in the data storage to 1 GB.

*   **Partial Copy**: Comes with 5 GB of storage but can only be refreshed every 5 days.

*   **Full-copy**: A full-copy of the production environment, but can only be refreshed once a month and is very expensive.

Both partial and full-copy sandboxes support templates, which allow you to say what object and data will be copied into the new sandbox.

Scratch orgs are similar to sandboxes, only they can be a copy of an existing sandbox, and they also expire automatically after 30 days. They are typically used by developers to test code or for concept development. Some functionality does exist in the Developer Edition org by going to **Setup | Scratch Orgs**.

Change sets

Having done work in a sandbox and tested it thoroughly, the new configuration can be moved to production or other sandboxes using change sets. This is the very basic form of configuration migration, and other tools such as *Copado, Gearset, AutoRABIT,* or *Harness* are often used as they give a lot more control over the migration. Salesforce also comes with DevOps Studio, which is relatively new to the Salesforce ecosystem and can be found by going to **Setup | DevOps Center** and pressing the **Enable** slider. However, change sets have been part of Salesforce for many years and are useful for simple deployments.

A basic overview of DevOps is covered in *Chapter 15, Further Readings*.

Conclusion

Salesforce has many features that are already built in, and this chapter covers many of them. Some are simply there to allow administrators to configure Salesforce correctly, whilst others offer functionality that may be additional to standard Salesforce functionality. The aim is to make sure readers are aware that Salesforce is extendible across many areas that they would otherwise not be aware of.

In the next chapter, we will delve more deeply into how to customize Salesforce using code. However, it is strongly advised to learn how to configure Salesforce using this book. Customization is not supported by Salesforce, so you can end up with a heavily customized Salesforce org that is not compatible with future requirements. As a general recommendation, do not customize Salesforce using code unless the organization fully understands that it is opting for a solution which may end up costing way more than the functionality is worth.

Multiple choice questions

1. **A sandbox can provide which of the following?**

    a. A copy of Salesforce without configuration

    b. A sample environment of Salesforce based on templates

    c. A copy of another sandbox

    d. A copy of the live production environment

2. **Salesforce has two convenient ways to create a web form, which are (choose any two):**

    a. Web-to-Case

    b. Web-to-Email

    c. Web-to-Lead

    d. Web-to-Contact

3. **Salesforce Knowledge requires which of the three configurations (choose 3):**

    a. Catalogues

    b. Categories

    c. Category groups

    d. Topics

4. **What are the features of a Salesforce path (choose 2):**
   a. To provide a confetti shower when it meets certain stages
   b. To give guidance to users
   c. To link the path to a picklist field
   d. To provide visibility to the values on the record

5. **Omni-channel is useful in Salesforce, but what features does it offer?**
   a. Giving agents the ability to accept or reject a case
   b. Routing enquiries based on channel, agent skills, and availability
   c. Combining with other Salesforce features to give 360^0 views of the customer
   d. Stopping unwanted support requests from coming into Salesforce

6. **Lightning Email Templates offer which of the following?**
   a. Include from email with subject lines
   b. Pre-headers, dynamic text, call to action features, preview the email, embed HTML, and view in mobile and desktop devices
   c. Show the details of recipients, including the social media accounts
   d. Allow Forward to all functionality with dynamic name tracking

7. **Advanced Currency Management has the following key feature?**
   a. Convert between various currencies
   b. Use the Salesforce default currency to change to the currency of the user
   c. The ability to set date ranges on currency conversions
   d. Use exchange rates in currency formula fields and other configurations, such as flows

8. **One of the key features of Omni-channel is:**
   a. The ability to configure many channels (such as social, email, and web) into Salesforce
   b. Omni-channel can be configured to handle many enquiries simultaneously
   c. Skills-based routing
   d. Omni-channel is able to integrate with other Salesforce products

9. **Salesforce can integrate with social media, such as WhatsApp, but this is best done:**
   a. Integrating your company ID on the WhatsApp ID field in the company setup
   b. Installing Social for Salesforce and logging in to the social media options

    c. Using Salesforce Messaging Settings and setting up a WhatsApp Business account

    d. Using Salesforce for social for the most popular social media accounts

10. **Contact roles provide the following functionality:**

    a. Allow various users to have different roles and profiles.

    b. Provide roles for contacts based on their current profile.

    c. The ability to have many-to-many relationships as a contact on various objects.

    d. Give users the ability to assign different Contacts to different features in Salesforce.

Answers

1	**d**
2	**a,c**
3	**b, c, d**
4	**a, c**
5	**b**
6	**b**
7	**c**
8	**c**
9	**c**
10	**c**

Join our Discord space

Join our Discord workspace for latest updates, offers, tech happenings around the world, new releases, and sessions with the authors:

https://discord.bpbonline.com

CHAPTER 11
Basics of Apex and Lightning Web Components

Introduction

This chapter is only a brief introduction to give an overview of how development is done and where it is needed. This chapter is aimed at getting you started, introducing you to core concepts, and pointing you in the right direction should you wish to take your learning further. Also, it is a personal choice to go down the coding route as a career path. Salesforce is great at configuration-based approaches to business requirements, but if there is a code-based approach, then many other platforms might be more suitable, such as *Microsoft .NET*.

This chapter also puts all the tools you will need to use at the end of it. This is because they are referenced throughout this book, but it would make a slow start if the first sections were about the tools and not about understanding the code. It is recommended that you set yourself up with the tools as needed. The basic tools are the Developer Console, **Visual Studio Code** (**VS Code**) with the Salesforce CLI extension, and often Postman or Swagger. These will be covered later in this book. The aim of this chapter is to give you enough information to get started coding in Salesforce, and also various resources available to developers to do their job.

https://code.visualstudio.com/

https://www.postman.com/

https://swagger.io/

Structure

In this chapter, we will cover the following topics:

- Apex and its usage
- Lightning Web Components
- Integration
- Developer Console

Objectives

The aim of this chapter is not to make you a dedicated developer but rather to show you what is typically involved and the resources you can go to if you want to go deeper. The aim is that by the end, you will have a reasonable understanding of how to customize Salesforce and what skills are required.

This chapter focuses on programming in Apex, which is Salesforce's own development language. This chapter also introduces key areas for using Apex, such as writing Apex classes and triggers, which form the foundation of custom logic and coded automation in Salesforce. It also involves building **Lightning Web Components** (**LWCs**) to create dynamic, modern user interfaces.

In addition, this chapter also includes how to use Apex to build **application programming interfaces** (**APIs**). These APIs enable Salesforce to communicate with external systems either directly or through middleware, allowing for seamless data exchange and integration between platforms.

The final section contains the use of the tools required to write code in Salesforce. This chapter is a high-level overview with many links to resources to get you started.

Apex and its usage

Salesforce uses Apex as its server-side compiled language for development, which cannot be achieved by configuration. In many ways, it is similar in language to Java or C# and allows developers to build customizations outside of what can be done with configuration. However, it is always worth checking with the business if the requirement is actually needed, since Salesforce can be configured to meet most of the requirements, and coding often complicates a project, adding to the **total cost of ownership** (**TCO**). Over time, this can build technical debt, which means a company may have many issues to resolve if the code is not well commented and documented.

Having said that, many developers love to do a great job in making Salesforce the best and push the boundaries of what can be achieved. There is a general rule of 80/20, meaning that

Salesforce orgs are generally 80% configured and 20% coded. If a Salesforce org is customized a lot, it can mean that the company is unaware of what can be achieved by configuration or that developers have been given free rein over the system.

For this reason, it is worth performing regular health checks on a Salesforce org as outlined in *Chapter 9, Various Salesforce Tools*.

Salesforce platform

Salesforce can offer a platform-only license, which removes most of the **customer relationship management** (**CRM**) capabilities, but is preferable for highly customized Salesforce orgs. This license is considerably cheaper than a CRM license, such as Sales or Service Cloud, since it removes the functionality associated with them. Using a Salesforce Platform license still provides access to core Salesforce features, such as accounts, contacts, reports, automation tools, coding development, and the ability to build Experience Cloud frontends.

Camp Apex

One of the best resources for learning Apex is **https://www.campapex.org/**. This is far more practical than Trailhead and is kept up to date with the latest coding features.

To access Camp Apex, follow the link above and press the **Connect** button under **Recent Org Connect** on the left-hand side. Refer to the following figure:

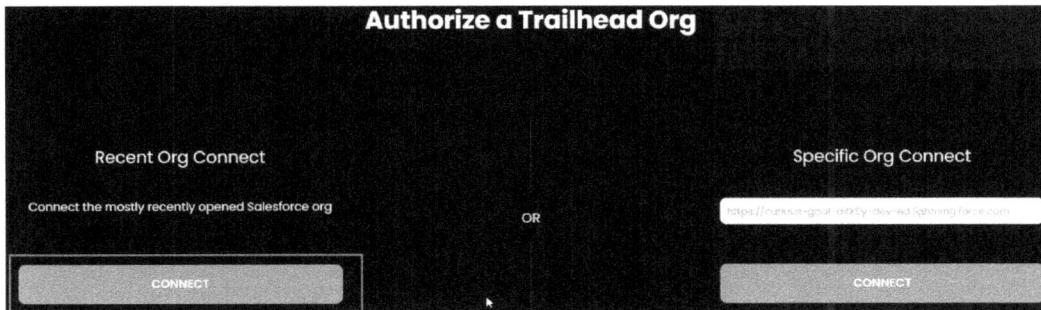

Figure 11.1: Camp Apex home page

Camp Apex is broken into four main areas, which are:

- Apex Fundamentals
- **Objectoriented programming** (**OOP**)
- Projects
- **Salesforce Object Query Language** (**SOQL**)

Camp Apex also makes learning Apex fun. It comes with interactive lessons, competitions, and projects, which allow you to choose configuration or custom development.

Coding basic terminology

The world of coding comes with its own language, too. It is helpful to understand some of the key terms outlined in the following section. It is not possible to make something that is complex sound simple, but the following are basic terms that will help you understand the language of Apex, as well as when other developers are discussing issues. For example, a developer would need to understand Salesforce governor limits and exception handling to ensure their code is efficient and reliable. The terms in the following sections are used by developers to translate business requirements into code they can write.

General terms

The phrase OOP covers a wide range of languages, such as C#, .NET, and Java, but also includes Apex. The concept is that you can build objects based on classes.

In the simplest terms, an object, such as an email you send, a photo on your phone, is just a copy of a class, which is code to say what the email or photo needs to contain.

Instantiation is an instance of a class and refers to the act of creating a new object based on the class.

An example of the above would be any time you press a **New** button in an application, for example, creating a new email. The email class may have properties such as header, subject line, body, and footer, and a method, such as send.

In summary, a class is a blueprint that defines what the object will become. Methods are functions inside the class that perform specific tasks on the object. An object can be reset or initialized using a specific method called a **constructor**. An instance is a single occurrence of a class.

After a while, you will see that OOP is everywhere. Every time you use a device, visit a website, create a new folder, or make a new document, you will see a new instance of a class.

Properties are essentially values stored within a class that are designed to hold specific types of information.

To illustrate properties, it could be that you are an instance of the human class. You have properties such as hair color, height, and language, with methods such as walking, swimming, or sleeping.

Working with data

As well as writing code, developers also must work with data. This is typically in two forms:

- **Salesforce Object Query Language** (**SOQL**) is used to query specific records from a single object.

- **Salesforce Object Search Language** (**SOSL**) is used to perform text searches across multiple objects.

The terms synchronous or asynchronous are mentioned here, but covered in more detail when referring to APIs. They often come up in discussions about triggers or classes since they are fundamental to development with APIs or the way in which Apex is processed.

- **Synchronous**: A message is sent from one system and is processed at the same time.

- **Asynchronous**: A message is sent and waits in the queue. This is sometimes referred to as **fire and forget**.

In Salesforce, Apex code is invoked synchronously, meaning it runs immediately and in the same thread as the action that triggered it, for example, when a button is clicked or a record is saved. However, Apex also provides asynchronous processing capabilities, which let you defer code execution to run in the background or at a later time, outside the context of the original trigger.

The reason it is mentioned here is that Apex runs asynchronously with various methods on how to run, such as queueable, schedule, batch, and future.

There are many other terms, but the above is used in almost all Apex development scenarios. For a complete reference, Google *Apex Developer Guide*, which can also come in a useful PDF version to download.

APEX caveats

There are many online communities and open-source sites that share code openly. Although this is great, it also has some inherent risk that the code may not be fit for purpose, and it could potentially put the project and company at risk. For this reason, all developers must understand every line of the code they are submitting before it goes into the live environment.

It is also impressive that it is possible to use ChatGPT for code generation, but it is important to understand the code before using it. An example is shown in the following figure of code for a trigger that generates an email when an opportunity is set to the status of Closed Won. It could be that this is better configured using Salesforce Flows, which would fit better into the overall configuration of the org.

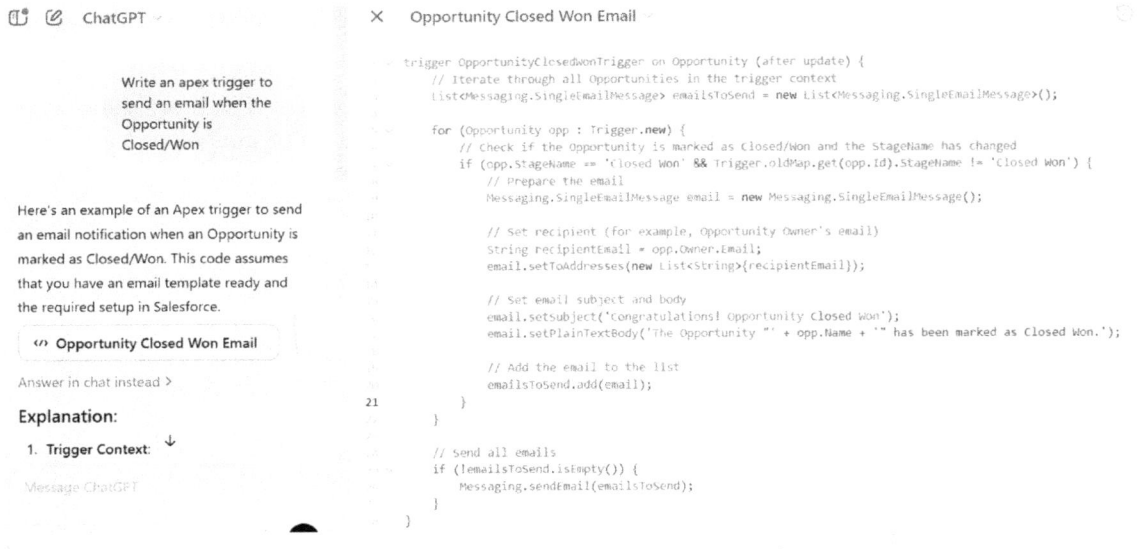

Figure 11.2: Using ChatGPT to generate code

OpenAI also allows developers to use Canvas. Canvas is a new interface for working with ChatGPT, which is an extremely useful way of writing code and provides real-time updates to your code with syntax correction and suggestions. Basic examples of where Apex is needed.

Note: The examples in the book are to give a broad overview. They should also allow you to know which areas of programming or integration are most relevant for you. However, since this is a big subject, online resources, such as Trailhead, are preferable as they will be kept up to date.

Apex is often used when business logic simply gets too complicated. For example, an opportunity discount may be based on a few related objects and require a precise order of execution. Other examples could be handling large data volumes, which require some data manipulation based on criteria, or Apex is often used in integrations or LWCs. In these scenarios, Salesforce Flows can become large and hard to manage, whilst code is clean and precise and has a logical structure outlined in this chapter.

There are three basic forms of development done in Salesforce:

- **Triggers**: These are written in Apex, which is used when a specific event, such as saving or updating an account record, occurs. They are triggered when something is done in Salesforce. When something happens in Salesforce, it is called an **event**. An event is typically after update or before insert and is used directly in the Apex code at the very start of the trigger. The name of the event describes when the event happens. Other useful events are:

  o **after insert**: This event triggers after a record has been successfully inserted into the database o   **after delete**: This event triggers after a record has been successfully deleted from the database

o   **after undelete**: This event triggers after a record has been successfully undeleted (i.e., restored) from the database

o   **before update**: This event triggers before a record is updated in the database

o   **before delete**: This event triggers before a record is deleted from the database

- **Classes**: Also written in Apex, these are generally reusable lines of code that can be called in Salesforce via many things, such as **Lightning Web Components** (**LWCs**), flows, integrations (APIs), etc. These are generally reusable, which means they can be called by any event or procedure. The fact that they are reusable means they have an instance. The term instantiation is used by developers to say the class is called. However, some classes are not reusable. In particular, if they are declared as private, which means they are not reusable outside the class in which it is defined. This will make more sense with practice.

- **LWCs**: These allow developers to build customized features for users or for Experience Cloud and can meet a variety of purposes. LWCs rely on traditional web skills such as **Hypertext Markup Language** (**HTML**), JavaScript, **Cascaded Style Sheets** (**CSS**), and Apex.

Other areas, such as web services, integrations, or schedulers, would require the developer to already have a reasonable understanding of Apex, so it is better to learn the basics covered in this chapter and seek reasonable online tutorials to cover areas of specific interest.

Accessing code in Salesforce

To find these three features in Salesforce, go to **Setup | Custom Code**, and you will find Apex triggers, classes, and Lightning components. It is worth simply opening these features to get an overview of what they look like. An example is shown in the following for an Apex class called `BookController`:

```
  Class Body | Class Summary | Version Settings | Trace Flags

  1    /* This is an example class with a description at the top
  2    which should include, who wrote the class, the date it was written, a
  3    description of what the class does and the business reason for it.
  4    It should also have a list of updates done with similar information.
  5    */
  6
  7    public with sharing class BookController {  // with sharing means it respects the user
  8       private Boolean isAvailable;
  9
 10       public BookController(){
 11          isAvailable = true;
 12       }
 13
 14       public Book__c addBook(String name, Decimal price){
 15          Book__c book = new Book__c();
 16          book.Name = name;
 17          book.Price__c = price;
 18          return book;
 19       }
 20
 21       public static void applyDiscount (Decimal discount) {
 22          Book__c[] books = [SELECT Name, Price__c FROM Book__c WHERE Price_
 23          if (Books!= null && books.size()>0) {
 24             for (Book__c b : books) {
 25                b.Price__c = b.Price__c - (b.Price__c*discount);
 26             }
 27          }
 28          update (books);
 29       }
 30    }
```

Figure 11.3: Example of a class that can be reused by invoking it

If you have a Developer Edition account, you might not see a lot, but the **Help** button on these pages is very useful for an introduction. If you are working in an existing Salesforce org, then you are likely to see a lot more.

There are other programmatic solutions to Salesforce that are outside the scope of this book. For example, **Salesforce Industries** (**SFI**) relies on a technology stack that is highly reliant on JSON, whilst Marketing Cloud uses AMP scripts. Heroku is useful for offloading heavy data processing and can use a variety of programming languages such as Java, Ruby, Python, PHP, JavaScript, and Go.

Apex basic syntax

Syntax simply means the language of the computer code. If you had to learn a foreign language, it would immediately appear complicated. It would take a long time to learn Greek, Chinese, or Hindi if you are unfamiliar with the language. However, computer syntax is comparatively simple and requires less knowledge and is more logical than spoken languages.

Apex is a block-structured language, meaning code is kept inside curly braces, i.e., {code here}. These blocks contain statements that end with a semicolon. Apex compiles, which means that when the class is instantiated, each statement is run sequentially and compiled into a form that Salesforce understands.

Apex syntax structure

Access to classes can be set as private, protected, public, or global, which limits the scope of where a class can be used. These are defined in the class and can also consider the user's own permissions using the with sharing or without sharing syntax.

Apex is also strongly typed, which means all variables and expressions need to be predefined. If you simply declare a variable without first declaring it, then Apex will throw an error.

Variables

Variables are simply containers for things such as numbers, text, and more complicated items such as collections, which are lists, sets, maps, and Salesforce objects. For example, a variable could be an integer, which is a whole number such as 12. Alternatively, there are other numbers, such as long or double, which give the number of decimal points and are useful for doing accurate calculations.

Text can be stored in a string variable, which has single speech mark (and not ") to contain it. For example:

```
strGreeting = 'Hello World';
```

Variables change their value as the code runs, so from the example above, **strGreeting** may later contain **'Welcome to the world'** and then **'Have a great day'**.

Naming convention

You may have noticed when doing configuration in earlier chapters of this book that when you create something, Salesforce generates an API name. These are the names of things you need to refer to in code and often end with the **__c** syntax, showing they are custom fields or objects. There are other extensions to names, such as **__r**, meaning it is a relationship.

Apex uses the common dot notation to indicate a relationship or dependency between words if they rely on each other. For example: **Person.Name** would be a person's name, whilst **Person. Age** would be their age.

Logic

Often, code needs to be able to make decisions; syntax for if, else, else if, and then are common in code, but they require syntax to make logical decisions. The operators such as and, not, equals, etc., are also very concise but use syntax such as:

- **&&** meaning and
- **||** meaning or
- **!=** meaning not equal to

Loops

Loops allow you to run code repeatedly until a condition is met. They use syntax like do-while or for. The golden rule of any loop is not to perform a lookup or SOQL operation inside the loop. This can cause problems with Salesforce performance and hitting API limits. The term **bulkification** is used to avoid this scenario and should be understood, although it is outside the scope of this book.

Test classes

Although Salesforce does allow you to write code in the live environment, it is generally best practice not to do this. This is to avoid any downtime or unpredictable results should a developer write some code that causes serious problems. Instead, development is typically done in a sandbox or scratch org and pushed into the live environment after testing.

This introduces the concept of a test class. These classes start with **@Test** syntax. When the code is run, if only 20% of the code is used, then it gets a test coverage of 20%. Salesforce does this to ensure the code is concise and useful. Salesforce only allows code to be deployed to production if it is over 75%. It is best practice to get this higher to contribute to the overall code coverage of your Salesforce org.

Hard-coding IDs

When writing code, it is tempting to put a hard-coded ID into it. For example, you could mention a record type or account ID, and it will work in the development environment, but would fail in production. This can be avoided by using code to look up the object using the **getRecordTypeByInfos** command or storing the value in a custom label.

Comments

A very important part of writing code is to help people understand it. It is extremely time-consuming to work out what a developer has done in code if they do not put comments in. Comments do not do anything other than say what the code does. However, it is useful to describe the code, say who and when it was written, then add comments inside the code as needed.

These can be either for a single line or a long sentence, as shown in the following:

- **Single line:** `Integer i = 1; // You can write anything after the this`
- **Long sentence:** `Integer i = 1; /* This comment can go over multiple lines until you've explained what the code means */`

Other Apex considerations

Programming in Apex is a massive subject, so this is only a quick guide to focus on gaining a basic understanding. Subjects such as wrapper classes, abstraction, and some other apex functionality are outside the scope of this book. However, this chapter is intended to give a good introduction to programming with Apex and some confidence in the core subjects and features.

Building a simple trigger

Triggers are different from classes. They are a lot simpler since they rely on an event happening to a specific object, such as creating a new record, updating it, or deleting it. Triggers are written by going into **Setup | Apex triggers**. An example is shown in the following:

```
trigger AccountBeforeInsert on Account (before insert) {
    // Loop through each Account record being inserted
    for(Account acc : Trigger.new) {
        // Convert the account name to uppercase
        if(acc.Name != null) {
            acc.Name = acc.Name.toUpperCase();
        }
    }
}
```

In the above, we can see that this trigger is for the **Account** object and fires **before insert**. This means that before the record is saved, it will convert the account name to uppercase.

Building cross-object trigger

When triggers get more complex, they need a helper class. A helper class is a separate class designed to help build in logic, such as validation rules. As such, the following code actually requires a helper class to support it.

The trigger in the following has two main features:

- When an account is updated, the trigger updates the field **Account_Status__c** on all related contact records.

- When a contact is created or updated, it updates the field **Number_of_Contacts__c** on the **Account** object.

The first trigger is:

```
trigger AccountContactTrigger on Account (after update) {
// Update related Contacts when an Account is updated
if (Trigger.isAfter && Trigger.isUpdate) {
        AccountContactHelper.updateContactsFromAccounts(Trigger.new);      }
}
```

The second trigger is:

```
trigger ContactAccountTrigger on Contact (after insert, after update) {
    // Update the Account field when a Contact is inserted or updated
    if (Trigger.isAfter && (Trigger.isInsert || Trigger.isUpdate)) {
ContactAccountHelper.updateAccountFromContacts(Trigger.new);
    }
}
```

Both of which require helper classes to ensure code reusability and cleaner triggers. For the chapter, all the code is stored in the BPB files with the link provided at the start of this book.

Building simple class

As mentioned, a class is a reusable blueprint of code that can be called in many places. As such, it requires a format that can receive information and be instantiated, meaning it will come to life. The following example calculates the total price of a product after applying a discount:

```
public class ProductCalculator {
    // Properties
    public String productName {get; set;}
    public Decimal originalPrice {get; set;}
    public Decimal discountPercentage {get; set;}

    // Constructor
    public ProductCalculator(String name, Decimal price, Decimal discount) {
        this.productName = name;
        this.originalPrice = price;
        this.discountPercentage = discount;
    }

    // Method to calculate the discounted price
    public Decimal calculateDiscountedPrice() {
        Decimal discountAmount = (originalPrice * discountPercentage) / 100;
        return originalPrice - discountAmount;
    }
}
```

You will notice in the class above the use of common syntax such as:

- **Public**: meaning the class is available to all records irrespective of the user

- **Get and set**: meaning the variable can get information and also write it

- **This**: Referring to the actual class

- **Method**: The actual calculation based on the variables

To enter the class into Salesforce, go to **Setup** | **Apex Classes** and press **New**. Enter the code above and press **Save**.

Next, go to the **Developer Console** via the Salesforce user interface, as shown in the following figure:

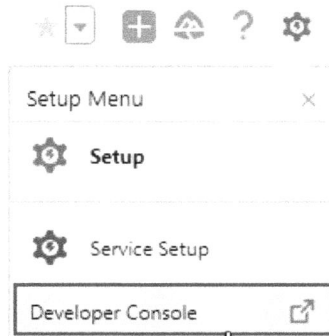

Figure 11.4: Getting access to the Developer Console

Once in, go to **File** | **Open** and select the class as shown in the following figure:

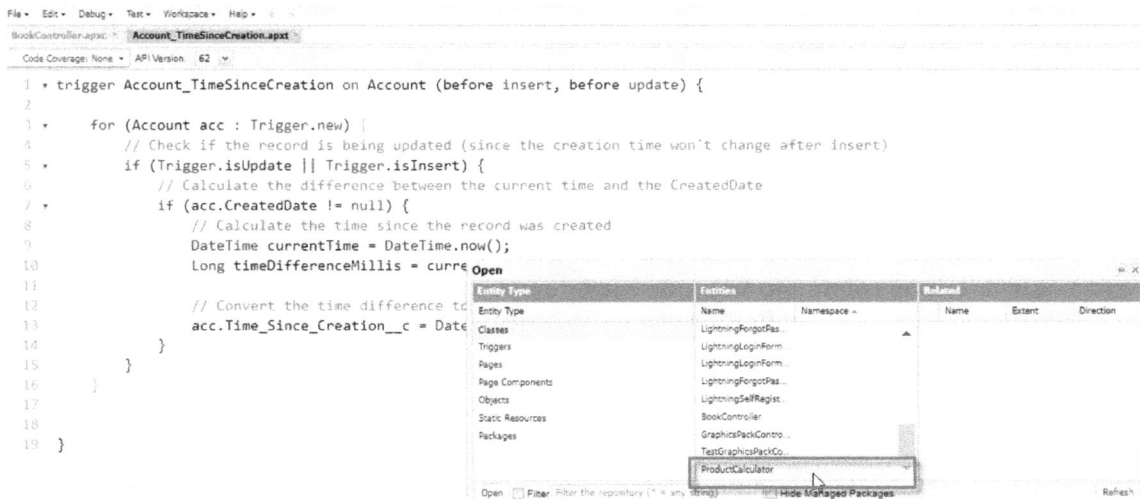

Figure 11.5: Opening a class in the Developer Console

From here, go to **Debug** | **Open Execute Anonymous Window**, as shown in the following figure:

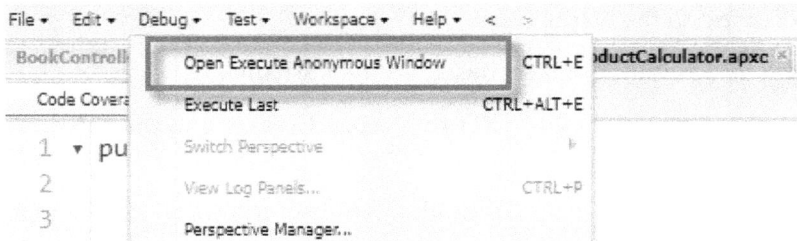

Figure 11.6: Using the Open Execute Anonymous Window

Enter the code from the class and press the **Execute** button, as shown in the following figure:

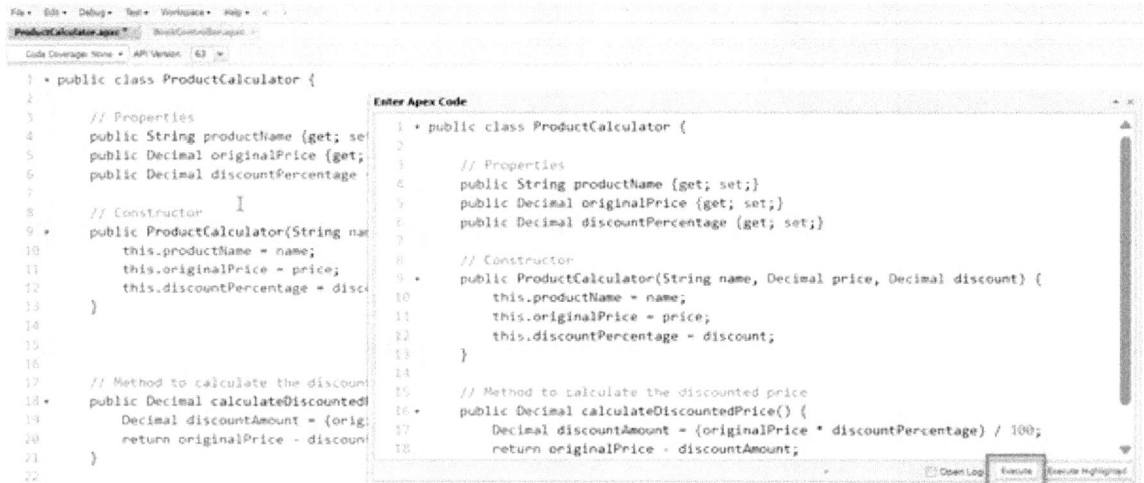

Figure 11.7: Running a class by pressing the Execute button

Although the code runs, it would be good to see what values are generated by the calculations in the class. To do this, we need to be able to display them. To do this, use the **System.debug** syntax, which can be entered to find out what values are being used in the code. This is very useful for debugging code and finding errors. To do this, go into the **Open Execute Anonymous Window** and enter the following code:

```
// Create an instance of the ProductCalculator class
ProductCalculator calculator = new ProductCalculator('Laptop', 1000, 10);
// Calculate the discounted price
Decimal discountedPrice = calculator.calculateDiscountedPrice();
// Output the results
System.debug('Product Name: ' + calculator.productName);
System.debug('Original Price: ' + calculator.originalPrice);
System.debug('Discount Percentage: ' + calculator.discountPercentage);
System.debug('Discounted Price: ' + discountedPrice);
```

This will show the following screen:

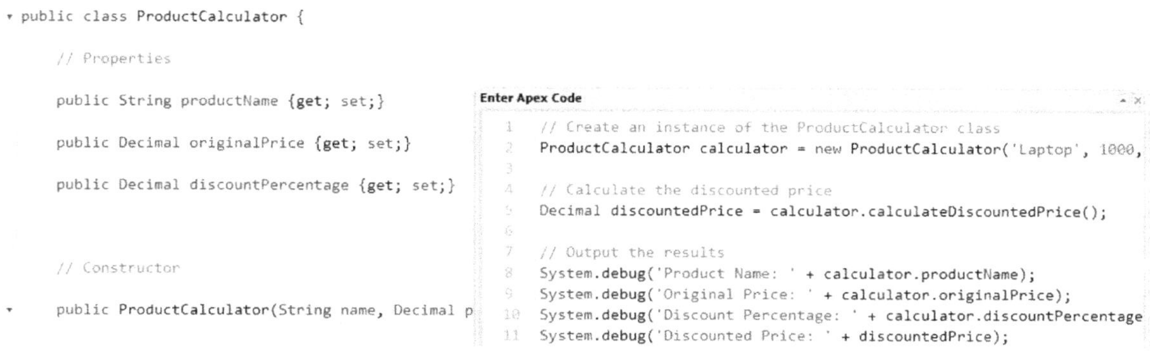

```
▾ public class ProductCalculator {

    // Properties

    public String productName {get; set;}

    public Decimal originalPrice {get; set;}

    public Decimal discountPercentage {get; set;}

    // Constructor
▾
    public ProductCalculator(String name, Decimal p
```

```
Enter Apex Code                                                        ▴ ×
 1   // Create an instance of the ProductCalculator class
 2   ProductCalculator calculator = new ProductCalculator('Laptop', 1000,
 3
 4   // Calculate the discounted price
 5   Decimal discountedPrice = calculator.calculateDiscountedPrice();
 6
 7   // Output the results
 8   System.debug('Product Name: ' + calculator.productName);
 9   System.debug('Original Price: ' + calculator.originalPrice);
10   System.debug('Discount Percentage: ' + calculator.discountPercentage
11   System.debug('Discounted Price: ' + discountedPrice);
```

Figure 11.8: Providing System.debug options for the class

Press the **Execute** button, and the code will run. Press the **Debug Only** option, as shown in the following figure to get a record of the order discount being applied:

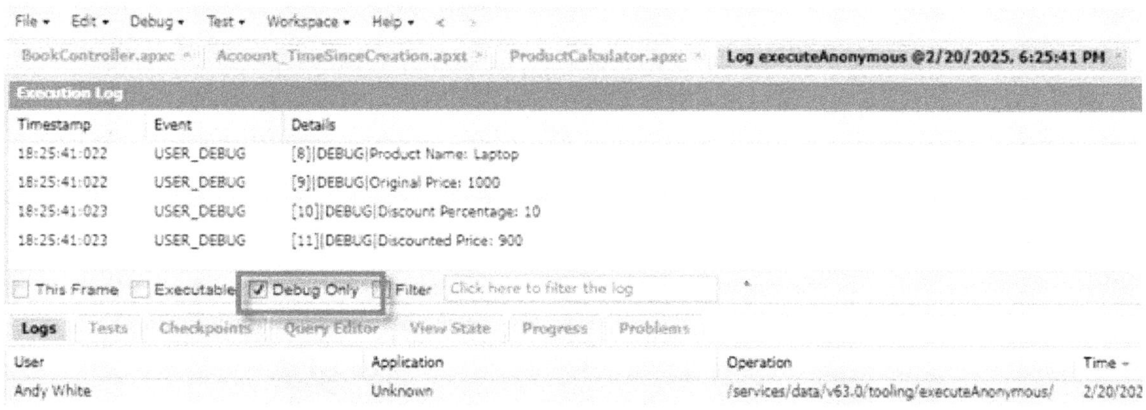

Figure 11.9: Viewing Debug Only in Developer Console

Lightning Web Components

LWCs build highly customizable parts to a webpage, be that for a Salesforce user or on Experience Cloud, or even part of a mobile app. There is a bit of history to LWCs, which readers should be aware of:

- Originally, customizations in Salesforce were done as Visualforce pages or even s-controls. There are still many of these in the Salesforce ecosystem.

- Salesforce moved to the Aura framework, which allowed for responsive design, but the skill set was bespoke to Salesforce, with various improvements offered by the successor, LWCs.

- Salesforce moved to LWCs, which combined basic web skills with Apex, giving a much better development experience as well as useful features such as being able to view dependencies between LWCs and tightly coupled data handling.

This is the brief history of development with Salesforce, but it may help put various online articles in context. In summary, LWCs combine basic web skills by including Apex and SOQL to create responsive web designs as illustrated in the following figure:

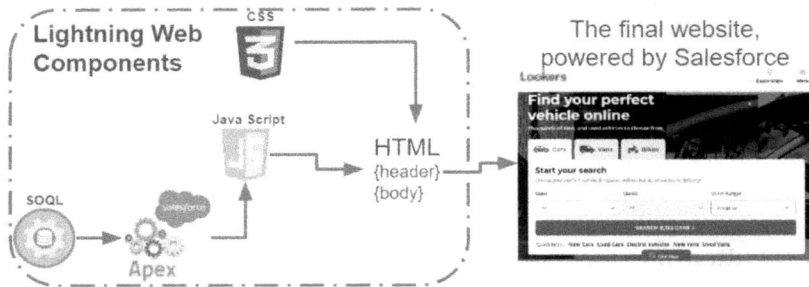

Figure 11.10: The basic construction of a LWCs

In the above illustration, LWCs are constructed out of a combination of:

- **Cascaded Style Sheets (CSS)** is a way of defining the look and feel of a website. For example, a font can inherit a font style as well as the corporate color.

- Allow Apex to generate SOQL to query the data in Salesforce and read or write to it as required.

- JavaScript runs in the browser, which means it is very fast at interacting with the user. This is run in the header of the webpage, meaning the user does not actually see it.

These combine to make a truly interactive webpage, which is based on Salesforce data and a look that can inherit the styles from the hosting website using CSS.

Lightning Web Component example

There are various online tutorials on building LWCs. For example, Trailhead has a simple **Hello World** example. Typically, they are done using an **integrated development environment (IDE)** like VS Code with SFDX, but the Developer Console will allow you to create a new LWC as illustrated in *Figure 11.10*.

The LWC structure will be as follows:

- **HTML (accountList.html)**: Displays the account data.
- **JavaScript (accountList.js)**: Calls the Apex method and processes data.
- **CSS (accountList.css)**: Basic styling.
- **Meta XML (accountList.js-meta.xml)**: Defines component visibility.

- **APEX controller (AccountController.cls)**: Fetches account records using SOQL.

The full code is kept in the book's code repository, outlined at the start of this book, shown in the following section.

HTML

As mentioned in the previous section, LWCs were introduced to replace Salesforce Lightning components as they were reliant on knowing the Aura framework. This provided greater security to customizations and used a more industry-standard set of languages; the most common is HTML.

The sample HTML code used in this example is pasted in the following:

```
<template>
    <lightning-card title="Account List">
        <template if:true={accounts}>
            <table class="slds-table slds-table_bordered">
                <thead>
                    <tr>
                        <th>Name</th>
                        <th>Industry</th>
                        <th>Phone</th>
                    </tr>
                </thead>
                <tbody>
                    <template for:each={accounts} for:item="acc">
                        <tr key={acc.Id}>
                            <td>{acc.Name}</td>
                            <td>{acc.Industry}</td>
                            <td>{acc.Phone}</td>
                        </tr>
                    </template>
                </tbody>
            </table>
        </template>
        <template if:true={error}>
            <p>Error fetching accounts: {error}</p>
        </template>
    </lightning-card>
</template>
```

JavaScript

As mentioned, LWCs were introduced to leverage languages more familiar to developers. If HTML is the basic structure of a webpage, then JavaScript is a language able to bring it to life, which can include simple formulas, libraries able to do form validation, creating interactive and dynamic content, and a lot more. The following is an example:

```javascript
import { LightningElement, wire } from 'lwc';
import getAccounts from '@salesforce/apex/AccountController.getAccounts';

export default class AccountList extends LightningElement {
    accounts;
    error;

    @wire(getAccounts)
    wiredAccounts({ error, data }) {
        if (data) {
            this.accounts = data;
            this.error = undefined;
        } else if (error) {
            this.error = error;
            this.accounts = undefined;
        }
    }
}
```

Cascading Style Sheets

CSS is a stylesheet language used to describe the presentation of a document written in HTML or XML. It controls the visual layout and appearance of web pages, including elements like colors, fonts, and layout. CSS allows developers to separate the content (HTML) from its presentation, making websites more maintainable and flexible.

The sample CSS code is pasted in the following:

```css
table {
    width: 100%;
    border-collapse: collapse;
}


th, td {
    padding: 8px;
```

```
        text-align: left;
        border-bottom: 1px solid #ddd;
}
```

Apex controller

An Apex controller is a server-side class written in Apex that is used to control the behavior of LWCs via Apex methods. It acts as the logic behind the user interface, allowing the component to fetch data, apply business logic, and respond to user actions.

The following is an example of an Apex controller for the **Account** object:

```
public with sharing class AccountController {
    @AuraEnabled(cacheable=true)
    public static List<Account> getAccounts() {
        return [SELECT Id, Name, Industry, Phone FROM Account LIMIT 10];
    }
}
```

Integration

IT systems need to communicate with each other. This happens all around you, from buying flight tickets to booking a holiday, or even simply sending an email or text message. The systems need to speak the same language, known as a **protocol**, and have information sent and received in a compatible format. This is where APIs come into play. They are the language spoken between systems to communicate.

A real-life example of this would be sending a letter. You would need to know:

- The name and address of the recipient
- Having a stamp or QR code, or similar
- Possibly add your address to the back of the letter
- If needed, special instructions such as fragile or this way up
- Some security, if needed, such as special delivery or a photo of the parcel at your door

This is the basic concept of sending information between systems. An API contains all the information required to send the information and confirm its delivery. It is the same for APIs. You need to ensure you have given the right details to ensure the information is received, and ideally, you would get a response. However, a bit like a letter, there are various ways to send and receive the information.

Application programming interfaces

Application programming interface (**API**) is the way in which Salesforce can send or receive information to another system. There are many public APIs that you can use to gain some familiarity, such as:

- **Google Maps API for Google Maps service: https://developers.google.com/maps**

- **OpenWeatherMap API for weather forecasts: https://openweathermap.org/api**

- **Genius API for song lyrics: https://genius.com/developers**

There are two basic ways that are constructed: **Simple Object Access Protocol** (**SOAP**) and **representational state transfer** (**REST**), but other methods exist, such as RAML and Pub/ Sub, which are not included in this book. REST is nearly always used by developers as it is faster, simpler, and works well with mobile devices. Platform events, which are based on REST principles, are now widely used. They help eliminate traditional point-to-point integrations commonly associated with standard REST APIs. As a result, this book will concentrate on REST.

There are a few basic terms that should be understood as they apply to both methods:

- **Synchronous**: Immediately send the message and ensure it has been received.

- **Asynchronous**: This is also known as **fire and forget**, which means it will wait in a queue and may be processed in part or in full.

- **Batch/Bulk**: The ability to send multiple records at once.

- **Payload**: This is the data that is sent between a client and an API server. It can be sent in a variety of formats, including JSON and XML.

- **Endpoint**: A dedicated URL that provides access to a specific resource, such as updating or retrieving data.

- **OAuth**: An open standard for accessing web resources and is commonly used to grant websites or applications access to information using tokens.

There are many other terms used when describing APIs, but these terms are used frequently.

SOAP vs. REST

Simple Object Access Protocol (**SOAP**) was one of the first integration protocols and has been used for many years, especially in large enterprises. It is an XML-based API and is often considered to be complicated. It has some advantages over REST, such as data migration and the ability to communicate with certain platforms and technologies.

REST is generally considered simpler, more lightweight, and suitable for many internet applications. The structure is like a webpage or email, as it contains:

- **Header section**: Information about the file and integration information.
- **Body**: The actual content that needs to be delivered.

REST relies on methods such as POST for sending data or GET for retrieving data. Other methods involve terms such as PUT, DELETE, PATCH, and others.

REST can also be written in XML or JSON. XML has some advantages as it is also a language, whilst JSON is an easy-to-read format.

A system-to-system integration, which is often called **point-to-point**, is simply one system talking to another. This can be done via a pre-built connector such as the Salesforce Marketing Cloud Connect. Many systems have pre-built connectors for Salesforce, which are generally available on the AppExchange or from the vendor. These keep life simple and provide an out-of-the-box solution.

However, as systems grow, this can get more complicated to manage, with the possibility of technical issues if not documented well and maintained. As a result, many large companies use middleware such as MuleSoft, Boomi, or Jitterbit, which can orchestrate the sending and receiving of data.

The following figure shows a simplified enterprise architecture that has middleware orchestrating the data between Salesforce Data Cloud and various external systems, such as *SAP* or *IBM*:

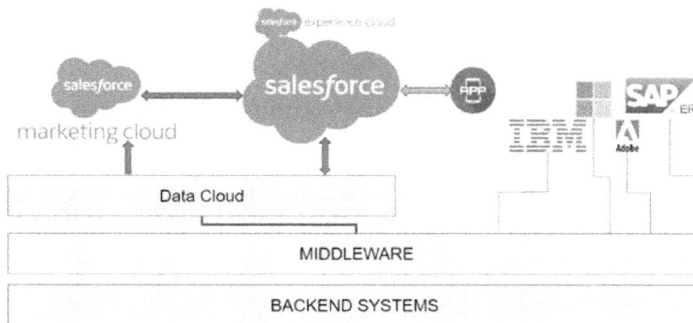

Figure 11.11: *A typical IT infrastructure*

In the above illustration, Marketing Cloud is connected by a red arrow. Data Cloud is connected by configuration in Salesforce using the Data Cloud Connector. This also provides data to Marketing Cloud. Middleware is used to send and receive data from other enterprise applications such as *SAP*, *Adobe*, and others.

In *Figure 11.11*, a legacy mobile app is the only point-to-point integration shown to the right-hand side of Salesforce, which remains from the legacy design. Also shown is Experience Cloud, which is built directly on top of Salesforce and exposes Salesforce Data on a public-facing website.

Salesforce provides various APIs to help developers perform their tasks. These are detailed by Salesforce in the API, use article found at: **https://help.salesforce.com/s/articleView?id=sf.integrate_what_is_api.htm&type=5**. The following table is a simplified table made from the article:

API name	Description	Data format	Communication
REST API	Uses REST	JSON, XML	Synchronous
SOAP API	Uses SOAP	XML	Synchronous
Bulk API 2.0	Uses REST for bulk data transfer	CSV	Asynchronous
Metadata API	SOAP for migrating configuration	XML	Asynchronous
Pub/Sub API	Very fast real-time integration	Binary	Asynchronous

Table 11.1: Summary of popular API formats

The above table is very oversimplified, and various languages can be used for developing APIs. However, these are the most common forms.

It is important to understand the differences in the APIs provided. If the business wants a real-time integration, then Pub/Sub would be required. If large data volumes need to be updated at the end of the day, then the Bulk API would be used on a daily schedule.

Example of a REST API

The first part of building the API is to provide the endpoint, which is used in the header section of the API. It will be in the format as follows:

GET: **https://your-instance.salesforce.com/services/data/v59.0/sobjects/Account/{AccountId}**

There is a full Salesforce REST developer guide available at: **https://developer.salesforce.com/docs/atlas.en-us.api_rest.meta/api_rest/intro_what_is_rest_api.htm**,which, which contains a reference section in the menu for all the URLs and endpoints available.

Although there are various forms of authentication, a popular one is based on OAuth 2.0. To do this, you need to include an access token in the request headers. This is done by using the Salesforce web server flow, which has the following two steps:

1. This flow is to get the authorization code
2. Get the access token

These steps are outlined in Salesforce documentation found at: **https://help.salesforce.com/s/articleView?id=xcloud.remoteaccess_oauth_web_server_flow.htm&type=5**, but are also provided in the following figure.

To setup a connected app, go to **Setup | App Manager** and press the **New Connected App** button, and select **Create a Connected App**, as shown in the following:

To use OAuth 2.0, create an external client app. As the next generation of connected apps, external client apps provide increased security and a better user experience. Learn more about connected apps and external client apps in Salesforce Help.

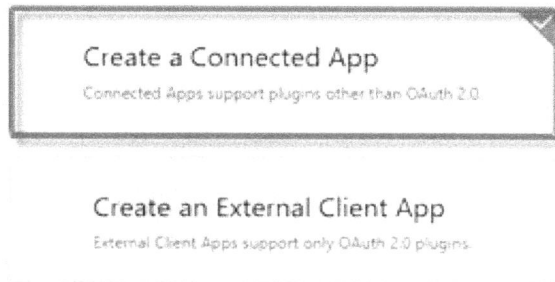

Create a Connected App
Connected Apps support plugins other than OAuth 2.0.

Create an External Client App
External Client Apps support only OAuth 2.0 plugins.

Figure 11.12: Building a connected app

Press **Continue** and give the app a name such as `Connecting Postman`, and enter an email address that is used to help if there are any failures, with an explanation of the problem.

Select the **Enable OAuth Settings** checkbox.

This requires you to enter a callback URL. Enter the URL of your Salesforce instance, stopping at force.com. For example, **https://doogle3-dev-ed.develop.lightning.force.com/**

The other option is what level of access to you wish to give this connected app. This could be updating or deleting records, but for this example, select **Full access (full)**, as shown in the following figure:

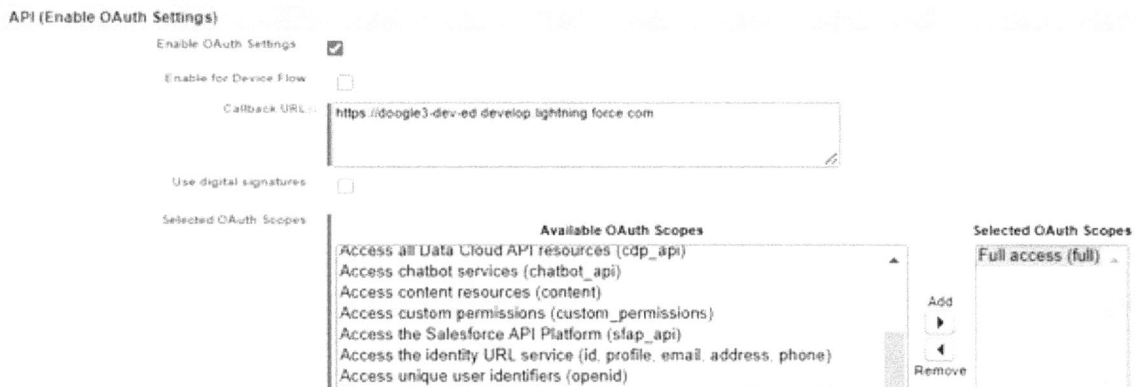

API (Enable OAuth Settings)

Enable OAuth Settings	☑
Enable for Device Flow	☐
Callback URL	https://doogle3-dev-ed.develop.lightning.force.com
Use digital signatures	☐

Selected OAuth Scopes

Available OAuth Scopes		Selected OAuth Scopes
Access all Data Cloud API resources (cdp_api)		Full access (full)
Access chatbot services (chatbot_api)		
Access content resources (content)	Add	
Access custom permissions (custom_permissions)	►	
Access the Salesforce API Platform (sfap_api)	◄	
Access the identity URL service (id, profile, email, address, phone)	Remove	
Access unique user identifiers (openid)		

Figure 11.13: Including OAuth in the connected app

Press **Save** and note that the following message informs you to wait for ten minutes before the connected app is available. Press **Continue**.

Wait for the app to appear in the App Manager and then press the **Manage Consumer Details** button, as shown in the following figure:

▼ API (Enable OAuth Settings)

Consumer Key and Secret   Manage Consumer Details

Selected OAuth Scopes   Full access (full)

Callback URL   https://doogle3-dev-ed.develop.lightning.force.com

Enable for Device Flow

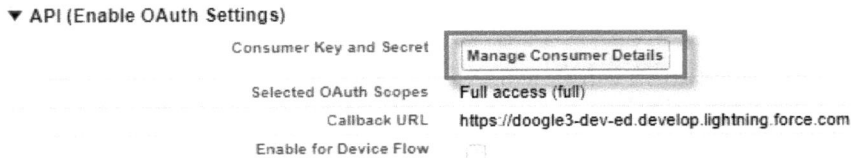

Figure 11.14: Getting key information about the connected app

This will give you **Consumer Key** and **Consumer Secret**, which are needed for the integration using Postman. Either leave the screen open or copy these to any plain text editor. Refer to the following figure:

Consumer Key   3MVG9YFqzc_KnL.xEqlfBX5EdlXbV3OWFDZdRGYYRLt_OugB9SWaxe.pXhLjcVfHIME_Z3fxqms9vHpNUbkUH

Copy

Consumer Secret   D183D139E4AF35199A23D612B93D5ABF908938386958FB9F3B644973276E5D58

Copy

Figure 11.15: Obtaining the Consumer Key and Consumer Secret for use in an integration

You have just created a connected app. Salesforce requires an additional step to verify the integration. You need to create a security token, which is done under your user profile, as shown in the following figure:

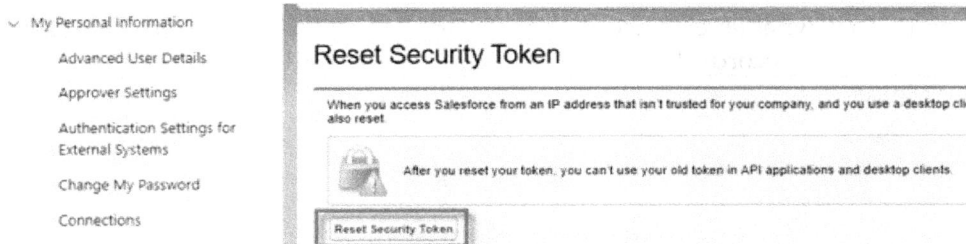

∨ My Personal Information

Advanced User Details

Approver Settings

Authentication Settings for
External Systems

Change My Password

Connections

Reset Security Token

When you access Salesforce from an IP address that isn't trusted for your company, and you use a desktop clie
also reset

After you reset your token, you can't use your old token in API applications and desktop clients.

Reset Security Token

Figure 11.16: Generating a security token

The final step in Salesforce is to go to **Setup | OAuth and OpenID Connect Settings** and slide the **Allow OAuth Username-Password Flows** slider, as shown in the following figure:

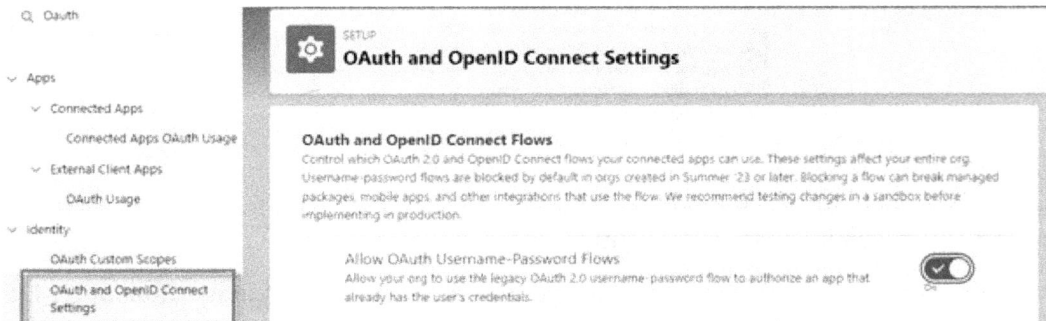

Q Oauth

∨ Apps

   ∨ Connected Apps

     Connected Apps OAuth Usage

   ∨ External Client Apps

     OAuth Usage

∨ Identity

   OAuth Custom Scopes

   OAuth and OpenID Connect
   Settings

SETUP

OAuth and OpenID Connect Settings

OAuth and OpenID Connect Flows

Control which OAuth 2.0 and OpenID Connect flows your connected apps can use. These settings affect your entire org.
Username-password flows are blocked by default in orgs created in Summer '23 or later. Blocking a flow can break managed
packages, mobile apps, and other integrations that use the flow. We recommend testing changes in a sandbox before
implementing in production.

Allow OAuth Username-Password Flows
Allow your org to use the legacy OAuth 2.0 username-password flow to authorize an app that
already has the user's credentials.

Figure 11.17: Enabling OAuth connected flows

Next, you need to go to Postman. Setting up Postman is covered in the final section of this chapter. In Postman, create a new collection by pressing the + button. A collection is simply a folder to keep the files. Refer to the following figure:

Figure 11.18: Creating a collection in Postman

To enable the integration, add **OAuth 2.0** to the **Auth Type** options, as shown in the following figure:

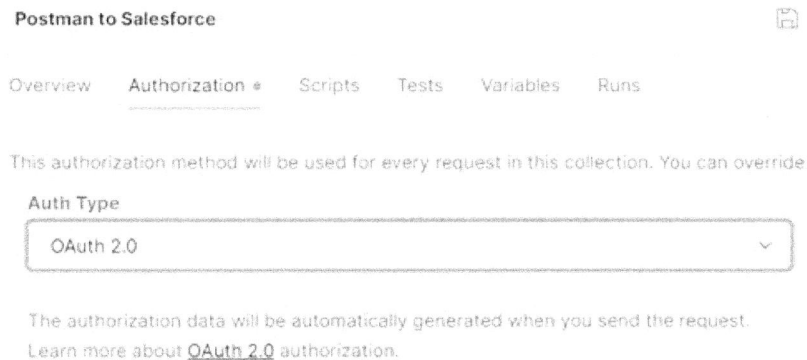

Figure 11.19: Setting the authorization type in Postman

Further down the same screen, you will see a section for **Configure New Token**. For **Grant Type**, select **Password Credentials** as shown in *Figure 11.20*.

You need to enter the **Access Token URL**, which is generally **https://login.salesforce.com/services/oauth2/token**

Note: If your Salesforce instance has a different domain, then you will need to use that with the same /services/oauth2/token in the URL.

Next, copy the **Consumer Key** value created previously and enter it into the **Client ID** field, and copy the **Consumer Secret** previously created and paste it into the **Client Secret** field.

Enter your **Username**, but the **Password** is made up of your login password, with the security token you have previously generated appended to the end. For example, if your password is **Hello!23** and the security token is **GyyrHvbFddDR**, then you would enter:**Hello!23GyyrHvbFddDR**.

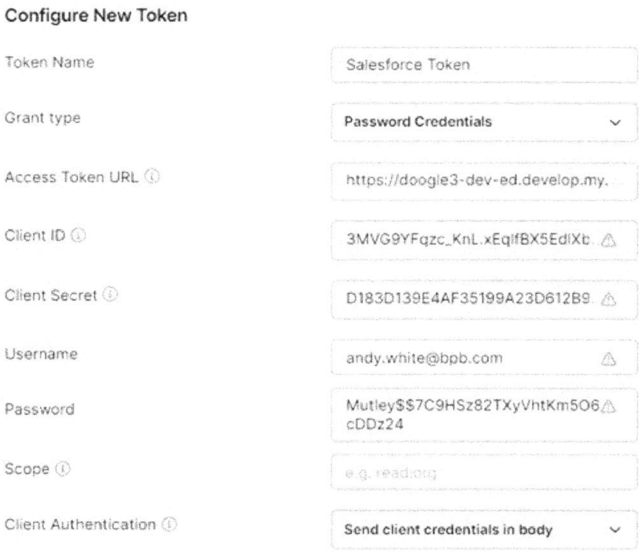

Configure New Token

Token Name	Salesforce Token
Grant type	Password Credentials
Access Token URL ⓘ	https://doogle3-dev-ed.develop.my.
Client ID ⓘ	3MVG9YFqzc_KnL.xEqlfBX5EdlXb ⚠
Client Secret ⓘ	D183D139E4AF35199A23D612B9 ⚠
Username	andy.white@bpb.com ⚠
Password	Mutley$$7C9HSz82TXyVhtKm5O6⚠ cDDz24
Scope ⓘ	e.g. read:org
Client Authentication ⓘ	Send client credentials in body

Figure 11.20: Key configuration in Postman

Finally, press **Get New Access Token** at the bottom of the page to generate the new token, as shown in the following figure:

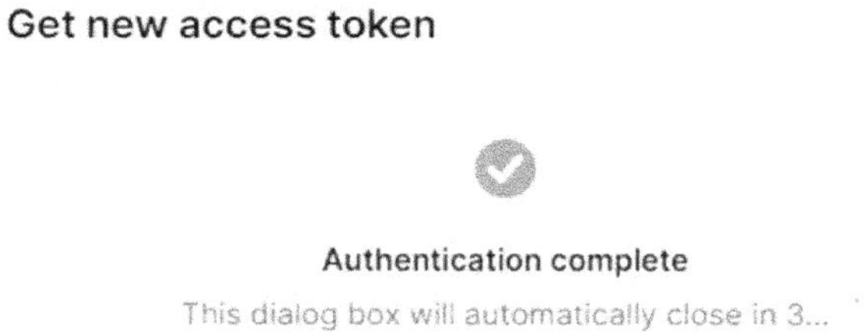

Get new access token

✓

Authentication complete

This dialog box will automatically close in 3...

Figure 11.21: Successful authorization confirmation in Postman

Press the **Use Token** button, which will then populate the **Current Token** field in the configuration. Refer to the following figure:

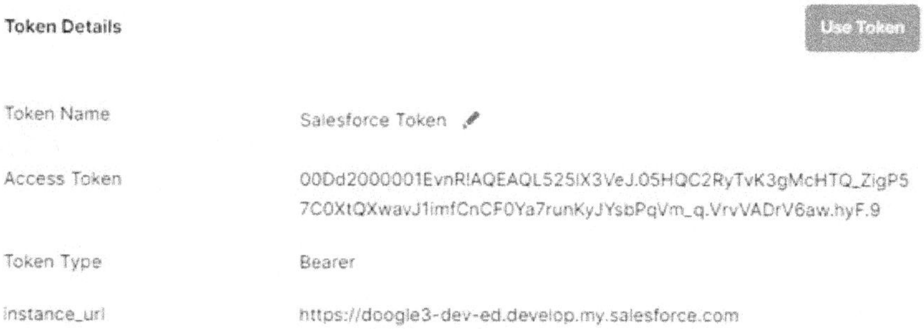

Token Details   Use Token

Token Name	Salesforce Token ✎
Access Token	00Dd2000001EvnR!AQEAQL525IX3VeJ.O5HQC2RyTvK3gMcHTQ_ZigP5 7C0XtQXwavJ1imfCnCF0Ya7runKyJYsbPqVm_q.VrvVADrV6aw.hyF.9
Token Type	Bearer
instance_url	https://doogle3-dev-ed.develop.my.salesforce.com

Figure 11.22: Viewing the Access Token in Postman

Note: **If you have any problems, then press the View Console button, which opens up the steps that were run when trying to create the access token.**

To test the connection, go to the collection and press the **Add a request** link, as shown in the following figure:

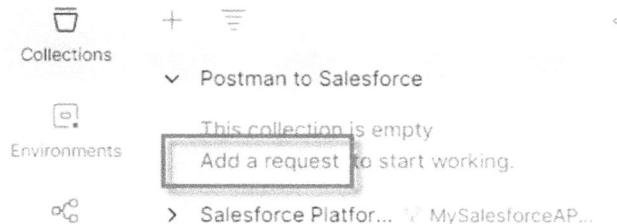

Figure 11.23: Testing the configuration by adding a request in Postman

Copy the following line into Postman, replacing **MyDomainName** with the one from your Salesforce org. There are many links in the Salesforce REST Developer's guide that you could use. The following link is for accessing the **Account** object:

https://MyDomainName.my.salesforce.com/services/data/v63.0/sobjects/Account

Set the method as **POST** to create an account and the input to raw and **JSON**, as illustrated in the following figure:

Figure 11.24: Configuration of Postman to add a record to Salesforce using the API

The text to create a new account is shown in the following:

```
{
    "Name":"Account created by Postman"
}
```

Finally, press the **Send** button, and you will see the return message for the newly created account with the ID. Copy the ID and return to Salesforce, and enter the ID into the URL. The newly created account is shown in the following figure:

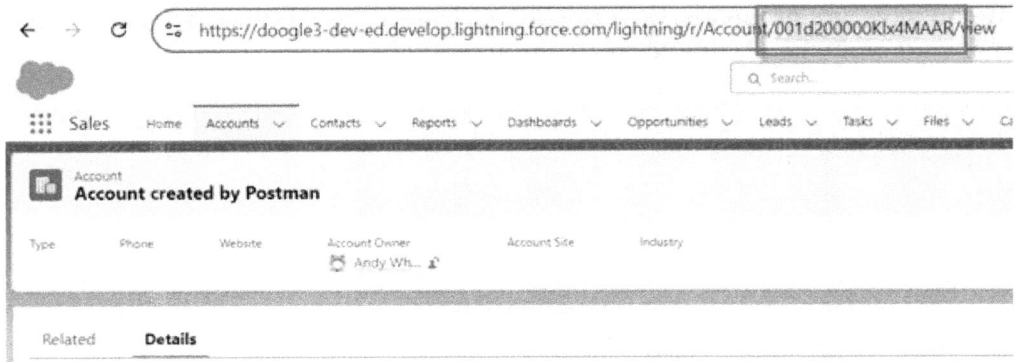

Figure 11.25: Checking the newly created account in Salesforce

Integration types

Some subjects are simply too good to leave out of this chapter, but the subjects are also so big that it is not possible to do them justice. A few features readers should be aware of are:

- **Pub/Sub integrations**: These integrations are not written in REST but rather based on an open-source framework called **Google Remote Procedure Call (gRPC)** and the HTTP/2 protocol. Pub/Sub API efficiently publishes and delivers binary event messages in the Apache Avro format. These are also referred to as **platform events**, which have a comprehensive guide found at **https://developer.salesforce.com/docs/ atlas.en-us.platform_events.meta/platform_events/platform_events_intro.htm**

- **OData**: **Open Data Protocol (OData)** integrations allow data to be displayed in Salesforce without storing the data in Salesforce. Effectively, they synchronize with an external system and retrieve data that has the appearance of being in Salesforce but only for the duration of the session. OData is often used when Salesforce users need real-time access to large datasets such as orders or transactions.

- **External objects**: Similarly to OData, external objects in Salesforce are like custom objects, but the data is stored outside of Salesforce. This allows users to access data from other systems without having to store a copy in Salesforce. External objects use OData to connect to the external system. The difference between OData and external objects focuses on visualization vs. integration.

- **Developer tools**: As mentioned at the start of this chapter, there are various tools required for development. The installation and use are covered briefly here. There are two distinct areas of development:

  o **Apex**: Salesforce development language

  o **APIs**: Generally written in SOAP or REST

The tools covered in this section are either about writing APEX or configuring integrations.

Developer Console

You may have noticed that in your Salesforce org, under **Setup**, there is an option for **Developer Console**. This opens a new window that gives you direct access to an IDE where you can create, debug, and test triggers, classes, and LWCs in your Salesforce org. Refer to the following figure:

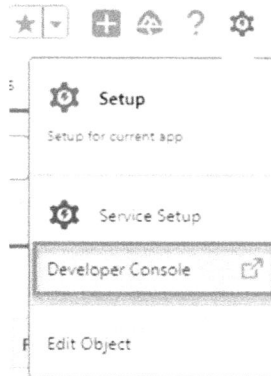

Figure 11.26: Access to the Developer Console directly from the Salesforce user interface

The development console does not require any configuration but has a simple-to-use interface for creating or editing code and much more. For example, if you go to **File | New**, you will see the ability to create many of the coded features in Salesforce, as shown in the following figure:

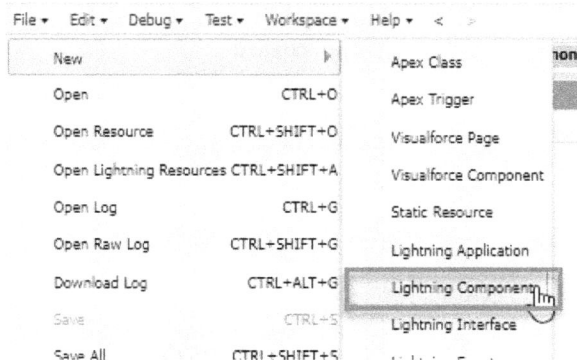

Figure 11.27: Creating new Lightning Component from the Developer Console

For example, to create a new LWC, select the **Lightning Component** option, which creates the necessary files and locations for HTML, CSS, and JavaScript, and options for Salesforce features such as Tabs, Pages, and Quick Actions. This is known as a **Lightning Bundle**, as shown in the following figure:

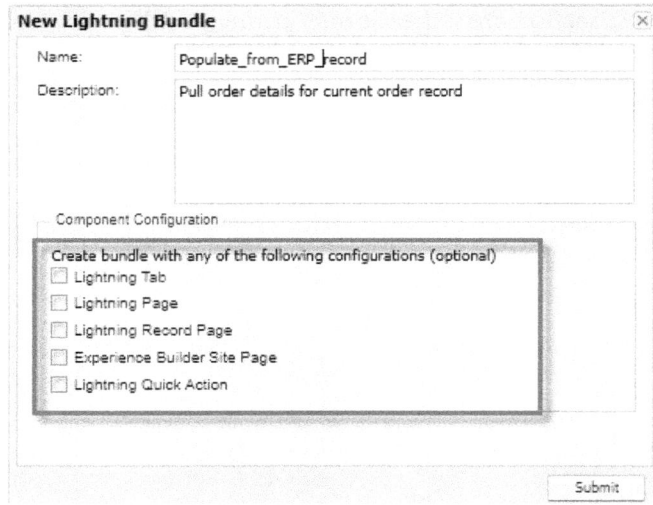

Figure 11.28: Selecting which features to build using the Developer Console

VS Code and the Salesforce CLI

VS Code is a free application that allows developers to write code. VS Code is an IDE. For it to work with Salesforce, you will also need to add the Salesforce extension as described in the following section.

First, download and install VS Code from **https://code.visualstudio.com/**. Simply, install VS Code as you would any other program. Once installed, you will see the following figure:

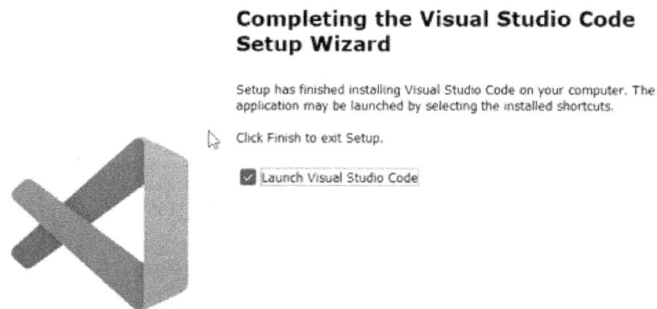

Figure 11.29: Installing VS Code

It is worth spending some time exploring VS Code before taking the next steps, as when VS Code is first installed, it will have a very basic layout. For example, you can change the look and feel, connect it with GitHub, and create a local folder or repository. There are many online tutorials, as per the example found at: **https://code.visualstudio.com/docs/getstarted/getting-started**

Installing the Salesforce extension pack into VS Code

Once VS Code is installed and you have familiarized yourself with the basics, go to the **Extensions** menu on the left-hand side and type in **Salesforce**, as shown in the following figure:

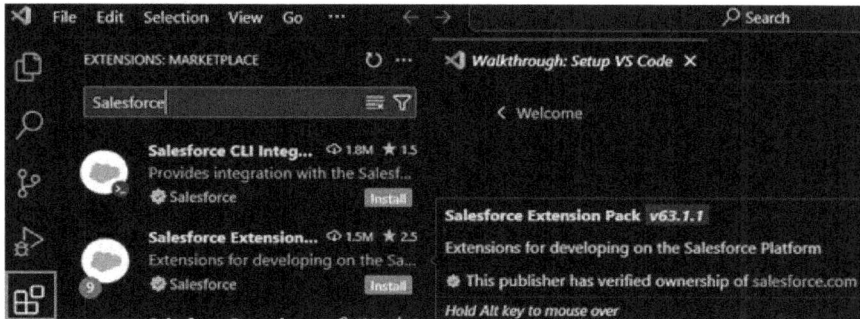

Figure 11.30: Adding the Salesforce Extension Pack to VS Code

There are many Salesforce options in the list, and they allow variations on what can be done. However, the **Salesforce Extension Pack (Expanded)** is generally the most popular. Refer to the following figure:

Figure 11.31: Selecting Salesforce Extension Pack

To check it is installed correctly, go to the **View** menu and select **Command Palette**, as shown in the following figure:

Figure 11.32: Opening the Command Palette

Type in **SFDX** and then **Create Project**, as shown in the following figure:

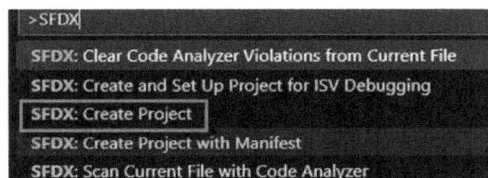

Figure 11.33: Creating a new Salesforce project in VS Code

This will give you a local repository where you can create classes, triggers, or LWCs. These are already in your Salesforce environment, and options to sync with the likes of GitHub.

Postman

Postman is a curious name, but it resonates that sending a letter requires some basic information, such as the name and address of the recipient and a stamp, etc. There is a lot of overlap between Postman and Swagger (mentioned in the following sections), but Postman is generally better at API checking, whilst Swagger is for writing APIs.

Installing Postman

To install Postman, go to **https://www.postman.com/downloads/** and press the installation button appropriate for your device. Once installed, you will need to register, as shown in the following figure:

Working with APIs simplified with Postman

Enter your work email

Your work email makes it easy for you to collaborate with your teammates.

Create Free Account

Figure 11.34: Registering your account with Postman

When you install Postman, you must create an account and grant permissions for public and private groups to access this app.

There is a public developer workspace that can be added to Postman, found at: **https://www. postman.com/salesforce-developers/salesforce-developers/overview**. From here, you can access a wide range of APIs for Salesforce by selecting the **Salesforce Platform APIs** menu option, as shown in the following figure:

∨ Salesforce Platform APIs

> 🗀 Auth

> 🗀 Bulk v1

> 🗀 Bulk v2

> 🗀 Composite

Figure 11.35: Selecting which Salesforce API to use with Postman

Press the **Fork** button at the top right-hand side of the screen, as shown below. Forking creates a copy of a specific version of an API in your account. For example, you can fork someone else's API as a starting point for your own API, or you can create a fork of your own API to experiment with changes without affecting the original API definition.

A fork is a new instance of an element that you can change without making any changes to the parent element. In Postman, you can fork collections, environments, and flows. Forking enables you to contribute to an element without having editor access for that element, as shown in the following figure:

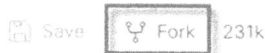

***Figure 11.36**: Creating a Fork*

Swagger

Swagger is a popular tool for developing APIs found at: **https://swagger.io/**

Swagger generates various files, which are shown in the following figure:

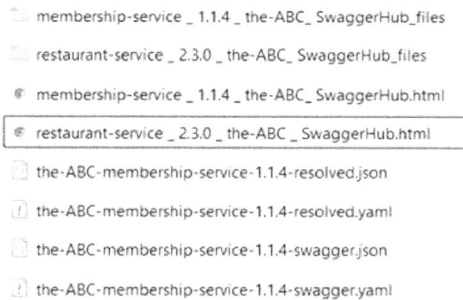

***Figure 11.37**: Typical files generated from Swagger Hub*

Although JSON and YAML are both structured files, YAML supports comments, which can make them easier to understand, as shown in the following figure:

```yaml
swagger: "2.0"
info:
  description: Membership service helps internal and 3rd party consumer create and
  version: 
  title: Membership Service
host: virtserver.swaggerhub.com
basePath: /the-ABC/membership-service/1.1.4
schemes:
- https
paths:
  /customer:
    get:
      tags:
      - Customers
      summary: Retrieves a list of customers assigned to your consumer
      description: "By passing in the appropriate options, you can search for cust
      produces:
      - application/json
      parameters:
      - name: searchString
        in: query
        description: pass an optional search string for looking up inventory
        required: false
        type: string
```

***Figure 11.38**: Example of a YAML file*

Conclusion

This chapter has given an overview of what is required for Salesforce development. It includes examples of triggers and classes, and an overview of other Salesforce areas such as LWC.

Also covered is an introduction to integrating Salesforce using APIs and an overview of the tools typically used.

There are many online tutorials to explore each subject based on the reader's interests.

In the next chapter, we will be looking at Einstein AI, which is Salesforce's AI offering, packed with features and the latest cutting-edge developments in AI.

Multiple choice questions

1. **The difference between a trigger and a class is:**

    a. Triggers are fired when a record is saved, whilst classes can run on any platform event

    b. Triggers run on an instantiation of an object, whilst a class runs when an event is fired

    c. Apex classes are blueprints for creating custom logic, while Apex triggers run in response to Salesforce events

    d. A class represents an object, whilst a trigger occurs when an object is updated

2. **Which of the following are methods in REST?**

    a. GET

    b. PUT

    c. DELETE

    d. PATCH

    e. All of the above

3. **Which one of the following is available directly from the Salesforce user interface?**

    a. Swagger

    b. VS Code

    c. Postman

    d. Developer Console

4. **If it is likely that the Salesforce org is going to be heavily customized, then which license type should you consider?**

    a. Configuration-only license

    b. Lightning license

    c. Salesforce.com basic license

    d. Platform license

5. **What is the main difference between SOQL and SOSL?**

    a. SOQL can be used in APEX, whilst SOSL cannot.

    b. SOQL is in a format similar to SQL, whilst SOSL uses JSON or XML.

    c. SOQL is used to query individual objects, while SOSL is used to perform searches across multiple objects.

    d. SOQL is only stored in Apex Classes, whilst SOSL can be used in triggers and classes.

6. **When writing a loop in APEX, one of the common mistakes is:**

    a. Ignoring governor limits when running the code

    b. Not giving an exit to the loop

    c. Performing data manipulation inside the loop

    d. Hard-coding IDs inside the loop

7. **OAuth and OData refer to the same set of features in Salesforce.**

    a. True

    b. False

8. **When configuring a connected app using OAuth you need which two items?**

    a. Integration user

    b. OAuth login credentials

    c. Consumer Key

    d. Consumer Secret

9. **What is the minimum percentage of code coverage allowed in a test class?**

    a. 50%

    b. 75%

    c. 80%

    d. 90%

10. **The variable type integer stores what kind of data:**

    a. Any number with up to 6 decimal points

    b. Negative and positive whole numbers without a decimal point

    c. Whole numbers between 0 and 6 million

    d. Numbers stored as text values

Answers

1	**c**
2	**e**
3	**d**
4	**d**
5	**c**
6	**c**
7	**b**
8	**c, d**
9	**b**
10	**b**

Join our Discord space

Join our Discord workspace for latest updates, offers, tech happenings around the world, new releases, and sessions with the authors:

https://discord.bpbonline.com

CHAPTER 12
Einstein AI

Introduction

This chapter gives you a high-level understanding of Salesforce AI. This has to be the main growth area in technology in general currently, and Salesforce is leading the way with incorporating it into its world-class **customer relationship management** (**CRM**). Salesforce has named the AI capabilities as Einstein, with various functionality enhancing the sales, service, marketing, development, automation, and more.

This chapter covers core concepts and a few examples. Many of the concepts should be researched to support the content of this chapter.

At the heart of Salesforce AI, there are some basic concepts, such as Ethical considerations that ensure that AI results are not biased or skewed, and that they do not favor or discriminate against individuals based on race, social status, or other demographic factors. Data quality involves making sure that the data used to train and generate AI models is both complete and representative of the broader population or use case. Poor-quality data will lead to inaccurate results and provide misinformation to the user or client. Trust is maintained by ensuring that sensitive data remains within Salesforce and is properly secured, preventing unauthorized access or exposure. This is maintained by encrypting data being sent to and from the AI provider.

When combined with actual Salesforce data and users' requests, customers or anything interacting with Einstein they will have a seemingly well-understood response to their requirement.

Einstein uses Salesforce's own native AI engine called **Atlas**. This can combine with other AI providers such as *OpenAI* and many others.

This chapter goes through core concepts and a few hands-on examples to get you started. It should be noted that this area of Salesforce is under continued development and will undoubtedly change. As such, this chapter is to give you a broad overview and sufficient detail to get you started.

It should be noted that this chapter has been the hardest to give practical advice since the menu options in Salesforce setup change on a regular basis, whilst the names used also change and the training material is often updated a long time afterwards. As such, this chapter is aimed to provide guidance as to what can be done.

Structure

This chapter will cover the following topics:

- Introduction to Salesforce AI
- Salesforce Einstein 1
- Enabling Einstein and configuring
- Einstein 1 Copilot for Service Cloud
- Other Salesforce AI capabilities

Objectives

The aim of this chapter is to give you a good understanding of core AI concepts, as well as setup Einstein in your own Salesforce org. This chapter will also go through some of the main features that are available with Salesforce and Einstein. Some of the features are to help with the sales process, such as lead scoring or opportunity insights, whilst others are on the service side, such as call summaries and **Next Best Action** (**NBA**).

There's also Einstein to help with development or building flows covered in *Chapter 6, Automating Salesforce with Flows*.

However, it is also important to understand key concepts such as **large language models** (**LLMs**) and **machine learning** (**ML**).

By the end of this chapter, you will have learned the core concepts of AI, how Einstein leverages these, and have a good understanding of the Einstein features in Salesforce.

Introduction to Salesforce AI

AI has undoubtedly become the latest thing in technology. If you simply look up **AI robots** or **Humanoid**, then you will find the most amazing applications of AI technology.

AI works by continually scanning vast amounts of data with algorithms that continually improve their own ability to interpret the data. We will go into this in more detail later in this chapter. The process known as **natural language processing** (**NLP**) and LLMs breaks large amounts of data into smaller pieces via a process known as **tokenization** and **vectorization**. These can then be compared and used to give two types of information:

- Predictive AI analyses existing data to make predictions or recommendations based on patterns or trends.
- **Generative AI** (**GenAI**) creates new content based on existing data or inputs.

Traditional search engines typically scan various websites for the best match to search words. AI works differently, using a process known as **retrieval augmented generation** (**RAG**), which puts the content from the various sites into a single returned result by combining the data.

Salesforce has, for many years, had some basic AI in the form of Einstein. However, Salesforce was leading in this area, offering many features simply unavailable in alternative CRM platforms. This meant Salesforce is ready to embrace the latest AI technologies, which represent the biggest technological shift in all industries and will dramatically change the way in which people work.

Salesforce AI has been traditionally referred to as Einstein and has covered many areas of the Salesforce platform with different terms to describe specific functionality. Einstein used in Service Cloud is often referred to as **Copilot**, but when specifically referring to features used by agents, Agentforce is the primary functionality. This includes voice recognition and integration into Data Cloud to provide predictive assistance to agents dealing with customers.

The previous offerings from Salesforce allowed businesses to build features such as **Einstein Next Best Action** (**ENBA**), which was able to assist agents in handling cases for customers. Einstein was able to provide real-time recommendations on complementary products and services, and many other use cases. Salesforce allows admins to combine Data Cloud with predictive analytics to give information that would be time-consuming to generate manually.

Although the logic is built using a combination of various configurations, such as Salesforce Flow, Apex, or prompts, the features can be built into the Sales or Service Console for agents or embedded into your Lightning Experience website or other external devices, such as a mobile app.

To assist in being able to understand Einstein, Salesforce includes an *Einstein Generative AI Glossary of Terms*, which covers many more keywords or phrases found here: **https://help.salesforce.com/s/articleView?id=sf.generative_ai_glossary.htm**

Salesforce AI certification

At the time of writing, Salesforce is offering both the AI Associate and AI Specialist certification training and exam for free. This is to ensure there are sufficient professionals available to implement the AI offerings Salesforce is providing.

Registration for the exam is done via Salesforce Training Academy, which is covered in *Chapter 13, Preparing for Salesforce Certifications,* as shown in the following figure:

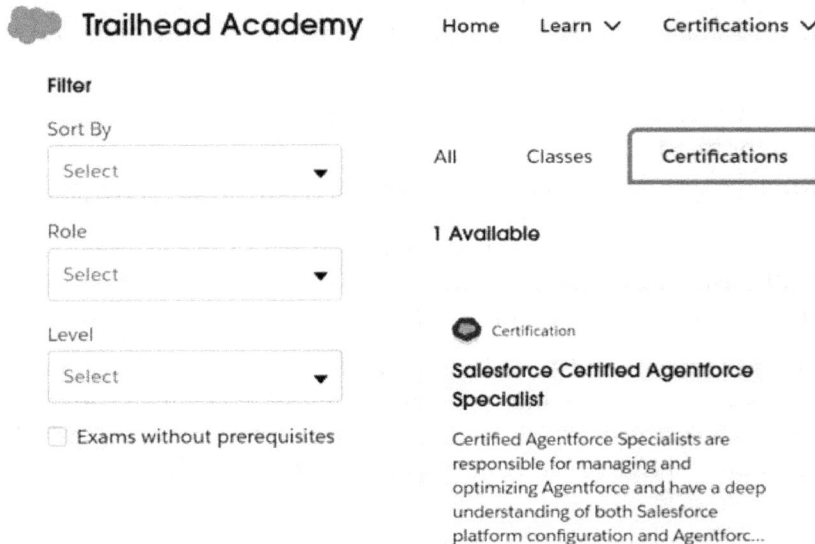

Figure 12.1: Registering for the Salesforce Agentforce Specialist exam

The AI Associate exam covers the basics of Salesforce AI with course material and training found at: **https://trailhead.salesforce.com/en/credentials/aiassociate**

The AI Specialist exam concentrates on more advanced features and some industry-specific questions. Training can be found at: **https://trailhead.salesforce.com/en/credentials/aispecialist**

Working of AI

In this section, we will go into more detail about the way in which Salesforce works with Einstein AI. Some of the concepts mentioned previously are conceptually very dense. In the following sections, you will be given a more detailed explanation.

Large language models

If you think about a simple task, such as catching a bus or train, there are many variables, such as the day, time, weather, and more complicated variables, such as traffic issues or whether you are walking, cycling, or driving to catch the bus or train. AI builds the connection between the variables and gives them a score or weighting. This allows the model to improve over time. In the above example, if the weather is bad and the roads are busy, then you will need more time to catch the bus or train. The bus is likely to be slowed down by bad weather, so your total journey will take longer.

As such, AI uses the variables to decide and gives them a weighting. This is illustrated in the following figure, where a request is made from the AI engine, which is then chunked into smaller pieces of information and then fed through the algorithms in the AI engine. This process is known as **tokenization**, which is the process of breaking down text into smaller units called **tokens**, which can be words, sub-words, or characters. Vectorization then converts these tokens into numerical representations (vectors) that the model can understand and process. Each piece of data is then given a weighting, which is illustrated by the thickness of the lines in *Figure 12.2*. The input is fed through multiple algorithms before returning the result. This combines to give an output that is a meaningful response to the request:

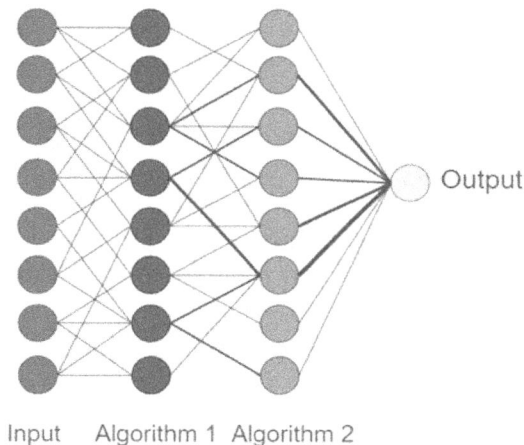

Input   Algorithm 1 Algorithm 2

Figure 12.2: Illustration of how an AI system works

Natural language processing

NLP is the means by which a device, such as a *Laptop, MacBook, Alexa* device, or similar, can understand speech and then use it to perform a task, such as getting you relevant information.

This process has a few distinct phases, such as breaking the text into keywords and removing unnecessary words in a process known as **feature extraction**. These are then analyzed using a process known as **computational linguistics**, where the meaning and even sentiment (such as *shouting* or *laughing*) allow the device to work out the meaning of the sentence or phrase. This is then fed into the LLM described in the previous section.

Retrieval augmented generation and grounding

Retrieval augmented generation (**RAG**) is an architectural approach that enhances the capabilities of LLMs by integrating them with data, such as Salesforce. This setup enables the LLM to access current and specific knowledge from Salesforce, resulting in responses that are augmented from Einstein as well as your CRM data.

AI is only as good as the context you give it, which is where grounding comes in. In Salesforce AI, grounding means connecting your AI-generated prompts directly to real, meaningful Salesforce data. It ensures that the model's responses are not solely based on its pre-trained data but are supported by the data relevant to the user's query. RAG serves as a method for achieving grounding by allowing LLMs to fetch and incorporate relevant data into the response. This is often used in Salesforce Prompt Builder, which is given a more detailed explanation later in this chapter.

Three types of AI

At a high-level, there are three types of AI available for use with Salesforce:

- **Private/Proprietary**: Einstein 1 is proprietary to Salesforce, meaning you have it available inside your Salesforce org. In other words, this is developed by Salesforce, including features from the Einstein 1 technology layer, and uses the Atlas Reasoning Engine.

- **Combined**: Salesforce has partnered with OpenAI and other AI providers, providing out-of-the-box GenAI capabilities to companies through direct access to OpenAI's enterprise-grade ChatGPT technology. Although this is great, there are security settings via Salesforce Trust to ensure the data from Salesforce is not used by OpenAI or stored outside of Salesforce.

- **Bring your own model**: As Einstein GPT is open and extensible, you can opt to use it alongside your own external models, such as *AWS SageMaker*. To do this, you need to use the Einstein Model Builder.

Salesforce allows you to add various models to leverage AI capabilities using Einstein Studio. There are also many AI tools generally available, with a short list grouped by categories as follows:

- **General AI**: ChatGPT, Claude AI, Perplexity AI
- **Productivity**: tl;dv, AudioPen, Notion, Goblin Tools, Scheduler AI
- **Customer success**: Second Native, Dante
- **Design and video**: Midjourney, Runaway, Leonardo AI, ElevenLabs, HeyGen
- **Marketing**: Pebblely, Pencil AI, Framer
- **Content**: Heypotenuse, PaperPal, Surfer, Lavender AI, Quillbot

OpenAI also has a range of plugins, which assist in certain areas; namely: Diagram AI, Prompt Perfect, Scholar AI, One Word Domains, ChatWithPDF, and KAYAK. These can be included in your AI solution either by adding them to your OpenAI account, building the integration, or using a connector available with OpenAI or the AppExchange.

Einstein

Salesforce typically uses Prompt Builders as the user interface to write actions and instructions, which can then be merged with company data. This is then sent to the AI model, where data can be masked and returned to Salesforce. The data is checked for toxic content and tracked in the Audit Trail as illustrated in the following figure:

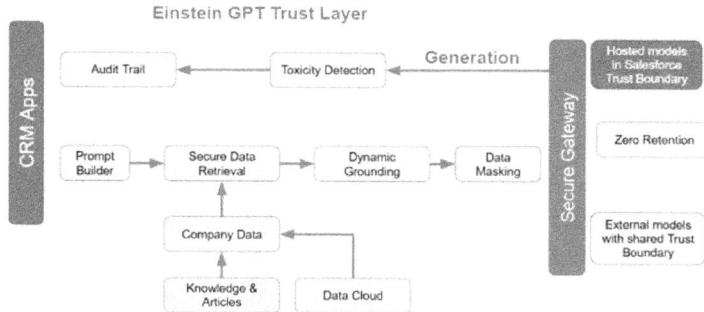

Figure 12.3: *Salesforce Trust Layer*

When you enter a question into ChatGPT, you could enter personal information such as your name, address, or names of friends or family. In the same way, when Salesforce integrates with an AI model, the data is sent, but companies have a duty to protect their data and the details of their customers. As such, the Einstein GPT Trust Layer illustrated above also has the ability to encrypt the data sent and leverage the zero retention capabilities to ensure the data is not stored in the AI model.

There is a difference between Salesforce Encryption at Rest and OpenAI's zero data retention policy, which lies in what data is stored, for how long, and for what purpose. Salesforce stores data securely, but for as long as it is needed in the database. The security model governs who can see what data. Whist OpenAI (or the AI platform selected) has a zero retention policy, which means it does not store or use the data in the LLM, and it is immediately discarded after processing the response.

In the illustration above, Salesforce has its own knowledge repository containing Knowledge and articles, which is outlined in *Chapter 10, Various Salesforce Features*. This can be integrated with Einstein to feed data into the response provided by Agentforce. This can be further enhanced using Data Cloud to provide proprietary company data to give an accurate response. At the time of writing, generating Knowledge articles from Einstein is still under rapid development with an inconsistent setup configuration. However, if you Google *Generating Knowledge articles with Einstein* it will give more up-to-date tutorials. AI uses the process of **grounding**, which refers to the process of connecting abstract AI representations of words or data to real-world meanings.

Salesforce Einstein 1

The key areas of Einstein 1 are:

- **Agentforce Copilot**: Perform a range of tasks, including providing recommendations based on Sales or Service. This can then be built into Einstein **Sales Development Rep**

(SDR) and **Sales Coach Agent** (**SCA**). Other tasks can be automated using your voice recognition.

- **Prompt Builder**: Groundings, actions, and plans go together with LLM to provide an intelligent response to users' or customers' questions.

- **GenAI in Salesforce applications**: Provides opportunity, lead scoring, and assists with time-consuming tasks such as email generation or even code writing.

- **Trust**: Since Salesforce has combined with OpenAI or other AI models, Salesforce data is used to generate the response. This needs encryption in transit and at rest so that confidential or sensitive data can be sent and not retained by the AI model.

- **Model Builder**: Combines future or existing business processes with recommendations for the best LLM tool to meet those requirements.

There is some overlap between some of these areas, but the above summarizes the Einstein 1 tools currently available.

At the time of writing, many AI tools are still under rapid development. As such, recommendations will vary wildly based on use case and recent innovations. Typically, Salesforce uses actions that can be predefined or custom. Some of the predefined features are:

- **Sales assistant**: The tool summarizes every step of the sales cycle in a side panel, from account research and meeting preparation to drafting contract clauses.

- **Sales emails**: The tool can automatically generate personalized emails for every customer interaction, using data from your CRM system.

- **Call summaries**: The tool automatically transcribes and summarizes calls and then sets follow-up actions based on the transcription.

Enabling Einstein and configuring

Trailhead has many resources for getting started with Einstein. If you search for Agentblazer, then you will find yourself with access to training materials and a pre-configured AI-enabled org at: **https://trailhead.salesforce.com/agentblazer**

Access to Einstein 1 Studio

To try out the new features of Einstein 1, you will need to register for a Salesforce playground called **Einstein 1 Studio**. This can be obtained directly from a few resources, such as:

https://trailhead.salesforce.com/promo/orgs/einsteinbuilder

There are a few other ways to get access to an Einstein playground.

A good place to start is to go to a Salesforce Trailhead and type in `Einstein 1` or `Copilot`. Next to the **Login** button at the bottom of a trail is the ability to register for an Einstein AI Playground org, as shown in the following figure:

Log In to Take This Quiz

Learn more about Einstein 1

See Einstein 1 in action

Start a free Einstein 1 trial today

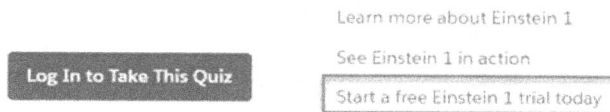

Figure 12.4: Gaining access to an AI-enabled Salesforce environment

Another way to get to the playground is to go to Trailhead and search for **Quick Start: Agent Actions** trail. Select this trail, and you will see a button with **Create Playground** as shown in the following figure. You will be emailed once the playground has been setup.

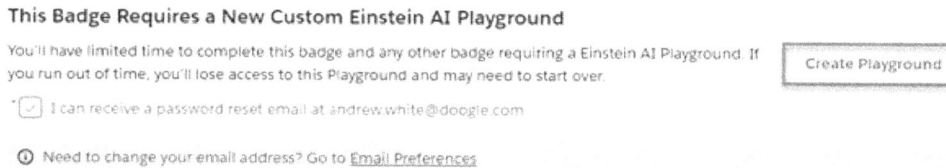

This Badge Requires a New Custom Einstein AI Playground

You'll have limited time to complete this badge and any other badge requiring a Einstein AI Playground. If you run out of time, you'll lose access to this Playground and may need to start over.

☑ I can receive a password reset email at andrew.white@doogle.com

ⓘ Need to change your email address? Go to Email Preferences

Create Playground

Figure 12.5: Another way to gain access to an AI-enabled Salesforce playground

A final way is via the partner learning camp found at **https://partnerlearningcamp.salesforce.com/**, which also has a variety of excellent tutorials to allow you to build out some of the more advanced features from Salesforce Einstein 1.

Note: **At the time of writing, the Salesforce playground will come with a few limitations, namely, the data in it is mock data, and that prompts are stand-alone, so they cannot be used with Salesforce Flow or Apex. As such, the AI features are there to be learned but not part of an end-to-end process.**

Enabling Einstein 1 in your Salesforce org

The setup menu is likely to change, so the instructions in the following are simply for guidance:

1. Ideally, you would enable Data Cloud in your Salesforce org, but in the playground configured previously, there are no Data Cloud licenses. To do this, go to **Setup | Permission Sets** and assign the Data Cloud Admin permission set to your user record.

2. Once in your org, go to **Setup |** select **Einstein Setup** and move the slider for **Turn on Einstein**, as shown in the following figure:

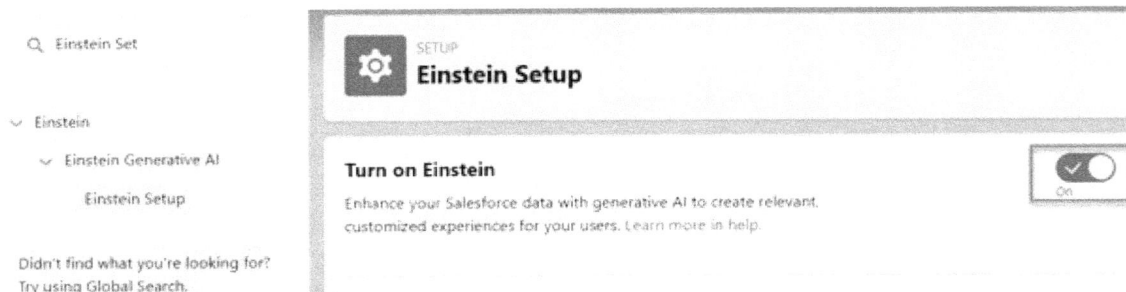

Figure 12.6: Enabling Einstein in a Salesforce environment

Einstein Prompt Builder

A prompt is just a question that you give to Einstein. This could be in the form of requesting a customer to attend an evening conference, which requires registration. This prompt can then be used in an email to provide personal content.

There are two additional steps required:

1. **Setup | Einstein for Sales**, then the option **Turn on Sales Emails** as shown in the following:

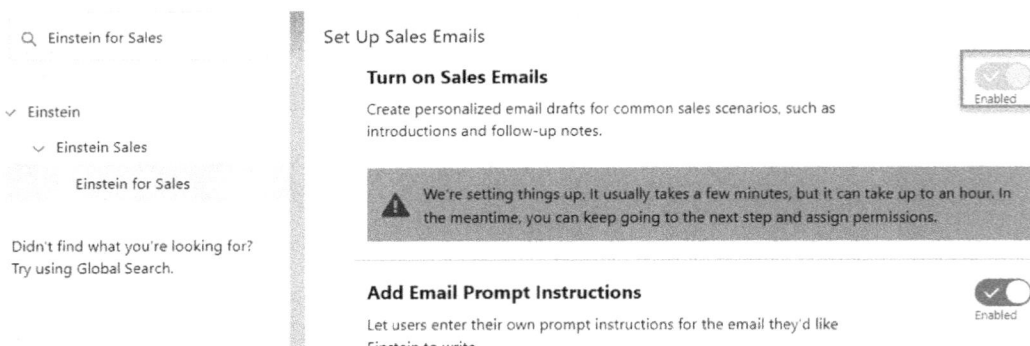

Figure 12.7: Providing access to sales emails

2. The final step is to add the following two permission sets to your user record, which are:

   a. **Prompt Template Manager**

   b. **Prompt Template User**

Note: **Users of the solution will need the Prompt Builder User permission set assigned to them.**

These are added by going to your user record and selecting the permission set link and adding them as shown in the following:

Permission Set Assignments   Edit Assignments

Action	Permission Set Name
Del	Work Summaries User
Del	Access Agentforce Default Agent
Del	Agentforce Default Admin
Del	Prompt Template User
Del	Prompt Template Manager

Figure 12.8: Allocating the necessary permission sets

Building a prompt template

There are currently 12 kinds of prompt templates available as described at: **https://help.salesforce.com/s/articleView?id=ai.prompt_builder_standard_template_types.htm&type=5**, but the list has more than doubled over the past year, so there will undoubtedly be more to come.

Some of the more useful prompt templates to be aware of are:

- **Case summary**: Summary of a case record with issue and resolution.

- **Field generation**: Users press a button to automatically allow Einstein to populate a field.

- **Flex templates**: Gather data from multiple objects.

- **Knowledge answers**: Allow prompts to have information taken from knowledge articles.

- **Record summary**: Summarize the contents of a record in one single field.

- **Work summary**: Give details on work that has been done by an agent, typically to assist with the after-call work.

As an example, if you have been asked to build a field generation prompt, you would do the following:

- Create a new field on the object to store the results from the field generation prompt. For example, create a new Text Area (Long) field called **Executive Summary** on the **Account** object, as shown in the following:

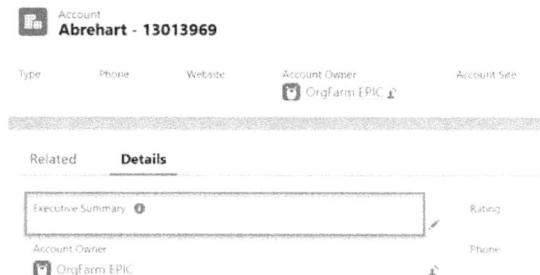

Account
Abrehart - 13013969

Type   Phone   Website   Account Owner   Account Site
                                      OrgFarm EPIC

Related   **Details**

Executive Summary   Rating

Account Owner   Phone
OrgFarm EPIC

Figure 12.9: Adding a field to capture the Einstein AI results

Then, go to **Setup | Prompt Builder** and press the **New Prompt Template** button as shown in the following figure. Select **Field Generation** for the prompt template type and add the newly created **Executive Summary** field for the **Account** object.

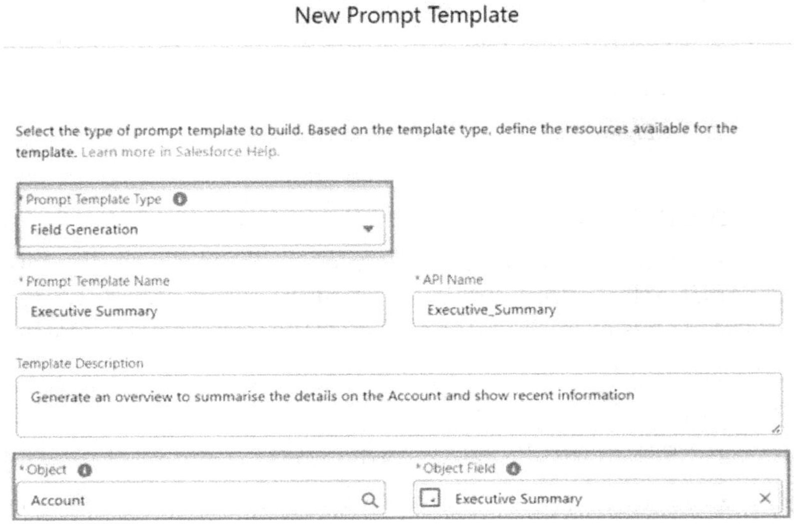

Figure 12.10: Creating a prompt template

- Once saved, add text to the Prompt Builder template as shown in the following figure. The field picker in the resources area allows you to decide what fields you wish to include in the template.

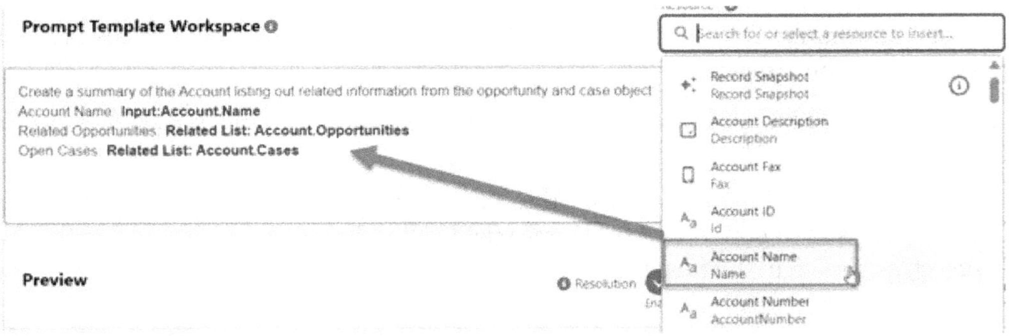

Figure 12.11: Adding variables to the prompt

Note: It is possible to call Salesforce Flow, Apex, and more from the options available.

- Finally, select an account to test the template on under the **Related Record** option. Note the number of AI models that are available on the right-hand side menu. Choose **OpenAI GPT 4**, although it is worth familiarizing yourself with the other models available. Refer to the following figure:

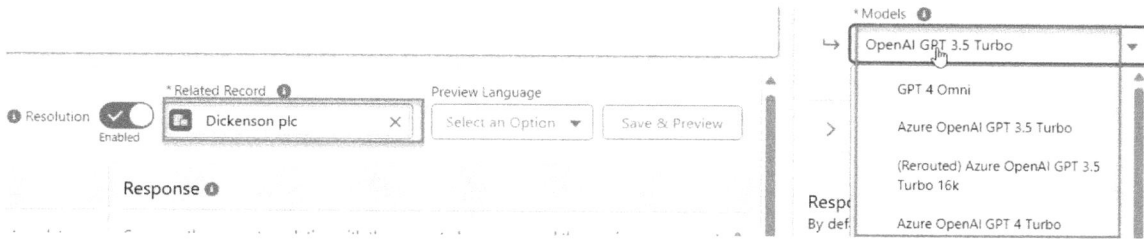

Figure 12.12: Checking the prompt and selecting the AI model to use

- Finally, press the **Preview** button to get a response matching the description based on the account selected, as shown in the following figure. Press the **Activate** button at the top of the page.

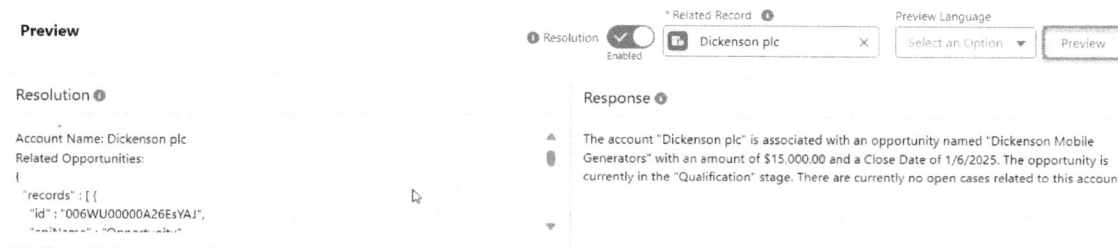

Figure 12.13: Viewing the send resolution message and reading the response

- To add the prompt to the page layout, first convert the page to a Dynamic Form. This was covered in *Chapter 3, Customizing User Interface,* but is described briefly in the following section.

- To do this, go to an account record and click **Edit Page** from the **Setup** menu. Press the **Details** tab and press **Upgrade Now** to convert the page into a Dynamic Form.

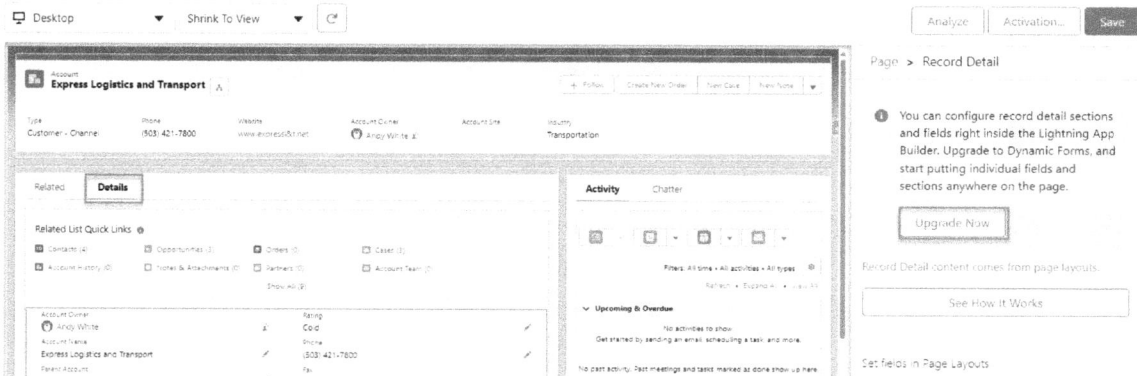

Figure 12.14: Adding the Einstein result to the page layout

- Finally, select the **Executive Summary** field on the page layout and select the **Executive Summary** in the **Prompt Template** field, as shown in the following figure, and press **Save** and **Activate**.

Related   **Details**

∨ Account Information

Executive Summary	⌂ + 🗑	Rating	
Executive Summary	⌄	Rating	✎
Account Owner		Phone	
Account Owner	✎	Phone	• ✎
Account Name		Fax	
Account Name	✎	Fax	✎

UI Behavior   ⓘ
◉ None
◯ Read-Only
◯ Required

✦ Einstein Generative AI
Prompt Template

| Executive Summary | ✕ |

Edit Template

Figure 12.15: Connecting the field to the prompt template

- Revisit the account record, and you will see a pen icon next to the field with sparkles next to it, as shown in the following figure.

  Note: If you do not see the pen icon, go back to the page layout, check that the prompt template is associated with the page, and re-activate the page layout. It can occasionally take a short while for the changes to take effect.

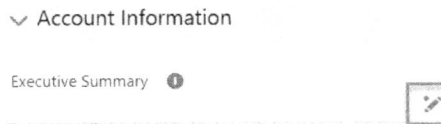

∨ Account Information

Executive Summary   ⓘ

🖉

Figure 12.16: Check that the Einstein button is active on the page layout

- The sparkle pen indicates that it is an Einstein-generated field. Press the icon, and Salesforce opens the Einstein interface with a **Use** button. Press this to generate the response required for the account record **Executive Summary** field, as shown in the following figure:

∨ Account Information

Executive Summary   ⓘ
Account Summary:
Account Name: Dickenson plc   🖉

Related Opportunities:
1. Opportunity ID: 006WU00000A26EsYAJ
Name: Dickenson Mobile Generators
Amount: $15,000.00
Close Date: 1/6/2025
Stage: Qualification

Open Cases: None at this time.

Figure 12.17: Viewing the results in the page layout

Einstein Prediction Builder

Einstein Prediction Builder allows you to enter simple phrases that can return either a yes or no option or a number. For example, you may wish to have the prediction of an opportunity being Closed Won based on similar opportunities. Alternatively, you may wish to find the likely value of an opportunity based on similar opportunities.

To do this, go to **Setup | Einstein Prediction Builder** as shown in the following figure:

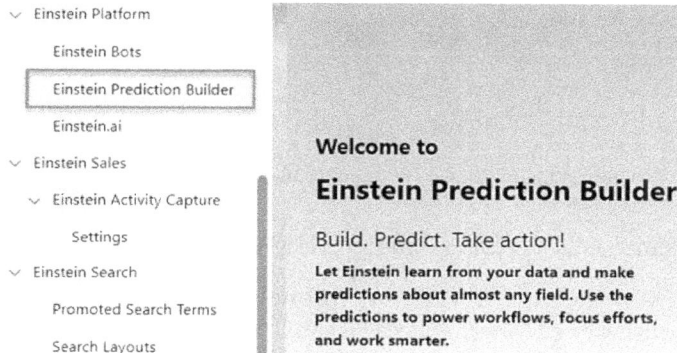

Figure 12.18: Enabling the Einstein Prediction Builder

Review the terms in the dialogue box and press the **Try Einstein** button. It may take a few minutes to be enabled.

Once enabled, press the **New Prediction** button and enter a description and the type of prediction you want to build, as shown in the figure:

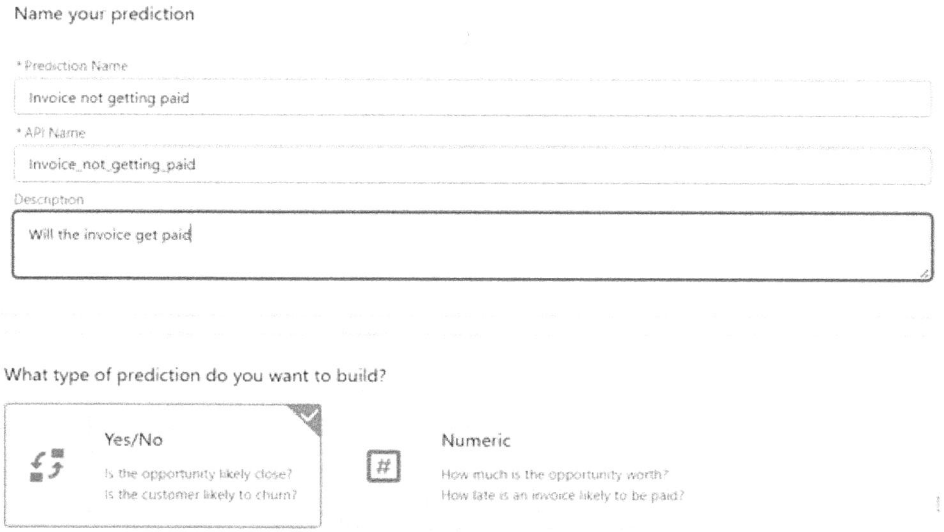

Figure 12.19: Configuring a prediction with a Yes/No outcome

In the next step, choose the object; for example, select the **Inovice__c** object. When asked which invoice records should Einstein consider, choose **All Invoices**. This option is useful if you wish to filter for certain types of records.

For the example of a **Yes** outcome, enter the values shown in the following figure:

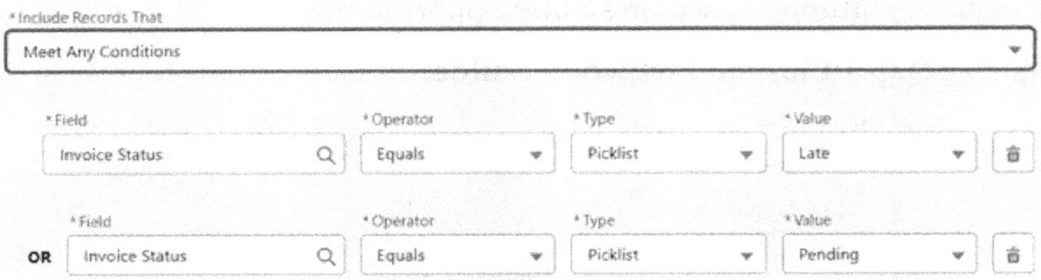

Figure 12.20: Configuring conditions to build the prediction

Similarly, add the example of a **No** outcome with **Invoice Status** equals **On Time**.

Add any fields you would consider that may influence the invoice being paid. Add the field name where the result will be stored, such as `Einstein Predicts Closed Won`.

Finally, press the **Build** button to activate the prediction. Note that in various playgrounds, there is insufficient data. If using the Einstein playground and basing the prediction on the invoice object, then the records to predict setting needs to be unchecked to base a sample on the remaining records, as shown in the following figure:

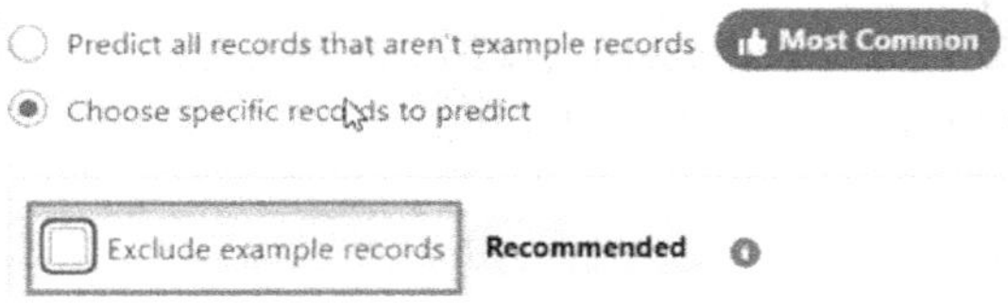

Figure 12.21: Excluding example records

Depending on the size of the data, it can take up to 24 hours to build the prediction. You will see the screen, as shown in the following figure:

Einstein is building your prediction...

It can take anywhere from half an hour to 24 hours to build your prediction depending on your data and settings. The notification bell tells you when building has finished.

Go to the list view in Setup to review your scorecard and prediction quality.

Go to Setup

Figure 12.22: Correctly configured Einstein Predictions

Once it has run, add the **Einstein Predictions** to your page layout by pressing **Setup** | **Edit Page,** as shown in the following figure:

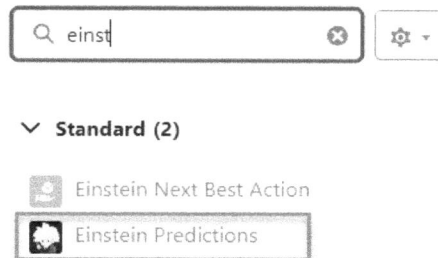

Q einst

⌄ **Standard (2)**

Einstein Next Best Action

Einstein Predictions

Figure 12.23: Adding Einstein Predictions to the page layout

You can find Einstein Lead Scores in Salesforce on the lead detail page or in the Einstein Score component in list views.

Einstein 1 Copilot for Service Cloud

Likewise, for Service Cloud, Einstein AI has some out-of-the-box features for assisting agents with their work, such as:

- **Service replies**: The tool can automatically generate personalized responses based on real-time data sources, such as your CRM data and other sources.

- **Knowledge articles**: The tool can automatically generate and update articles based on the latest real-time data from support interactions.

- **Work summaries**: Create concise and informative summaries of service cases and customer engagements based on the details of the case and the customer's history.

- **Mobile work briefings**: The tool summarizes critical information about each appointment before field service teams arrive, helping them to work more efficiently.

- **Call summaries**: The tool automatically transcribes and summarizes calls and then sets follow-up actions based on the transcription. Keywords and sentiments can be stored as part of the summary.

Assessing your current Salesforce org for Einstein

If you are using an existing Salesforce org, then before you can use Einstein 1 with Salesforce, you need to ensure the company's data is protected. Admittedly, Salesforce has already added multiple security layers, but when ChatGPT or other third-party vendors are using the data, then the data is encrypted by Salesforce Trust, so the data is not accessed unintentionally, and the results can be returned to Salesforce securely without leaving any data in ChatGPT or the chosen model.

To enable Salesforce Trust, you should view the Trailhead on the subject, but they are outlined below. Google *Salesforce Trust and meet the Einstein Trust Layer*.

Start by doing the assessment in your Developer Edition org for Sales or Service Cloud, as shown in the following figure:

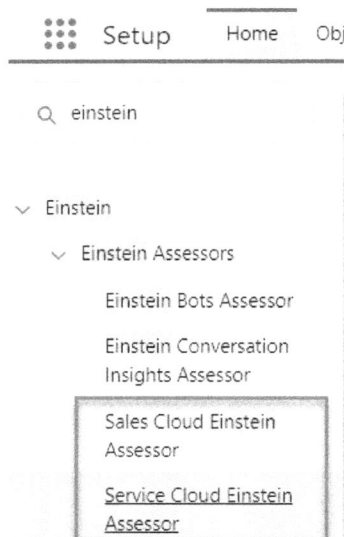

Figure 12.24: Assessing if your Salesforce org is compatible with Einstein

Complete the assessment for Bots, Sales, and Service Cloud. An example is shown in the following figure:

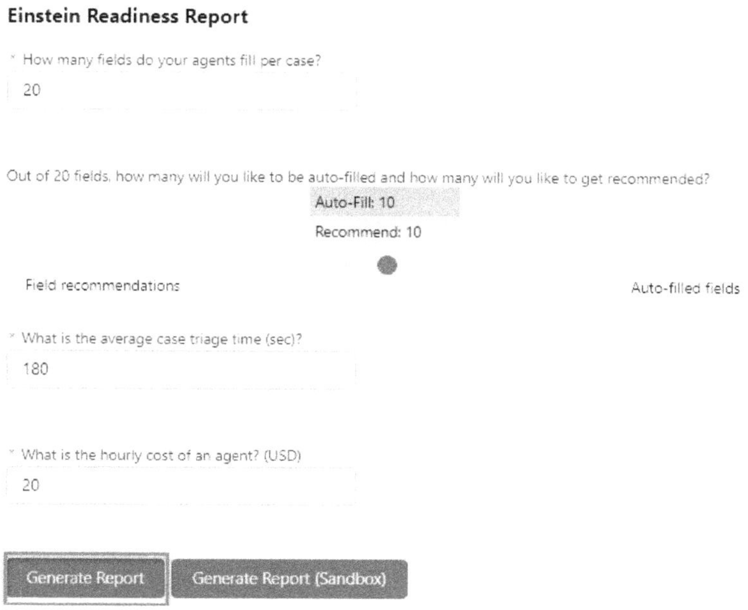

Einstein Readiness Report

˅ How many fields do your agents fill per case?

20

Out of 20 fields, how many will you like to be auto-filled and how many will you like to get recommended?

Auto-Fill: 10

Recommend: 10

Field recommendations   Auto-filled fields

˅ What is the average case triage time (sec)?

180

˅ What is the hourly cost of an agent? (USD)

20

Generate Report | Generate Report (Sandbox)

Figure 12.25: Generating an Einstein Assessment report

This will generate a report, which is sent to your email inbox with a link to the results:

Hooray! Your personalized Sales Cloud Einstein Readiness and ROI Estimation Report is available

The report is available from the Files tab in Salesforce.

Get ready for artificial intelligence (AI) for sales! With Sales Cloud Einstein, your team's sales productivity is supercharged at every step of the sales process with key predictions, intelligent recommendations, and timely automation.

Check out the new ROI estimations for selected functionalities.

Figure 12.26: Final steps of having Einstein enabled in your existing Salesforce org

Other Salesforce AI capabilities

The examples in this chapter are aimed at basic features in Sales and Service Cloud. The following is a list of other areas where Einstein can be used to build AI capabilities in various Salesforce clouds. The following table contains a list of various Salesforce clouds and the Einstein AI capabilities available for each cloud. If you Google each capability, you will find a whole range of products that are available to use:

Cloud	Einstein AI capabilities
Sales	Close plan, find similar opportunities, meeting follow-up email, forecast guidance, call explorer, sales emails, Einstein Search, search answers, call summaries, contact suggestions, Einstein Activity Capture, sales emails, Einstein for Formulas
Service	Knowledge creation, service replies, GenAI surveys, knowledge creation, work summaries, Einstein Search, search answers, Einstein conversation mining, service replies, work summaries, Einstein for Formulas
Marketing Cloud	Co-create with Einstein, Einstein's assistant
Data Cloud	Einstein segments
Field Service	Pre-work brief
Salesforce Industries (SFI)	Contracts AI, tools available in Sales and Service Cloud
Commerce	Concierge, Einstein return insights, page meta tags, smart promotions, predictive sorting, product recommendations, commerce insights SP, AI tools from Sales and Service Cloud
Developers	Various modules are covered in the following link: **https://www.salesforce.com/uk/artificial-intelligence/developers/**

Table 12.1: A list of Einstein capabilities applicable to different Salesforce clouds

Conclusion

Enabling Einstein in your Salesforce org allows many repetitive tasks to be automated and gives insightful information to decision makers.

This chapter covers some of the basics and hopefully gives a start to configuring Salesforce with AI. Einstein has addressed many of the common issues with dealing with customers and configuration.

However, this area of technology is still rapidly developing to the extent that configuring Salesforce will undoubtedly change each month. As a result, this chapter is to convey core concepts rather than a how-to guide.

In this chapter, the Salesforce AI certifications were recommended as they are currently free. In the next chapter, there will be a more comprehensive guide to taking Salesforce certifications and a guide to succeeding in becoming a well-certified Salesforce professional.

Multiple choice questions

1. **Salesforce has its own in-built AI capabilities called:**
   a. Columbus
   b. Atlas
   c. Euston
   d. Newton

2. **When Salesforce sends data to an external AI provider, what options are available? (choose 2)**
   a. Encryption method
   b. JSON format of the reply message
   c. The model to use
   d. Sample data

3. **Einstein Prediction Builder can give a response in various ways. What two options are available?**
   a. Numeric
   b. Text field
   c. Yes/No field
   d. An AI response

4. **The strongest Salesforce principle for using Einstein is:**
   a. Data quality
   b. Integration models
   c. Configuration settings
   d. Integrity

5. **To connect a prompt to a page layout, you need to:**
   a. Set the page to Dynamic Form
   b. Connect the prompt template to the field
   c. Activate the page in the page layout builder
   d. Set the page to the Einstein layout

6. **If you ask Einstein what its favorite color is, and it responds blue, this is an example of what?**
   a. Informative AI
   b. Generative AI
   c. Predictive AI
   d. Collaborative AI

7. **The two permission sets required to use Prompt Builder are:**
   a. Prompt Template Administrator
   b. Prompt Template User
   c. Prompt Template Manager
   d. Prompt Template Builder

8. **Einstein connects company data with LLMs using the process of:**
   a. Prompt creation
   b. Grounding with data retrieval
   c. Augmentation
   d. Compliance

9. **The Salesforce Trust layer encrypts sensitive data so it is not stored by the AI model.**
   a. True
   b. False

10. **In Agentforce, call summaries do which of the following:**
    a. Give information such as call duration, priority, and weighting time
    b. Provide a score for providing feedback on the call
    c. Capture key points, next steps, and customer feedback for agents and supervisors
    d. Show key statistics such as customer satisfaction and Next Best Action

Answers

1	**b**
2	**c, d**
3	**a, c**
4	**d**
5	**b**
6	**c**
7	**b, c**
8	**b**
9	**a**
10	**c**

CHAPTER 13
Preparing for Salesforce Certifications

Introduction

Salesforce certifications are your way to validate your knowledge and experience with Salesforce. They are recognized by businesses to distinguish themselves as someone committed to them and getting the most out of Salesforce.

Some certifications are generic, whilst others are specific, such as **Salesforce Industries** (**SFI**) or Commerce Cloud.

This chapter gives you insight into gaining the certifications that are right for you and your career.

Structure

In this chapter, we will cover the following topics:

- Overview of Salesforce certifications
- Study tips and resources
- Maintaining your certification

Objectives

By the end of the chapter, you will familiarize yourself with what Salesforce certifications are and how to navigate your way to certifications relevant to you and your chosen career path. You will also be able to register for the certifications and learn how to maintain them.

There is also relevant advice on helping you to make the right career choices and interview tips.

Overview of Salesforce certifications

Salesforce allows you to be certified in many areas. Typically, you will start off as a Salesforce Administrator. This is possibly the most useful and relevant certification, and a great way to get started. Employers will often require that you be certified in this as a foundation level. From here, you can choose your career path. You may wish to go down the developer route, but it is worth being confident in configuration, as coding a solution should be avoided unless something cannot be done using configuration.

Certification paths and requirements

Salesforce certifications start with various foundation certifications you can get with one or two years of experience. However, there are some certifications you can only get if you have got a foundation certification. Salesforce illustrates this concept of a certification pyramid to reflect your level of expertise, as shown in the following figure:

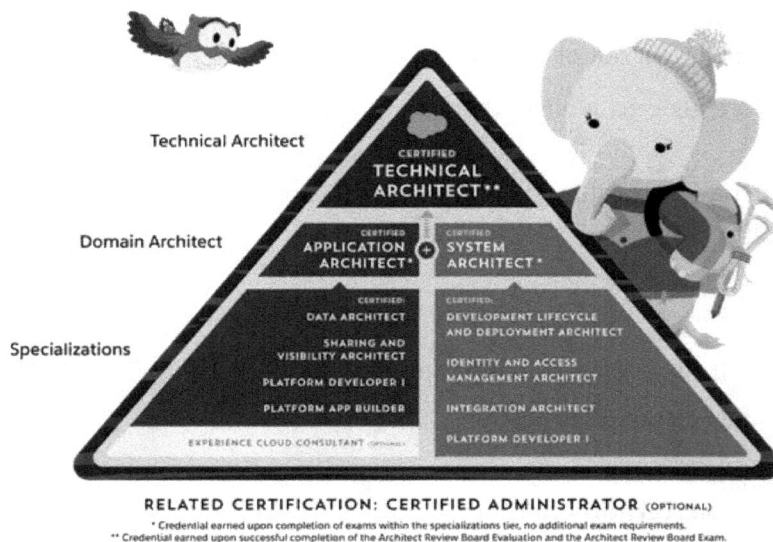

Figure 13.1: Salesforce certification pyramid

In the pyramid illustration, you work your way up via two routes:

- The left-hand side is more about configuration, but not to be taken lightly. Each level builds upon the one beneath it. The aim is to become an Application Architect.

- The right-hand side is more about being a developer, customizations, and integrations. Again, each level requires the certification beneath it. The aim is to become a System Architect.

In both cases, there are options for how you wish to steer your career path. For example, to be a domain architect, such as an Application Architect, you would first need to do the Sharing and Visibility Architect exam, but in order to do this, you should at least have either the Salesforce Administrator certification.

At the top of the pyramid is the **Certified Technical Architect (CTA)** certification. This is a very prestigious certification requiring deep Salesforce and industry knowledge, and an exam in front of the Salesforce Architect review board. It is worth doing the free practice exam readily available online to see the level of knowledge required.

Having said that, it may be worth avoiding being a CTA, since it could also limit you to being a Salesforce techie, whilst at a similar level in many companies, a director, executive, or similar can offer a wider range of opportunities and can be agnostic to technical solutions.

There are many other Salesforce certifications, some being relatively easy, others requiring months or years of experience and study. In most cases, there is a study guide with the necessary links and resources to guide you through.

Many exam certifications require maintenance exams to keep you up-to-date. Reminders should be emailed to you, but a more reliable way is to periodically check your certification status as outlined in the section *Maintaining your certification*.

Study tips and resources

Salesforce offers study guides for the exams, which are free to download. In the study guide, you will get links to the various resources Salesforce offers, which are specific to the exam. Trailhead (**https://trailhead.salesforce.com/**) provides a lot of training, including examples, study guides, and course material. Other useful training material can be found in the following:

- *Udemy* with various Salesforce courses aimed at administrators, platform developers, and architects.

- *Focus On Force* is dedicated to Salesforce learning with great course material.

- *PluralSight* with various Salesforce courses aims more towards developers and integration architects.

These resources are worth paying for as they are kept up-to-date and have the necessary information and practice exams.

There are numerous communities and forums that also contain interactive training materials. Examples of these are *Salesforce Ben, LinkedIn Learning,* and *Reddit.*

Notice that the exam questions are typically from a much larger pool of questions, so you cannot guarantee which questions you will be asked. As a result, it is wise to do quite a few mock papers and always exceed the pass mark. This will ensure you have a solid understanding and a good chance of passing.

If you are lucky enough to work for a Salesforce partner (i.e., a company that has an established relationship with Salesforce), then you should also get access to **https://partners.salesforce. com/pdx/s/**, which will give additional resources. However, you will not be at a disadvantage if you do not have access, as the training material should give you everything you need. However, having access to Salesforce partners does give you a community to ask questions and share knowledge and experience if you wish.

Registering and taking the exam

Salesforce has recently launched its new certification experience within Trailhead Academy, which can be found at **https://trailheadacademy.salesforce.com/**. This now serves as a central hub offering personalized dashboards, recommendations, preparation resources, and registration.

Exams are done either at a specific test center, online at home, or in the office. Many Salesforce exams are delivered using an independent company called *Pearson VUE*, which has partnered with Salesforce to provide the secure, proctored exam and certification services.

Once you get access to Salesforce Academy, go to **My Account | Profile**, and you will see the following screen:

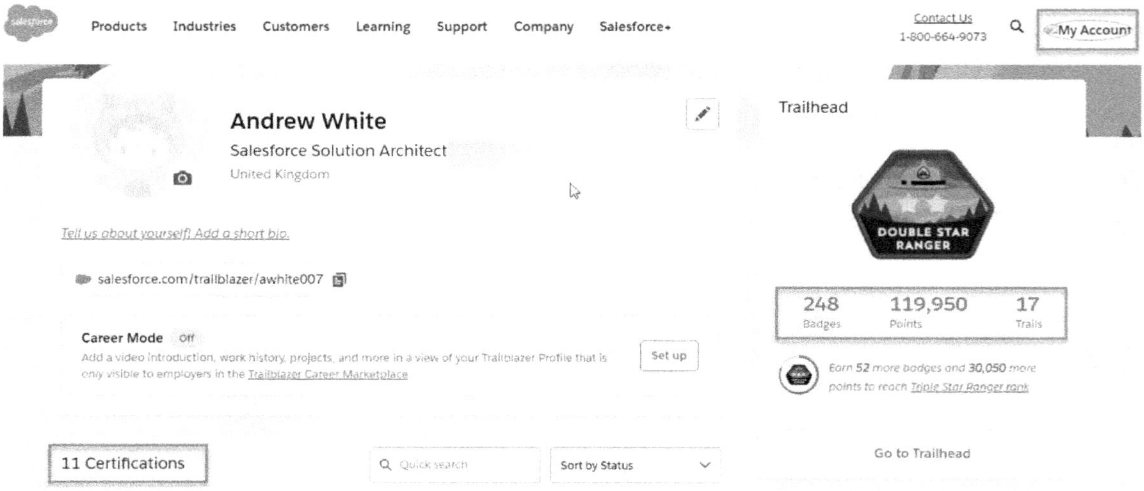

Figure 13.2: Trailhead Academy

In the above figure, you will be able to see a list of your certifications, how many badges you have achieved using Trailhead, as well as basic information about yourself.

First, ensure your details are entered correctly and make sure the email address associated with the account is an email address you own and not a work-related email. This is to ensure you keep your certifications should you change employers. This also helps to link various trails since you may be working in different environments, and it is important that you get the necessary credit for completing a trail. There are also other features of the Salesforce Academy that allow potential employers to see your progress and achievements.

Another important field to complete is the company field. This is found in your user profile section. This will ensure that your certifications contribute to their status as a Salesforce partner. Many companies rely on this to gain the necessary status with Salesforce, which can be Base, Ridge, Crest, and Summit, where Summit is the highest level of achievement for a company.

Registering for a Salesforce exam

To register for an exam, go to the Trailhead Academy and select **Learning | Learning on Trailhead | Salesforce Certification** as illustrated in *Figure 13.3*:

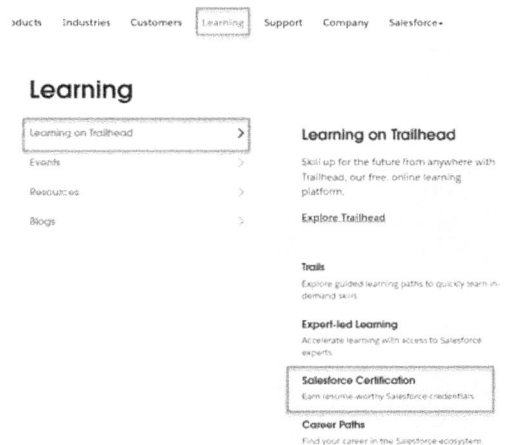

Figure 13.3: Accessing Salesforce Certification

Find the certification you are interested in, which will take you to a page with the study guide, the necessary trails to complete, as well as the option to register for the exam, as shown in the following figure:

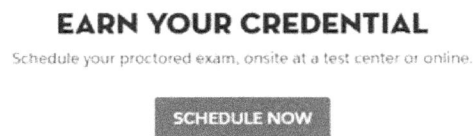

Figure 13.4: Registering for an exam

Note: **Many companies will also pay for you to do the certifications, so check with your employer if this is possible. The prices for each certification are given when you register for an exam.**

Onsite proctored

If you choose to take the exam using the onsite proctored option, then you will attend an exam center at a specific location. You will need to take two forms of ID and the exam code sent via email as proof that you are registered for the exam.

It is important you take your exam reference code with you, as the people in the exam center will need to look you up to setup the exam, since they will also be overseeing many other people doing exams for various subjects such as AWS, Google, and more.

Onsite proctored exams will typically be in a private room or a booth without any outside disturbance. You will have several cameras in the exam area. Your exam proctor is a person online sharing access to the laptop who will first ask you a few basic questions and ensure that you do not have any devices or potentially compromising equipment. They will also be available during the exam. You are usually provided a piece of paper and a biro.

Online proctored

If you choose to take the exam at home or in an office, you are required to empty the room and show that no other applications are running on your laptop. Typically, you will need to provide some ID and have the proctor confirm that you have met these requirements. It is not unusual to have to do a floor walk around the room and show that there is nothing under your desk or inside any drawers. They will also be able to monitor your activities during the exam. You are not allowed to talk during the exam.

Exam format and expectations

The exams have a typical format of a series of questions with multiple choice answers. You can mark questions to review later and return to them if you have time. The time remaining is displayed on the screen. It is up to you to remember how long the exam takes and monitor your progress.

If you fail the exam and need to retake it, then the questions will change for your next attempt. For this reason, many online cheat sheets should be ignored, and it is better for you and the people you work with if you genuinely learn the subject you have chosen to get the certification for.

It is evident when someone has a certification but no real understanding of what they are doing in Salesforce, so it is strongly advised to pass the exam by having a genuine understanding of the subject. Suppose you meet someone who has more than 20 certifications, but a very limited practical understanding of Salesforce. This is often because they have worked at a company with an internal repository of exam questions and answers. This does the company a disservice since they are putting people on projects who will end up costing the company and the client many times more than the cost of genuinely sitting the exams.

Showing off your new certification

When you pass the exam, make sure you enter the company you work for in your Salesforce Academy profile, as it contributes to your company's success. This is done in the **Company** field on your profile. Many companies can see how many certifications their employees have, which contributes to their overall status as a Salesforce partner. Check that the name you enter for the company is correct, as some companies may have different names depending on your location.

Connect your certifications with LinkedIn

Also, place your certification on LinkedIn. This will raise your profile and attract better employment opportunities.

There are two methods, so either do the following method or check the next section, which will perform the procedure automatically.

The exact method seems to depend on how your LinkedIn account is setup. The recommended approach is:

1. Go to your LinkedIn profile.

2. Scroll down to the **Licenses & certifications** section.

3. Press the + button.

4. Add as many details regarding the certification as possible.

5. Press **Save**.

An example of certifications showing on LinkedIn is shown in the following figure:

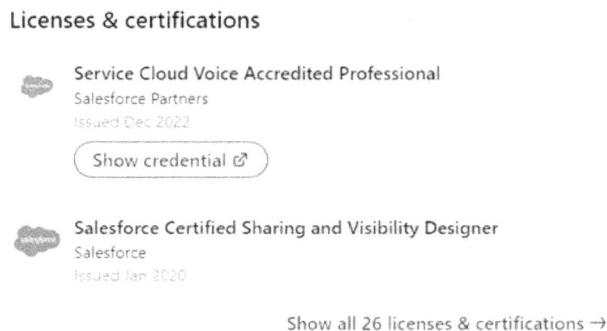

Licenses & certifications

Service Cloud Voice Accredited Professional
Salesforce Partners
Issued Dec 2022

(Show credential ⌐)

Salesforce Certified Sharing and Visibility Designer
Salesforce
Issued Jan 2020

Show all 26 licenses & certifications →

Figure 13.5: Showing your certifications on LinkedIn

Maintaining your certification

You can see an overview of your collected Salesforce certifications and those of others by going to: **https://trailhead.salesforce.com/en/credentials/verification/** (or Google: Salesforce certification status).

This will bring up the screen in the following:

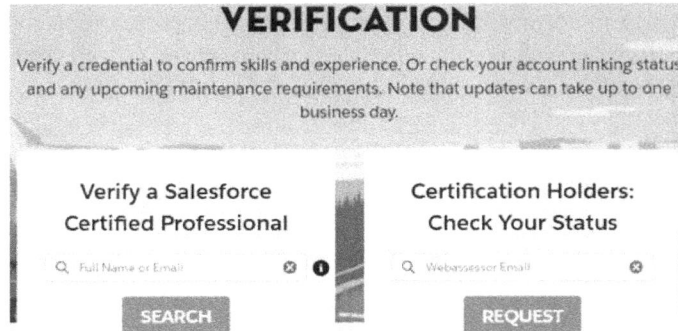

Figure 13.6: Checking your certifications or other Salesforce professionals

You can either check on someone's certification or check your status, as shown in the following figure:

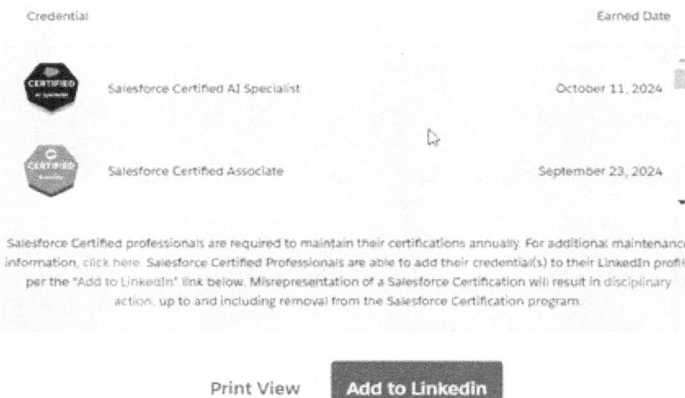

Figure 13.7: Viewing your certifications

As mentioned in the previous section, this is also a good way to add your certifications to LinkedIn. Pressing the **Add to LinkedIn** button requires you to enter your LinkedIn profile ID and verify using the communication preferences you have stored in your LinkedIn account.

Job interview tips

The golden rule for all job interviews is to be honest. Prepare, learn who's on the interview via LinkedIn, and visit the company's website. However, what every company is looking for is simply your experience, success stories, and what you can bring to them that makes you stand out. Be aware that the job description typically emphasizes particular technical skills, such as SFI, CPQ, or softer skills, such as customer-facing or being able to engage with the sales team.

If you are new to Salesforce, then be honest but say that you realize the benefits Salesforce brings, and you have succeeded in other technologies that are transferable. After all, it is a lot easier to learn a technology than to change an attitude. If you have limited experience, then talk about what you would like to achieve. If you have a bad experience, then that can also be a benefit, as it shows lessons learned.

Your CV should be short (approximately two pages), but highlight your success and responsibilities, and not just what you did. After all, doing something does not show how you added to the role, show initiatives you took, how you built the team, established rapport, and why the project was a success because of what you did.

Career path

Having chosen to further yourself using your Salesforce certifications, there are many routes to a career. You can either work for a single company, which gives some stability, or work for a consultancy, often referred to as a **system integrator** (**SI**), which refers to a company that specializes in bringing together different technologies from various vendors. These range from small or boutique companies to global corporations. They offer a huge variety of end companies to work for, and you will tend to learn increasingly quickly. There are advantages and disadvantages to both. This will give you a vast range of experience, typically working on two to three large projects a year, as well as the opportunity to engage with several customers throughout the year.

There is further advice given in the final bonus chapter, which gives some experience and the wisdom of hindsight on this subject.

Conclusion

This chapter should show you how to start your journey as a Salesforce professional. The emphasis is not only on getting certified but also on selecting the journey you wish to take as a Salesforce professional. There are always options to change based on experience and industry trends.

This chapter also gives advice on gaining the certifications, but also making sure you get the recognition from social platforms and your employer.

Certifications are always best done by not only learning the course material but also building the configuration in a Salesforce org. This way, you can confidently give valuable advice to colleagues but also get the satisfaction of doing your job well.

In the next chapter, we will look at the broader Salesforce ecosystem to give insight into the various products that are offered. The aim is to give you some choice in where you steer your career path.

Multiple choice questions

1. **Salesforce certifications are in the following format:**
   a. Online proctored with questions specifically for working online
   b. Onsite proctored with a pen and paper to answer the questions
   c. Onsite proctored, where you attend with ID and proof of registration
   d. Online proctored with an onsite proctor with you

2. **Salesforce offers many exams which could be taken in the following order:**
   a. Platform App Builder, Application Architect, CTA
   b. Sharing and Visibility Architect, System Architect, CTA
   c. Integration Architect, Application Architect, CTA
   d. Platform Developer 1, Integration Architect, Application Architect

3. **When you pass a Salesforce certification you should: (chose 2 answers)**
   a. Post it on all your social media accounts
   b. Link your Trailhead Academy account with LinkedIn
   c. Ensure the 'Company' field is filled in correctly on your Trailhead Academy profile
   d. Reclaim the certification expense

4. **The best way to study for a Salesforce exam is: (chose 2 answers)**
   a. Review the current Salesforce release notes
   b. Get as many Salesforce dump exams as possible
   c. Do the recommended training material
   d. Practice the training material in a separate Salesforce org

5. **Once you have successfully completed a Salesforce certification, you have it for the rest of your career.**
   a. True
   b. False

Answers

1	**c**
2	**a**
3	**b, c**
4	**c, d**
5	**b**

CHAPTER 14
Broader Salesforce Ecosystem

Introduction

The following sections are ordered by the most popular separate clouds that Salesforce offers. Many of them are built on the Salesforce Lightning Platform and often referred to as **native**. Others were bought by Salesforce through a company acquisition, so they rely on a connector to plug them into the Salesforce ecosystem. For example, Marketing Cloud was previously known as **ExactTarget** before Salesforce acquired it, and it can have various studios that can be added to it. It is a separate platform and not built natively in Salesforce, but rather integrates with Sales and Service Cloud using the Marketing Cloud Connect. Sales and Service Cloud can have **Revenue Lifecycle Management** (**RLM**) and **Service Cloud Voice** (**SVC**) added to it. Some products span across various Salesforce products, such as Data Cloud or Tableau, and so are given their own section accordingly.

This chapter does not cover every Salesforce product. Each one is potentially a book in its own right, but this chapter does cover the Salesforce products most frequently used and emphasizes products that are compatible with each other to provide a more comprehensive and sophisticated solution.

For example, companies that have mobile field engineers would benefit from **Field Service Lightning** (**FSL**) in Service Cloud. This allows site visits to customers' locations and provides an efficient way of planning the route. This could also be combined with other Salesforce products depending on the business requirements.

Structure

This chapter covers the following topics:

- Overview of the Salesforce ecosystem
- Salesforce Marketing Cloud
- Marketing Cloud Account Engagement
- Service Cloud Voice
- Revenue Cloud and RLM
- Salesforce Industries
- Commerce Cloud and Revenue Cloud
- Revenue Lifecycle Management
- Configure, price, quote
- Heroku
- Customer data platform and Data Cloud
- MuleSoft
- Field Service Lightning

Objectives

The objective of this chapter is to understand what the various Salesforce products do and how they work together. Each product is designed to be compatible, and companies can choose how they wish to build out a solution. This chapter is written to give you a reasonable understanding of what is required to set each product up and a description of the features provided. In addition to understanding what each product does, it is also important to understand the level of effort required when adding a product to your Salesforce ecosystem. Some products are comparatively easy to setup, such as **Marketing Cloud Account Engagement (MCAE)**, whilst others can take months or years to master, such as **Salesforce Industries (SFIs)** or RLM.

However, by the end of this chapter, you will have enough information to gain a basic working knowledge with the aim of empowering you should you wish to take your knowledge further.

Overview of the Salesforce ecosystem

Salesforce offers a suite of products, and Sales and Service Cloud are just two of them. The others are designed to work with Sales and Service Cloud but provide additional functionality to the business. This chapter is a very brief overview of what they are, what they do, and how they work.

For a full list of Salesforce products, go to: **https://www.salesforce.com/uk/products/**, which should show you the most popular Salesforce products as shown in the following figure:

Figure 14.1: Salesforce products, including Sales and Service Cloud, amongst others

It should be noted that Salesforce changes the names of its products more frequently than most people would like. The assumption is that the new name encompasses a new suite of features or technology. Perhaps the only two products that have not had a rebranding exercise done to them are Sales Cloud and Service Cloud.

Each of the products would be a book, and experts will undoubtedly challenge this simplistic view on them, but it is worth having an awareness of what they do and how they fit together in the broader ecosystem of Salesforce.

The list of products shown above does not include additional features for each product. For example, to the Sales and Service Cloud, you can also include:

- Salesforce Maps

- Salesforce FSL

- Service Cloud Voice

- SFI

- Certinia and many more

There is a good article on the products available at Salesforce Ben, found at: **https://www. salesforceben.com/salesforce-products/**

Note: **If you are working in a Salesforce Sandbox environment that has already purchased licenses for new Salesforce products, then you can copy the licenses into the sandbox. This is done by going: Setup | Company Information | Match Production Licenses. This will ensure that the features in the live production environment match any work that you are about to do.**

Getting access to Salesforce products

Many of the products can be used for trying out. The trial orgs or playgrounds are available at: **https://developer.salesforce.com/free-trials#browse**

Trailhead (**https://trailhead.salesforce.com/today**) offers many resources, which are available in the **Learn** tab or as shown in *Figure 14.2*. Many of the tutorials in Trailhead will require you to use an org specifically pre-configured with features from various Salesforce products. In addition, it is possible for Salesforce to provision an org if you are a customer with specific needs to do so. For example, Marketing Cloud does not have a training environment, but there is a simulator in Trailhead for building interactive forms found at: **https://dfc-data-production. s3.amazonaws.com/files/ti/thi/THI-000120/index.html**

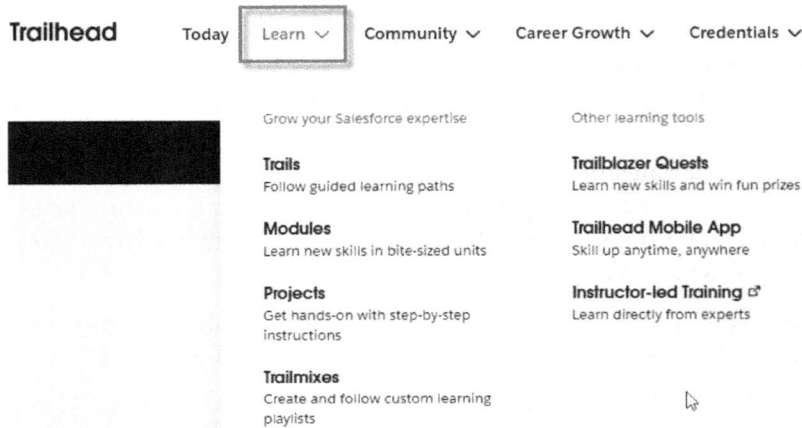

Figure 14.2: Getting access to training for various Salesforce products via Trailhead

You can also register with Salesforce partners. You will need to link your Developer Edition org to Trailhead and then go to **https://partners.salesforce.com/** and login using the Salesforce option. This will then give you access to various communities. For example, the **Actives Groups** menu will give you access to other people's experiences in using Salesforce products and often give you access to them.

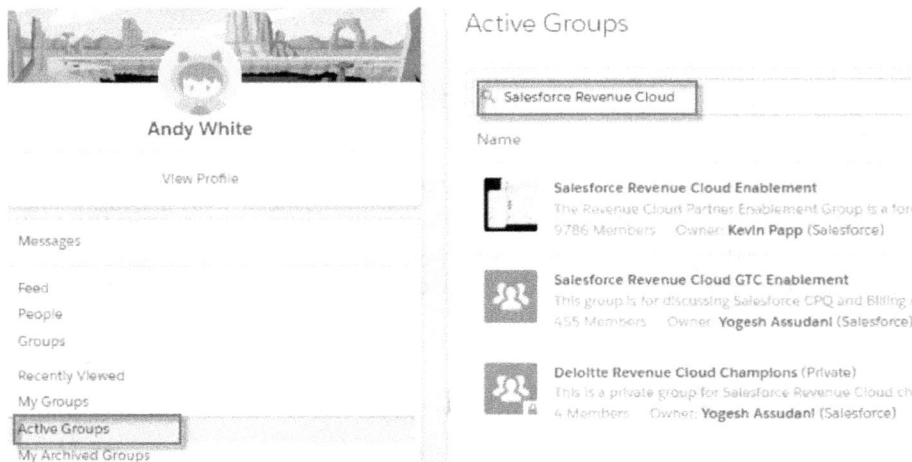

Figure 14.3: Joining an active group in the Salesforce partner portal

Salesforce Marketing Cloud

Marketing Cloud is possibly the third largest cloud from Salesforce, outside Sales and Service Cloud. This is a **business to customer** (**B2C**) platform that targets engagements to individuals, purchasers, and the public via various channels such as social media, email, SMS, and more. It is used for mass marketing but can include social listening, WhatsApp, and AI.

Marketing Cloud integrates with Salesforce Sales and Service Cloud using a dedicated connector, but can be used in conjunction with Data Cloud or a **customer data platform** (**CDP**) to give an enhanced view of engagements with contacts stored in Salesforce.

Marketing Cloud can be driven by Salesforce campaigns or reports to provide a list of customers to engage with. It might sound counterintuitive to use campaigns or reports, but this is an easy way to segment contact data for marketing campaigns. These can be fed into Marketing Cloud for various marketing activities.

Marketing Cloud is not built on the Salesforce Lightning platform, though, and as such, it is quite different from Salesforce Sales and Service Cloud and generally requires a different skill set. The chapters in this book will not really be much use in configuring Marketing Cloud, but there are many online resources to assist.

Marketing Cloud key features

Marketing Cloud was formerly known as **ExactTarget** until its acquisition by Salesforce in 2016. Since then, Salesforce has either acquired or built additional features, which are referred to as **studios** in Marketing Cloud. Due to the fact that Marketing Cloud has an entirely different history from other Salesforce products, it is not built on the Salesforce platform and, as a result, is almost completely different in the way it works from other Salesforce products. For example, custom code is done via AMPscripts and not Apex, and the closest equivalent to a Salesforce Sandbox is Marketing Cloud business units. In addition, the various features and studios are generally related to each other using Contact Builder, with many nuances in the way these features are configured and interact.

The following sections discuss the various Marketing Cloud key features.

Marketing Cloud studios

When you first get access to Marketing Cloud, you can see the various studios across the top of the screen. Each menu may have sub-menus depending on the context. Refer to the following figure:

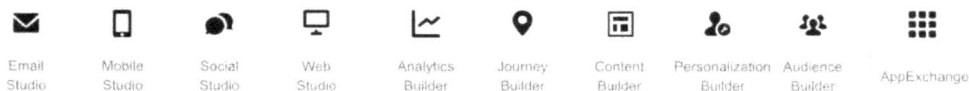

Figure 14.4: *The various studios available in Marketing Cloud*

The list of various studios available in Marketing Cloud is provided in the following figure, but it will also depend on what features have been paid for:

- **Email Studio:** This allows users to do mass email sends to a segmented list of recipients. It can track the email journey and measure the success of the email campaign. Emails can have dynamic content, so images or text in the email are tailored to the recipients' demographics, such as age, gender, interests, etc.

- **Mobile Studio:** This allows users to create, send, and monitor SMS, MMS, push notifications, **Rich Communication Services** (**RCS**), and in-app messages. This can also be extended to WhatsApp Business Platform, which allows marketing users to create personalized messages to recipients.

- **Advertising Studio:** This allows you to align online advertising with **customer relationship management** (**CRM**) data, and use audience segmentation and analytics to create personalized campaigns that can be added to *Facebook, Twitter (X), Instagram, YouTube, Google Ads, Pinterest, LinkedIn*, and more.

- **Automation Studio:** A broader tool for automating data management tasks and marketing activities, including those that might be part of Journey Builder. It allows you to create marketing automation and data management activities and add them to Journey Builder. Journey Builder has a logical flow interface where marketers can build logic into multi-channel campaigns based on recipients' demographics or interactions. Journey builder is shown in the following figure, which starts with a data extension and then emails are sent. They then take various routes available depending on whether the email recipient opened the email within a certain time period.

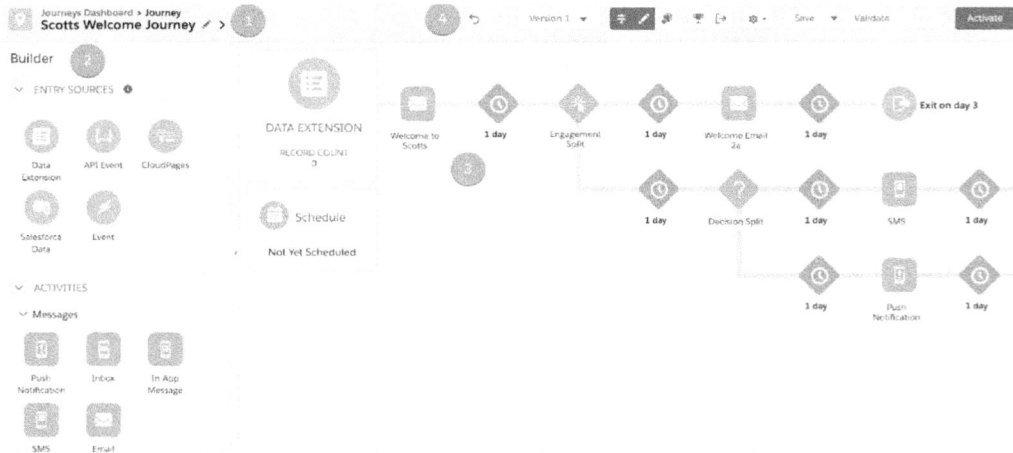

Figure 14.5: Journey Builder in Marketing Cloud

- **Interaction Studio:** Visualize, track, and manage customer experiences with real-time interaction management, which could be an offer to purchase an item based on their recent online activity.

- **Social Studio**: This is included, although it has since been deprecated. At the time of writing, there is no official reason other than that Salesforce has similar functionality by integrating into *Sprout Social* (**www.sproutsocial.com**). However, Social Studio had social listening capabilities that allowed users to see what was being said about them on numerous social media channels and then manage strategic responses accordingly.

- **Web Studio**: This allows users to build:

  o **Landing pages**: These are pages used in response to clicking links in emails or messages. They are typically embedded as part of a larger corporate website.

  o **Microsites**: Like landing pages, but form a smaller section of an existing webpage. For example, they can be added to a subscriber's webpage or embedded into a social feed.

Various features to be aware of with Marketing Cloud

Marketing Cloud is a bit of a beast when you first get access to it. The following is a short summary of some of the key terms and items to be aware of:

- **Data extensions**: These are essentially the same as a table, meaning they are a structured way to store and organize data.

- **Attributes**: Often referred to as **Contact Attributes**, these are essentially the same as fields in a data extension.

- **Contact Builder**: It is wise to leverage Contact Studio to ensure that your contacts in the Marketing Cloud have a single source of reference. This allows you to do multi-channel marketing communications such as email and SMS, but ensures the customers' preferences and engagements are kept against a single record. Typically, the subscriber key is used to reference any other data extensions or other customer details. It is worth noting that Contact Builder is sometimes confused with Contact Studio. Contact Builder is the central hub for organizing, managing, and connecting data for a unified contact view. Contact Studio, on the other hand, is a broader term encompassing various tools within Marketing Cloud for managing and interacting with your contacts, including Email Studio, Mobile Studio, and Social Studio.

- **AMPscripts**: This is the code used by Marketing Cloud and follows a syntax that starts and ends with **%%**, such as **%%=LowerCase(Name)=%%**.

  AMPscripts can be added to an email in the header or footer, in line with the email body, or in other areas of Marketing Cloud.

- **Business units**: These are additional copies of Marketing Cloud that exist within the parent instance. Each one has a unique **Member ID** (**MID**) number and effectively separates out functionality between different areas of the business. For example, one business unit might be used for training purposes, the other by a third-party marketing company, and the parent business unit owned by the business for its real marketing activities. Content and some features can be shared between business units.

- **SAP**: Sender Authentication Package (SAP), which is an additional feature to help with email deliverability, also provides a custom domain in marketing material sent out so it appears to come from an organization and not Marketing Cloud.

- **A/B testing**: A generic marketing technique for sending out two email or SMS campaigns and comparing the response.

- **IP warming**: The process of sending out mass emails in increments from small to large over time. Typically, the most likely recipients are sent first. This is to avoid getting your Marketing Cloud instance blocked by email delivery companies.

- **Send definition**: Combines the sender profile and delivery profile into an email to control who sends it and how it is delivered.

- **Scope by user**: An important setting in the connector from Marketing Cloud to Salesforce to enforce the correct visibility into the report or campaign used in sending mass emails from Marketing Cloud.

Marketing Cloud Account Engagement

MCAE was previously known as **Pardot** (pronounced par-dot) and is similar in many ways to Salesforce Marketing Cloud in terms of what it is trying to achieve. The difference is that MCAE is aimed at B2B marketing and lead generation. It is comparatively simpler to setup than Salesforce Marketing Cloud, but it provides lead nurturing accompanied by lead scoring to automate engagement with potential customers, typically via email. One of the main features is Engagement Studio, which has a visual flow of a marketing journey with logic built into it to steer the engagement down predefined paths.

Setting up Pardot

Setting up Engagement Studio typically requires building:

- **Programs**: Programs are automated workflows that help businesses nurture leads and customers. They look very similar to Marketing Cloud's Journey Builder. They can include email campaigns, pre-sales programs, and onboarding programs. A program is illustrated in *Figure 14.6*.

- **Events**: These are either physical events or online events, for which invites are sent to possible attendees with follow-up features to nurture the lead into a new prospect.

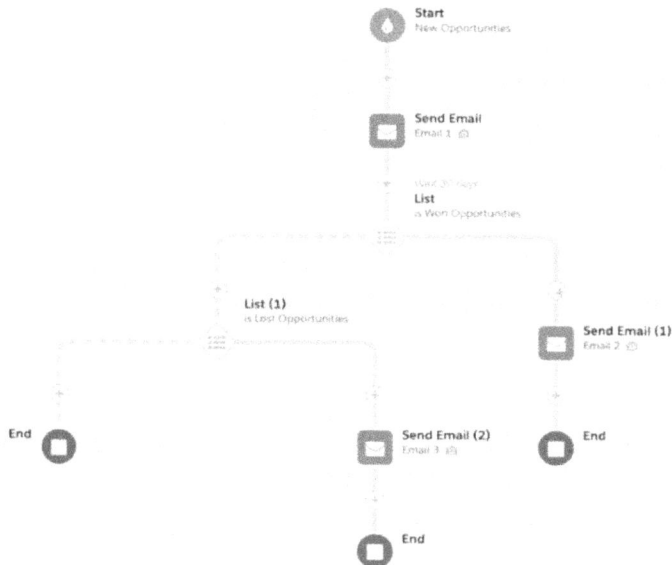

Figure 14.6: A program in Engagement Studio to nurture new prospects via email

When the lead (or prospect, as it is often referred to) qualifies, it is then passed to Salesforce for further engagement.

MCAE is also like Salesforce Marketing Cloud since it requires a connector to send and receive data from Salesforce.

Service Cloud Voice

SVC is Salesforce's **Contact Center as a Service** (**CCaaS**) offering. It is to allow many people to call the customer service help number and be connected to the next appropriate agent, i.e., the person who answers the call in a call center. There are alternatives to SCV, such as *Genesys*, which may offer more suitable features depending on the business requirements.

With SVC, it is comparatively simple to setup with a very graphical interface to create a flow that allows you to configure the logic required to receive an inbound call and assign it to the correct queue or person.

By integrating with Salesforce, SVC can use the data in Salesforce to answer the call and greet you with your name and options about your recent purchases, cases, or other related information.

Understanding how Service Cloud Voice works

SCV is about 80% AWS and 20% Salesforce. It leverages Amazon Connect, which provides call center functionality while leveraging Salesforce data such as contact details, recent orders, or cases. This is fed to Amazon Connect to help identify the customer or their reason for calling. The agent is also able to see this information in the Service Console and various Salesforce features to provide the complete solution.

SCV comes with Amazon business support as standard. This means that you will normally get a meaningful response to a query within 24 hours. If you do not use business support, you may not get a response at all.

Amazon Connect provides the following basic features:

- Some available inbound numbers that also give you options for dialing codes and locations.

- Basic call center values such as the hours of operation, language to use, and users.

- Flows to build logic into the call script, such as options to press on your phone, waiting times, queue assignment, and other features.

- Agent skills, availability, and queue configuration, such as agent allocations.

- Integration via AWS Lambda to push or pull data to or from Salesforce. SCV comes with some pre-built connectors that work with Contact Attributes in Amazon Connect. Contact Attributes are key-value pairs to assign values to variables.

- Call center manager insight to call volumes, agent productivity, and basic call center statistics such as **average handling time (AHT)** and more.

Some of the more sophisticated features from AWS are:

- Sentiment analysis to understand if a caller is happy or getting angry.

- Call transcription (voice-to-text) from Amazon Lex to record what a caller said in a script.

- Text-to-voice using Amazon Polly, which provides various voices and dialects to provide voice messages from scripts.

One useful configuration tip is to simply configure the Salesforce Service Console so that the contact record already has related records, such as cases or orders. This means that when you configure SVC to automatically display the contact record, then other relevant information is displayed, and no further configuration is required.

Setting up Service Cloud Voice

Once Service Cloud licenses are provided in your Salesforce org, you need to do the following steps. In Salesforce, under **Setup | Voice | Amazon Setup,** follow the five-step wizard:

1. Setting up omni-channel is not strictly required, but it is covered in *Chapter 10, Various Salesforce Features.*

2. For the root user, you can use your email address for demonstration, but be aware that the root user is difficult to change, so it is better to use an agreed-upon email address with the customer. This step can take several minutes to complete.

3. Assigning the permission sets and feature licenses with **Voice** in them to the users required to use SCV.

4. Even though you have assigned the permission sets to the users, you still need to go into **Setup | Voice | Amazon Setup** and add the users to the contact center.

5. Finally, activate the call center. This will provide you with a link to access it.

Once you have access to Amazon Connect, the screen gives the various steps to configure the call center, such as inbound number selection, operational hours, members, queues, and call flows. The detailed configuration is outside the scope of this book, but a few tips are given in the following:

- Do not change the name of flows with the name example or sample at the beginning of their name. It is better to copy these if needed.

- Enter plenty of play prompts in the flows to diagnose issues. More complex issues can be debugged using AWS Cloud Watch.

- To migrate flows between different instances of Amazon, you can simply export them as a JSON file and import them into the new environment. Re-assign the **Amazon Resource Name** (**ARN**) numbers as needed. Any blocks with a small red warning symbol need further consideration.

- If setting up a large call center, check the number of concurrent calls. At the time of writing, the easiest way to do this was to add a large number into the Amazon Connect settings, which will return an error saying what the maximum number of concurrent calls is allowed. If this number is less than the number of anticipated users or concurrent calls, then you need to request that Amazon increase it.

Although setting up SCV is relatively straightforward, an example flow is shown in *Figure 14.7*, which manages a call center across various geographies with many products and a broad range of customers. Flows also have subflows, which means that the actual flow is likely to be larger. A sub-flow could be if the agent needs to divert the caller or whisper when the agent can talk to a colleague to get advice.

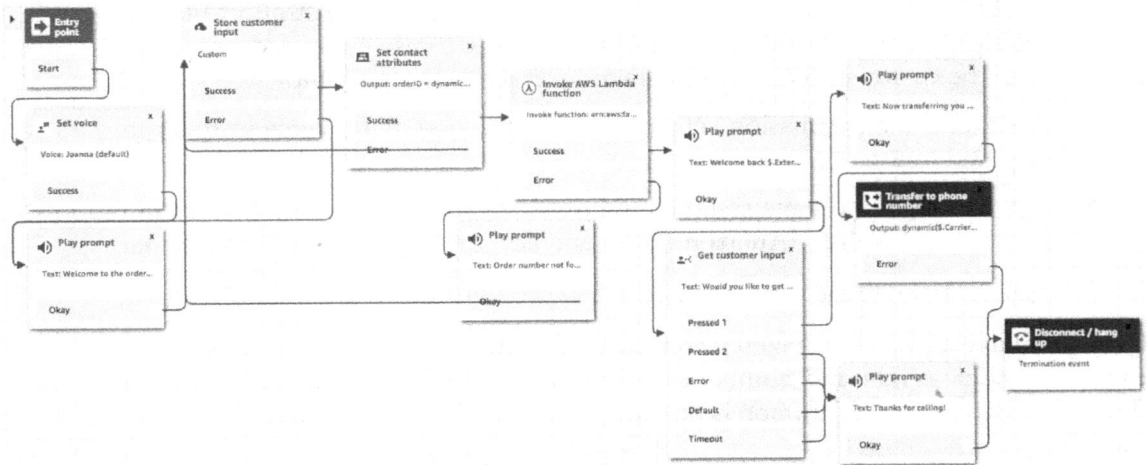

Figure 14.7: Example of a call flow using Salesforce SVC

The above is a relatively simple call flow. Working from left to right, the Set voice block allows you to choose what voice and language you want the prompts to be in. All the Play prompt blocks use this voice and allow you to simply type text, which is converted into natural language. The Set contact attributes is useful for storing variables in the call flow, which are stored in key-value pairs. The Invoke AWS Lambda function does a call-out to Salesforce. For example, if the caller's phone number is stored in Salesforce, then this is used to retrieve the contact record and related information, such as existing cases or orders. From here onwards, it is simply a case of setting the queue and transferring to the queue for an agent to pick up the call.

If a call flow is not working, then a simple call flow can be used for testing. This would be an inbound number assigned to a queue, and the developer is the only person in that queue. This can be useful for trying to resolve issues with Lambda settings or other AWS settings.

Revenue Cloud and RLM

Salesforce offers a suite of tools that initially appear to have a lot of overlap and similar terminology. The next few sections will show these different products and how they provide various features, but in summary, **configure, price, quote** (**CPQ**) automates and streamlines the quoting process for sales teams. Users can configure products with a highly configurable range of options. The final quote can then be sent to the customer.

Although CPQ is not going to disappear overnight, Salesforce is phasing out its older CPQ solution (previously referred to as **SteelBrick**) in favor of Salesforce Revenue Cloud, which was formerly known as **RLM**. Salesforce is actively transitioning customers from CPQ to Revenue Cloud, which offers a more comprehensive approach to revenue management.

Revenue Cloud is designed to manage the entire revenue lifecycle, including CPQ functionality, contract management, billing, and revenue recognition. One of the advantages of Revenue Cloud is that it is native to the Salesforce solution, being built on the core platform. This means it doesn't come as a separate package that can be installed or upgraded like older Salesforce CPQ (which was a managed package). Instead, it is directly integrated into the Salesforce platform, offering better flexibility and scalability.

Revenue Cloud includes:

- RLM with a new CPQ, order management, product catalogue, and price management, with optional features such as contract management.
- Vlocity
- Salesforce Billing

When these are put together, Revenue Cloud can conceptually be seen in the following figure:

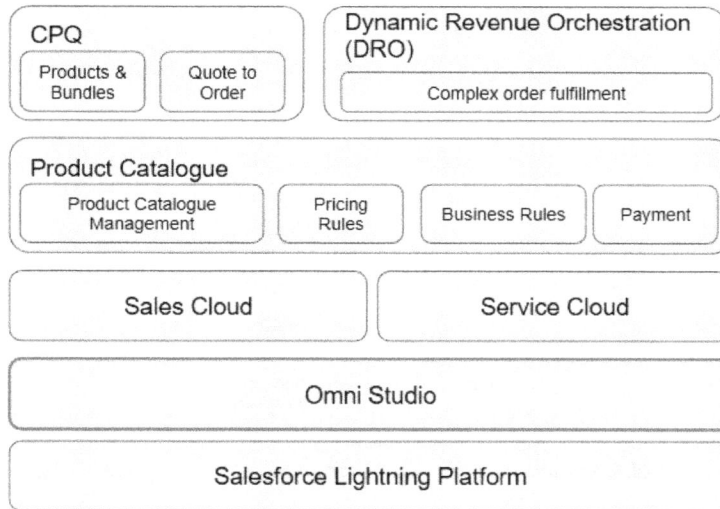

Figure 14.8: *The tech stack used for Revenue Cloud*

In the above figure, the Omni Studio layer is emphasized because a lot of functionality that comes out of various products is via Omni Studio. This was originally part of a suite of tools from a company called *Vlocity*, which pre-built various Salesforce products around various industries. Since the functionality was required across many products and the technology can be used independently of other products, Salesforce moved Omni Studio onto the core platform. However, Vlocity is often referred to as **Omni Studio** or even an essential part of SFI, all of which are correct terminology.

Figure 14.8 can help with understanding various Salesforce products, where features and terminology can get a bit confusing.

Salesforce Industries

SFI was originally built by Vlocity and refers to a suite of pre-configured versions of Salesforce, each one aimed at a specific industry. The list of industries can be found at: **https://www.salesforce.com/uk/solutions/industries/**

The following figure shows the current list of SFI, each one having a configuration specifically designed to meet the needs of the industry:

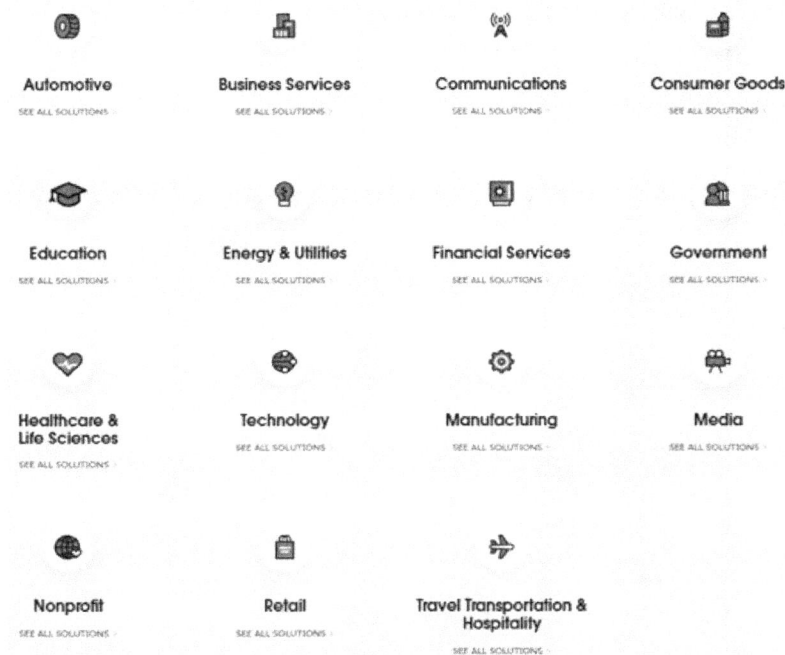

Figure 14.9: Various industries that have an SFI cloud developed for them

In a very simplistic way, all the various industry clouds have the same overall structure and architecture as illustrated in the following figure:

Figure 14.10: Overview of SFI structure

In the above figure:

- Salesforce is the standard Salesforce CRM used throughout this book.

- Vlocity is a suite of tools and components as described in the next section.

- Automations are pre-configured flows to align with industry standard procedures and best practices. This can also include other customizations such as Apex classes, **Lightning Web Components (LWC)**, and more.

- Additional objects are included to allow functionality typical for that industry.

Vlocity

Vlocity is a suite of tools that allow developers to build highly detailed user interfaces with logical scripts to coordinate the user's data entry or retrieve data from Salesforce. This consists of the following features:

- **OmniScripts**: Logical steps that FlexCards follows or interacts with DataRaptors or Integration Procedures. They define the logic used in building out the solution.

- **FlexCards**: Graphical tiles, which can be heavily customized but are driven by the logic in the OmniScript.

- **DataRaptors**: These read or write to a single Salesforce object and perform basic **Data Manipulation Language (DML)** procedures.

- **Integration Procedures**: These interact with many types of data, including REST APIs and Apex classes, and multiple objects.

The four features above are the building blocks of Vlocity, which are used extensively in SFI as well as other Salesforce products:

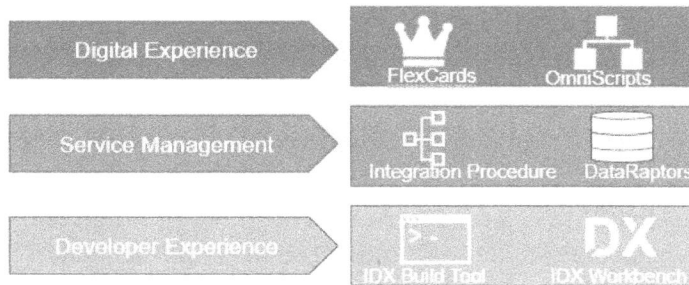

Figure 14.11: Overview of Vlocity

Also illustrated above are the developer and deployment tools, which are needed since Vlocity uses its own JSON-based metadata format, and deployment is typically done via the IDX Build Tool, Salesforce CLI, or the Vlocity IDX Workbench. Although there are suitable tools (such as Harness, **https://www.harness.io/**), Vlocity comes with its own tools for deployment, described as:

IDX Build or IDX Workbench: These help with Vlocity deployment. However, at the time of writing, deployment is a complex task if run in parallel with other Salesforce configurations, and standard DevOps tools such as Gearset, AutoRABIT, and Copado are bound by limits in

Salesforce APIs. For this reason, deployment tools such as Harness (**https://www.harness.io/**) are often used, or a pure scripting-based approach suitable for GitHub or GitLab.

Using a combination of the above, it is possible to build highly configurable data-driven flows that steer users through complicated data entry or retrieval.

Omni Studio also has an additional capability called **OmniOut**, which allows users to embed the results of Vlocity within external applications such as websites, storefronts, online advertising, or mobile apps.

Commerce Cloud and Revenue Cloud

Salesforce Commerce Cloud, Revenue Cloud, and **Revenue Lifecycle Management** (RLM) are all Salesforce products that help businesses manage their revenue. The main differences between them are the scope of their functionality and how they are built:

- **Salesforce Commerce Cloud**: A product that helps businesses manage their e-commerce. It is aimed towards companies selling their products online and comes with a storefront. Originally, the storefront was SiteGenesis, but it has evolved into the **Storefront Reference Architecture** (SFRA) to a sophisticated **Progressive Web App** (PWA) built on React. There are two versions of Commerce Cloud, one built for B2B (formerly known as **CloudCraze**), which is built on Salesforce, and the other for B2C (formerly **Demandware**), which integrates with Salesforce.

- **Revenue Cloud**: A product that provides a 360° revenue management solution, which includes product management, billing, and revenue recognition. This has been superseded by RLM but is still a Salesforce product.

- **RLM**: A product that provides end-to-end solutions for the revenue generation lifecycle. RLM includes processes like lead generation, CPQ, invoicing, and revenue analysis. It also includes Vlocity to allow highly visual product and pricing configuration.

The key difference is that RLM is more recent than the other products and provides a solution for the entire revenue generation lifecycle, including sales, billing, and finance.

Revenue Lifecycle Management

RLM is a relatively new Salesforce offering that combines the best of Vlocity with configurable product and pricing combinations and intuitive CPQ capabilities.

The heart of RLM has **Product Catalog Management** (PCM). To access this, go to the **App Launcher** and select **Product Catalog Management** as shown in the following figure:

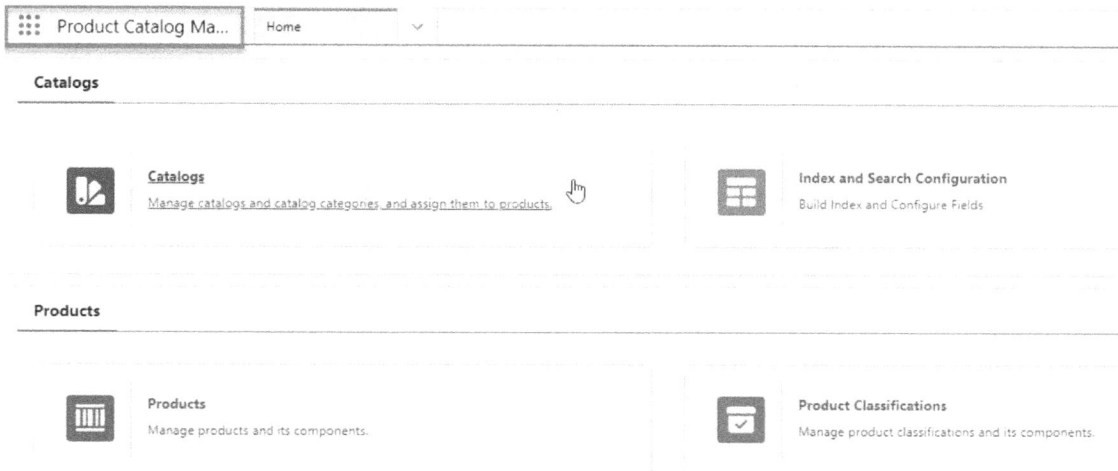

Figure 14.12: PCM Home page

Figure 14.12 contains the following features:

- **Catalogs**: Organize products by categories and add them to the catalogue.

- **Products**: All the products or services that are sold. Products are referred to as **static** or **dynamic**, where dynamic products can be bundled before or during the sales process.

- **Index and search configurations**: Speed up searches with large product catalogues.

- **Product classifications**: Define a large catch-all term that will allow you to group many products, such as hardware or software.

- **Product selling models**: Various time frames used in selling or billing, such as months or annually.

- **Attributes**: Build variables to hold regular product information, such as screen size or processor speed.

- **Attribute categories**: For organizing many similar attributes, such as brand or manufacturer. These can also be used as sub-categories, such as printer type.

- **Picklists**: A reusable picklist value that can be used for attributes to standardize values.

- **Qualification rules**: Logic builder for products that can be bundled or excluded from a sale.

- **Product configuration rules**: Certain restrictions, such as if a customer is eligible for a discount or a product is not suitable for certain countries.

- **Qualification rules procedures**: Manages the sequence in which product category and product qualification rules are applied.

Setting up Revenue Lifecycle Management

The best place to start is by setting up a catalogue. This is done by going to the **Product Catalog Manager** and selecting catalogs as shown in the following figure:

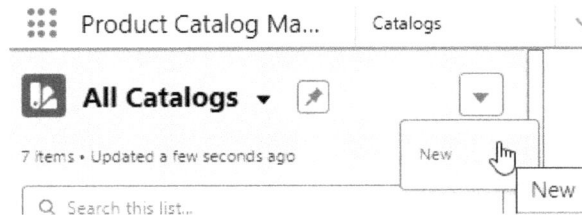

Figure 14.13: Adding a new catalog

Give it a name such as `Online Shop` and feel free to add the effective start and end dates. The dates would only be used if you were to add qualification rules. From here, add a **Category** such as **Online merchandise**, to get to the screen shown in the following:

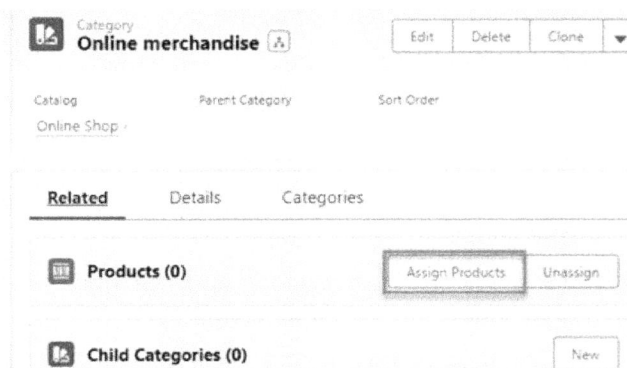

Figure 14.14: Assigning products to the new catalog

Assign several products that are to be available in the online shop. Note, there are a few fields to be aware of, which are found on a product record:

- **Product type**: This is setup on creation of a product and cannot be changed afterwards.
- **Configure during sale**: Allowing the products to have other products added to them during a sales process.
- **Display URL**: Allows you to add an image of the product, which will display in the catalogue or online shop.

The following figure shows that on the product record, you have the combination of choices between a simple or a bundled product, and then for both product types, you can have static or configurable sales options:

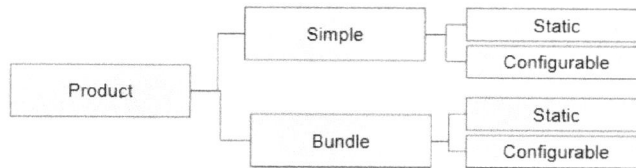

Figure 14.:15: *Core concepts in configuring product bundles*

To create and manage the product catalogue, there are a few key things to remember:

- When creating a product that could be a bundle now or in the future, make sure the product type is set to Bundle, as it saves reworking.

- Every product needs to have a product selling model option, which is on the related list. These are needed to allow pricing for the order.

- A product does not necessarily need to have a price book, category, or product component group, but these will help when configuring the pricing engine.

An example of a configured Bundle is shown in the following figure, where the information shown is also available from the related tabs:

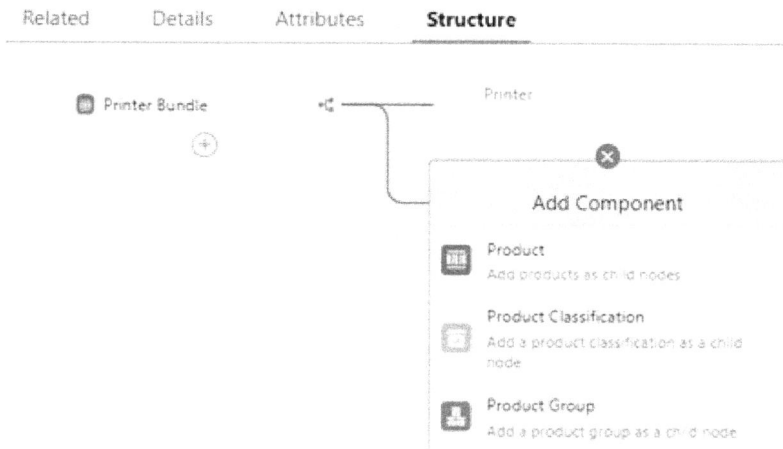

Figure 14.16: *Configuring bundles and components*

Revenue Lifecycle Management data model

It can be helpful to understand the data model to grasp the basic configuration. Although there are many more objects than shown below, the following figure illustrates some of the core objects and the relationship between them:

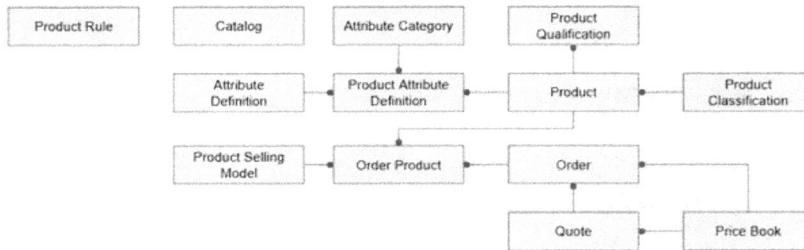

Figure 14.17: RML logical data model

Configure, price, quote

Salesforce CPQ refers to extending the default Salesforce sales process. This originated from a company called *Steel Bricks*, which was bought by Salesforce. It has been officially retired by Salesforce, but there are many companies that will use it. To replace CPQ, Salesforce now offers RLM, which includes a newer version of CPQ but also uses Vlocity, which is described above.

Configure, price, quote overview

From the first few chapters in this book, you may have noticed that once a lead is converted to an opportunity, then the logical next steps would be to fulfil the opportunity by creating a quote, then an order, and either getting the customer to pay upfront or to go through the corporate billing and payment process. Finally, the sold items are moved onto the asset object, which means the products have been sold but now belong to the account that purchased them. This can be helpful to maintain the ongoing relationship with the customer as well as offer **service level agreements (SLAs)** to maintain the products sold.

Salesforce CPQ is based around managing these steps, although the payment function can either be done by adding a suitable payment app or by using Salesforce RLM instead. RLM is covered in the following section of this chapter.

Configure, price, quote feature overview

CPQ includes the ability to move from an opportunity to transfer the data onto the quote object. Multiple quotes can be generated, but only one is considered to be the primary quote. This can be sent to the customer and generated into an order. Depending on the way your company works, the order can then be fulfilled and an invoice generated in Salesforce for payment.

CPQ has two core concepts:

- **Pricing rules**: Allow various scenarios for complex pricing calculations and adjustments based on specific conditions such as the volume ordered, customer status, or other factors. Pricing rules use **AND** or **OR** logic to define the rule and the order in which the rules are executed.

- **Product rules**: This shows how products could be grouped or should not be grouped. These are referred to as bundles, which contain related products. For example, a bundle could be a laptop, charger, and travel case, with options to include a separate screen or headset.

CPQ sells assets or subscriptions. An asset is a physical object, whilst a subscription could be a service or skills. Many companies sell both. Another consideration is the unit of time the company can work with. This could be months or days, but it fundamentally affects the way in which CPQ calculates prices and the subscription and renewal features in CPQ.

Configure, price, quote key configuration

Core CPQ configuration is done by going to **Setup** | **Installed Packages** | **CPQ**, then the **Configure** link, as shown in the following figure:

| Uninstall | Configure | Manage Licenses | ⬇ | Salesforce CPQ | Salesforce CPQ 242.2 | SBQQ | Active Unlimited | 0 |

Description
Salesforce CPQ simplifies configuration and ensures pricing and quoting accuracy. Sales reps reduce errors, improve prod

Figure 14.18: Accessing basic Salesforce CPQ configuration

This brings up the following tabs, which are outlined in the following: This will take you to the main configuration panel with the following tabs:

- **Documents**: How documents should be displayed and saved.

- **Groups**: Typically, how bundles (groups of products) are grouped.

- **Line editor**: View and modify settings for creating quotes. For example, whether you can delete multiple lines at once or view product bundle grouping as a hierarchy.

- **Plugins**: Include additional functionality available from Salesforce at: **https://developer.salesforce.com/docs/atlas.en-us.cpq_dev_api.meta/cpq_dev_api/cpq_plugins_parent.htm**. They typically provide specific functionality, which is often not needed, for example, Heroku integration.

- **Pricing and calculation**: This requires the unit price scale, which is the number of decimal places used in doing the calculations.

- **Subscriptions and renewals**: As illustrated in *Figure 14.19* below, the calculations can be done based on various options. This is typically **Month + Daily**, which allows the calculations to be performed in multiple months with a ratio of any additional days. The field **Subscription Term Unit** is also a key field, as the calculations are always done in these units.

- **Quote**: Key fields for how long a quote is valid for, and the ability to remove options if not needed from a quote.

- **Order**: The ability to provide multiple orders and set default values based on the quote.
- **Additional settings**: These can help with CPQ performance, such as sorting products in memory and improving browser performance.

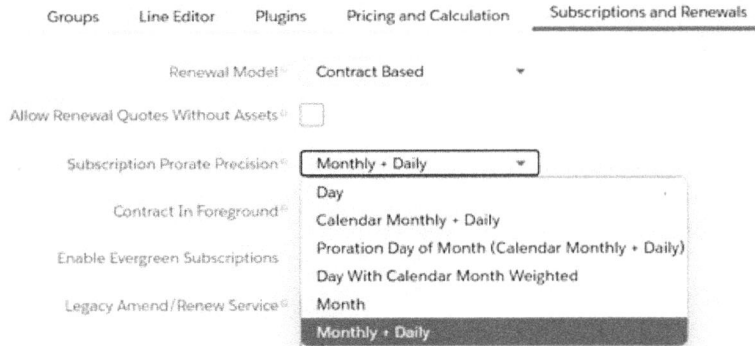

Figure 14.19: Setting the right pricing model for Salesforce CPQ

Configure, price, quote logic model

To understand CPQ, it can be helpful to think of the logical model that CPQ uses to enable the functionality. This is not the same as an object model, but rather the logical flow that needs to be considered when building out CPQ. The following figure has a main flow working from left to right, with Salesforce objects shaded in grey. The vertical lanes show what needs to be considered in succession to enable a successful configuration of CPQ:

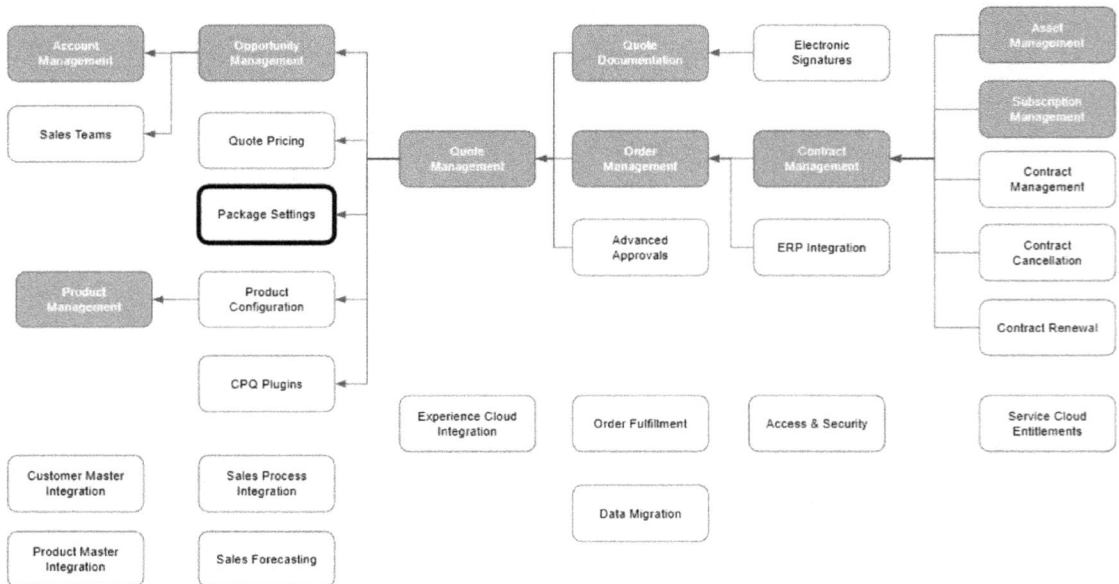

Figure 14.20: Logical flow through Salesforce CPQ

In the above figure, the grey blocks are for standard objects, and the Package Settings block is the configuration steps required by going to the CPQ configuration as described in *Figure 14.18.*

Heroku

Heroku is a Salesforce product, but it is built on various AWS components. It can meet many uses, but the typical scenario would be to offload intensive processing from Salesforce. For example, if a customer wants to check their purchase history over the past year on their phone, they need summary information. This could be to check your pension performance or to look at vouchers for a supermarket.

Heroku is a **platform as a service** (**PaaS**) that also supports a variety of languages and frameworks like Node.js, Ruby on Rails, Django, and Spring. Heroku can also support languages for building a frontend app using languages like Java, Ruby, Python, PHP, JavaScript, and Go.

The Heroku Platform uses the container model to run and scale all Heroku apps. The containers are referred to as **dynos**. Dynos are isolated, virtualized Linux containers, a bit like having a virtual machine able to build and deploy your app.

The following figure shows a typical use case for Heroku to provide Salesforce data for a mobile app or device.

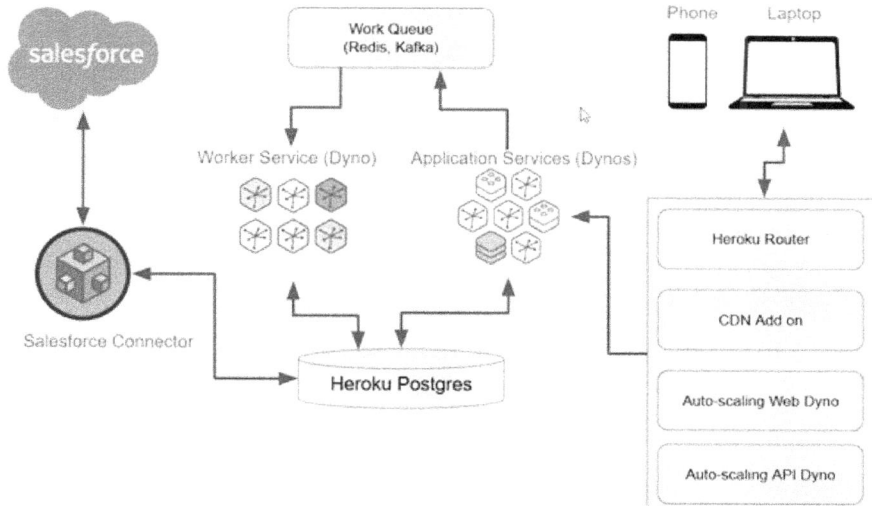

Figure 14.21: Example of a Heroku implementation for using Salesforce with a mobile app or device

In the above, apps are deployed from Heroku, for example, using the Salesforce Mobile **software development kit** (**SDK**) and are available on the *Apple Store* or *Google Play*. The app is segmented between a UI layer and a data layer managed by the auto-scaling web dyno and auto-scaling API dyno. These retrieve the necessary information from the application service dyno, which in turn can either pull/push data to Heroku Postgres or the work queue for jobs that do not require an immediate response.

Postgres is kept up-to-date with Salesforce using the Salesforce Connector, which can be run in batch mode based on recently modified Salesforce data. Salesforce is still the master data record for the system. The data in Postgres is typically for immediate use in the app, such as in-store purchases, restaurant vouchers, supermarket coupons, or pension performance summaries. These services can be accessed directly using internal DNS or a messaging layer to broker the communication by leveraging one of the Heroku Add-ons.

Two features to be aware of are Heroku Data Sync and Private Spaces. These are two distinct features within the Heroku Platform, addressing different needs for managing applications and data. Heroku Data Sync, specifically Heroku Connect, focuses on synchronizing data between Salesforce and Heroku Postgres, enabling seamless data flow and manipulation. In contrast, Heroku Private Spaces provides a dedicated, isolated environment for running Heroku applications and their associated data services, enhancing security and control.

The work queue is used for processes that do not require an immediate response (such as restaurant reservations). Redis provides data storage and can be used for caching, real-time analytics, session storage, and message brokering. These are managed by Kafka for data pipeline management.

Customer data platform and Data Cloud

CDP is an industry phrase that typically means getting your data in one place for marketing or CRM purposes. Salesforce has its own version of this called **Data Cloud**, which was acquired from a company called *Genie*. It is a dedicated platform that can ingest and process vast amounts of data, which can be used across multiple Salesforce instances. It is not the same as **master data management** (**MDM**) or data lakes (typically unstructured data suitable for various purposes). Instead, Data Cloud can connect multiple Salesforce products and provide a single view, and coordinate data usage.

This provides a single data platform to support various Salesforce projects and provides a unique ID for each contact in Data Cloud, which is used for pairing CDM with other Salesforce products. Having a unique ID for every contact allows Data Cloud to manage a whole variety of purposes, from email to e-commerce.

MuleSoft

MuleSoft is a Salesforce API middleware platform:

- Middleware means it sits in between dedicated applications (or a group of applications with point-to-point integration between them) and the broader Enterprise Architecture.

- API means it uses standard internet protocols (i.e., an agreed format for the message) to send data between the systems. Typically, REST or SOAP, but **publish/subscribe**

(**Pub/Sub**) pattern for event-driven architectures is increasingly common along with platform events for real-time updates, such as a train ticket confirmation.

MuleSoft is a Salesforce product, but the skills are outside the scope of this book, and typically MuleSoft developers are certified professionals with deep working knowledge of API strategies. It is configured using the MuleSoft Anypoint Studio application. MuleSoft works in a similar way to any middleware, such as Jitterbit, Informatica, and many others, which is the structuring of API messages using the three layers illustrated in the following figure:

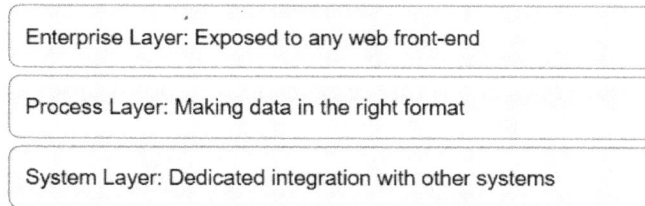

> Enterprise Layer: Exposed to any web front-end
>
> Process Layer: Making data in the right format
>
> System Layer: Dedicated integration with other systems

Figure 14.22: MuleSoft core structure

These three layers allow MuleSoft developers to connect APIs and either modify them (in the Process Layer), expose them in the Enterprise Layer, or update other external systems in the System Layer.

This is managed in Anypoint Studio as illustrated in the following figure:

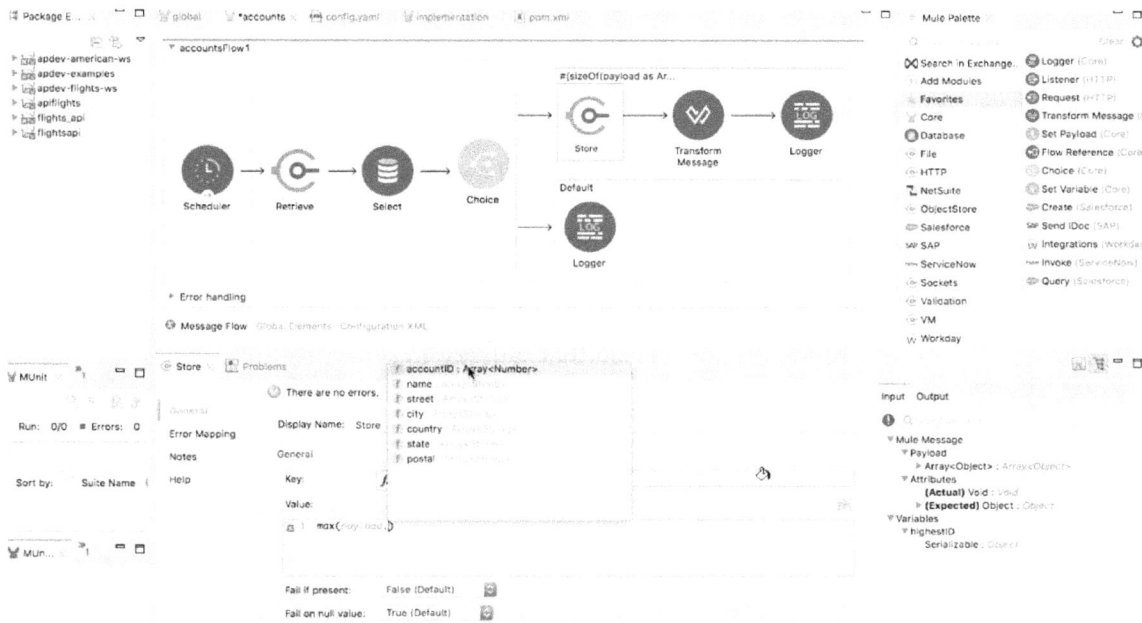

Figure 14.23: Anypoint Studio user interface

Field Service Lightning

FSL focuses on *the Traveling Salesperson Problem,* which is a classic optimization problem where a salesperson must visit multiple locations on a list exactly once and return to the starting point, whilst also minimizing the total distance traveled. People who do deliveries or onsite services need an efficient way to travel and collect or deliver supplies. FSL combines travel and product or supply information to allow users the best route with real-time updates on their mobile device.

FSL leverages the following two Salesforce features:

- **Salesforce territories**: It means that users can avoid boundaries as well as plan around delivery between warehouses or teams.

- **Mobile app**: FSL has full mapping functionality to allow users to see a plan for their delivery schedule. The app is highly customizable.

The general rule for FSL is to stick to the out-of-the-box functionality. A business may require specific requirements, but it is generally better to avoid configuring it beyond the intended purpose.

In terms of how many FSL projects are live and employable, then it is comparatively few, so these projects tend to be for more niche opportunities. The rule learned from most FSL projects is to keep it simple, stupid. Do not customize it too much, as there will be built-in limitations to Salesforce's functionality.

Conclusion

In this chapter, some of the various Salesforce products have been introduced. There are still many products not covered, but those included are the main products encountered in typical Salesforce products. The list will continually change or be renamed by Salesforce. The aim is not to give you a deep understanding but a reasonable chance of understanding the broader Salesforce ecosystem.

Salesforce is a continuously evolving service that will try to offer products to assist in many areas of a business. It is up to each business to decide which products best fit their requirements.

This chapter would have given you a reasonable and practical overview of these products and compared the differences between them.

Multiple choice questions

1. **What two products does Salesforce offer for marketing automation? (choose 2)**
    a. Automation Studio
    b. Marketing Cloud

    c. Engage Online

    d. Marketing Cloud Account Engagement

2. **Vlocity is often referred to as:**

    a. Performance cloud

    b. Industry cloud

    c. Omni-channel

    d. OmniOut

3. **Heroku is a collection of AWS products which work together in:**

    a. Silos

    b. Dynos

    c. Biros

    d. Gyros

4. **MuleSoft can integrate with any API exposed interface and orchestrate the messages using:**

    a. API orchestrator

    b. Middleware APIs

    c. Transactional interface

    d. Anypoint Studio

5. **RLM configures products and price books using standard Salesforce objects.**

    a. True

    b. False

6. **SVC is a single solution for call center management. Some of the key features are:**

    a. Integration with AWS and Salesforce via Lambda

    b. Real-time call transcription and sentiment analysis

    c. Call Flows to manage the logic in call routing

    d. All the above

7. **If working in a test sandbox environment, then you can copy the new licenses to the sandbox by:**

    a. Requesting assistance from Salesforce

    b. Pressing the Match Production Licenses button under Company Information

    c. Installing the new features from the AppExchange

    d. Raising a case with the vendor of the product

8. **Marketing Cloud stores data in tables known as:**
   a. Objects
   b. Data retentions
   c. Data extensions
   d. Data repositories

9. **Data Cloud is a Salesforce product, which:**
   a. Provides a single customer view of all customers
   b. Gives data to various Salesforce products using a unique ID for every customer
   c. Allows users to see Salesforce data from other systems
   d. Give a real-time view of all customer interactions

10. **Vlocity has core features which include:**
    a. OmniScripts
    b. DataRaptors
    c. FlexCards
    d. Integration Procedures
    e. All of the above

Answers

1	**b, d**
2	**b**
3	**b**
4	**d**
5	**a**
6	**d**
7	**b**
8	**c**
9	**b**
10	**e**

CHAPTER 15
Further Readings

Introduction

This chapter is for additional information that will be useful when working for a company. It is to assist in understanding the way projects are implemented and how they are structured. There is also some insight based on experience that may be useful.

This chapter also contains personal experience, which is not found online, but may prevent you from learning at your own expense.

Structure

In this chapter, we will be discussing the following topics:

- Structure of a system integration company
- DevOps
- Keeping on top of Salesforce
- Career advice

Structure of a system integration company

All companies are different and will have their own way of working. A **system integration** (**SI**) company is a firm that specializes in building out IT systems for other organizations. This is not to be confused with an individual who may refer to themselves as an SI, which is their profession. They can also be referred to as **solution providers**, **integration and service partners**, or even just **consulting partners**. Essentially, they focus on making various technologies work together seamlessly. Typical companies include *Capgemini, IBM, TCS, Accenture, Deloitte, Cognizant, EPAM, Infosys,* and many smaller companies often referred to as **boutiques** since they specialize in particular business areas or technologies.

Every company will have strengths and weaknesses. Some are hugely expensive but will have all the employees in the client office, whilst others use an offshore model where most of the work is done. Others have a combination of the two or use a near-shore model, which leverages employees who work remotely but are not too far away.

However, many SIs tend to have a typical structure as outlined in the following figure:

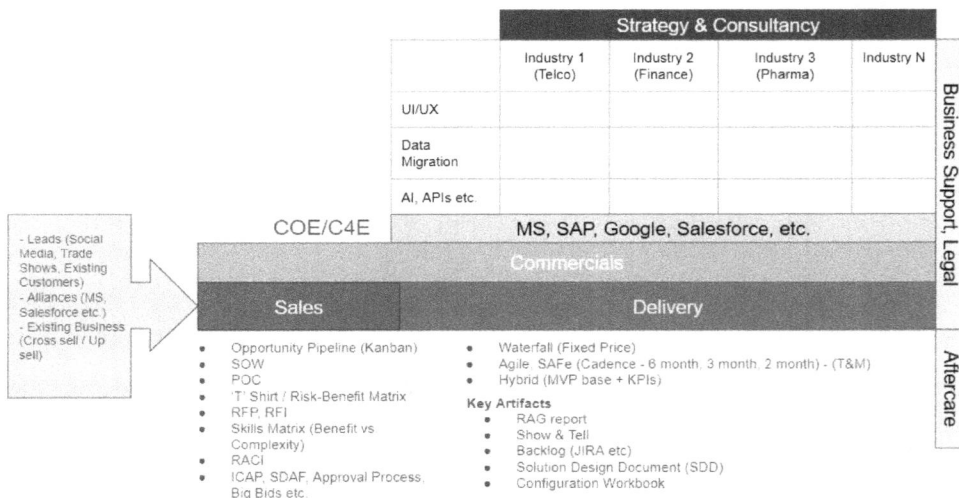

Figure 15.1: The typical structure of an SI company

In the figure above, Sales is on the left, which represents new business opportunities that can come from a variety of sources. As you move to the right, the projects are defined and aligned for Delivery. Above the Delivery, you have support from experts in a particular industry, such as Telco, Finance, or Pharma. There are also teams that specialize in a particular area of technology, such as Salesforce, but this could also be AI, middleware, or data integrations.

Beneath the diagram are typical documents used in the process, which are outlined later in this chapter. There is often a group called the **Center of Excellence** (**COE**) or **Center for Enablement** (**C4E**) that works to ensure that the business model is working correctly and ensures best practices are used in sales and delivery of projects.

The exact structure would depend on the size and budget of the project, the in-house skills of the SI, and the operating model as outlined in the following section. There is also feedback from the customer to help improve the way the practice works. As such, the Salesforce practice is a continually evolving system, keeping the latest Salesforce technologies involved in sales and delivery, and making sure the customers are kept happy.

SI operating model

There are three basic types of operating models:

- **On-shore**: This is when the SI has people based in the client's office or readily available. This tends to be the model used by boutique companies or more consultative companies. This has a stronger client engagement but also tends to be more costly for the client.

- **Near-shore**: This tends to have a few people in the client's office for direct engagement, but leverages people working in geographies nearby who are able to engage with the client but will not be in the office. This helps to reduce cost and has fewer barriers than an offshore model.

- **Off-shore**: This model has larger teams working in countries that may be in a very different time zone and have a different culture. The primary aim of this is to reduce cost. The golden rule of offshore is *you get what you inspect, not what you expect,* meaning there is a potential for misunderstanding between the client and the delivery team.

This is summarized in the following table:

Model	Advantage	Disadvantage
On-shore	• Closer collaboration between teams. • Better for high-risk projects.	• More expensive.
Near-shore	• Reduced cost compared to on-shore. • Possible to select the vendor in a similar time zone.	• Possibility of misalignment by time zone or communications.
Off-shore	• Leverage cheaper day rates. • Suitable for clearly defined projects. • Potential to work around the clock with multiple teams. • Access to a global talent pool.	• Time zone misalignment. • Risk of cultural misunderstandings. • Harder to enforce quality control.

Table 15.1: Comparison of delivery models

SI delivery model

There are various delivery models, but they fall into two basic types:

- **Waterfall**: Projects are clearly defined with explicit requirements. The term waterfall refers to a linear and sequential approach where each project phase must be fully completed before moving on to the next.

- **Agile**: This relies on iterations of delivery and demonstrations of progress to the client. There is a daily scrum meeting where people discuss what they are doing. Terms such as **burndown chart** and **Kanban boards** are used. This provides more flexibility in what is delivered in a project.

An illustration of a waterfall project plan is shown in the following figure:

Project Name: Salesforce Einstein

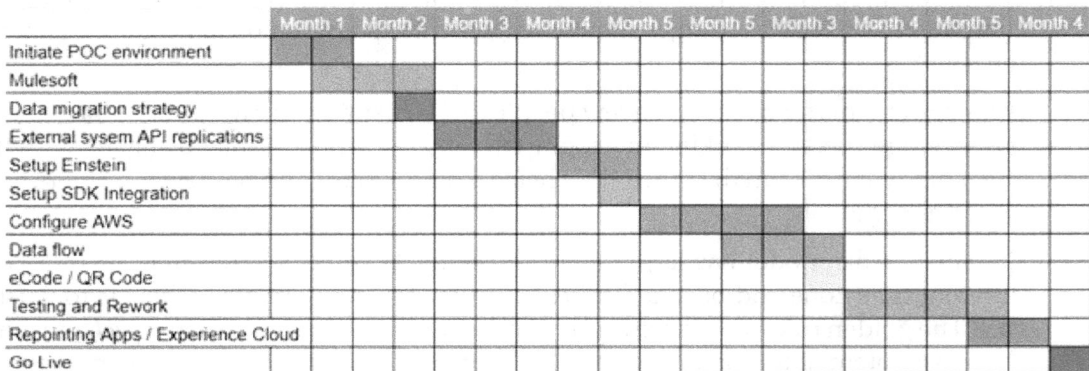

	Month 1	Month 2	Month 3	Month 4	Month 5	Month 5	Month 3	Month 4	Month 5	Month 4
Initiate POC environment	██									
Mulesoft		██								
Data migration strategy			██							
External sysem API replications				██						
Setup Einstein					██					
Setup SDK Integration						██				
Configure AWS							██			
Data flow								██		
eCode / QR Code										
Testing and Rework									██	
Repointing Apps / Experience Cloud										██
Go Live										██

Figure 15.2: Illustration of a project delivery using the waterfall

Scrum basics

Agile is by far the most common delivery method, but many companies seek to lock in key aspects of delivery using high-level requirements known as **epics**. There is also a trade-off between a fixed price project, or time and materials, where a client may not wish to have a budget absorbed by a project taking too long, vs. a client having a project delivered that does not meet expectations. Some more innovative methods include shelving upfront payment for a good **return on investment** (**ROI**), meaning the responsibility to deliver a successful project is shared between the SI and the customer. This can help customers who wish to avoid a highly expensive project but also carry the risk.

The core concept of scrum is continuous development based on sprints. A sprint will be two to four weeks, during which various tasks are sized using T-shirts, which simply gives them a comparative level of complexity relative to each other. T-shirts are often sized by small, medium, or large, but the Fibonacci sequence is also a popular method of sizing T-shirts.

A solution architect will draft the design and assign it to the appropriate developer or Salesforce Administrator to configure. The daily standup is a meeting where the team says what they have done the previous day, what they are doing today, and any issues blocking them. These are managed by the scrum master, who can see the progress of the team and the burndown chart showing if they are on track for the sprint. At the end of the sprint, the work is generally pushed into the delivery pipeline to be combined with work from other teams.

An example of a burndown chart is shown in the following figure:

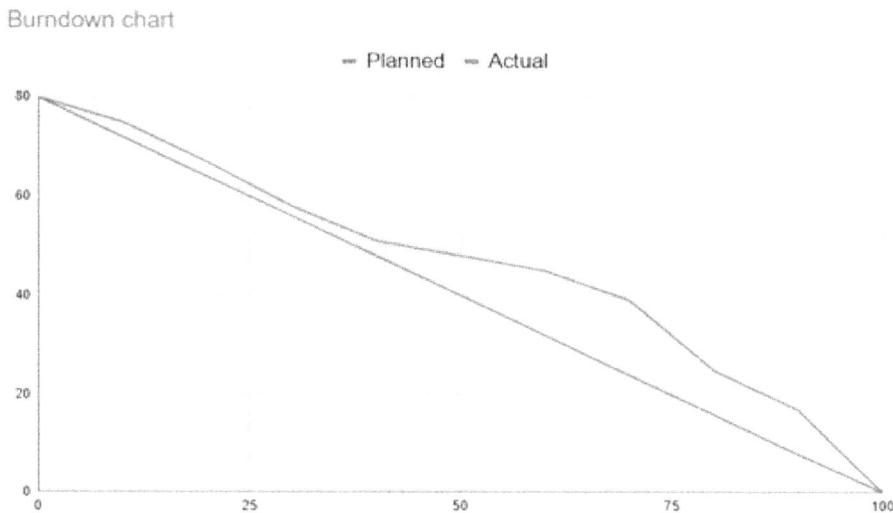

Figure 15.3: Scrum burndown chart

Since projects can be anywhere between small and huge, there are variations on using scrum with agile, particularly on very large projects. The **Scaled Agile Framework (SAFe)** is a structured approach for scaling agile and scrum for large enterprises. It allows multiple agile teams to coordinate and deliver value together using processes such as Agile Release Train, Program Increment, and Scrum of Scrums.

Standard documentation

In this section, some of the typical standard documentation is explained. These are typically used to help run the teams, give progress reports to the customer, or simply gather requirements in a way to assist in the design and delivery of projects.

RAG reports

In both models, there are some key documents, such as a **Red, Amber, or Green (RAG)** report, which indicates the progress of the project. An example of a RAG report is shown in the following figure, which shows the status of key parts of the project and whether they are getting better or worse. It would be up to the project manager or scrum master to maintain the RAG report on a weekly basis, and it is generally not a good idea to go straight from green to red, since that shows a lack of insight into the project progress.

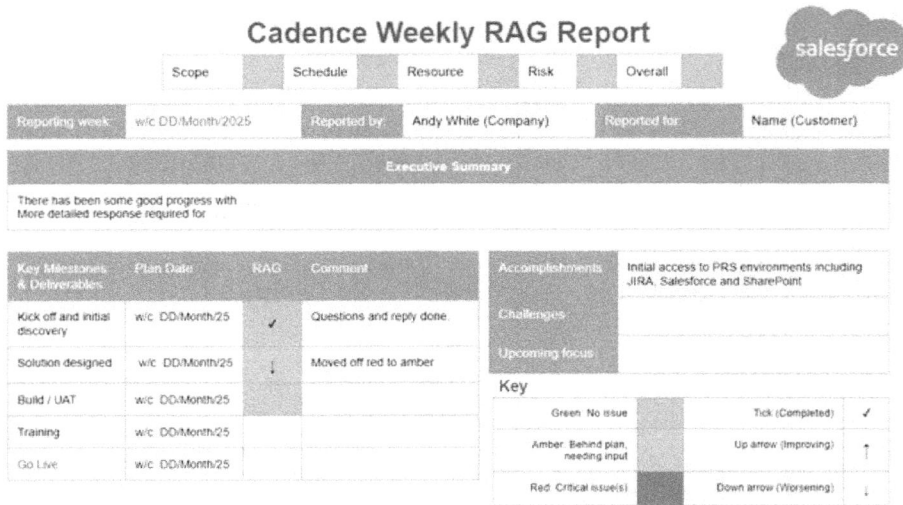

Figure 15.4: A typical RAG report

Statement of work

The **statement of work (SOW)** is the official document that kicks off the start of a project, a large phase, or an existing project. The document typically defines what is in scope for the project or what is out of scope. It is important that key members of the team have read and understood it because if a project is derailed, it is often because the team has taken on work not in the SOW, or they have not done the work they are contractually obliged to do.

SOW should include sufficient detail about what specific features of Salesforce are required and the expected high-level requirements. They are not a detailed design document, nor would they include details about what objects in Salesforce will be used, but they should include statements about what the business is expecting from Salesforce in terms of which of the products will be implemented, outcomes, and expected functionality.

You may not be given much choice in which projects you work on. It is often helpful to read the SOW before, as this will give you insight as to what the customer is requiring, as well as an indication of the team structure.

Other documents

There will be many other documents involved in defining and managing a Salesforce project. From the start, there will often be a **request for proposal (RFP)**, or **request for information (RFI)**, and as a project progresses, there may be **change requests (CRs)** for the ongoing support of the system, typically bound up in a service contract. Other documents often include a **Solution Design Document (SDD)**, which ideally is tied back into the SOW requirements as well as the various user stories that have come out of the design and delivery process.

User stories should be in the following format:

As a … [the role of the user], I want … [an action] so that … [a benefit]. This format helps the team to design solutions that meet the business requirements. Some examples could be: *As a sales representative, I want to see my open opportunities on a dashboard, so I can prioritize my tasks. As a customer service agent, I want to easily log cases, so I can track customer issues.*

As the project progresses, the user stories are often accompanied by the configuration workbook, which may include technical details that are only relevant for the delivery team. Ideally, the high-level requirements in the SOW are broken into epics, which are then further broken down into user stories. These can be referenced in the configuration workbook for continuity. This can prove invaluable if a project starts to veer off course or the customer is not convinced that everything in the SOW has been built. Keeping accountability also boosts customer satisfaction and can help focus the business and the delivery team on keeping the project going smoothly.

SI team structure

Depending on the size of the project, the team structure would vary. A typical project might have 10 to 20 people involved, but a larger one may have over 100. Some of the key roles are:

- **Project or program manager**: Ultimately responsible for coordinating delivery and reporting to the client. A program manager will often be on larger projects or multiple projects, with two or three project managers on each project. A project manager would typically be involved in the day-to-day running of the project. They would be responsible for overseeing the team and keeping the project running on time and on budget.

- **Business analyst**: Someone who can understand the business and put requirements in a way that can be understood by other team members. A good business analyst would also have a reasonable understanding of the technology being used, i.e., Salesforce. A business analyst is often heavily involved at the start of the project for gathering the requirements. These are often mapped out in diagrams with swim lanes, which are organized by actors (i.e., people in the company) or by the technology or data flows. A good business analyst will be capable of thinking through the business problems and not just repeating the same processes.

- **Scrum master**: Responsible for coordinating the daily scrum meetings and managing communication between the team and business. They would typically be involved in the project backlog, as well as assigning the work to individuals in the team.

- **Architect**: This can be a technical architect, solution architect, enterprise architect, or others. They play a key role in the overall design of the solution. They have a high-level overview of what is going to be achieved in the project, as well as an excellent working knowledge of Salesforce and other technologies. They should also be aware of the various design patterns that Salesforce recommends, found at **https://architect. salesforce.com/.**

- **Administrator or developer**: They are hands-on in building the solution. They work with the project manager and scrum master to organize the delivery of the work. Ideally, the administrator can meet most of the requirements by configuration, leaving the developer to only do the work that cannot be configured.

There are many other roles, but terms like stakeholder or C-suite generally refer to key people from the client side. Other terms, such as **subject matter expert** (**SME**), refer to people required on a project for expertise in a particular area.

When dealing with stakeholders or senior executives, it is highly advisable to be very careful how you conduct yourself. They will often be under a lot of pressure, and any casual comments can have a negative impact on the project. It is far better to use a consultative approach in conversations to listen to their concerns and ensure they are understood by the delivery team.

DevOps

Development and Operations (**DevOps**) simply means how you deploy from a development environment into the production live environment. If you have only a small project, then this is a relatively straightforward process, and you can use Salesforce change sets to deploy between environments. However, change sets have limited functionality and, on larger projects, are incapable of viewing development in other environments, leading to merge conflicts from combining different delivery workstreams. As a result, more powerful DevOps tools are used, such as Gearset, Copado, Harness, or AutoRABIT.

Salesforce launched the *DevOps Center* in 2022 to address this gap in its product offering. Having worked on several large Salesforce deployments, the tools listed above still seem to be favored, or in some cases, a purely script-based approach is used using the Salesforce **command line interface** (**CLI**) to automate tasks like deployments, validations, and managing changes across environments.

Gearset is generally considered to be easier to use but may lack some of the sophisticated functionality of Copado. For this reason, Copado is often used for larger enterprise projects since it has sophisticated automated tests, granular migration, including code comparisons with deployment validations. The Salesforce DevOps Center is native to Salesforce and is a huge improvement, and it shows Salesforce's keenness to address a badly neglected gap in its offering. All tools typically use GitHub or GitLab as a repository for metadata to allow the new configuration to be pushed between sandboxes, as well as integration with Jira or Azure DevOps.

Salesforce deployment structure

The following figure shows a typical setup for a large project. The important feature to note is that there are six small projects, two medium projects, and one large project. This allows the deployment of the small projects every month, the medium project every three months, and the large project in a six-month interval. This then means that every six months, all the sandbox environments can be refreshed from production, which keeps them all synchronized.

This process is illustrated in the following figure:

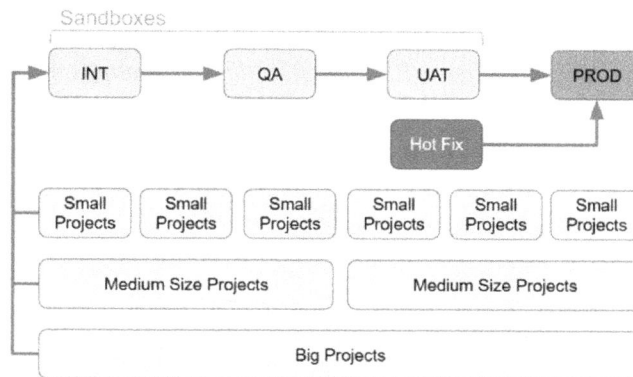

Figure 15.5: A typical delivery pipeline

In the above figure, all development is done in sandboxes. This includes the Small, Medium, and Large Projects. The first combined environment is often called **integration** (**INT**). This is a good time for the administrators and developers to resolve any conflicts from the combined source environments. There is a phrase known as **left shift**, which means the INT environment should be used to resolve as much as possible, including integrations or possible data issues, since resolving them later will incur greater complexity and could delay the project. Once the INT environment is fully configured, the push through into other sandboxes is often handled by a delivery manager. This is to ensure that the correct processes are in place and the solution can be signed off.

The names and number of sandboxes will change between companies and project complexity, but typically:

- **INT**: Refers to the integration of all the development environments.
- **Quality assurance (QA)**: It is often called a test, and is typically for internal approval of the configured solution.
- **User acceptance testing (UAT)**: This is used for signing off on the configuration by the business.
- **Production (PROD)**: The live environment.

Also shown is a Hot Fix sandbox, which can be used for any emergency remedial work.

Keeping on top of Salesforce

A great way to keep on top of Salesforce is by registering for Dreamforce. This is an annual event that showcases the latest developments with Salesforce. Dreamforce then goes on tour with the Salesforce World Tour, which gives you a chance to get involved with various activities.

Three times a year, Salesforce automatically updates in your org. Beforehand, you will get a release note informing you of what has been included in the update. It is highly recommended to subscribe to **https://www.salesforceben.com/** to get regular updates, which are easy to read. Another helpful resource is the *Release Readiness Trailblazer group*, which will go through the new features of Salesforce.

Although it is good to keep on top of the releases, it can be difficult to understand them in context. As a result, it is helpful to go through every option under **Setup**. For example, the current **Setup** menu is shown in the following figure:

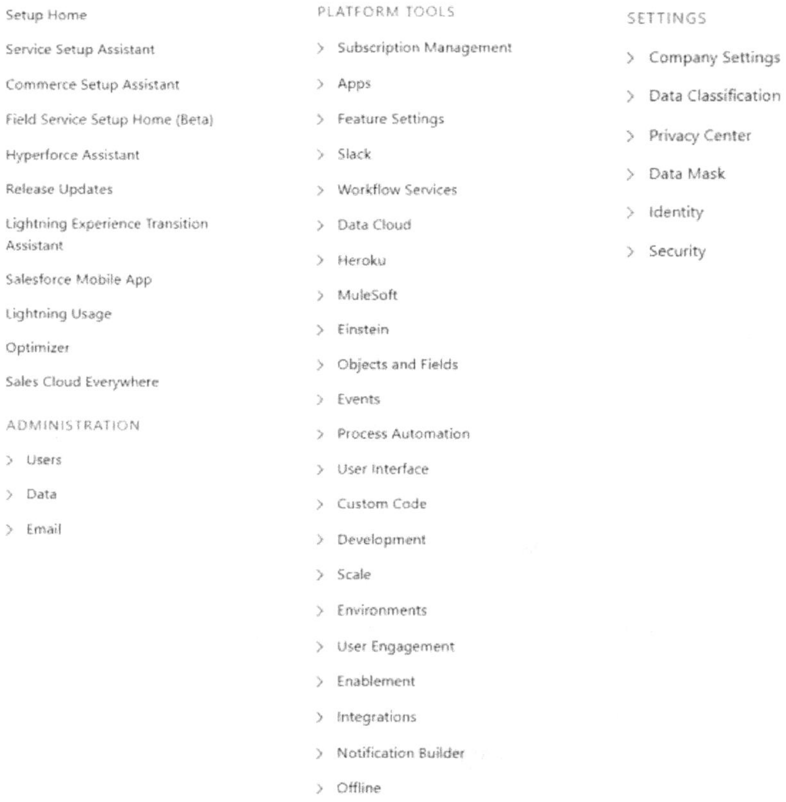

Setup Home	PLATFORM TOOLS	SETTINGS
Service Setup Assistant	> Subscription Management	> Company Settings
Commerce Setup Assistant	> Apps	> Data Classification
Field Service Setup Home (Beta)	> Feature Settings	> Privacy Center
Hyperforce Assistant	> Slack	> Data Mask
Release Updates	> Workflow Services	> Identity
Lightning Experience Transition Assistant	> Data Cloud	> Security
Salesforce Mobile App	> Heroku	
Lightning Usage	> MuleSoft	
Optimizer	> Einstein	
Sales Cloud Everywhere	> Objects and Fields	
	> Events	
ADMINISTRATION	> Process Automation	
> Users	> User Interface	
> Data	> Custom Code	
> Email	> Development	
	> Scale	
	> Environments	
	> User Engagement	
	> Enablement	
	> Integrations	
	> Notification Builder	
	> Offline	

Figure 15.6: Salesforce Setup menu items to learn

Career advice

Although this book is primarily to give you a solid understanding of Salesforce, the various products, and how to work with them, it is also useful to have some understanding of the way various companies work. The experience in the following sections may prove useful, so you can be a success in your career and may save you from going through some of the painful experiences outside, simply by having a good working knowledge of Salesforce.

Different types of companies

The best companies are generally able to allow you some freedom to design a project, and you have a collaborative team to rely on. The worst companies are simply forcing you to do something because they assume you understand their business, and they are resistant to alternative designs that may be simpler and reduce complexity. In this case, you end up building an overcomplicated Salesforce solution to replicate their legacy system, which does not take advantage of many Salesforce features that would greatly benefit their business. If possible, build out a **proof of concept (POC)** in a recently refreshed sandbox to demonstrate what could be done and show that the total cost of ownership can be reduced by reconsidering the design.

There is also a huge difference between working for a smaller boutique company, where you will get to know more people but may have to do a wide variety of roles, and working for a larger company, where you may only do the same type of work on every project. The larger companies may offer better salaries and incentives, but it is a personal choice for the type of company you may wish to work for.

Industry types

Some industries are a genuine pleasure to work for. These are the likes of media, hospitality, and leisure, since these people tend to genuinely enjoy their job and are open to doing things differently. Some other industries, typically Financial Services, are often high-pressure, with little time to explain their requirements, and often involve a lot of pressure to deliver a project to the customer's satisfaction.

Avoid projects with major technical debt

If you are starting with a new customer who has an existing Salesforce org, it is always worth doing a health check on the existing Salesforce org before starting a project. It may be that the level of technical debt in their Salesforce org is so great that the project would be impossible to deliver, and you will not be thanked if it fails.

For example, the Salesforce org may have 100s of custom objects, numerous triggers firing on the same event, many redundant fields, and a poorly configured security model. In which case, this needs to be resolved before you start any additional configuration, which may simply make things worse.

Jobs that appear too good to be true

If you decide to work for a system integration company that delivers Salesforce projects for customers continuously, then be wary of a job offer that is *too good to be true*. It is typically in the form of a great salary with an immediate start date. It could be that you accept the offer only to find out that when you start at the company, they had not actually won the project for which they had employed you. In which case, it is likely that you will be shown the way out without any apology. The company has nothing to lose by aligning you for a potential new project, but if they do not win it, then you have everything to lose. This messes up your career, not to mention family life, and it might be hard to return to your previous employer or to get a job if you are currently without work.

For this reason, it is advisable to either stay in a role for a minimum of two years or check with the new employer that the work they have aligned you for is actually happening, and get written evidence for this, or ask to speak with the project manager.

An employer will have nothing to lose if they hire and fire you without notice and only because they did not win a project, which has nothing to do with you. Depending on your local employment law, you do get paid if the company is at fault, but it is usually only a month's salary, which often is not long enough to get a new position.

Working with stakeholders

When on a project, there will be people who are significant to the project's success. It is good advice to keep them up to date on progress and inform them of any issues. It is often risky to be as friendly as possible with stakeholders and only give them the good news. This strategy does not work, as there will be increasing levels of stress put on yourself while you defend an underperforming team. It is better to be open and honest about the progress of a project rather than build a gap between what is happening and the reported progress. Regular show and tell demonstration of progress helps the stakeholders to see what has been achieved, and motivates the team doing the work. Another risk of being too friendly with customers at an early stage of the project is that you never want to tell a joke to the customer that is so funny that you then have to explain it to **human resources (HR)**.

Working with tech gurus

Another common pitfall is when the team is very technical but resorts to coding instead of using Salesforce's out-of-the-box configuration. Many projects have been made overcomplicated since the team immediately resorts to a code-based solution. The strength of Salesforce is that most things can be configured. This means that it is kept up to date as Salesforce does the various releases. A code-based project requires time and effort to maintain, which often results in a Salesforce environment getting worse over time. A good solution architect will steer the team in a configuration-based approach and possibly build out a POC for the business to check that the solution is fit for purpose.

Conclusion

This chapter is written to help give you context for the way in which IT projects are delivered and to understand the way many companies structure themselves. It also shows you how to engage with the two extremes of the technical guru to the executives in a company, who will have different ways of thinking.

The beginning of this book was to help you make a start in Salesforce and then guide you through getting started and building on that knowledge. The final chapters are to give you the broader context of various Salesforce products, and this chapter focuses on the areas that you would need to know so you understand the broader context of how different companies work and how you can succeed in your career.

Index

www.ingramcontent.com/pod-product-compliance
Lightning Source LLC
Chambersburg PA
CBHW061742210326
41599CB00034B/6759